Cranach – The Early Years in Vienna

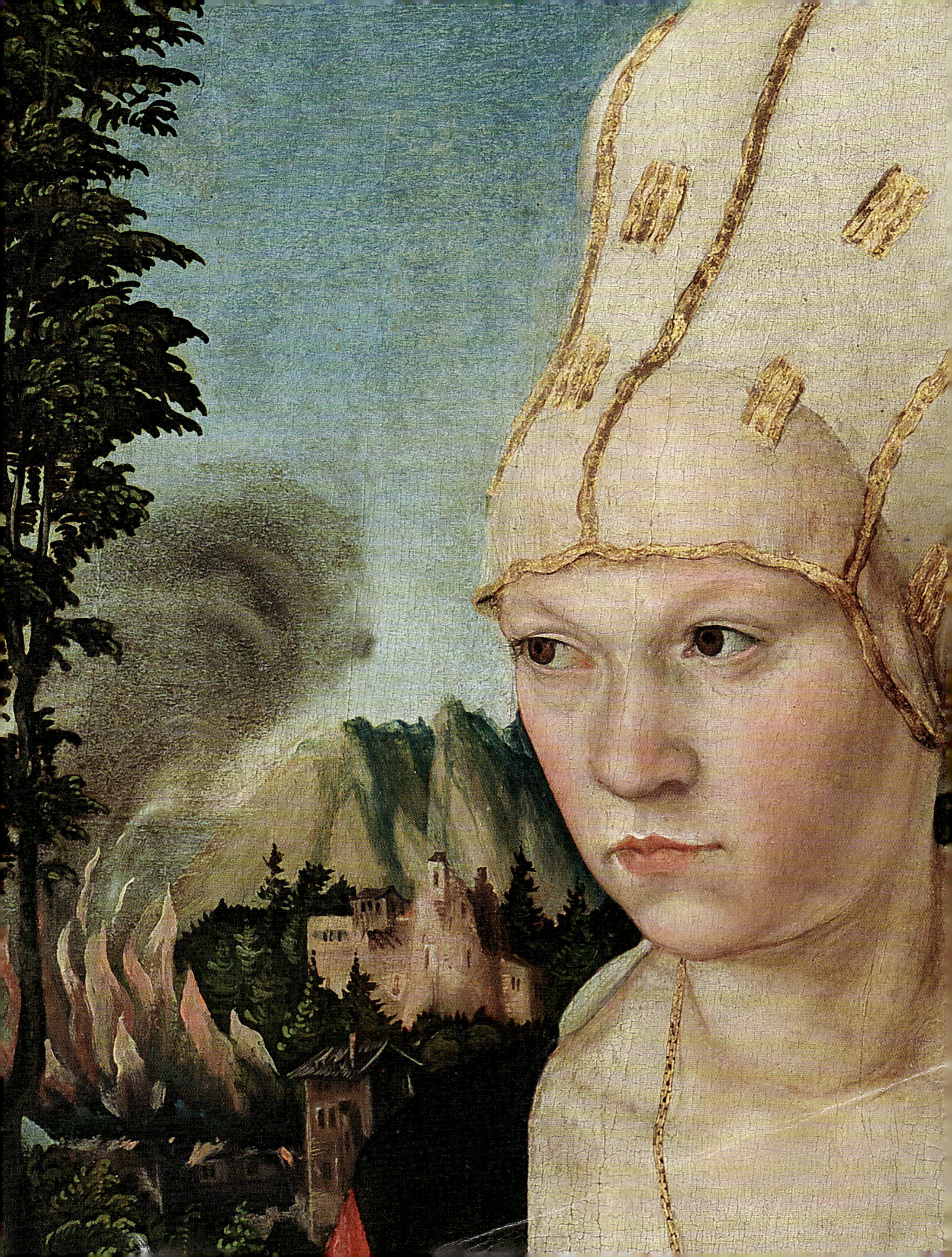

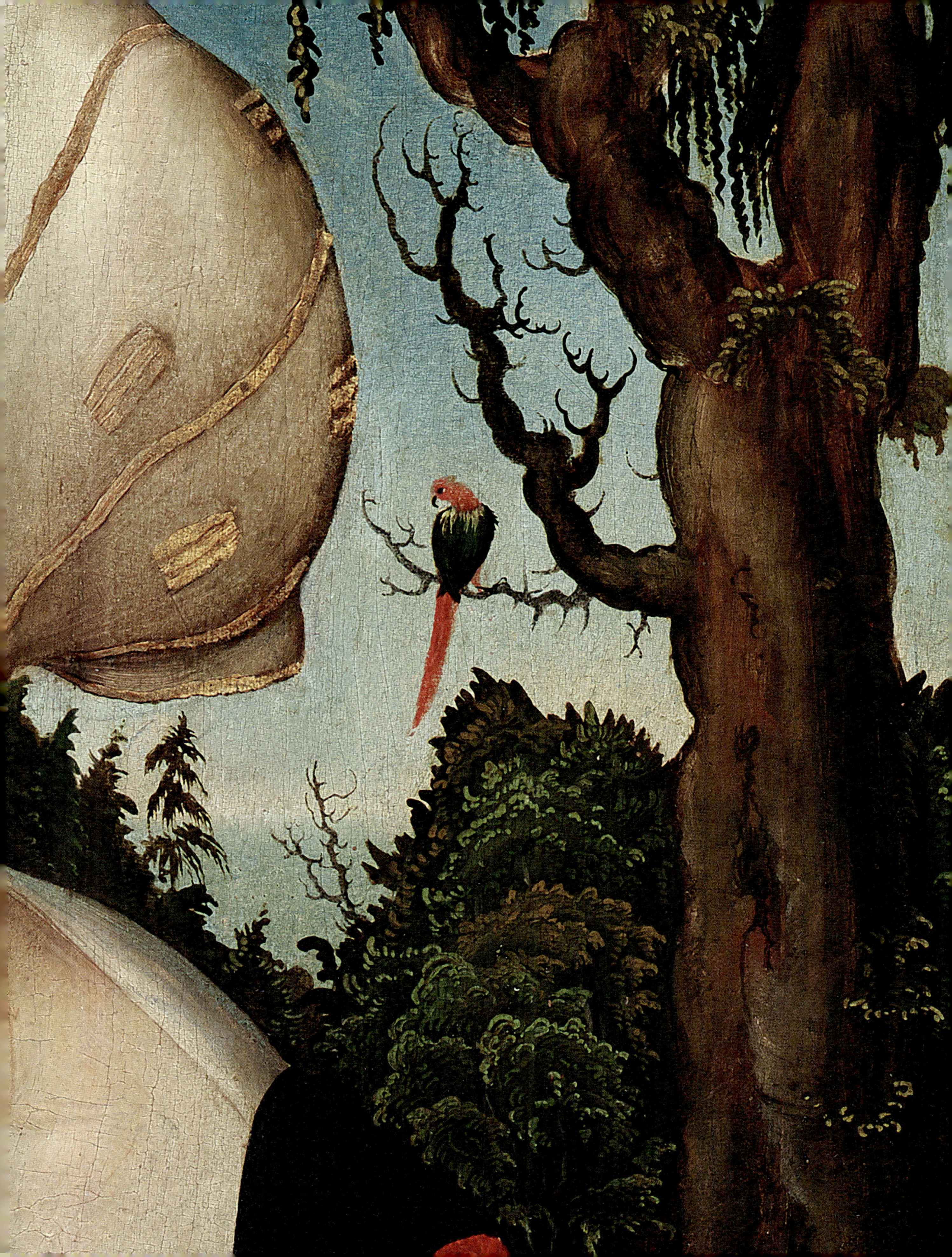

KUNST
HISTORISCHES
MUSEUM
WIEN

Cranach

The Early Years in Vienna

Edited by Guido Messling and Kerstin Richter

Sammlung OSKAR REINHART 'AM RÖMERHOLZ' Collection
FEDERAL OFFICE OF CULTURE

Schweizerische Eidgenossenschaft
Confédération suisse
Confederazione Svizzera
Confederaziun svizra

Swiss Confederation

Federal Department of Home Affairs FDHA
Federal Office of Culture FOC

LENDERS

We want to express our thanks to the following institutions and colleagues for lending us works for the exhibition:
Kunstmuseum Basel: Josef Helfenstein & Bodo Brinkmann
Staatliche Museen zu Berlin, Kupferstichkabinett:
Dagmar Korbacher & Michael Roth
Herzog Anton Ulrich-Museum, Brunswick:
Thomas Richter & Thomas Döring
Hessische Hausstiftung, Kronberg: Markus Miller
Staatliche Graphische Sammlung München:
Michael Hering & Achim Riether
Germanisches Nationalmuseum, Nuremberg: Daniel Hess & Claudia Valter
Albertina, Vienna: Klaus-Albrecht Schröder & Christof Metzger
Österreichische Galerie Belvedere, Vienna:
Stella Rollig & Björn Blauensteiner
Gemäldegalerie der Akademie der bildenden Künste Wien:
Sabine Folie & Claudia Koch
Österreichische Nationalbibliothek, Vienna:
Johanna Rachinger & Andreas Fingernagel
Kunsthaus Zürich: Christoph Becker & Philipp Büttner

We also want to thank all the authors of the exhibition catalogue and Georg Josef Dietz (Berlin), Andreas Dobler (Eichenzell), Gábor Endrődi (Budapest), Babette Hartwieg (Berlin), Stephan Kemperdick (Berlin), Jürgen Kleidt (Munich), Tristan Kobler (Zurich), Dieter Koepplin (Basel), Johanna Kopp (Vienna), Fritz Koreny (Vienna), Teresa Krah (Vienna), Armin Kunz (New York), Selma Kurtagić (Vienna), Florence Le Bègue (Winterthur), Astrid Lehner (Vienna), Georg Lendorff (Zurich), Hanspeter Marty (Zurich), Olivier Masson (Zurich), Benjamin Mayr (Vienna), Thomas Müller (Basel), Julia Neubauer (Vienna), Michaela Noll (Vienna), Elke Oberthaler (Vienna), Martine Passelaigue (Paris), Sabine Pénot (Vienna), Thomas Ritter (Vienna), Martin Schawe (Munich), Christina Scheublein (Winterthur), Agnes Stillfried (Cairo), Andreas Uldrich (Vienna), Gerhard Veigel (Vienna), Karin Zeleny (Vienna), Valentina Zingg (Winterthur)

Contents

Foreword

There have been countless exhibitions on Lucas Cranach the Elder (1472–1553), especially during the last few years, but this is the first to examine the beginnings of the career of this exceptional artist. The main reason for this is that no more than two dozen panels, drawings and woodcuts by him have survived from the few years we know he spent in Vienna just after the turn of the sixteenth century. It is not only their small number and rarity that distinguishes these works from the mass-production characteristic of Cranach's time in Wittenberg, where he moved in 1505 to become court painter to the Electors of Saxony; it is their at times almost raw expressivity that differentiates them so dramatically from the courtly-elegant manner typical of Cranach's later works. With their artistic power and often unconventional compositions and solutions, Cranach's Viennese works are both among the most exceptional artworks from the early sixteenth century and the greatest treasures of the museums that house them today.

The Oskar Reinhart Collection "Am Römerholz" in Winterthur and the Kunsthistorisches Museum Vienna are the only museums in the world to hold two early paintings by Cranach, apart from the Gemäldegalerie Berlin whose celebrated *Rest on the Flight into Egypt* (1504) Cranach presumably painted only after he left Vienna. It is therefore more or less a given that this ambitious project should be led by the collections in Vienna and Winterthur. Our successful collaboration has allowed us to explore new aspects of the early Cranach, incorporating the findings into the two high-calibre exhibitions mounted in Winterthur and Vienna respectively. In this context, the portraits of the Viennese humanist Johannes Cuspinian and his wife Anna, which were acquired by Oskar Reinhart, will for the first time in many decades leave their home and temporarily return to the place where they were painted. The exhibition also presents important loans from other public and private collections, but these two portraits and the two paintings owned by the Kunsthistorisches Museum form the focal point of the show, which offers a unique comprehensive overview of the early oeuvre of this exceptional artist. The exhibition will be shown in Winterthur from 12 March to 12 June 2022 before moving to Vienna.

We would like to thank all public and private collections for loaning us their treasures. It goes without saying that the light-sensitive works on paper and parchment, as well as some of the extremely fragile panels, can only be shown at one of the two venues. This is why we decided to focus on religious works in Vienna and on portraits in Winterthur, something that also reflects the two museums' respective holdings. In Switzerland, the presentation of the Cuspinian diptych will be augmented by selected older models and more-or-less contemporary portraits by Cranach and his circle.

The Oskar Reinhart Collection "Am Römerholz" would like to thank the Swiss Federal Office of Culture for its active support of this collaboration.

The curators involved in this project vouch for its quality. The Kunsthistorisches Museum Vienna was represented by Guido Messling, who was involved from the start in this collaboration and whose exceptional knowledge of artist and period laid the solid basis for new research on the early Cranach. Katja Baumhoff, together with the management of the collection in Winterthur, developed the exhibition there with great commitment and dedication. We would like to thank them and the other authors of the exhibition catalogue, namely Björn Blauensteiner, Andreas Fingernagel, Sabine Heiser, Claudia Koch and Erwin Pokorny for exploring various aspects of Cranach's sojourn in Vienna such as the art of printing and publishing, the role of guilds, earlier pictorial traditions, and the influence of humanist ideas, as well as the relatively late discovery of Cranach's small early oeuvre. We are confident that this catalogue represents an important contribution to research on Cranach, and we want to thank everyone who helped make it possible. Karin Zeleny, Martine Passelaigue and Agnes Stillfried did an excellent job editing and translating the exhibition catalogue. We would like to express our gratitude to all members of staff at both museums for their commitment to this at times complex project, especially Benjamin Mayr for his highly-competent coordination of this publication, Michaela Noll for the beautiful layout, Florence Le Bègue for securing the image rights and her work as a registrar, and Julia Neudorfer for her accomplished handling of the challenging exhibition management.

They and many others in and outside our two museums have made this ambitious project possible, which offers a new look at this early, almost wild phase in Lucas Cranach's oeuvre.

Kerstin Richter
Director of the Oskar Reinhart Collection "Am Römerholz", Winterthur

Sabine Haag
Director General of the Kunsthistorisches Museum Vienna

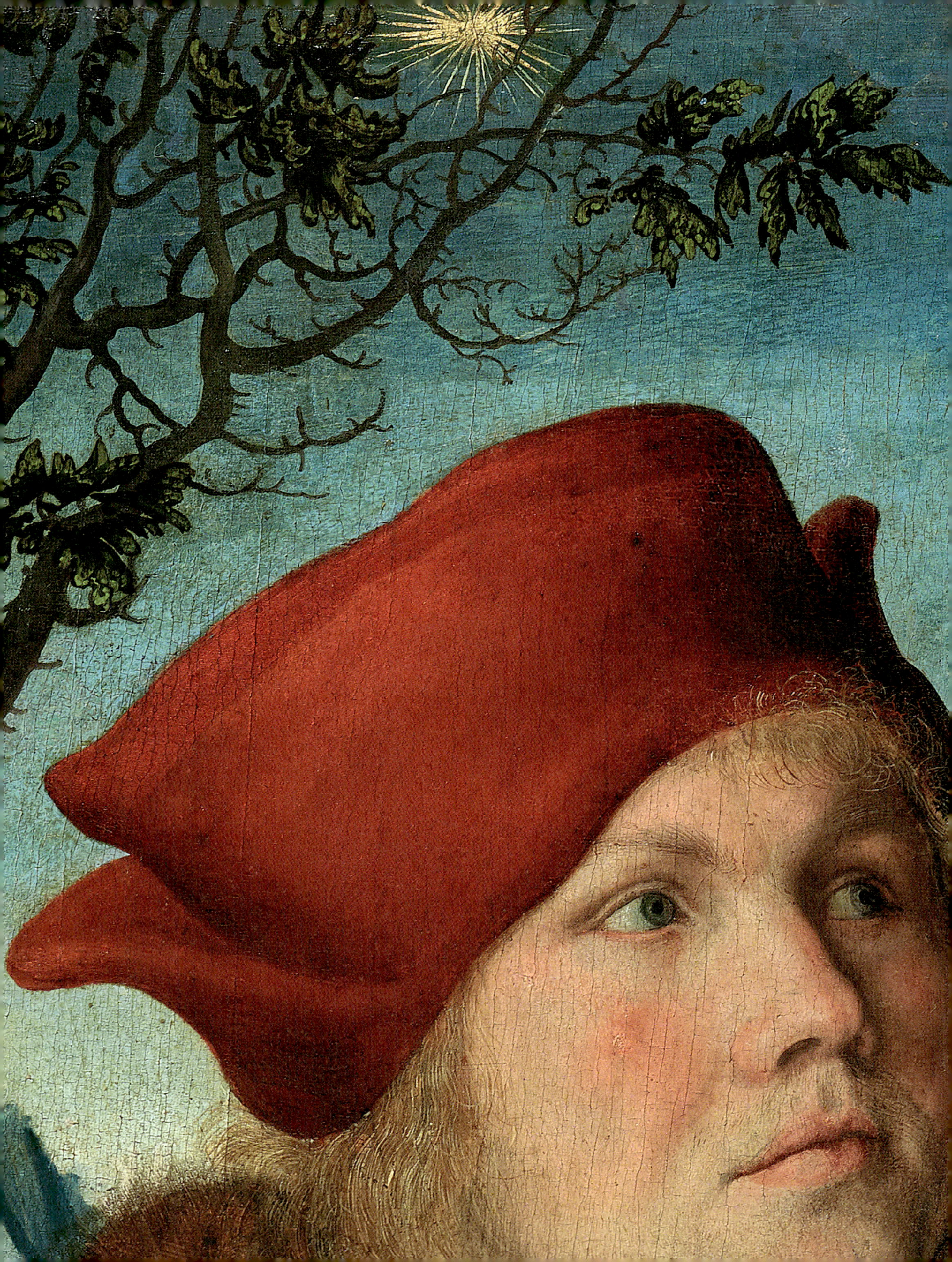

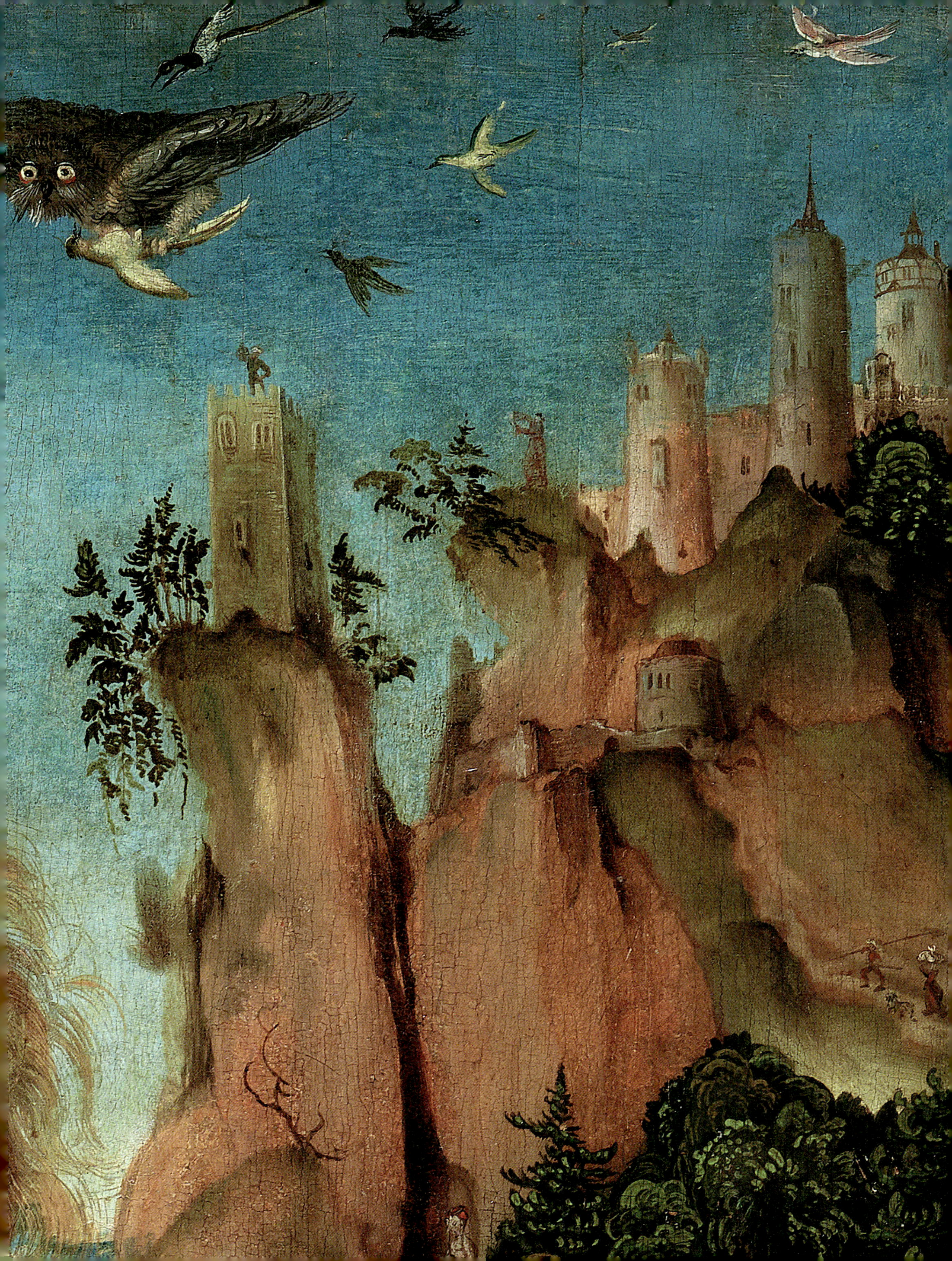

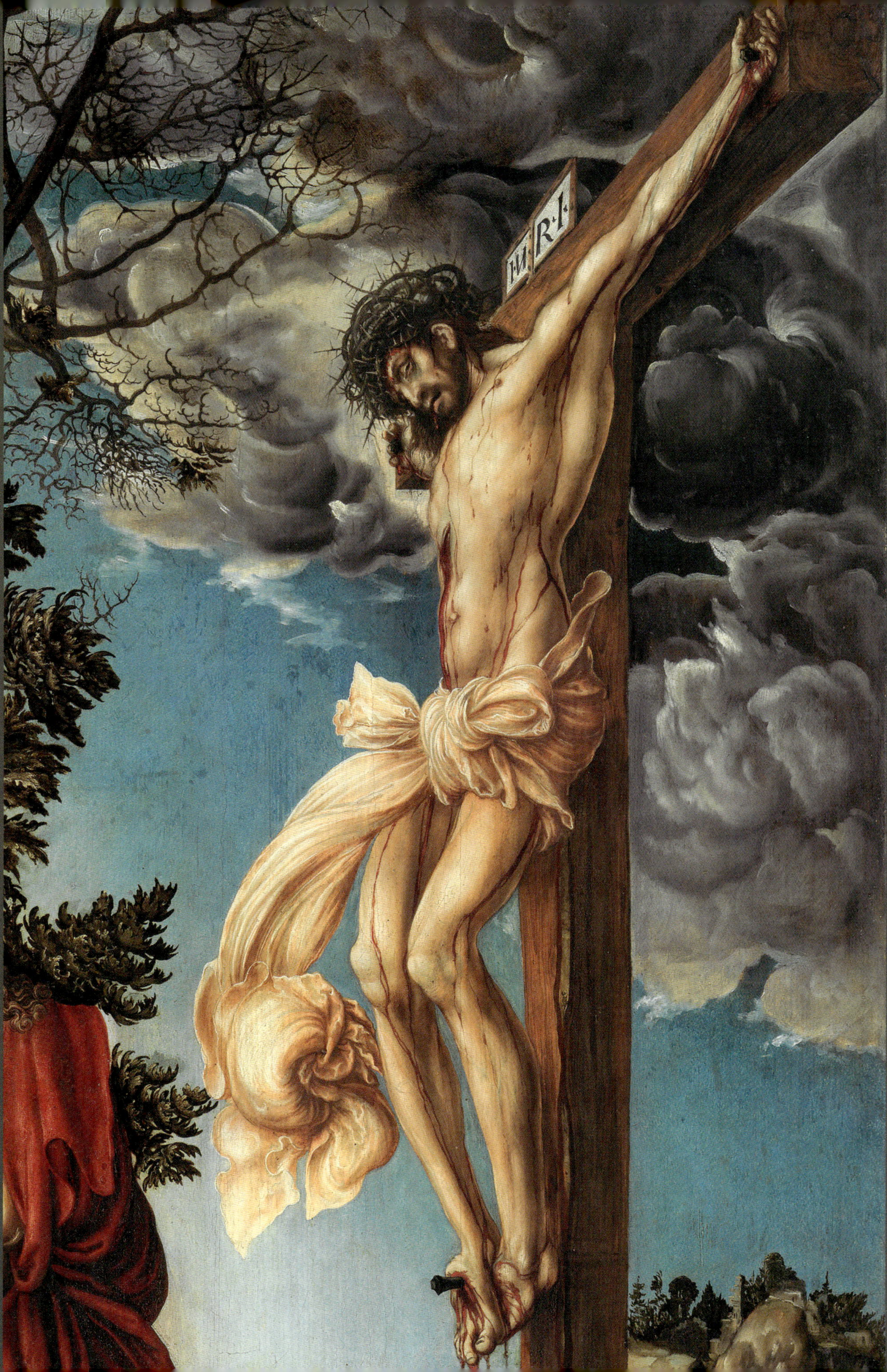
I·N·R·I·

Guido Messling

Cranach's Beginnings. Known Facts and Assumptions

As with many of his fellow Renaissance painters, we know very little about the beginnings of Lucas Cranach the Elder (1472–1553). The fact that he is today regarded as one of the most popular artists of the sixteenth century is the result of his long and highly productive time as court painter to the Electors of Saxony, a position he assumed in 1505 and held until his death. Cranach's time in Wittenberg (and later in Weimar), during which he, a close friend of Martin Luther's (1483–1546), literally put a face on the Reformation, is also extensively documented. But only a handful of panels, woodcuts and drawings, which are either on show in this exhibition or discussed in this catalogue, bear witness to the fact that he spent the first years of the sixteenth century in Vienna. Some of the patrons who commissioned these works, local reflexes in them, or their provenance suggest that Cranach produced them in Vienna; others are stylistically closely related to them.[1] But sadly not a single document from these years has yet come to light, one that affirms the painter's sojourn in Vienna in black and white, so to speak – all we have are some later remarks by people close to him that seem to confirm this retrospectively.[2] This contrasts with the first decades of Cranach's life, about which we have at least some biographical information that provides us with a vague timeline. We know that he was born in 1472 in Kronach, a small town in Upper Franconia, after which he called himself from 1504 onwards.[3] But we have not the slightest idea what kind of works the young artist created before appearing, around 1500, almost from nowhere when he began producing his brilliant Viennese paintings.

Both the fact that Cranach was around thirty years old and their artistic and technical virtuosity suggest that they are not the work of a novice. In 1556, Matthias Gunderam (c.1529–1564), a generally reliable Cranach biographer who was also a native of Kronach, noted that young Lucas studied with his father, Hans Maler, who taught him the "artem graphicam" (something like the art of drawing).[4] We may assume that the father too worked as a painter (something also suggested by his surname: Maler = painter in German), but he may also have been, for example, a sculptor.[5] After these basic instructions, his pupil will have gone on to train in the workshop of another master before setting off as a journeyman. Matthias Weniger is surely correct that the loss of almost all late-gothic panels produced at Kronach and its environs probably put paid to Cranach's earliest works.[6] It is, however, interesting to note that a statue of St John – according to the signature a work produced in 1498 by Hans Hartlin for the parish church at Kronach – already exhibits the expressive and deeply-cut, tube-like drapery that is surprisingly similar to Cranach's earliest extant works. This outstanding statue gives us an inkling of the "tools" the young artist learned in his artistically perhaps not so parochial hometown (fig. 1).[7]

In 1495, 1496 and 1498 Cranach was a witness in a court case in Kronach though this does not necessarily mean that he lived and worked there permanently, especially because at least one of the dates was set taking the painter's absence into account. By this time his years as an apprentice and journeyman may have been over for a number of years, and he could well have moved to some other inspiring town.

(ALMOST) ALL ROADS LEAD TO NUREMBERG

The most likely hypothesis is still that all this took place at Nuremberg. In the late fifteenth century, the free imperial city, located around a hundred kilometres south of Kronach, was a charismatic artistic centre. In many respects this was Bamberg's loss; the city was the residence of a prince-bishop who also ruled over Cranach's birthplace. A survey of the extant paintings produced by workshops active in Bamberg shortly before the turn of the sixteenth century reveals nothing that could have taught an ambitious young artist anything more than technical skills.[8] One exception is perhaps the workshop run by the outstanding painter and engraver who signed his works with the monogram "LCz", and who can probably be identified as Lorenz Katzheimer. Cranach may have been impressed by the narrative expressionism of this artist who seems to have been active in Bamberg around 1490/1500.[9] At Bamberg he probably saw also earlier works by Hans Pleydenwurff (c.1420–1472), who had relocated to Nuremberg in 1457 (see cat. 1). The woodcuts that Cranach created in Vienna do not bridge the gap that separates them from the few formally somewhat modest contemporary book illustrations produced at Bamberg. But the calendar dial to identify the dominical letter that Cranach designed in 1503 for the *Passau Missal* (it was commissioned by Johannes Winterburger, a printer from Vienna) proves that his work was informed by a Bamberg incunable (see cat. 23). His solution does not only presuppose the calendar dial included after 1490 in several liturgical books published by Erhard Ratdolt, a native of Augsburg, but the pendentives filled with ornamental foliage also show that he was familiar with the version (equally dependent on Ratdolt) included by Johann Pfeil from Bamberg in his *Ratisbon Breviary* (1495; fig. 2).[10] Like the sole figurative woodcut of this incunable, the calendar dial also seems to have been designed in the Nuremberg workshop of Michael Wolgemut (1434–1519), which is where Cranach may have come across it.[11]

A young, ambitious foreign artist was probably also attracted by the fact that there was no painters' guild at Nuremberg, which made it much easier for him to find employment. Reflexes of works produced by artists in Nuremberg in compositions Cranach created during his sojourn in Vienna strongly suggest that he spent some time in the Franconian metropolis shortly before the turn of the sixteenth century. Here, he seems to have moved in the circle of Albrecht Dürer (1471–1528), who at the time was already in contact with both the arch-humanist Conrad Celtes (1469–1508) and Frederick the Wise, Elector of Saxony, whose court painter Cranach would become. The "Schleissheim Crucifixion" of 1503 functions as the chief witness for this: here, Cranach has clearly borrowed the exceptional lay-out and individual details from the depiction of the same scene in Dürer's *The Seven Sorrows of the Virgin*, a panel he presumably painted around 1495/98 for Frederick the Wise, Elector of Saxony (figs. 3 & 4).[12] If Cranach had not already met the elector before the turn of the sixteenth century, he must have seen this panel in Dürer's workshop during his time in Nuremberg, although he probably did not work there.[13] Veit Stoss was also still in town working on the reliefs for the *Volckamer Monument* in St Sebald, which he completed not later than 1499. Cranach must have been fascinated by this sculpture because the head of the rapt St John and the saint's folded hands in his woodcut depicting *The Agony in the Garden* derive from Veit Stoss's relief

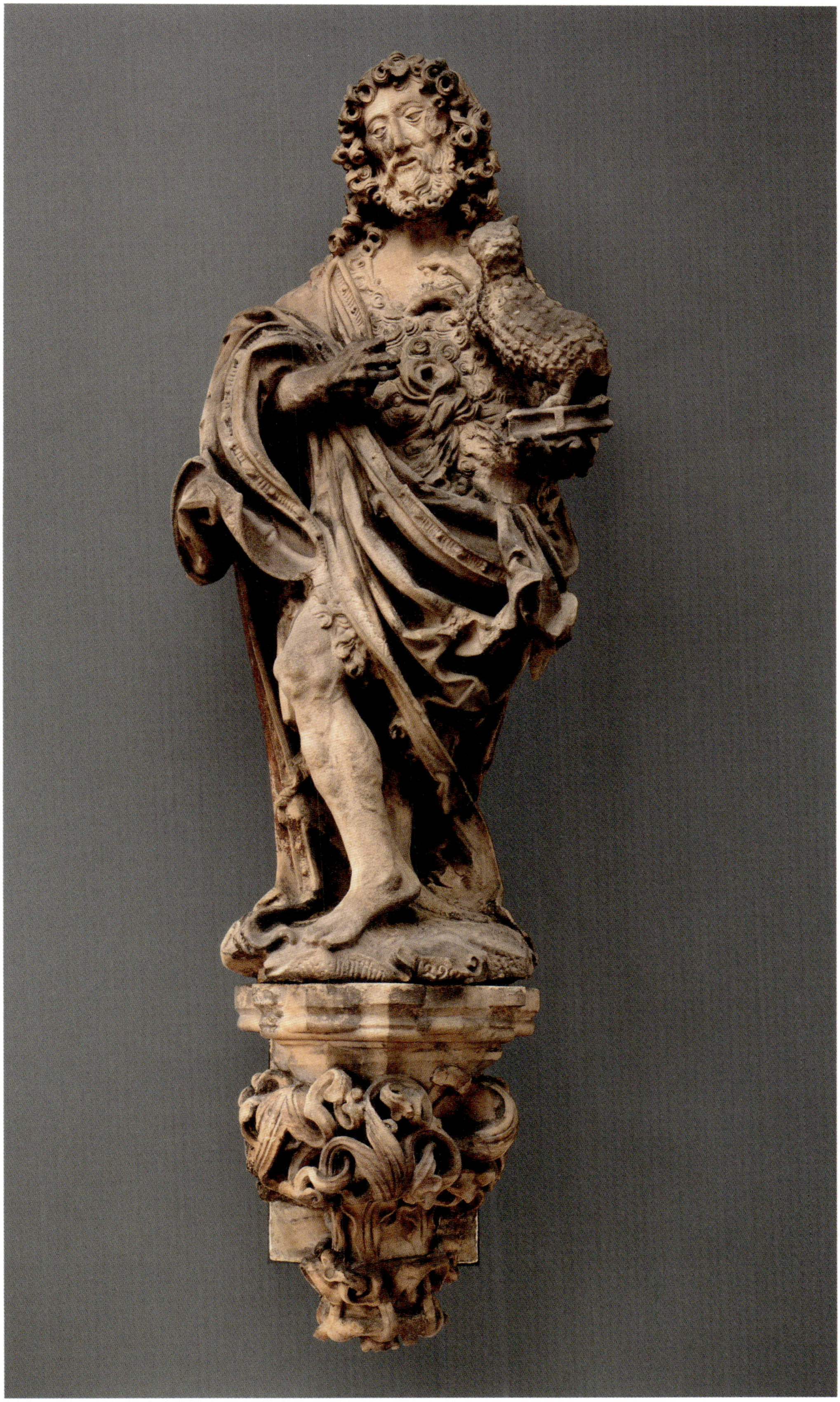

Fig. 1
Johannes Hartlin,
St John the Baptist, 1498.
Katholische Kirchenstiftung Kronach, on loan to the Bayerisches Nationalmuseum Munich, Zweigmuseum Fränkische Galerie, Veste Rosenberg, Kronach

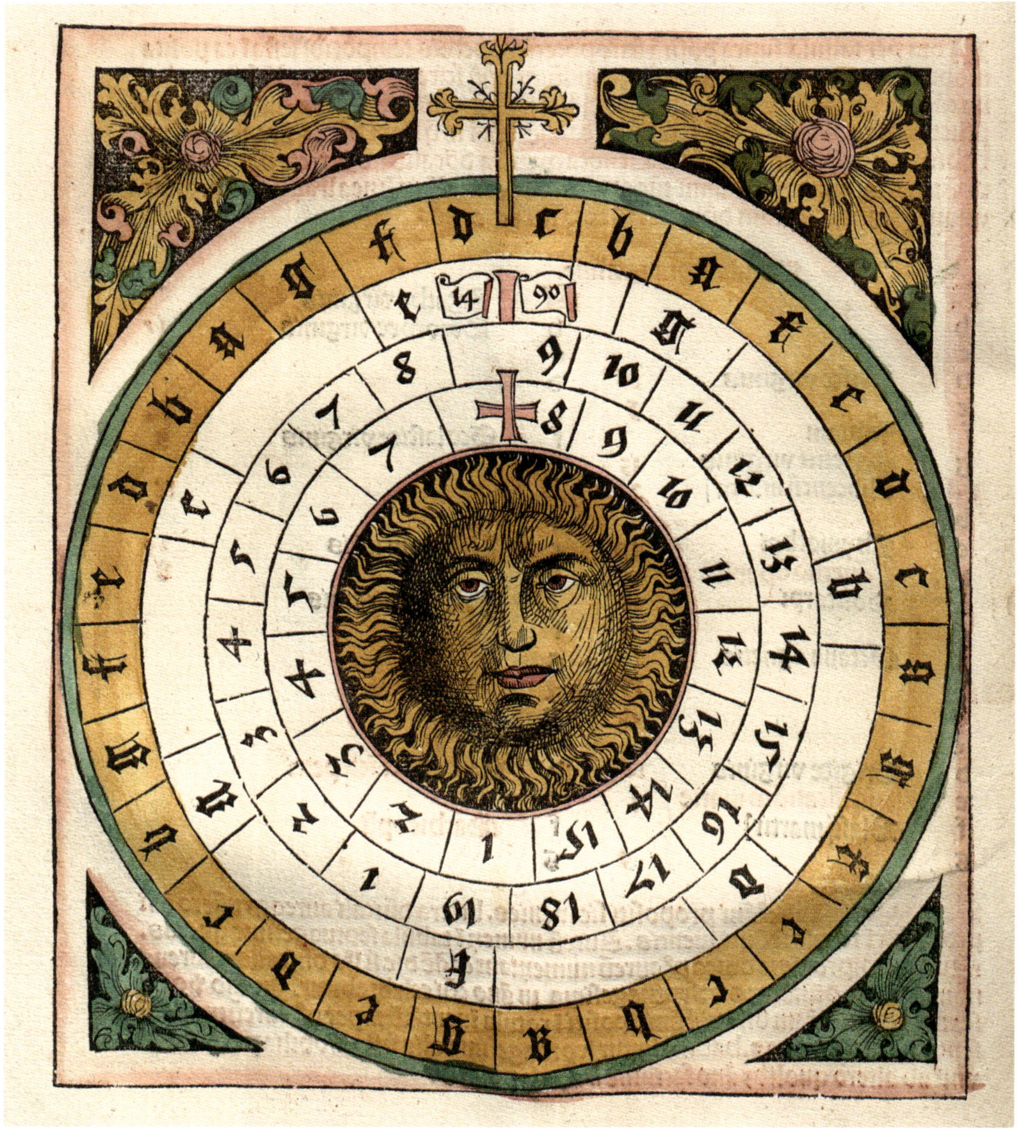

Fig. 2
Workshop of Michael Wolgemut (design), calendar dial to identify the dominical letter, woodcut in *Breviarium Ratisponense*, Bamberg (Johann Pfeil) 1495. Bayerische Staatsbibliothek, Munich, 2 Inc.c.a. 3185-1,1/9

of the same subject (figs. 5 & 6).[14] And, last but not least, we should mention the anonymous artist from Dürer's circle who composed the canon woodcut in the *Revelationes sancte Birgitte* in 1500, which clearly informed Cranach's crucifixion in the *Passau Missal* (figs. 7 & 8).[15] However, there remains the possibility that Cranach first saw this print from Nuremberg in Vienna, which eliminates it as a terminus post for his departure from Nuremberg. But he freely borrowed individual gestures, hand signals, or compositional details from all three works that appealed to his desire to create the emotional and dramatic pictorial language that so clearly pervades the works he produced in Vienna.

But these borrowings may just as easily be explained by a shorter sojourn in the Franconian metropolis, just as some of Cranach's other early works suggest a knowledge of the works of Michael Pacher in Salzburg, or works produced by the Frueauf workshop in Passau.[16] However, individual (technical) idiosyncrasies in Cranach's handling in his earliest paintings and drawings suggest he spent some time in the workshop of a master active in Nuremberg. For example, on some of his panels he used a reddish ground or imprimatura; rarely found in works by other German or Netherlandish masters, it is a somewhat regular feature in contemporary panels produced at Nuremberg, most of which originated in the circle of Michael Wolgemut and Dürer.[17] Connected with this, we find a similar pale red tone in the paper used for the two drawings showing the two thieves crucified with Jesus, generally regarded as early works by Cranach (cat. 4 & 5). In Germany, such red-tinted paper is very common in Franconia, coming into regular use there in the middle of the fifteenth century; towards the end of the century, we encounter it most frequently in drawings that originated in Wolgemut's workshop.[18] Wolgemut produced both panels and designs for woodcuts, and from 1486 Dürer trained in his large workshop; there Cranach could have learned about the division of labour and how to run a large workshop, something he made good use of when organising his own workshop at Wittenberg. It is also interesting to note that both Dürer and Wolgemut were among the Nuremberg artists favoured by the Elector of Saxony, with Wolgemut producing a "Taffel" (a panel, presumably a winged altarpiece) for his princely patron in 1503/04.[19]

Dürer was almost the same age as Cranach and, unlike Wolgemut, has to be eliminated as a possible master of Cranach's, but the influence of his art on the latter's Viennese works cannot be overestimated. With his *Apocalypse*, published in 1498, the early prints of his *Large Passion*, and some magnificent individual sheets, Dürer set new standards for the medium of woodcuts. Cranach's large Viennese woodcuts clearly respond to these folio-size prints with their never-seen-before love of details and technical brilliance. Cranach was obviously just as impressed by Dürer's pathos and his dynamic linear handling, clearly visible in the calligraphic branches.[20] But compared to his contemporaries, Cranach employed a more expressive formal idiom that results in grotesquely distorted bodies or seems to animate all pictorial elements to the same degree. These dynamisations, which are most marked in his depictions of nature, make Cranach one of the precursors of the so-called Danube School.[21] And his iconographic solutions for established Christian subjects are equally exceptional.

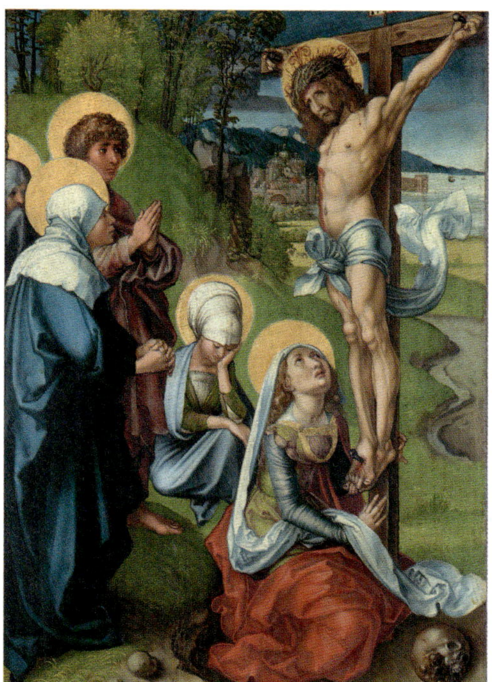

Fig. 3
Albrecht Dürer, *The Crucifixion* (from the panel *The Seven Sorrows of the Virgin*), c.1495/98. Staatliche Kunstsammlungen Dresden, Gemäldegalerie Alte Meister, inv. 1880

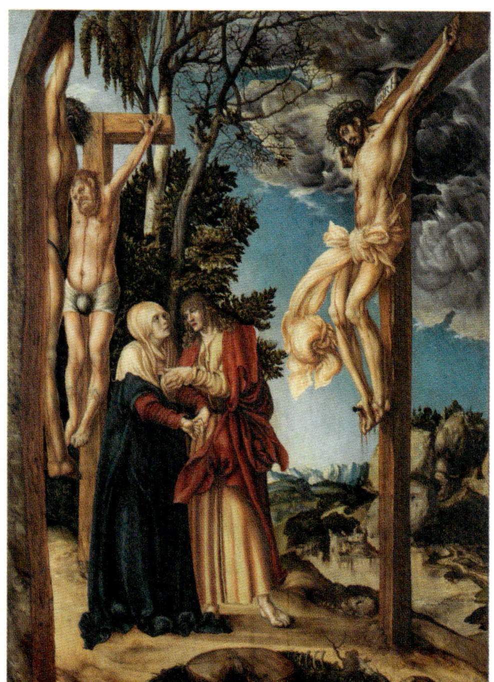

Fig. 4
Lucas Cranach the Elder, *The Lamentation of Christ ("Schleissheim Crucifixion")*, 1503. Bayerische Staatsgemäldesammlungen, Alte Pinakothek, Munich, inv. 1416

Fig. 5
Veit Stoss, *St John Asleep*, before 1499 (detail from *The Agony in the Garden* relief of the *Volckamer Monument* in Nuremberg, St Sebald)

Fig. 6
Lucas Cranach the Elder, *St John Asleep*, c.1500 (detail from fig. 6, essay Heiser)

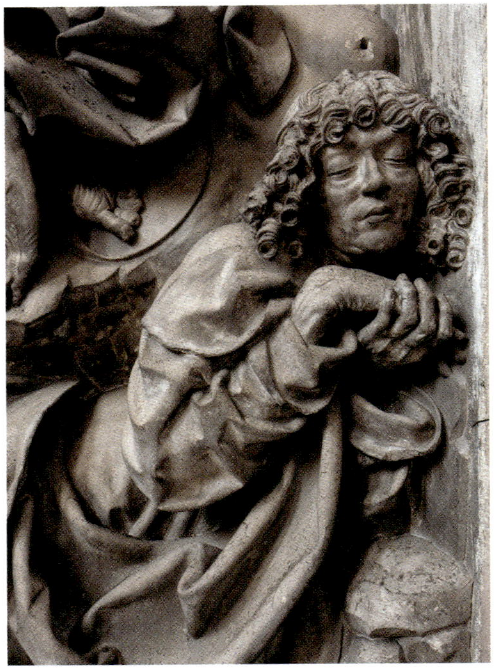

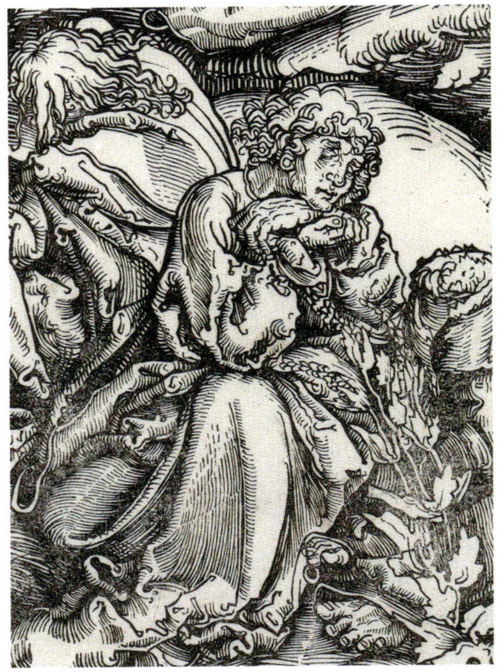

Nothing comparable was being produced in Vienna at that time (see the essay by Björn Blauensteiner) – but there is an artist with a similar outlook who was working outside the city's gates, so to speak, and he too was an immigrant: at more or less the same time, Jörg Breu the Elder, a native of Augsburg, was executing the painted panels for three winged altarpieces commissioned by three monasteries in the environs of Vienna: for Zwettl in 1500, for Aggsbach in 1501, and for Melk shortly afterwards.[22] In 1501, Breu seems to have run or been connected to a workshop active at Krems, a city near Melk without a painters' guild. The panels produced by the master from Augsburg are less atmospheric, and their compositions still rely on building blocks, but their expressive and raw attitude and forcefully-modelled faces are pretty close to Cranach's. We can easily imagine – but sadly not prove – that Cranach encountered some of Breu's works, or maybe even that the two met at some point.[23] Breu's Austrian oeuvre is somewhat erratic, with sudden stylistic changes. He is the younger of the two artists, and only his final retable, completed around 1502 for Melk Abbey shortly before he returned to Augsburg, documents a deeper familiarity with Dürer's woodcuts. He grappled with Dürer's works in a merely superficial way, resulting in a calming of his previously rather bold and reckless compositions.

Cranach's Viennese works, however, reveal no such rupture. On the contrary, they reflect a gradual evolution, although even Cranach's earliest works document his ability to make use of Dürer's pictorial ideas to express his own feeling for form. After entering the Augsburg workshop of Ulrich Apt the Elder in 1493, Breu presumably travelled via Passau or Salzburg to Lower Austria, where he was belatedly exposed to Dürer's prints. The slightly-older Cranach, however, must have studied them in detail during his sojourn in Nuremberg. This is why there have been countless attempts to identify individual works produced at the turn of the sixteenth century by followers of Dürer in Nuremberg as early works by Cranach. And although none of these suggestions survive closer analysis, the stylistic details of a painting like *Portrait of a Young Man* (Hessische Hausstiftung, Kronberg, see cat. 11) forge a surprisingly strong link between Dürer's and Cranach's portraits.[24] In addition, the internal animation and sharp verisimilitude of Dürer's *Portrait of Oswolt Krel* (1499; Munich, Alte Pinakothek) is closely related to the portraits Cranach produced not long afterwards.

We should now take a closer look at a contemporary woodcut (c.112 × 95 mm) that also oscillates between Dürer and Cranach (fig. 9). Depicting pilgrims imploringly gazing at the Woman of the Apocalypse on an altar surrounded by votive offerings, it was designed for the title page of a booklet of miracles recorded at the Shrine of Our Lady at Altötting. This collection of miracles connected with the famous Bavarian pilgrimage church was written by Jacob Issickemer, a native of Würzburg who became a canon at Altötting in 1494 and had the book printed in Nuremberg around 1497/98.[25] And while the content of this now rare publication has been repeatedly discussed in connection with cultural and/or religious-historical questions, Max Geisberg was, it seems, the only one to attempt an art-historical appreciation of this remarkable woodcut, even believing it to be an early work by Dürer.[26] And although the depiction demonstrates impressive powers of observation, and the various head-types and drapery-motifs are closely connected with the *Apocalypse* prints, it lacks the readability and precise forms characteristic of Dürer – perhaps the reason why Geisberg's attribution seems not to have gained much traction with fellow art-historians.

This print is even closer to Cranach's work (the earliest extant one dates from not much later) than the other woodcuts produced around 1500 by Dürer's circle in Nuremberg, which is why we would like to suggest it as a possible first work by our artist. However, because of the expressive design of Cranach's Vienna woodcuts, similarities between them and the frontispiece appear much less obvious than with his later prints produced at Wittenberg. In addition, comparable crowded prints are at least twice as large and accordingly much more detailed. If the craftsman who carved the image in our pilgrim's booklet really did follow faithfully the drawing given him by the artist who had designed it, then the curved hatching in the men's

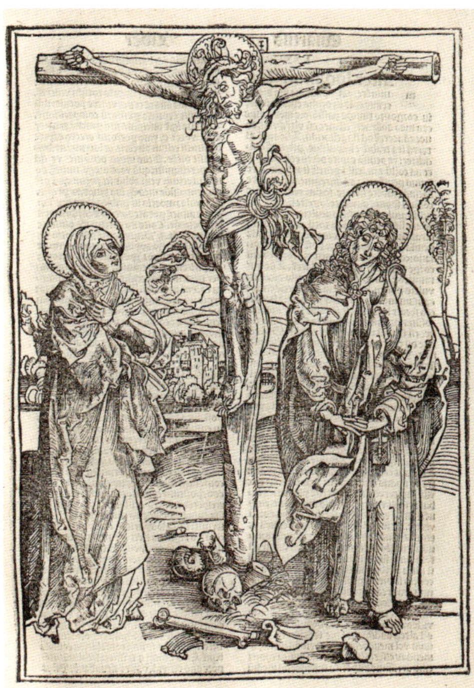

Fig. 7
Circle of Dürer (design), *The Crucified Christ with the Virgin and St John the Evangelist*, canon sheet woodcut in the *Revelationes sancte Birgitte*, Nuremberg (Anton Koberger) 1500. Bayerische Staatsbibliothek, Munich, 2 Rar. 424

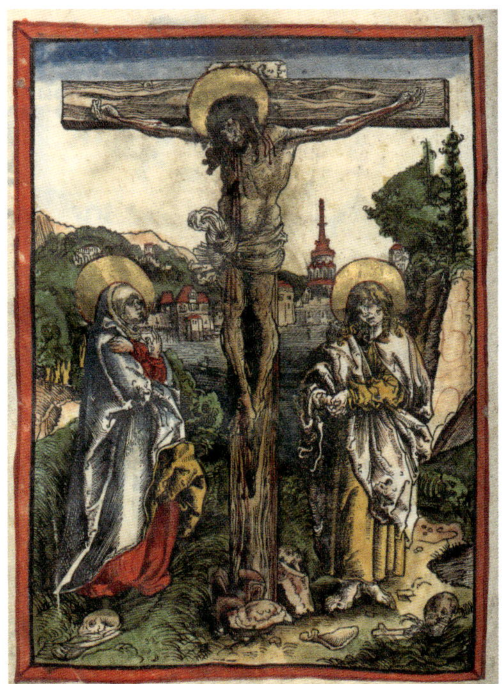

Fig. 8
The Crucified Christ with the Virgin and St John the Evangelist, canon sheet woodcut in the *Missale Pataviense*, 1503 (cat. 25)

Fig. 9
Lucas Cranach the Elder? (design), *Pilgrims before Our Lady of Altötting*, title page woodcut of Jakob Issickemer, *Das buchlein der zuflucht zu Maria der muter gottes in alten Oding*, Nuremberg (Kaspar Hochfeder) 1497/98

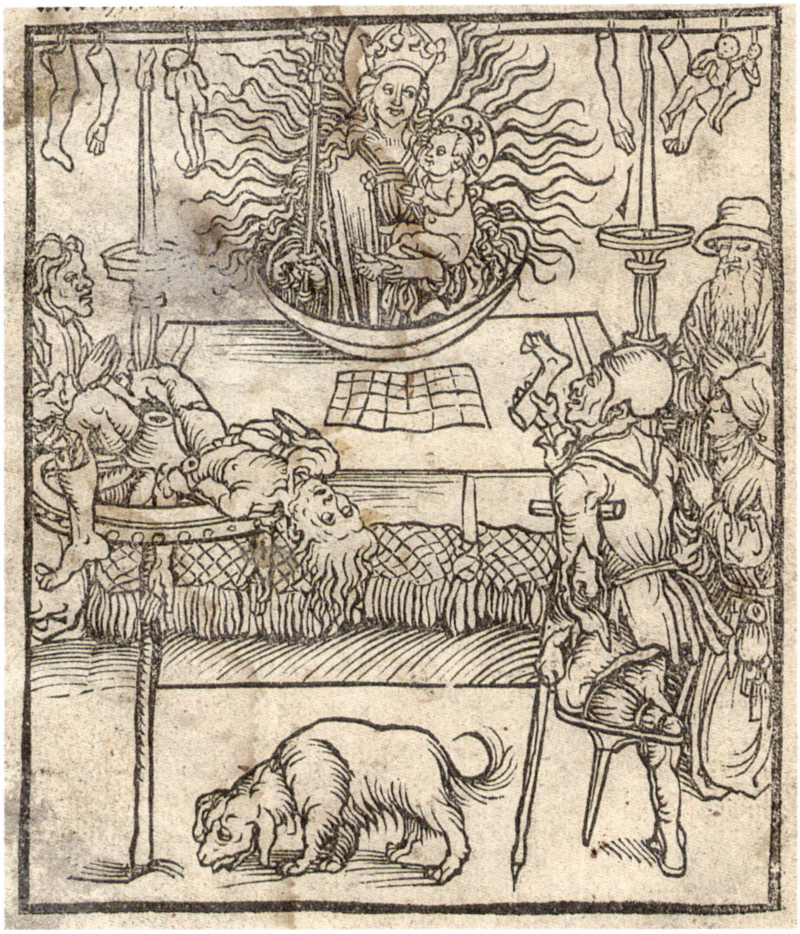

heads and the blazing seams that seem to shadow the contours (see, for example, the arm and the legs of the man with the amputated foot) are surprisingly close to Cranach's handling – compare, for instance, the mourners in his *Calvary* woodcut of 1502 (cat. 3), or the chiaroscuro drawing *St Martin* (1504; cat. 27), which is only a little larger and has a similarly linear feel. There are also a number of additional compositional similarities – see, for example, the repoussoir figure of the kneeling beggar and the flat handling of the pictorial elements where a compact group of figures is again paired with the aligning foreshortened architecture. And finally, there are two "Cranach-esque" motifs: the man broken on the wheel, the scene's drastic brutality and the upside-down perspective are an apparent precursor of the bodies scattered on the ground in the large *Mount of Calvary* woodcuts produced in Vienna (cat. 2 & 3), and, secondly, the dog sniffing round the foot of the base of the wheel. The latter is not really Cranach's invention (the ancestor of this and many related canines first appears in Schongauer's engraving *The Adoration of the Magi*) but its striking verisimilitude and especially its curly tail have much in common with many of the countless dogs in Cranach's later works. A much later woodcut produced at Wittenberg, which may or may not have been designed by a member of his workshop, even features a hound in the foreground whose individual details seem to derive from the very same study (fig. 10).[27]

Fig. 10
Lucas Cranach the Elder or workshop (design), *Christ and the Canaanite Woman* (from a series of eight illustrations of the Creed and the Lord's Prayer), c.1520/25. Staatliche Kunstsammlungen, Kupferstich-Kabinett, Dresden, inv. A 1905-378

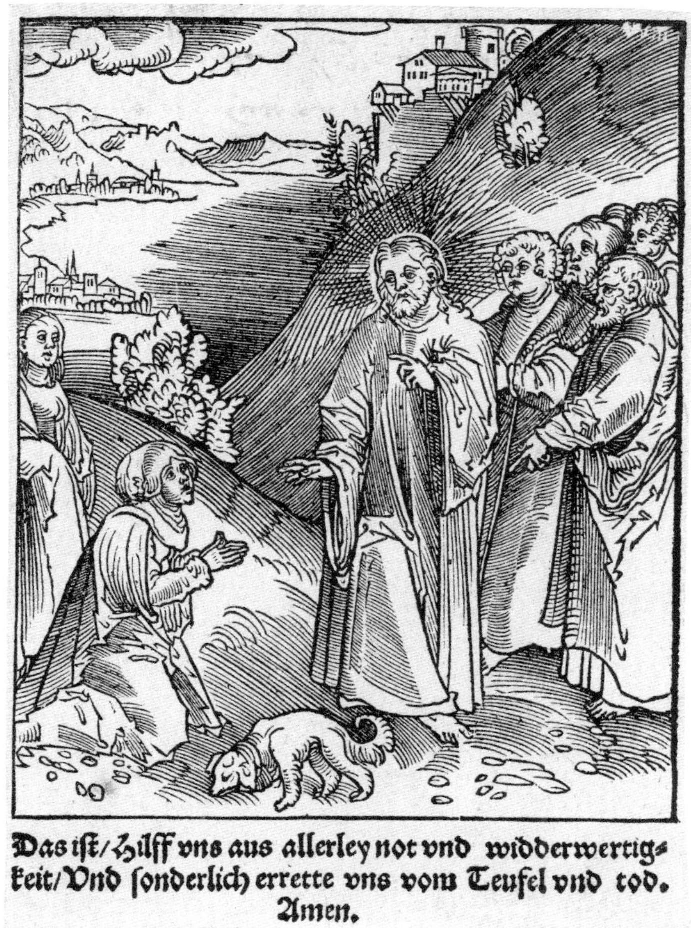

If Cranach designed the woodcut for the Altötting booklet and was in contact with its author, it would support a long-held assumption, namely the reason the artist moved to Vienna soon afterwards. Before he became a canon in Altötting, Issickemer taught and lectured in Vienna. This may be why a "Jeronimus Issehamer de Otting" enrolled at Vienna University in 1509, and a "Guolfgangus Yssikemer de Ȯtting" the following year. Their unusual surname suggests they were related (sons?) to the canon.[28] From extant paintings and copies we know that Cranach's patrons in Vienna came from the city's bourgeoisie and especially its leading humanist circles, for whom he produced portraits, small-scale devotional paintings, and woodcuts. In 1497, Emperor Maximilian I had called Conrad Celtes to Vienna University, where he joined his friend Johannes Cuspinian and where in 1501 he founded the Collegium Poetarum, a college for poets. In the winter semester 1500, Cuspinian served as rector and shortly afterwards he and his wife sat for their portraits by Cranach. Hoping for (more) such commissions from the newly-constituted humanist milieu may have been the main reasons why Cranach, who seems to have known some Latin, moved to Vienna.[29] Here, too, there are additional connections to Nuremberg, where Celtes had been the first humanist to be crowned Poet Laureate by Emperor Frederick III, and where he met Dürer and other humanists. Residing in Vienna since 1497, Celtes continued to publish some of his most important books in Nuremberg, among them the first edition of the writings of Roswitha von Gandersheim (1501), which he dedicated to his patron (who subsequently made Cranach his court painter) Frederick the Wise, Elector of Saxony, and *Quattuor libri amorum* (1502). Dürer was involved in the woodcuts illustrating both publications. It seems that, unlike Nuremberg, Vienna at the turn of the sixteenth century had no artists skilled enough to produce such sophisticated portraits and woodcuts, and we may assume that Cranach – encouraged by these men of letters he had become acquainted with in Nuremberg – moved there in the hope of filling this very gap.

1 Flechsig 1900, 9, was the first to point out that Cranach must have worked in Austria and Vienna, as evidenced by the Hungarian types in his undated *Mount of Calvary* woodcut (cat. 2), and Scheurl's 1509 eulogy (see note 2). See also the summary of all these arguments in Vogel 1909. 1501 is generally cited as the year in which Cranach arrived in Vienna, which is based on a source that tells us that he was still at Coburg in 1501. But it seems the "Lucas Maler" mentioned in this document is not our artist (see Hambrecht 1995). And in 1996, Kunz was able to expose the occasionally repeated story that Cranach had accompanied Frederick the Wise on a pilgrimage to the Holy Land in 1493 as a legend based on a fake document.

2 In his 1509 eulogy on Cranach, Christoph Scheurl, dean of the University of Wittenberg, mentions that Cranach worked in Austria (*Oratio doctoris Scheurli attingens litterarum prestantiam, necnon laudem Ecclesie Collegiate Vittenburgensis*, Leipzig [Martin Landsberg] 1509, here: fol. A2r). We also have Melanchthon's report of a sadly undated statement by the artist that he had been very ill in Austria 32 years earlier (»sehr kranck zu Wien in Osterreich«). See Philipp Melanchthon, *Opera Quae Supersunt Omnia* (Corpus Reformatorum, vol. XX), Brunswick 1854, col. 593–594, no. CCLXI. See also Koepplin 1973, 42–46.

3 Cranach's date of birth (1472) is testified in several ways, including his celebrated portrait in the Uffizi Galleries painted by his son Lucas the Younger in 1550 and inscribed with the sitter's age (Friedländer & Rosenberg 1979, no. 425). Schepers 1994, 48–49, however, has suggested that the artist may have been born a few years later; ditto recently Vaisse 2019.

4 A faksimile of Gunderam's report in exh. cat. Wittenberg 2011, 58–61, the quote is on 59. For a German translation see Lüdecke 1953, 84–88.

5 See Heiser 2002, 44–46; Weniger 2018, XXXI.

6 For events in the diocese of Bamberg, see Franz-Duhme 1994.

7 For this artwork, see most recently Weniger 2018, XXXfl., figs. 1–3.

8 Seven painter's workshops are recorded in Bamberg in 1501, see Baumgärtel-Fleischmann 1968, 28.

9 See Hörsch 1994, 105–107, and Weniger 2018, XXXI–XXXII, who also rejects the repeatedly-voiced idea that the monogramist can be identified as Cranach.

10 For Pfeil's breviary see Geldner 1964, 68, 93, no. 37 and fig. on 74; for illuminated manuscripts from Bamberg, see also Hengelhaupt 1994. Dörnhöffer was the first to realise that Ratdolt's composition served as Cranach's most important template (Dörnhöffer 1904, col. 182–185, fig. 39). See also Endrődi 2018, 88–91.

11 For both prints, see Stadler 1913, 78.

12 Anzelewsky 1971, no. 26. Though patron and intended destination remain obscure, we know that Dürer's panel was in Saxony in the sixteenth century. See Goldberg & Heimberg & Schawe 1998, 159–161.

13 Dürer set up as an independent master around 1495/96, but he would not initially have taken on assistants. And Scheurl would surely have mentioned it in his 1509 eulogy if Cranach had worked with the famous Nuremberg master (see note 2); Koepplin in exh. cat. Basel 1974, 118.

14 For Stoss and the *Volckamer Monument*, see Albrecht 1997, esp. 92–97 and 110–117.

15 Exh. cat. Basel 1974, 135 and cat. 64, 67 (Dieter Koepplin); Schramm 1934, no. 610.

16 For Cranach's relationship with Pacher, see most recently Heydenreich 2007, 313–315, who also thinks Cranach may have worked in the latter's workshop; for Frueauf, see Weniger 2018, XLIII–XLVI. The Polish costumes in some of the works produced in Vienna led Anzelewsky 1999, 125–134, to suggest that Cranach may have visited Poland or Cracow at the turn of the sixteenth century.

17 See Heydenreich 2007, 97, 101–103, 315–317; see also Teget-Welz 2018, LI–LIII; cat. Nuremberg 2019, no. 40, here and note 5 (Katja von Baum, Sebastian Schmidt).

18 See Buck & Messling 2011, XVIII–XIX.

19 The sources are in Gurlitt 1895, 113.

20 See Koepplin in exh. cat. Basel 1974, 135.

21 For more on this, see the essay by Sabine Heiser, esp. 68.

22 See Menz 1982.

23 For Breu and Cranach, see most recently Weniger 2018, XLV; Teget-Welz 2018, LIII.

24 For this portrait, see Anzelewsky 1971, 31; exh. cat. Vienna & Munich 2011, cat. 58 (Thomas Kuster) and most recently Teget-Welz 2018, LIII. Koepplin's suggestion that Cranach may have been responsible for the illustrations in the *Revelationes sancte Birgitte*, printed in 1500 by Anton Koberger at Nuremberg, should be rejected because woodcuts designed by the same

artist also appear in books published at a later date in Nuremberg. See Dieter Koepplin in exh. cat. Basel 1974, see cat. 68; Rainer Schoch refutes this suggestion in Schoch & Mende & Scherbaum, vol. 3, see no. A34. For the so-called Benedict Master whom Koepplin 1977b has tentatively identified as Cranach, see most recently and comprehensively Scholz 2009 (who does not mention Koepplin).

25 *Das buchlein der zuflucht zu Maria der muter gottes in alten Oding*, Nuremberg (Kaspar Hochfeder), after 15 October 1497 (the date on which the author dedicated it to Johannes Graf). The booklet must have been published before 1498, the year Hochfeder moved to Metz. See GW M15397; ISTC ii00217000; Bauer 1964/65; Van der Vekene 1974, 24, 55, no. 38 (edition), 168–169, no. 54 (woodcut); and Signori 1999, esp. 56–66.

26 Geisberg 1939, 142, fig. 50.

27 Woodcut: Hollstein 1959, no. 67h (112 × 93 mm [image]). For dogs in Cranach's oeuvre, see most recently the contributions and illustrations in exh. cat. Innsbruck 2018.

28 Issickemer mentions that he taught "in gynnasio viennensi" (i.e. at the university) in his dedication to Georg Stuchs, a printer from Nuremberg who had published the *Salzburger Obsequiale* (fol. A2r) in 1495. For the cited names listed in the university register, see Gall & Szaivert 1967, 359 and 373.

29 In 1509, Andreas Karlstadt praised the painter's Latin utterances as "full of wit" ("Cuius ab ore fluit sermo latiusque sagaxque") in a poem. Quoted from Scheurl 1509 (see note 2), fol. C5r, for a German translation see Lüdecke 1953, 55–56.

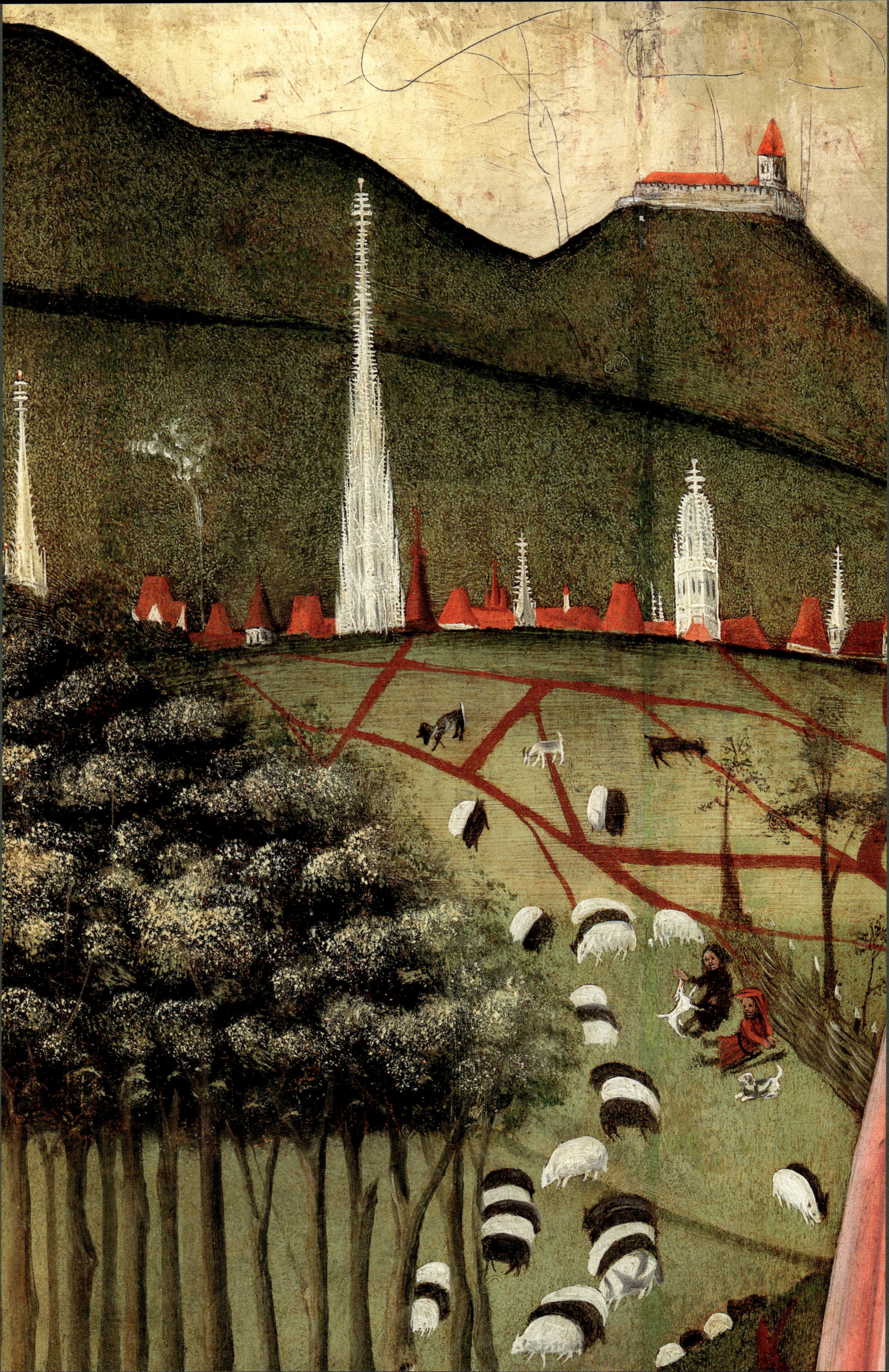

Björn Blauensteiner

Cranach's Vienna. Guild Regulations and Artistic Environment

In his *Nuremberg Chronicle* of 1493, Hartmann Schedel praises Vienna as the wealthiest, most populous, and oldest city on the Danube, and includes a woodcut of its skyline spread over two pages (fig. 1).[1] At the time, Vienna was enjoying a respite after going through several turbulent decades.[2] First, the city was at the centre of a struggle that pitted Emperor Frederick III against his brother Albrecht VI, who wanted to become Duke of Austria following the death of the heir to the throne, Ladislaus the Posthumous, in 1457. This fraternal conflict culminated with Albrecht laying siege to the emperor holed up in the Hofburg, the ducal palace in Vienna, in 1462, and only ended with Albrecht's death in 1463. Early in the following year the inhabitants of Vienna pledged allegiance to the emperor, which would involve the city in the next armed confrontation, this time with Matthias Corvinus, King of Hungary. In 1477, Hungarian troops laid siege to the Austrian capital for the first time, and after a second siege conquered it in 1485. When Matthias Corvinus died in Vienna in 1490, the city again fell to Emperor Frederick III and his son Maximilian, who had been crowned King of the Romans in 1486. This marked the beginning of a relatively quiet period for the city until the Ottoman siege of 1529, though it saw an outbreak of the plague in 1506. It has been estimated that at the turn of the sixteenth century Vienna had around 20–30,000 inhabitants, making it the by far largest and most populous city in the Habsburgs' domains and one of the great metropolises of the Holy Roman Empire, whose most populous city was Cologne with around 40,000 inhabitants.[3] Vienna's population stagnated in the unsettled second half of the fifteenth century, and many sectors of its increasingly specialised job market began to complain of a lack of trained workers, which made Vienna an attractive destination for immigrants from the politically-stable 1490s onwards.

The political and economic situation presumably also influenced Cranach's decision to try his luck in Vienna.[4] But what was his (legal) status, and how did he earn a living during his stay in the city?[5] Cranach was already about 28 years old when he moved to Vienna around 1500. We can preclude that he worked as an apprentice, especially in the light of prominent commissions like the portraits of Cuspinian and his wife (cat. 12 & 13). This also makes it highly unlikely that he was employed as a subordinate journeyman in the workshop of some Viennese master.[6] So we have to assume that Cranach operated in Vienna as a free master. This is, however, contradicted by the fact that Cranach was probably still unmarried at the time and that he never seems to have become a citizen of Vienna:[7] according to the guild regulations effective around 1500, only painters who could prove that they were married and living with their

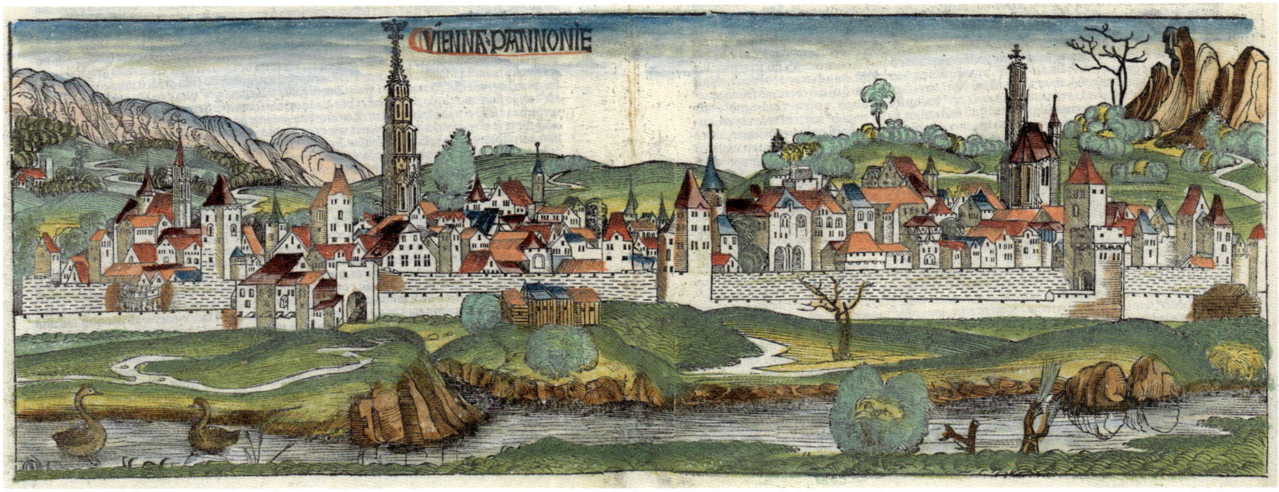

Fig. 1
Michael Wolgemut, *Vienna seen from the North ("Vienna, Pannonie")* from the Nuremberg Chronicle published in 1493, (hand-coloured) woodcut. Wien Museum, Vienna, inv. 169582

spouse and who had acquired citizenship were allowed to settle there as free masters.[8] This suggests Cranach was a travelling journeyman who pursued his profession without having obtained either citizenship or his master-craftsman's certificate, and who could therefore be prosecuted under guild regulations.[9] However, students and faculty of Vienna University, whose impressive student body hailing from Hungary and Southern Germany Schedel explicitly mentions,[10] fell under the autonomous university's jurisdiction and not the city's.[11] The university connections of Cranach's prominent patrons presumably protected him from lawsuits instigated by the local painters' guild: in the winter semester 1500/01, Johannes Cuspinian was vice chancellor of Vienna University, i.e. supreme judge in academic matters, later becoming superintendent, the ducal supervisor of the university's jurisdiction. In 1504, Johann Stephan Reuss, who was presumably also painted by Cranach (cat. 15), was elected vice chancellor; the latter also repeatedly served as dean of the Law Faculty (1500, 1504/05, 1509). In 1478, Johannes Fuchsmagen, who probably commissioned Cranach to illustrate a *Filocalus* copy (cat. 7) and perhaps also the *St Jerome*, a painting dated 1502 (cat. 6), was both dean of the Arts Faculty and a member of the *Sodalitas Danubiana*, which was founded by Conrad Celtes. And Johannes Winterburger, the Viennese publisher of books illustrated with Cranach's woodcuts (cat. 22–26), oversaw the printing of most university publications. Regardless of his personal status, we may therefore assume that thanks to his commissions from this privileged circle of patrons, Cranach was not subject to the city's guild regulations.[12] Perhaps Cranach was even able – in analogy to later examples of craftsmen and artists working for the court, which freed them from the restrictions imposed by the city's guilds[13] – to accept external commissions without fear of prosecution thanks to his status as a kind of university painter. Although we do not (yet) have any documentary proof, Cranach's special status under local guild regulations is probably best explained by his documented closeness to Vienna's university circles.

Painting in Vienna in the second half of the fifteenth century[14] is closely related to Early-Netherlandish painting. This is already true of the most important extant pictorial ensemble that we know was produced in Vienna in the middle of the fifteenth century, the retable for the high altar of the city's Carmelite church.[15] The focus on realistic details and atmospheric vistas in the so-called *Albrecht Altarpiece* may derive from paintings produced along the Upper-Rhine and in Swabia,[16] works by artists like Konrad Witz and Hans Multscher who, in turn, were inspired by the Early-Netherlandish *ars nova*. The panel depicting the *Meeting at the Golden*

Gate includes the earliest known view of Vienna and its environs (fig. 2). The so-called Albrecht Master produced not only the *Albrecht Altarpiece* but probably also, for instance, the epitaph of Johannes Geuss, a canon of St Stephen's Cathedral and vice chancellor of Vienna University who died in 1440. While the undulating drapery and delicate modelling of these works still echo the International Style prevalent at the beginning of the century, *The Virgin with Saints and the Patron Casper Hornperger* in the church of Maria am Gestade, dated 1462,[18] and the retable for the high altar of the Schottenkirche,[19] dated 1469 on one of the panels, are closer to Early-Netherlandish painting. In addition to fastidiously handled details and stacked landscapes constructed using colour perspective – two of the panels again include views of Vienna (fig. 3) – the *Schotten Altarpiece* also features drapery with harder creases as well as protagonists with haggard features and solemn poses. Ultimately these characteristics can be traced back to Rogier van der Weyden and Dieric Bouts, probably indirectly adopted via Hans Pleydenwurff's workshop in Nuremberg.[20] It seems quite symbolic that the *Schotten Altarpiece* served as the high altar of the church where the members of the city's painters' guild met because the retable functions as a summary of the styles prevalent in Vienna and its environs until the end of the century.[21] For instance, the epitaph of Jodok Hauser (d. 1478) in Vienna's Minoritenkirche (Friars Minor Conventual Church) (fig. 4), for which the painter Hans Siebenbürger received payment in 1479,[22] is closely related to the style favoured by the Schotten Workshop. Handling, pale flesh colour, and composition of the *Hauser Epitaph* are closely related to a *Woman of the Apocalypse* in St Stephen's Cathedral,[23] which is based on a woodcut by Schongauer and which was allegedly erected near a pillar of the nave by a Viennese burgher in 1493.[24] Also related is a small *Crucifixion Diptych* in the church of St Florian Monastery that, as documented by the inclusion of depictions of St Stephen's Cathedral and Hofburg Palace, was produced in Vienna as well and that may also be by Siebenbürger.[25]

Fig. 2
Albrecht Master, *The Meeting at the Golden Gate*, c.1438/40. Klosterneuburg Abbey, Stiftsmuseum, inv. GM 25

Fig. 3
Schotten Master, *Rest on the Flight into Egypt*, c.1469. Museum im Schottenstift, Vienna

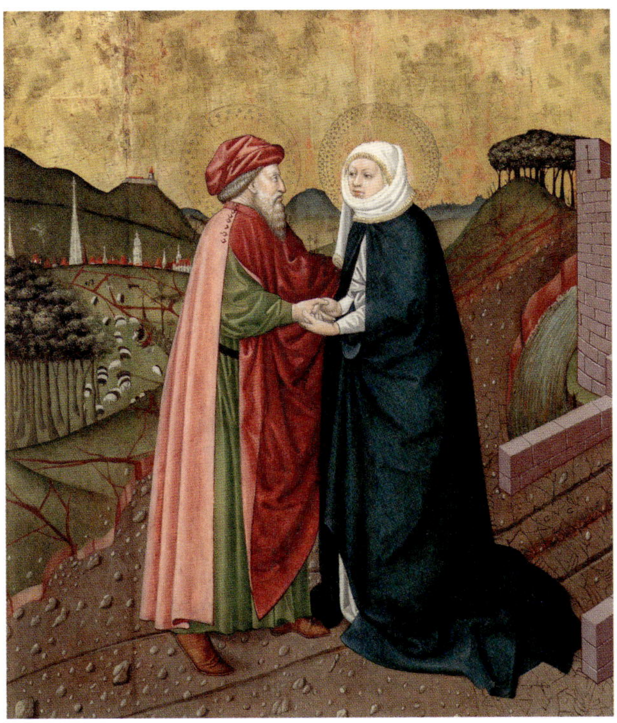

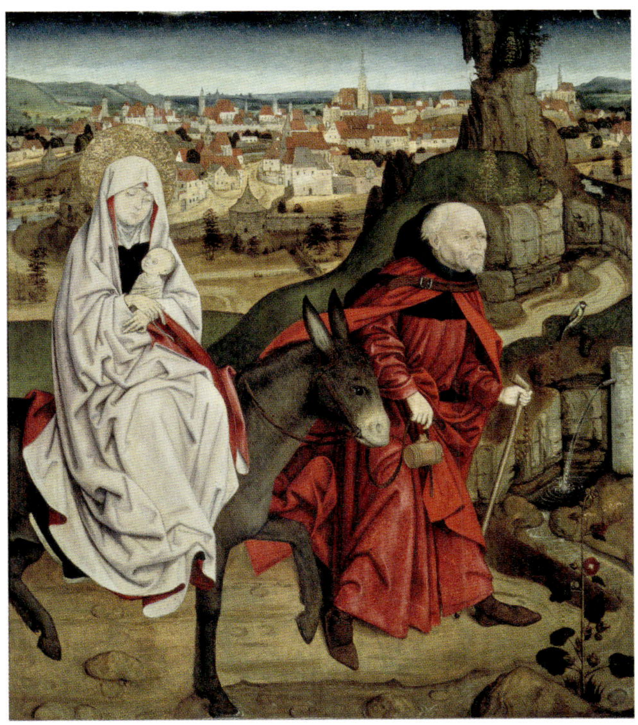

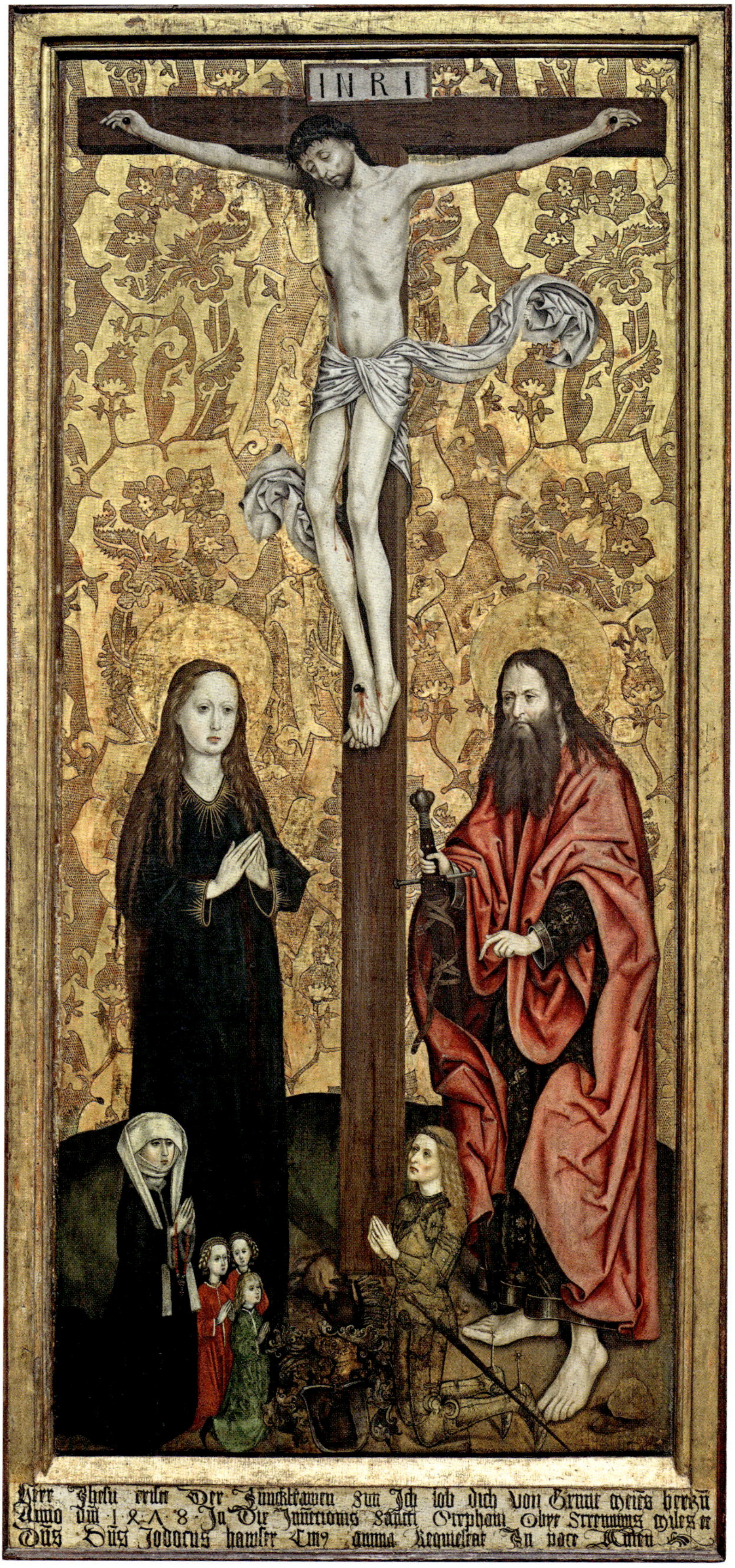

Fig. 4
Hans Siebenbürger,
Epitaph of Jodok Hauser,
c.1478/79. Belvedere,
Vienna, inv. 4850

A number of other works from the final quarter of the fifteenth century can also be attributed to the Schotten Master and his circle, because they too were clearly produced in Vienna and its environs.[26]

Vienna's relatively rigid guild regulations and the changing political situation may be why painting in Vienna in the second half of the fifteenth century remains somewhat homogenous and dominated by the Schotten Workshop and its filiations. There are, however, also a number of stylistically divergent works, among them the *Virgin with Saints and the Patron Jörg von Pottendorf* painted in 1467, or the *Epitaph of Jesse Sax* from 1473, both in the parish church of Ebenfurth located south of Vienna; here, features and facial types, drapery, and handling are closer to works produced by the Albrecht Master than those of the Schotten Workshop.[27] This older tradition is also reflected in the works of the so-called Lehrbüchermeister (Master of the School Books), Vienna's leading illuminator in the second half of the fifteenth century.[28]

Another outlier is the so-called *Babenberg Family Tree* dated 1489 in the church of Klosterneuburg Monastery, which was probably commissioned for the tomb of Duke Leopold III of Austria, a scion of the Babenberg family canonised in 1485.[29] Conceived as a profane triptych with wings spanning eight metres, this work, for which the painter Hans Part received payment in 1491,[30] is truly remarkable. The structure of the central panel is also exceptional, featuring vegetal medallions, each of which contains a Babenberg duke in a landscape setting, with many also including realistic views of identifiable towns (fig. 5). These medallions are joined by the branches of a tree, its trunk embedded in a landscape that covers the entire central panel. In the *Babenberg Family Tree*, landscape is accorded an even more prominent role than in the other examples of fifteenth-century Viennese painting after the *Albrecht Altarpiece*.

A look at works in other media undoubtedly produced in Vienna in the late fifteenth century shows that they too received important impulses from Nuremberg. The earliest woodcuts in the books published by Johannes Winterburger are closely related to works by Michael Wolgemut, who took over Hans Pleydenwurff's workshop after the latter's death.[31] The baptismal font in St Stephen's Cathedral also represents a direct connection to Franconia: for the outer reliefs, clearly informed by Schongauer's engravings, artists from Nuremberg were asked for a brass template before the stone was carved by Ulrich Auer in Salzburg in 1481.[32] Reliefs produced in Vienna in the last third of the fifteenth century exhibit a similar linear quality and a preference for crinkled folds – see, for example, the carved sacramental scenes on the crown of the font[33] (temporarily "misused" as a pulpit ceiling),[34] or the *Christ on the Mount of Olives* relief on the south wall of the Apostles' Choir of St Stephen's Cathedral.[35]

However, the *Christ on the Mount of Olives* group on the outside wall of St Blaise's Chapel in St Michael's Church[36] is an almost Renaissance-like outlier in contemporary Viennese art production with its wet, clinging draperies. The highly original motifs and extremely expressive figures of the choir stalls of St Stephen's,[37] dated 1486 but sadly almost completely destroyed in the Second World War, are also exceptional, although most of the carving is rather pedestrian. And we should also mention Niclaus Gerhaert's life-size depiction of Emperor Frederick III,[38] its masterly realism identifying it as perhaps the most important sculptural artwork produced in Austria at that time. In 1493, the marble slab was transported from Wiener Neustadt to St Stephen's Cathedral to serve as the lid of Frederick's tomb.

In his overview of Gothic painting in Vienna, Erick Strohmer described Cranach's *Schotten Crucifixion* (cat. 1) as a "great revolution", with a „highly destructive storm" blowing through it.[39] The painterly handling, the soft draperies, and the enormous expressiveness of Cranach's early paintings have almost nothing in common with works produced in Vienna in the late

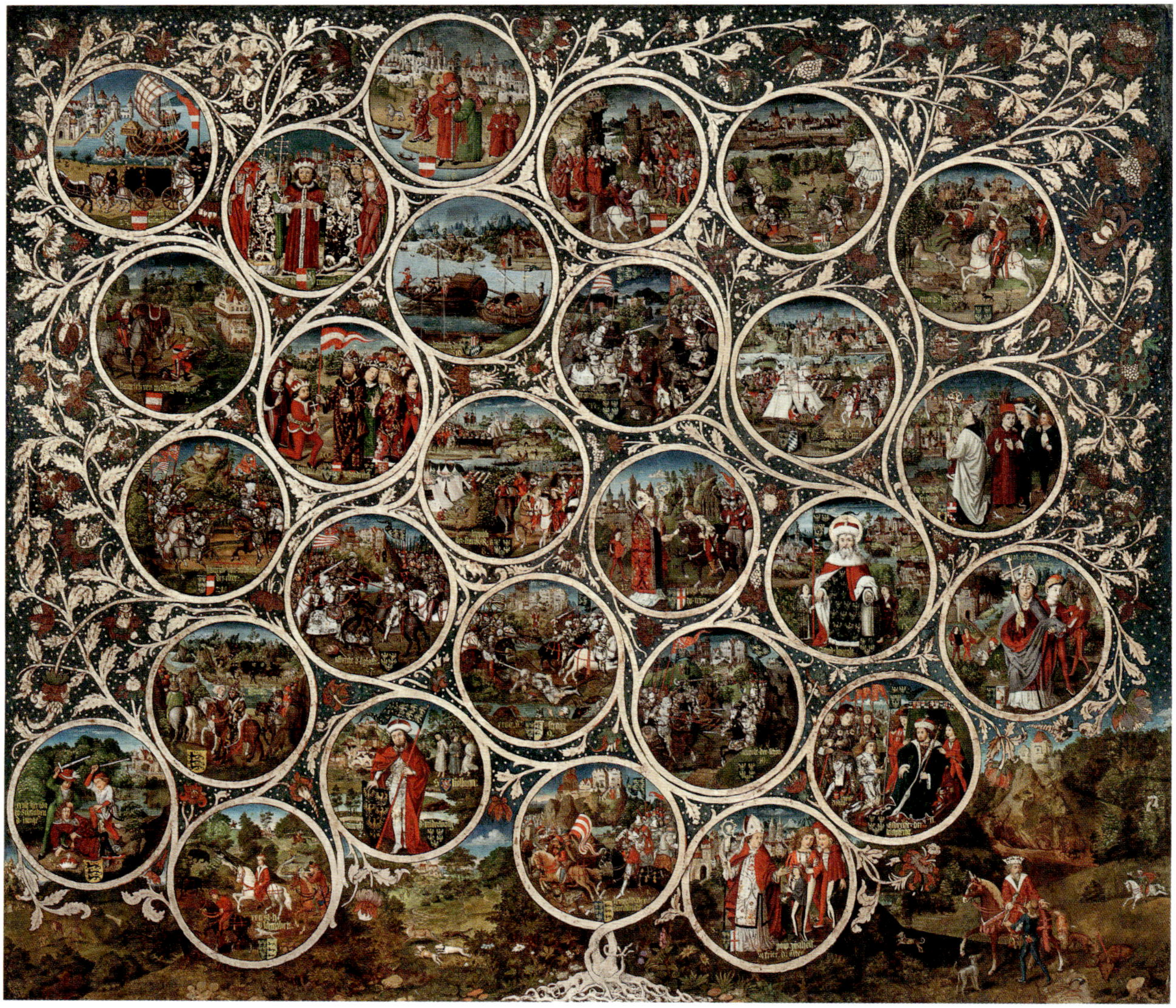

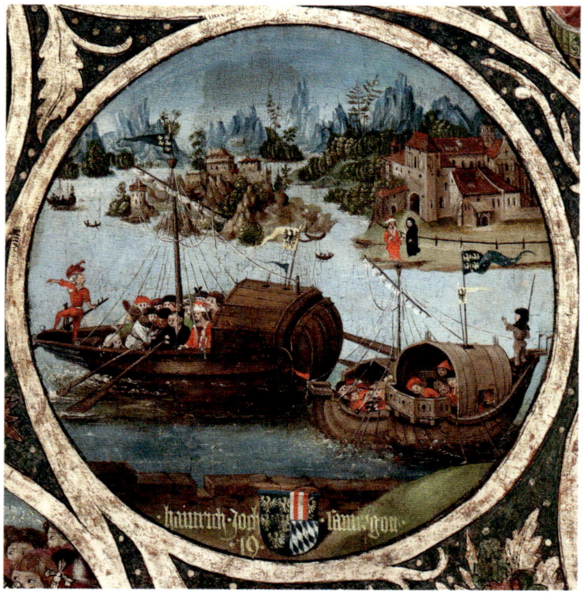

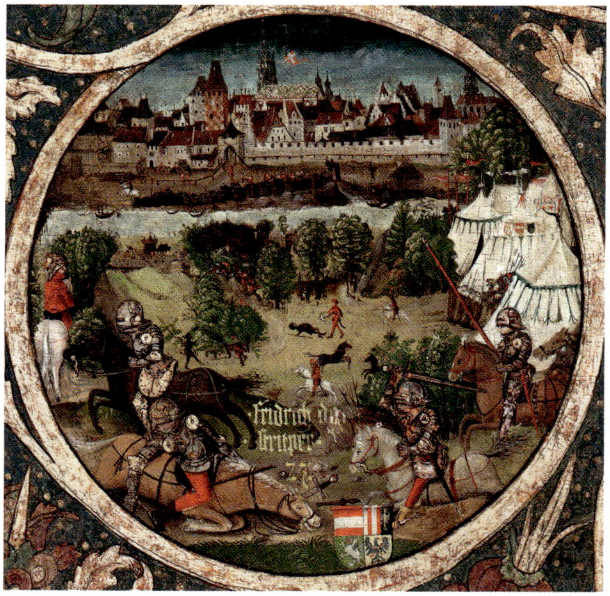

Fig. 5
Hans Part, *Central Panel of the Babenberg Family Tree*, c.1489. Klosterneuburg Abbey, Stiftsmuseum.
Detail bottom left: Henry II, Duke of Austria on a pilgrimage and in front of the Schottenkirche in Vienna;
detail bottom right: Frederick II, Duke of Austria during the Battle of the Leitha River with a view of Vienna in the distance

fifteenth century – but Cranach's art greatly impacted the contemporary art scene in Austria's capital. One of the works bearing this out is the panel depicting the Viennese burgher Paul Vink and his wife as witnesses to Christ's crowning with thorns (fig. 6).[40] The anonymous but probably Viennese artist commissioned by Vink – perhaps to commemorate the death of his wife in 1504 – clearly based this work, which may have been destined for the *Gottesleichnamsbruderschaft Sankt Stephan* (Fraternity of the Body of Christ St Stephen), on Cranach. His templates seem to have been the figures in the *Schotten Crucifixion*, produced only a few years earlier, which is best seen in the group assembled around the Virgin in the centre of the composition. Changes to the outside wall of the former treasury of St Stephen's Cathedral document that Viennese sculpture too received "decisive impulses" from Cranach's sojourn in the city.[41] Above a series of scenes from the Passion – produced around 1470/80 by a painter from the circle of the Schotten Workshop – was installed, around 1520, a series of sandstone reliefs (identical in format) that depict the corresponding episodes in stylistically contrary ways.[42] By

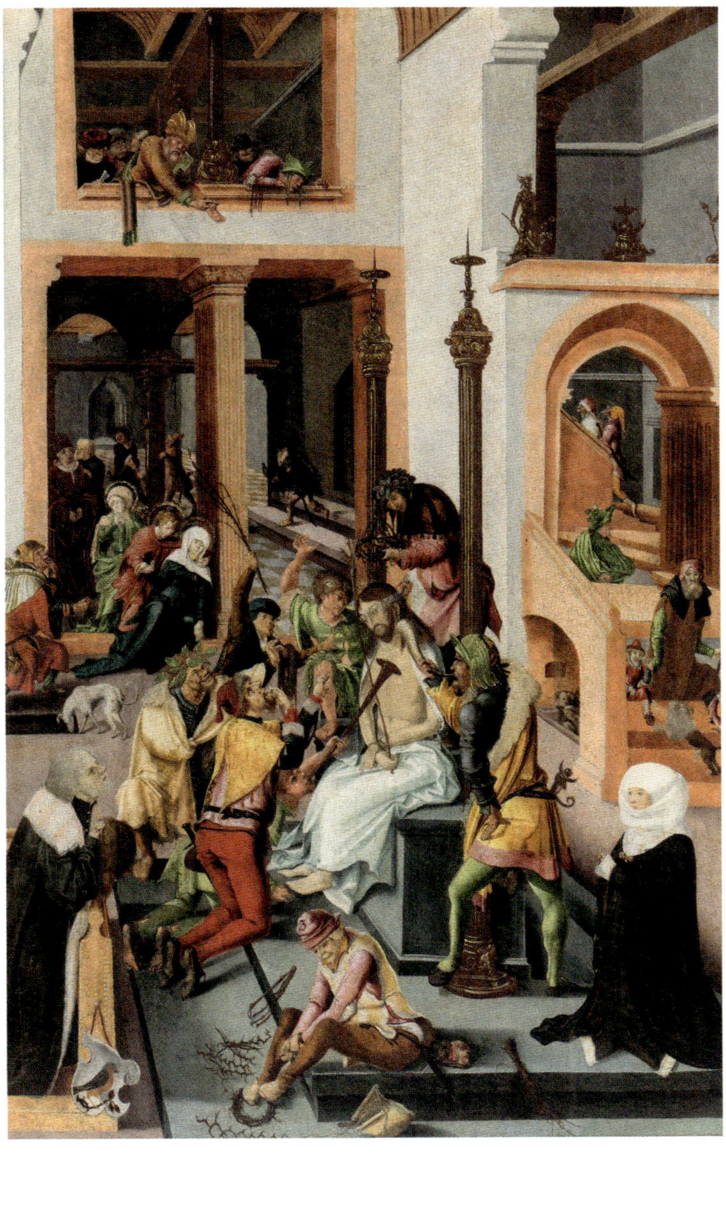

Fig. 6
Viennese artist (?), *The Mockery of Christ with the Donor Paul Vink and his Wife*, c.1505/10. Dom Museum, Vienna, inv. L-59 (on loan from the Archdiocese)

now, décor and architectural motifs derived from classical antiquity have entered Viennese art,[43] and the Schotten Workshop's rigid renderings of figures and drapery, which had dominated artistic production for decades, have been replaced by a softer and more expressive approach, for which Cranach's early work provided a template. This means that, from an art-historical point of view, the Vienna Cranach left behind when he moved to Wittenberg was very different from the one he had arrived in only a few years before.

1 Schedel 1493, fol. XCVIIIv–XCIXr.
2 For a history of Vienna from the second half of the fifteenth century to the first Ottoman siege of the city, see Dürigl 1975/76; Csendes 2001; Csendes & Opll 2021, 130–205.
3 Niederstätter 1996, 22–25; Perger 2001, 206–209.
4 See the essay by Guido Messling.
5 See also Heiser 2002, 52–56. I would like to thank Andreas Zajic for his suggestions regarding this question.
6 In general, journeymen were employed for only about three months, and they had to leave the city immediately if they were unable to obtain work in another workshop. See Gneiß 2017, 96; for information on Vienna's fire regulations of 1458, see Hollnsteiner 1937, 80.
7 The receipts from the fees payable on obtaining citizenship are recorded in the Oberkammerrechnungen der Stadt Wien, Wiener Stadt- und Landesarchiv, Sig. 1.1.1.B1, series 55–60. For the years 1498–1501 and 1503–1504 (the receipts for the years 1502 and 1505 have not survived) the Christian name Lucas appears only once: the vintner Lucas Hofer in 1504.
8 Guild regulations applied not only to painters but also to silk embroiderers, glass makers, gold-beaters, and printers (*Aufdrucker*) – it seems the rules also applied to publishers as Johannes Winterburger is listed as an *Aufdrucker* in the records of 1496 and 1500; see Perger 2005, 263. For the complete text of the guild regulations adopted on 18 June 1446, see Gneiß 2017, 294–296 (no. 150). See also the supplementary agreement dated 31 January 1468 according to which painters, silk embroiderers, gold-beaters, and printers were not allowed to work ("nichts arbaiten"), neither secretly nor publicly ("haimblich noch öffentlich"), until they had obtained their citizenship, among other requirements, Uhlirz 1896, CLXXX–CLXXXI (no. 15378).
9 Haupt 2007, 33–36; Gneiß 2017, 151–152.
10 Schedel 1493, fol. XCIXr.
11 See Mühlberger 2001, esp. 324–325, 360–364, 368–369.
12 Cranach himself is not listed in the university's register, see the archive of Vienna University, Matricula Universitatis Vindobonensis (1451–1548), sig. M3; Protocollum Inclytae Nationis Rhenanae (1415–1582), sig. NR 1.
13 For craftsmen working for the court, whose ad personam privileges also allowed them, in selected cases, to work for patrons who did not belong to the court without having to fear falling foul of the city's trade regulations (*hofbefreite Handwerker*), see Haupt 2007, esp. 13–26. It seems this instrument was already very popular in the sixteenth century; we know, for example, that in 1572 Emperor Maximilian II passed (now lost) regulations for court merchants, grocers, and craftsmen; see Haupt 2007, 16. For craftsmen removed from the city-guild jurisdiction by an imperial writ of protection (*Dekretisten*), see Haupt 2007, 32–33. For the special treatment of sixteenth- and seventeenth-century artists by the law, see also Bredekamp 2008, esp. 9–23 and – regarding Veit Stoss – 23–28.
14 See Pächt 1929, 8–22; Benesch 1930/32; Strohmer 1955; Seidl 1987; Madersbacher 2003.
15 Today, the retable is in the St Sebastian's Chapel of Klosterneuburg Abbey. For the ensemble and its history, see Röhrig 1981; Madersbacher 2003, 415–417 (no. 189; Michael and Thomas Rainer).
16 For the Albrecht Master's handling and style, see Rosenauer 1981.
17 Today, the painting is in the Dom Museum in Vienna. See Rosenauer 1981, 114, pl. 34; Madersbacher 2003, 417–418 (no. 191; Michael and Thomas Rainer).
18 Hornperger, who died in 1460, was the representative of the Diocese of Passau in Vienna; this suggests the painting was commissioned for the church of Maria am Gestade, which was Passau's official church in the city until the Diocese of Vienna was canonically established in 1469. For the painting, see cat. Vienna 1987, no. 68 (Arthur Saliger); Madersbacher 2003, 413.
19 The eight depictions of the Passion from the closed view and thirteen of the originally sixteen scenes from the life of the Virgin from the first opening have survived. Today, the majority of the paintings are in the Museum im Schottenstift in Vienna, and two are in the Belvedere (*Adoration of the Magi* and *Lamentation*). See cat. Vienna 1971, nos. 62–63; Reiter 1994; Koller 1994; Madersbacher 2003, 419–421 (no. 194; Michael and Thomas Rainer).
20 See, most recently, Suckale 2004, esp. 367–379.
21 For the Guild of Saint Luke in Vienna, see Löw 1907.

22 Today, the painting is in the Belvedere in Vienna, see cat. Vienna 1971, no. 59. For the panel's provenance and its attribution to Siebenbürger, see Perger 1973; Perger 1980.
23 Tietze 1931, 282–287, fig. 261; engraving: Bartsch no. 28.
24 Ogesser 1779, 141.
25 Suckale 2004, 365–367.
26 The artist who produced the epitaph for Florian Winkler, which was once in the cathedral in Wiener Neustadt, was presumably also in contact with the Schotten Workshop. For the painting (today in the Museum St. Peter an der Sperr in Wiener Neustadt), see Madersbacher 2003, 423 (no. 197; Michael and Thomas Rainer). The so-called Meister der Heiligenmartyrien (Master of the Saints' Martyria) is also connected with the traditions of the Schotten Workshop and is believed to have worked in Vienna, his *Notname* deriving from three panels now in the Belvedere, see cat. Vienna 1971, nos. 81–83; Madersbacher 2003, 425 (no. 199; Michael and Thomas Rainer). For more attributions to the Schotten Workshop, see Seidl 1987, vol. 1, 19–100.
27 For both paintings – today in the Liechtenstein Collection and the Wien Museum respectively – see Benesch 1930, 159–164, and cat. Vienna 1984, no. 1/88.
28 See Pfändtner 2011.
29 For the ensemble, now in the Stiftsmuseum Klosterneuburg, see Röhrig 1975; Madersbacher 2003, 423–425 (no. 198; Michael and Thomas Rainer).
30 Röhrig 1975, 10.
31 They include the frontispiece of the *Wiener Praktik* published in 1495 (Gollob 1925, figs. 29, 31; Gollob 1926, 11–14), the woodcuts depicting scholars in the two grammar textbooks printed in 1499 and 1500 respectively (Gollob 1926, 38, fig. p. 42; Gollob 1929, 28, fig. pl. VII), and the illustrations in the *Wiener Heiltumsbuch* of 1502 (see most recently Cárdenas 2021, 149–182, 428–437, 470–471).
32 Tietze 1931, 328–329; Oettinger 1949, 45–47.
33 Oettinger 1949, esp. 7–22.
34 Schlosser 1925, 10, 15, 19–21, figs. 47–59.
35 For the ensemble, said to have been dated 1502 and commissioned by the merchant Lienhart Lackner, see Tietze 1931, 359–361, fig. 398.
36 According to one source, the group was commissioned in 1480 by Hans Siebenbürger and his wife, who had it set up in the old St Michael's cemetery, see Perger 1980, 148; Perger 2005, 201.
37 Klebel 1925. An entry in the (lost) Viennese Kammeramtsrechnungen from 1484 apparently identified the choir stalls as a work by the carver Wilhelm Rollinger, see Klebel 1925, 21; Perger 2005, 166.
38 Exh. cat. Frankfurt & Strasbourg 2011/12, cat. 5 (Stefan Roller); Rosenauer 2017.
39 Strohmer 1955, 197.
40 For the painting (now in the Dom Museum in Vienna), see cat. Vienna 1987, no. 70.
41 Plieger 2018, 237.
42 For the wall paintings, see Lanc 1983, 7–16 (Ivo Hammer). Three of them have been removed and are today in the Wien Museum in Vienna, see exh. cat. Vienna 1975, cat. 252. For the reliefs, see Plieger 2009.
43 The earliest examples of classical architectural elements, decoration and calligraphy in Vienna are two architectural sculptures from the late 1490s: a lunette pediment inscribed with capital letters in a Renaissance script and embellished with a décor comprising loops and rosettes from 1497, and a *tabula ansata* dated 1498, see Blauensteiner 2021, 27. First commissioned in the first decade of the sixteenth century, the so-called humanists' epitaphs represent the most important vehicle for the reception of classical antiquity in Vienna, see Friesen 1989.

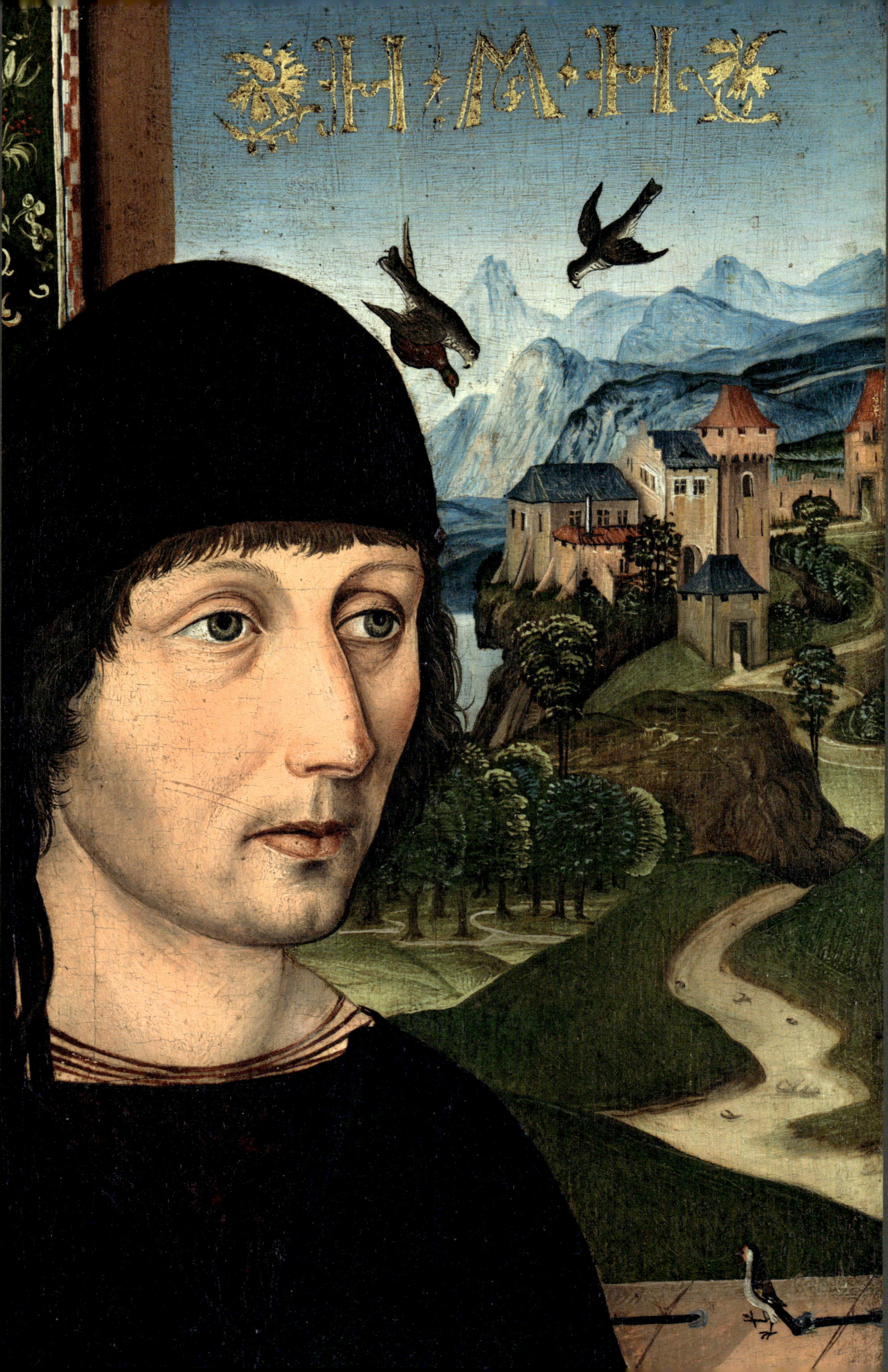
H · M · H

Kerstin Richter

Unmistakable. On Portraiture in Germany and the Low Countries before 1500

Portraits as an independent genre can be traced back to classical sources. In his *Naturalis historia*, Pliny the Elder recounts the legend of the daughter of the potter Butades of Sicyon who drew the silhouette of a departing friend on the wall.[1] This description focuses on one of the most important functions of a portrait: taking the place of an absent person, and – should that person be dead – his/her memoria. Leon Battista Alberti refers to Pliny in his *De Pittura* (On Painting), published in 1435, describing the art's divine power to help visualise an absent or deceased person, even if he or she lived many centuries earlier.[2] This, he writes, brings the artist acclaim. In the introduction to his book on painting, Dürer, who owned a Latin manuscript copy of Alberti's treatise, elaborates on painting's two functions: it serves, on the one hand, "the churches" because it can "depict the suffering of Christ". But painting also "preserves the appearance of people after they have died".[3] However, this memoria-function was not restricted to portraits, it could also be achieved through things like recalling the person's name and his/her function(s) or honours, inscriptions, or his/her coat of arms.[4] Sometimes these signs were combined, for example in funerary sculpture or epitaphs. In the fourteenth century, we increasingly find portraits of donors included in religious compositions, thus combining painting's two main functions as outlined by Dürer – though intercession definitely played a more prominent role. Portraits commissioned by members of the ruling elite focus on the princely ideal rather than verisimilitude. The sitter is depicted as the holder of an office in his dynastic legitimisation with the insignia of authority and power. He is identified by his clothes, his coat of arms and inscriptions, the insignia of his elevated status and rank. The depiction of the sitter was informed by the accepted canon denoting his social rank. There was no wish for a physical-mental identification of the individual by capturing his/her real appearance. This changed in the fourteenth century, which saw the evolution of a bourgeois society whose closeness to the court offered justifications for commissioning a portrait but who lacked the traditional badges of rank. From now on, the foremost criteria of painted documents of bourgeois existence were verisimilitude and realism. However, this new form of individualisation is not a sign of the slowly evolving sense of individuality, as is often maintained in older art-historical literature.[5] Pictorial conventions in these early portraits continue to rely on formulaic elements, and these likenesses remain visible documents of the sitter's social and familial status. Nonetheless, we notice an increase in realism and a growing psychological understanding. We can only speak of an autonomous portrait if the sitter is presented as him- or herself rather than as a representative or example expressed through a dominant reference.[6] His/her appearance must be highly distinctive and atypical and be the main subject of the painting. These

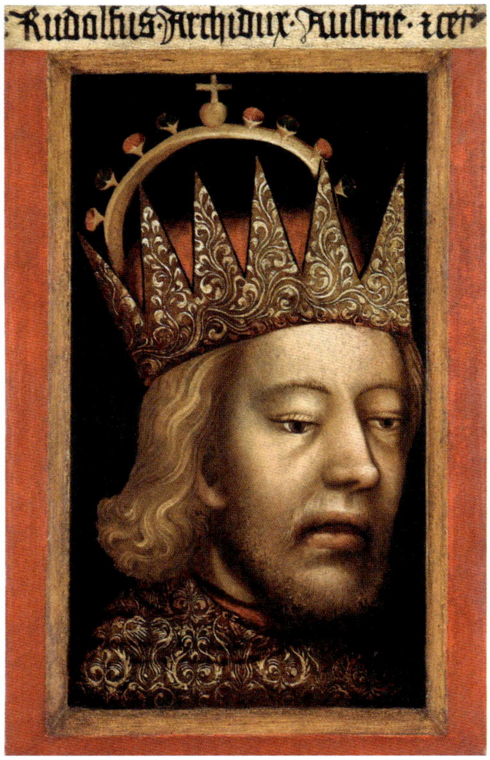

Fig. 1
Anonymous artist, *Rudolf IV, Duke of Austria*, c.1360/65. Dom Museum, Vienna, inv. L-II

first autonomous likenesses were beginning to be called "portraits" – earlier versions were known as "imago", "icon", "figura" or "effigies".[7] Two portraits of rulers must be regarded as the earliest extant proto-autonomous likenesses: one is a portrait of John II, King of France in profile by a presumably French artist. It is generally dated to 1350/60.[8] The portrait is clearly informed by ancient medallions and coins, a form of depiction long the most popular in Italy. In the *Portrait of Rudolf IV, Duke of Austria* painted around 1360/65, the sitter turns his head to face the viewer, which is quite innovative (fig. 1). The three-quarter view allows us to differentiate between the direction of his gaze and that in which his body is facing. This tension of the torso is also connected with the potentiality of movement, and together with the expression of his mouth and eyes, this greatly helps to animate the composition. The anonymous painter is generally located among the artists working for the court of Emperor Charles IV in Prague, with the frescoes in Karlštejn Castle and the triforium sculptures in St Vitus's Cathedral functioning as important precedents for this form of presentation.[9] Clearly this painting, which formed part of Rudolf's tomb and which shows him wearing the then still contentious archducal coronet symbolising a title he had "invented", carries a powerful political message. The image is still mainly informed by a lack of individuality and the prominence given to the sitter's dynastic claims, which is why we cannot speak of a fully autonomous portrait, even if this use of formulaic elements allows us to identify the duke.

In Germany this strong beginning long ploughed a lonely furrow, unlike at the Burgundian court. The courtly portrait of an anonymous, richly attired lady or princess painted around 1410/15 still continues the tradition of the classicising portrait in profile. It is surprisingly close to the portraits Pisanello produced thirty years later, and it is generally attributed to a Franco-Flemish artist.[10] Truly revolutionary are the well-known portraits by Robert Campin (c.1375–1444) or the Master of Flémalle and those by Jan van Eyck (1390–1441), though their frequently debated but still unclear dating makes an uncontested timeline all but impossible. In the *Portrait of a Stout Man*, which has also been attributed to Rogier van der Weyden, the sitter turns to face the viewer (fig. 2). Every detail and peculiarity of his skin is captured without flattery or idealisation, his powerful presence is almost too big for the painting. The location of his body, however, remains unclear, and his highly individualistic head almost touches the frame. The face feels like a realistic mask with an animated warm gaze. The two extant versions of this private portrait suggest it was intended for different branches of the family to remember the sitter and preserve a realistic likeness of his appearance.[11] Jan van Eyck's sitters occupy a similarly restricted space but are generally placed before a dark background. His earliest dated (1432) portrait of a man is inscribed "Léal Souvenir" on the parapet, which clearly

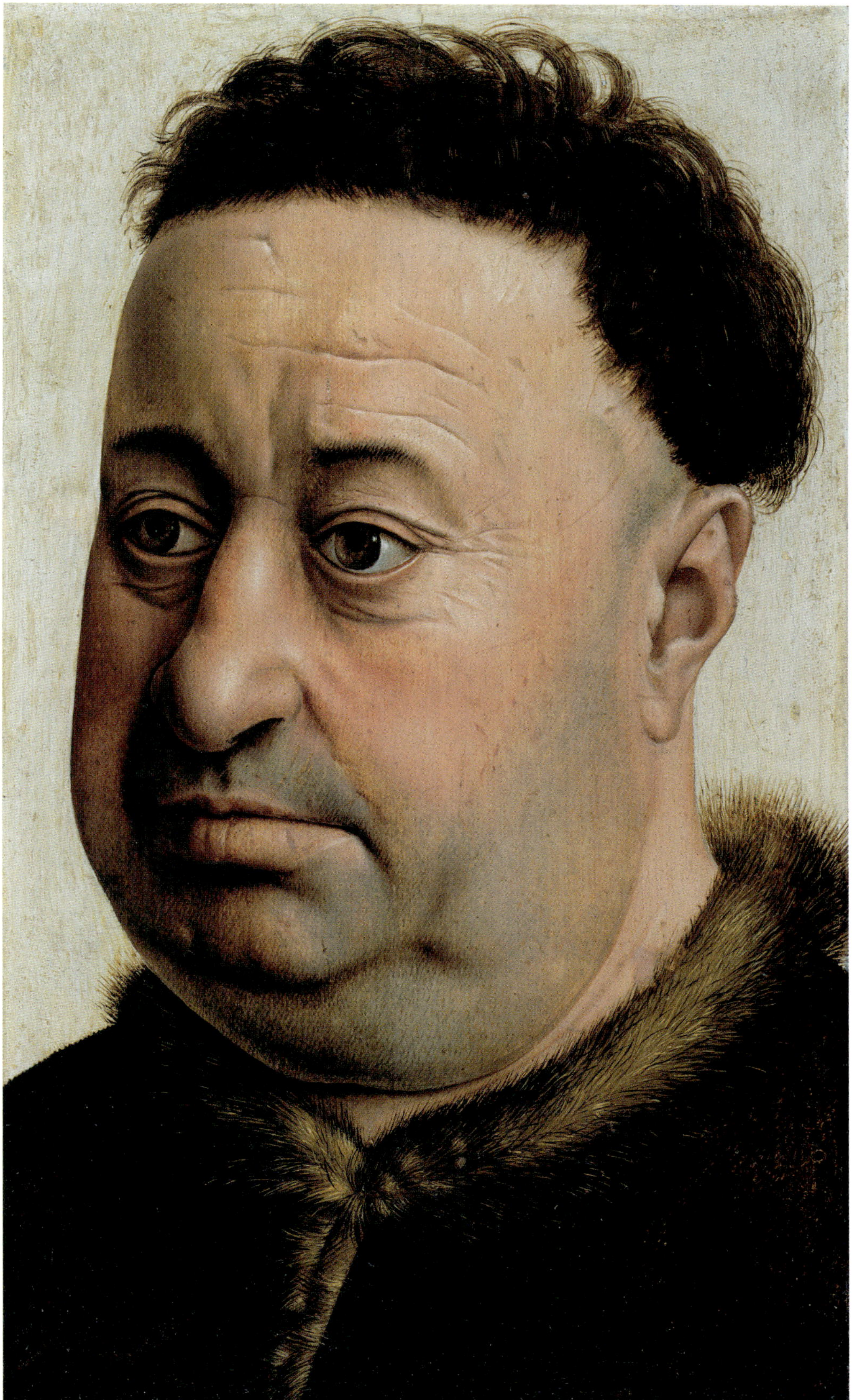

Fig. 2
Attributed to the Master of Flémalle, *Portrait of a Stout Man*, c.1440. Staatliche Museen zu Berlin, Gemäldegalerie, inv. 537A

indicates its memorial function (fig. 3). In his empirical handling Jan van Eyck emphasises every detail. The profusion of these countless fastidiously rendered individual elements results in their concatenation at the expense of the overall appearance. He creates facial landscapes designed to produce uniqueness. This verisimilitude results in a levelling of social distinctions and a reduced coordination of all details in the overall appearance. The heads are, for example, frequently much larger than the sitters' bodies. Unlike van Eyck, Rogier van der Weyden (1399/1400–1464) focuses in his portraits on his sitters' characteristic features. He follows a more linear presence and uses a pattern to subtly alter his sitters' appearance to fit a common ideal. Clearly, his patrons liked such stylisations combined with a reduction of surface phenomena. Smoother surfaces elevate the sitter, and this emphasises differences in rank again; his sitters remain defined by their social status and religion and within a norm they embody in their temporal existence. This type of portrait with a reduced empirical verisimilitude functioned as the template for the subsequent development of Flemish-Netherlandish art in the works of painters like Petrus Christus, Dieric Bouts, and Hans Memling. Earlier patrons were placed before a neutral, generally dark background, but Petrus Christus (1415/20–1472/73) was the first to create interiors for his sitters – see, for instance, the atmospheric *Portrait of a Young Woman* painted around 1470.[12] The space around the sitters begins to grow, and they are increasingly depicted as half-length figures who make eloquent use of their arms and hands. The latter are frequently placed on the edge/frame of the painting or a parapet that creates a plane boundary facing the viewer, and they seem to reach out to the latter. Dieric Bouts (1410/20–1475) takes this pictorial concept one step further by placing his sitters in the niche of a room with a window offering a vista of the surrounding landscape (fig. 4). This innovation may have been informed by similar compositions in prints showing the Virgin Mary.[13] Both window frame and the corner of the room create an orthogonal structure that supports the figure. At the same time, the bright, contrasting landscape adds depth and space. The sitter becomes part of his/her surroundings and is reflected in them. This constellation allows the artist not only to anchor the sitter but to tell us something about his/her mood through the landscape, and to introduce additional elements to describe his/her character and temperament. Interior portraits with a landscape vista became the most popular type of portraits in both the Low Countries and Germany. Next, the sitter is placed in a panorama-like landscape, an innovation first introduced by Hans Memling (c.1433–1494). Early portraits in which background landscape and sitter are still surrounded by a thin architectural frame give way in the 1470s to portraits without any mediatory architecture.[14] As with Bouts, here too religious painting served as

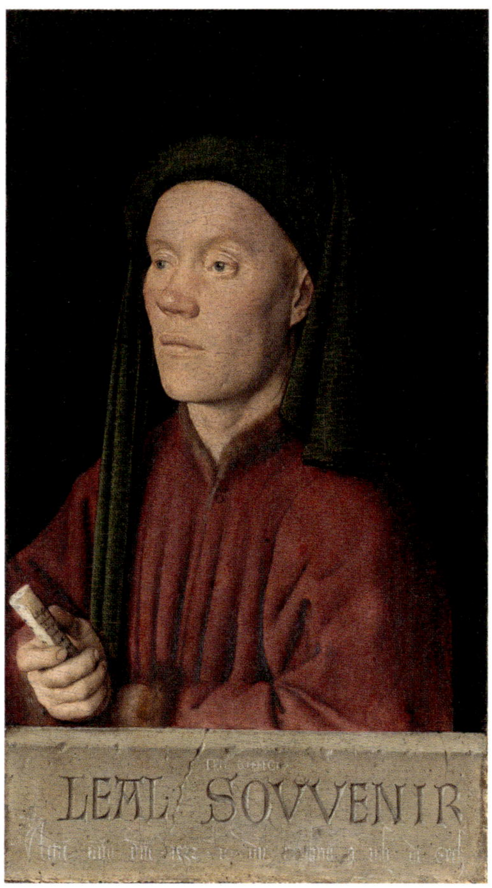

Fig. 3
Jan van Eyck, *Portrait of a Man, "Léal Souvenir"*, 1432. The National Gallery, London, inv. NG290

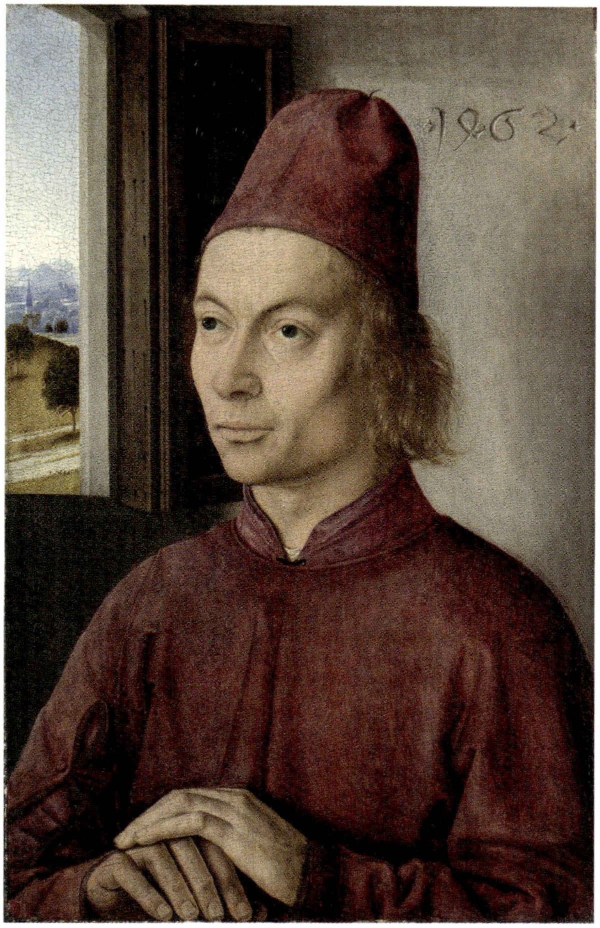

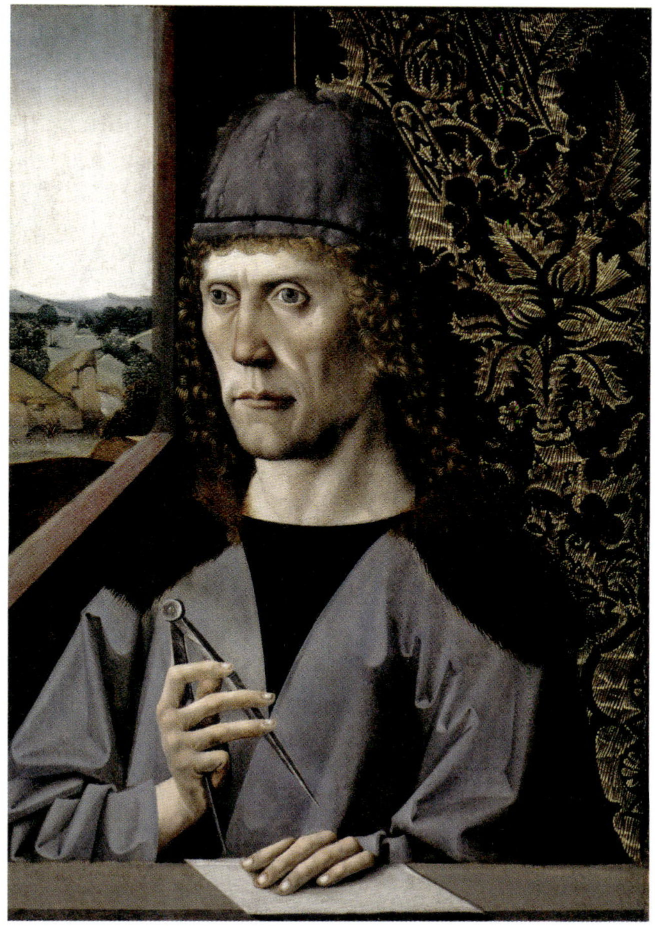

Fig. 4
Dieric Bouts, *Portrait of a Man (Jan van Winckele?)*, 1462.
The National Gallery, London, inv. NG943

Fig. 5
Bavarian Master, *Portrait of an Architect*, c.1480.
Kunstmuseum Basel, inv. 1597

inspiration, with Rogier van der Weyden's *Braque Triptych* with its half-length figures placed before an open landscape probably functioning as a model.[15] Memling used this composition to animate the more neutral areas of his generally black-clad sitters through the landscape, and the calmer blue of the sky to set off the head containing the vital elements that allow us to identify him/her. The artist brilliantly combines a close-up view of the sitter with a panorama view of the distant landscape. Portraits with landscape backgrounds were especially popular with the wealthy foreign merchants who resided in Bruges, particularly those from Italy, presumably because Netherlandish artists were celebrated for their ability to depict nature. After their return to Italy, they and their acquisitions influenced local artistic production – see, for example, the works produced by Perugino and Botticelli.

In Germany, a different evolution in portraiture began around 1460 which was informed by ideas that had been developed in fully-articulated Netherlandish portraiture. Hans Pleydenwurff's powerful *Portrait of Georg, Count of Löwenstein* (c.1456) is an early example of a German artist adopting these novel ideas. He depicts the count as a half-length figure who has been interrupted in his reading of a breviary and raised his eyes to gaze surprised and reverently at a vision.[16] The latter fills the companion panel of this diptych, a depiction of the Man of Sorrows on a gold ground presumably executed by Pleydenwurff's workshop.[17] The concept of a devotional diptych with the half-length portrait of a donor derives from Rogier van der Weyden. The sitters adopt a devotional pose and turn to gaze at the divine apparition, generally the Virgin Mary, on their right. Though the two spheres were initially separated by differing backgrounds and handling, they are soon both located in a bourgeois interior. The best example is Memling's *Diptych of Maarten van Nieuwenhove* (1487) with its complex spatial concept.[18] In Germany there are but few other examples of devotional diptychs after the Löwenstein portrait.

As in the Low Countries, bust- or half-length three-quarter view portraits set before a neutral background in a narrow pictorial space were initially the most popular in Germany. Green was the dominant background colour, presumably providing a complementary contrast to the sitter's skin-tone, followed by red and blue. Neutral backgrounds remained the most common until well into the sixteenth century. A certain bluntness and exaggeration in the depiction of mimetic qualities are typical of German portraits. They lack the smoothness that became common in the Low Countries after Rogier van der Weyden. Most of these panels measure less than 60 cm in height, and, as we know from contemporary written sources, were not displayed on a wall but wrapped and stored in chests or placed on tables.[19] A sole painting case or sheath has come down to us.[20] The main function of portrait panels was documentary and to a lesser extent display and representation. Southern Germany – especially Nuremberg, Munich, Ulm, Augsburg and Frankfurt – was the stronghold of German portrait painting after 1460. Most of the sitters were clearly members of the wealthy bourgeoisie even if only a handful of names have come down to us. Attributes like a pair of dividers or a coiner's die indicate offices or professions, but numerous sitters clutch rosaries which removes them from the purely mundane. The successful compositional concept of placing the sitter before a window, which Bouts had introduced in the Low Countries, became increasingly popular in Germany too (cat. 30). One of the earliest examples is the *Portrait of an Architect* from Bavaria (c.1480) that may have served as the inspiration for portraits with landscape vistas in Bavaria and Franconia (fig. 5). This painting already includes a typical feature of German portraits: a (flat) cloth of honour made of richly-patterned gold brocade hung behind the sitter and covering part of the background. These textiles emphasise the contrast between interior and outside, between depth and pictorial plane. Their light reflexes imbue the painting with grandeur and lustre. We can, however, only speculate about possible connections between these cloths of honour and the documented contemporary habit of decorating (and heating) rooms with textiles.

One of the most beautiful portraits combining a landscape background and a cloth of honour – both transport ambiguous heraldic and symbolic meanings – is by Michael Wolgemut (1434–1519), with whom Dürer was apprenticed. His *Portrait of Levinus Memminger* (c.1485) features a detailed mountainous landscape with falcons hunting above (fig. 6). At the beginning of his career, Albrecht Dürer (1471–1528) placed his sitters both in the corner of a room with a landscape vista and in combinations with cloths of honour. In his half-length self-portrait of 1498 he stands, turning slightly, before a window giving us a view of a distant mountain range. Attired in choice contrasting clothes, his gloved hands folded, Dürer scrutinises us with a quizzical gaze. With its exquisite handling, this panel is regarded as a highpoint of portraiture in Germany before 1500 (fig. 7). In contrast to interiors with landscape vistas, Memling's idea of placing a sitter before an open landscape background was taken up only rarely by German artists (see cat. 11).

Double portraits of engaged or married couples are surprisingly common in German painting. They were either executed on a single wide panel – a peculiarity of German portraiture – or as a pair on two complementary panels. The latter concept originated in the Low Countries. The oldest fully articulated works are a pair of portraits, dated to around 1435 and attributed to Robert Campin, in which both well-lit partners are placed before a dark

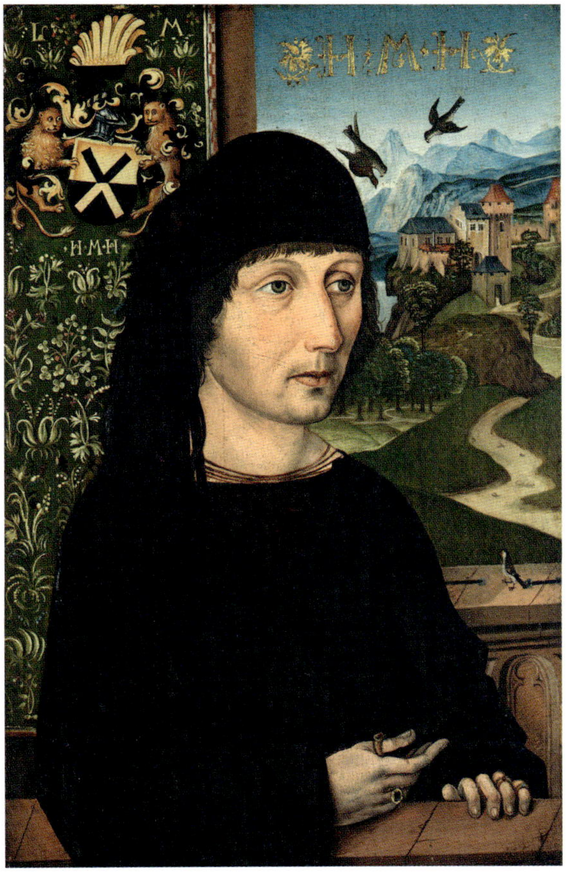

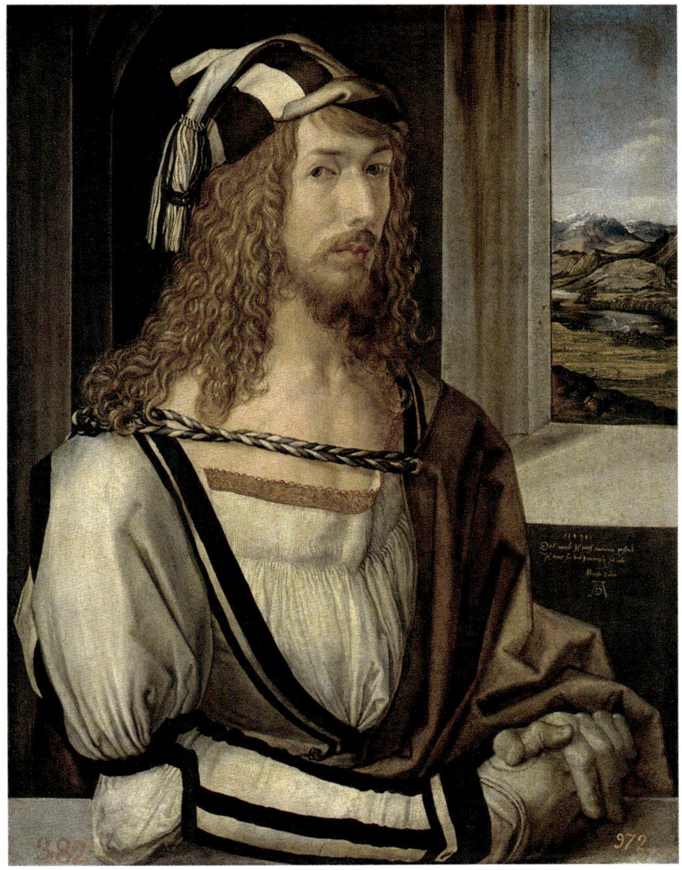

Fig. 6
Michael Wolgemut, *Portrait of Levinus Memminger*, c.1485. Museo Thyssen-Bornemisza, Madrid, inv. 440

Fig. 7
Albrecht Dürer, *Self Portrait*, 1498. Museo del Prado, Madrid, inv. P002179

background, facing each other in three-quarter views.[21] Many of the extant portraits presumably once had a, now lost, companion piece. This is particularly true of portraits in which the sitter clearly turns to face someone, or in which he or she clutches an attribute like a ring or a flower that can be connected to nuptials or matrimony. Carnations often function as a symbol of marital fidelity, but other options are, for instance, roses, forget-me-nots, pansies or lilies-of-the-valley. The use of related compositions, inscriptions or arms indicate a sitter's bond with his or her partner. The dividing frame naturally interrupts the continuing elements that connect the two likenesses.[22] The fact that most patrons continued to prefer two separate portraits is presumably best explained by the way they were "used", because these companion portraits formed "portrait boxes" that could be closed like a book, with one portrait resting upon the other.[23] The panels were joined with hinges, straps or rings. Only a few panels have survived in their original frames, the vast majority lost their original utilisation concept. When opened, the man usually occupied the heraldically more prominent left side; the rare exceptions to this rule reflect either marked differences in rank or honour a deceased partner.[24] Closed, these portraits offered additional opportunities for dynastic display, with the reverse(s) often featuring the alliance arms created by the sitters' union, which again emphasised the legal act of the marriage being celebrated on the obverse(s). Other options for the reverse(s) were skulls or *transis* that functioned as a warning of transience and a refutation of possible accusations of vanity (see cat. 29). The lack of shared actions or gestures in these companion portraits – unlike, for example, tombs showing the dexiosis – increased the importance of a common composition or a continuous landscape background. Dürer's only portrait diptych

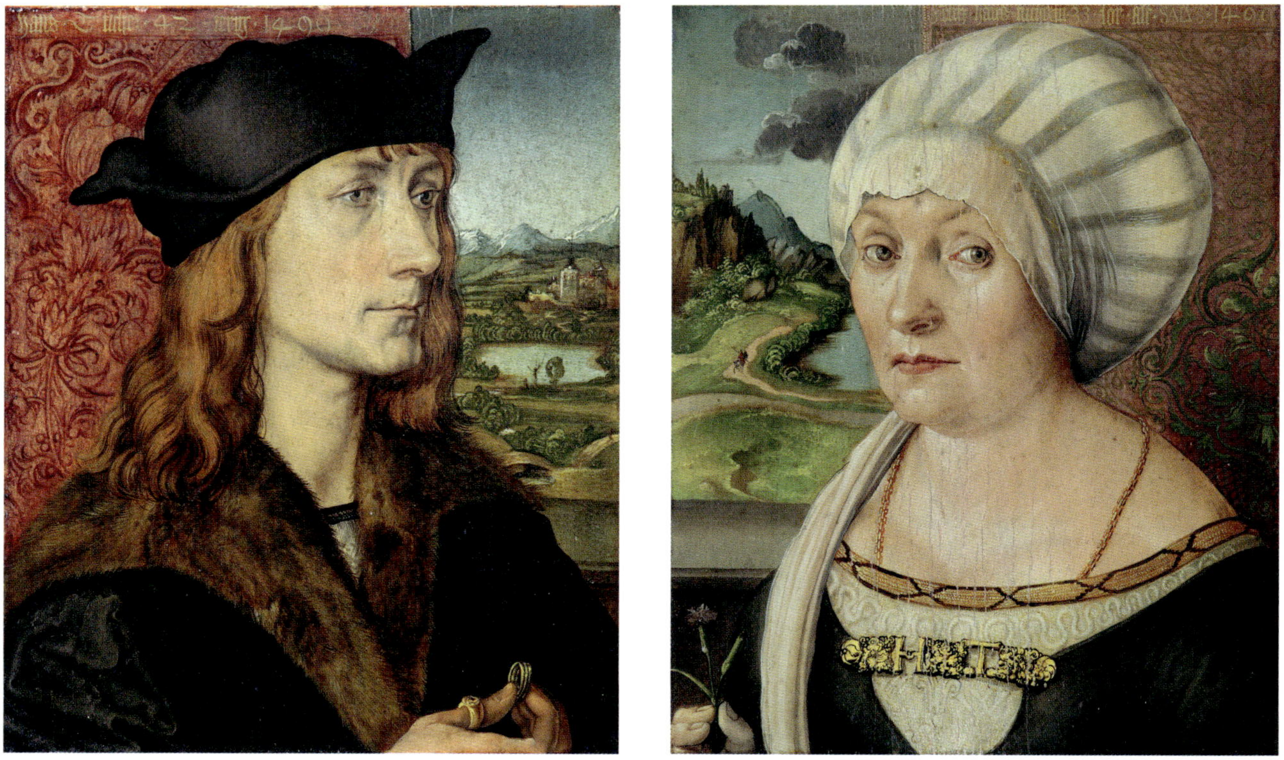

Fig. 8
Albrecht Dürer, *Portraits of Hans XI Tucher and Felicitas Tucher*, 1499. Klassik Stiftung Weimar, Schlossmuseum, invs. G 31 and 32

to have survived in its original condition features continuous interiors and landscape vistas that connect the sitters, with paths in one panel continuing in the other (fig. 8). Inscriptions, gestures and jewellery (especially the brooches decorated with his initials) document this reciprocal connection.[25] The earliest extant example of a pair of sitters placed before an open landscape was produced in Italy: Piero della Francesca's (1416/17–1492) *Diptych of Federico da Montefeltre and Battista Sforza* (c.1473/75) presents the married couple in profile before a kind of world landscape.[26] The reverses feature allegorical triumphal processions celebrating the spouses' virtues. These innovations concerning portraiture and landscape were introduced more or less simultaneously in Italy and the Low Countries; the question about who influenced whom (or not) continues to be debated.

A comparison with Dürer's *Tucher Diptych* in Weimar illustrates Cranach's innovations: he was the first artist north of the Alps to relinquish a framing architecture and place his sitters in companion portraits not in front of, but embedded in the landscape. His *Portrait of Johannes Cuspinian* (cat. 12) is also far removed from the traditional portrait of a bridegroom. Clutching a folio and gazing heavenwards, Cuspinian is clearly more in tune with his ideas and thoughts, which are symbolically reflected in the landscape, than with his wife. Though Cuspinian's portrait is closer to the tradition of the emerging humanist portrait, for this commission Cranach made innovative use of – and this undoubtedly reflects his patron's wishes – the conventions of companion portraits.

1 Pliny the Elder, *Naturalis historia*, vol 35, chapter 43.
2 Leon Battista Alberti, *De Pictura*, Liber II, 25, in: Bätschmann & Schäublin 2000, 235–236.
3 "jm dinst der kirchen [...] angetzeigt werden das leiden Christi", and "behelt awch dy gestalt der menschen nach jrem absterben"; quoted in Rupprich 1966, 109.
4 For more on the arms, see Belting & Kruse 1994, 45–48; Beyer 2002, 113.
5 See, for example, Buchner 1953, 9; Dülberg 1990, 169; for a dissenting opinion, see Reudenbach 1996.
6 Boehm 1985, 22–24.
7 Ibid., 45.
8 Musée du Louvre, Paris, inv. RF 2490.
9 See Buchner 1953, 9, no. 1.
10 National Gallery of Art, Washington, D.C., inv. 1937.1.23.
11 The second portrait is now in the Museo Thyssen-Bornemisza, Madrid, inv. 74.
12 Staatliche Museen zu Berlin, Gemäldegalerie, inv. 532.
13 For example: Master E.S., *Madonna at the Window*, c.1460, engraving, L 73.
14 For more on the evolution of portraiture, see Campbell 2005.
15 Rogier van der Weyden, *Braque Triptych*, c.1452, Musée du Louvre, Paris, inv. RF2063.
16 Germanisches Nationalmuseum, Nuremberg, inv. Gm128.
17 Kunstmuseum Basel, inv. 1651.
18 Memlingmuseum – Sint Janshospitaal, Bruges, inv. O.SJ0178.1.
19 Dülberg 1990, 60–65.
20 Dülberg 1990, 77–78.
21 The National Gallery, London, invs. NG653.1 and NG653.2.
22 Hinz 1974, 146.
23 For the term, see Dülberg 1990, 81.
24 Piero della Francesca's diptych could serve as an example for a deceased partner taking precedence.
25 For the Tucher portraits, see Hirschfelder 2012.
26 Gallerie degli Uffizi, Florence, invs. 1615 and 3342.

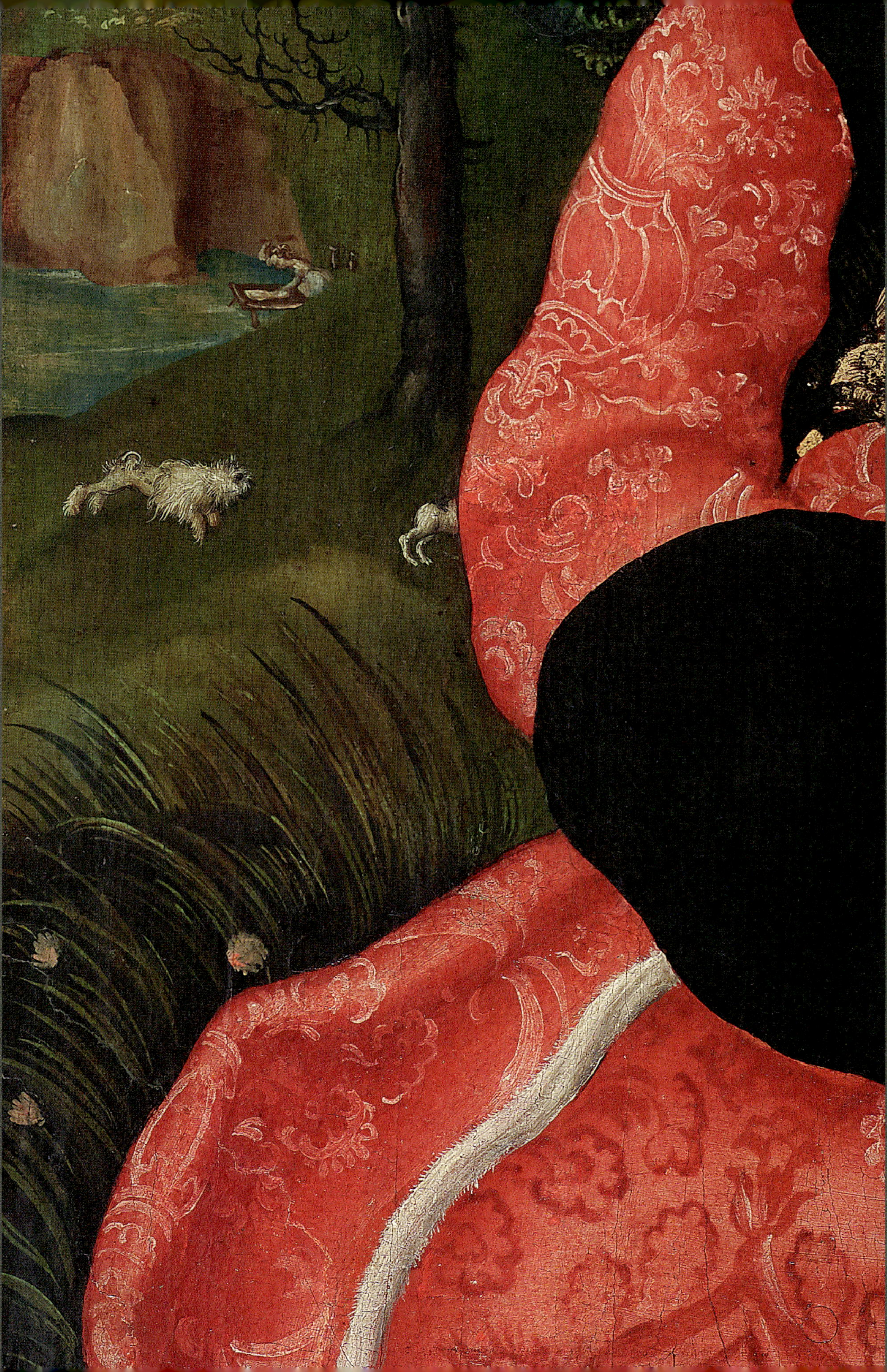

Katja Baumhoff

Green Pastures. The Image of Nature in Viennese Humanism

Verdant tufts of grass are growing next to the two sitters in the Cuspinian double-portrait now in the Oscar Reinhart Collection (cat. 12 & 13) because the sitters are not, as one might have expected, comfortably seated in a room with a landscape visible through a large window behind them, but out in the open. Even their seats – both have settled on a grassy bench – are part of the nature that surrounds them.

Embedding his sitters in the landscape is both a novelty in portraiture north of the Alps, and a direct key to understanding Cranach's attitude to Nature and that of his circle – the topic explored in this essay. How is landscape depicted in Cranach's early works? In what way is Cranach's understanding of Nature informed by contemporary socio-political concepts and rooted in the history of ideas? What is the subtext of the depictions of nature in Cranach's early works?

Lucas Cranach spent the first few years of the sixteenth century in Vienna where he became acquainted with the city's leading humanists.[1] Scholars and humanists close to Maximilian I became his most important early patrons; from them Cranach absorbed ideas and a body of thought, and his artistic implementation and transformation of these ideas provided them, in turn, with new impulses.

In the German Empire, humanist ideas were primarily disseminated through court circles and the arts faculties of the universities.[2] The main humanist strongholds were the court at Prague, the imperial free city of Nuremberg – the latter was where in 1487 Emperor Frederick III named Conrad Celtes, celebrated as the "German arch-humanist", poet laureate[3] – and Vienna. At the turn of the sixteenth century, Vienna University, founded in 1365 by Rudolf IV and supported by Maximilian, became a magnet for Germany's humanist intellectual elite. For example, from 1497 onwards, the poet laureate Celtes taught "Eloquence and Poetry" at Vienna's Faculty of Arts; he also founded the *Sodalitas litteraria danubiana* the year he arrived in the city, a society that Cuspinian (who was portrayed by Cranach) joined too.[4] The "sodalitates" formed a kind of mystery cult: members of these secret societies focused on deciphering and interpreting sacred symbols in the Christian sense, while also fostering an attitude of dissociation from "profane" society.[5] Four years later, in 1501, Celtes helped found the *Collegium poetarum et mathematicorum;* supported by Maximilian, its aim was to serve and advance humanist academic life at Vienna University.

Following an encyclopedic concept of science, subjects such as Astronomy and Mathematics, Rhetoric and Philosophy were taught at this new institution, also known as the "fifth faculty". The privilege of naming a poet laureate was also transferred to this new college, a right from which Cuspinian profited directly when he was crowned "poeta laureatus" in Vienna in 1493, an honour that also allowed him to give lectures on "Poetry and Rhetoric" at Vienna University.[6]

The socio-political consequences of Maximilian's choice of Vienna as his capital cannot be overestimated, because the Habsburg's affinity with humanist ideas and his patronage of Vienna University had far-reaching consequences for the careers of members of the university-bourgeois scene. In addition to traditional careers – until now reserved for the aristocracy – this offered new opportunities for social advancement through education; opportunities that a number of Cranach's patrons made good use of.[7]

Cranach was connected in many ways to faculty members and the humanists patronised by Maximilian – these were the circles in which he moved and which provided him with opportunities to win new patrons with his novel pictorial concepts. In addition to the Cuspinian double-portrait and a similar portrait-diptych of a jurist and his wife (cat. 15 & 16), another link between Cranach and the humanist university scene in Vienna are the prints he produced for the Viennese publisher Johannes Winterburger.[8] Woodcuts like *St Stephen* (cat. 22), the calendar dial to identify the dominical letter (cat. 23), and a canon illustration depicting the crucifixion (cat. 24 & 25) bear eloquent witness to Cranach's humanist-inspired willingness to engage with iconographic innovations.

In addition to the woodcuts he designed for Winterburger, Cranach was probably commissioned by Johannes Fuchsmagen, a diplomat and imperial councillor, to create the twelve depictions of the months for a late-antique *Filocalus* calendar (cat. 7).[9] Fuchsmagen may also

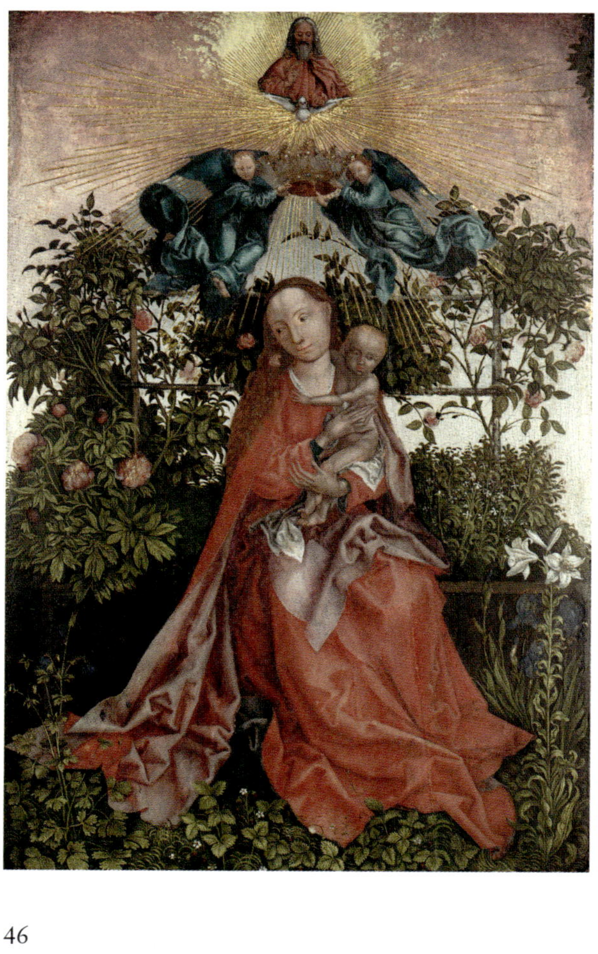

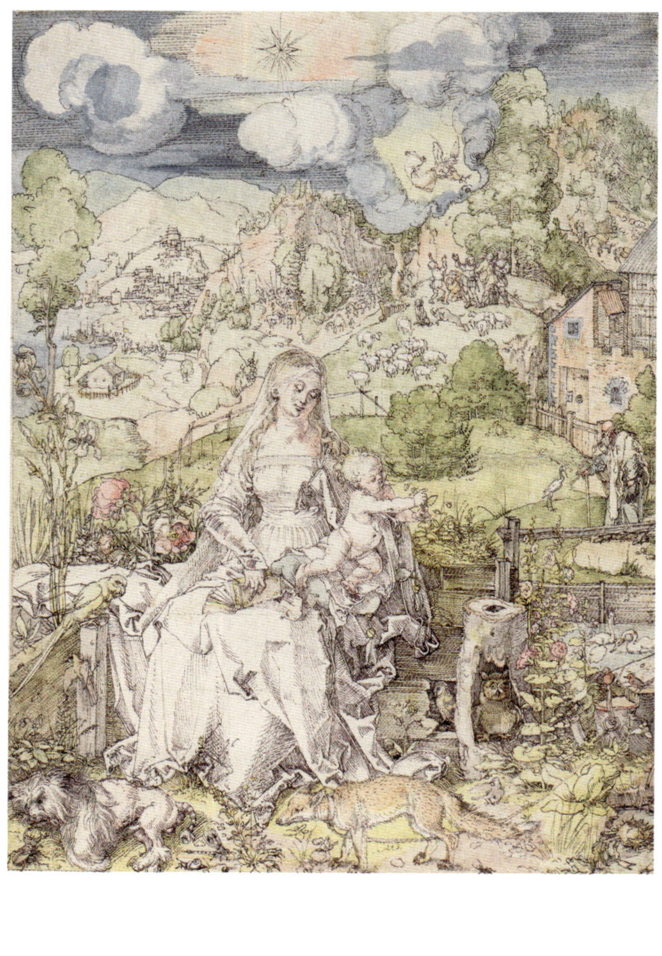

have been the patron for whom Cranach painted the *St Jerome* (cat. 6). Fuchsmagen, in turn, dedicated his earliest known poem to Cuspinian – these crisscrossing links show that the members of these humanist circles knew and respected one another, and Cranach clearly profited from his patrons' support and extensive networks.[10]

Like their fellow humanists in Germany and Italy, humanists in Vienna were striving for a balance between their ideas and Christian teachings. At the turn of the sixteenth century, the natural sciences were only just beginning to emancipate themselves from religion, and the humanist idea of Nature found itself between the poles of empirics and symbolism, between new and traditional knowledge.[11] For centuries, the study of nature could only be justified through religion; every creature was regarded as a reflection of the divine mystery of creation, as well as a concrete religious-moral symbol – the allegorical reading of Nature was still omnipresent.[12] An even rudimentary outline of coeval humanist ideas would go beyond the scope of this essay, but to understand Cranach's image of Nature one must bear in mind that at the turn of the sixteenth century strands born of different histories of ideas ran side by side. Traditional Christian interpretations, the rediscovery and growing appreciation of classical authors, together with a politically-motivated reevaluation of German ideals and the resulting disengagement from Italian models encountered a fast-growing interest in the empirical observation of nature.

Conrad Celtes's popularisation of the *Germania* topos is a perfect example of this merging of descriptions of nature, the reception of classical antiquity, and cultural-political interests. With the support of Maximilian, Celtes began in 1493 to give lectures at Vienna University on Tacitus (AD c.58 – c.120) and his book *Germania*. In this work, the ancient Roman author describes an arboreous Germany (which naturally had little in common with the real state of German forests in classical antiquity, which had by then already been subjected to extensive deforestation) and its "uncivilised" inhabitants.[13] Tacitus saw clear advantages in the way these "barbaric Germans" lived – he describes how friendly and social they are, that they are unfamiliar with both gold and silver, and that, unlike the Romans, they do not know corruption.[14] Celtes's *Germania generalis*, an ideologically adapted, patriotic interpretation of the ancient text, was published in 1500, and in his Odes he describes a "forest beloved of the Muses", juxtaposing it with the "city despised by poets".[15] Celtes's remarks led to a cultural reappraisal of the German forest – conjuring up an alternative classical past that was at least equal to the Italian one.[16] The context to this is, of course, Maximilian's claim to imperial legitimacy and the glorification of the House of Habsburg.

Cultural-political reasons that expedited the dissemination of the German forest-myth encountered a growing interest in field studies and illustrations. Konrad von Megenberg (1309–1374) wrote his *Book on Nature* – the first-ever scientific book on nature written in German – between 1348 and 1350, but 150 years later it continued to be republished in new, now also printed editions. Conceived as a pharmaceutical reference book, it also offers information on the symbolic and allegorical qualities of individual plants and animals (including, for instance, discussing the mythical character of mermaids); we can safely assume that at the turn of the sixteenth century a copy or perhaps even a printed edition of this book was in Vienna and well-known in university circles.[17] Additional books on natural science such as *Gart der Gesundheit* (Garden of Health; 1485), or the *Hortus sanitatis* (1491) met a growing interest in the characteristics of fauna and flora, and this went hand in hand with an appeal to readers to look for themselves, to ask critical questions, and to make their own attributions. This burgeoning interest in field studies is reflected in art – religious scenes move out of doors,

Fig. 1
after Martin Schongauer, *Madonna and Child in a Rose-Bower*, mid-16th century. Isabella Stewart Gardner Museum, Boston. Copy of the still-uncut painting by Schongauer from 1473, which is now in Colmar

Fig. 2
Albrecht Dürer, *Madonna of the Animals*, c.1506. Albertina, Vienna, inv. 3066

depictions of plants, forests, and nature take up increasing amounts of pictorial space and may be regarded as precursors of (autonomous) landscape painting. At the turn of the sixteenth century, however, naturalistic depictions were still a long way off: as a child of his time, Cranach was less interested in depicting nature for its own sake than anchoring it in the reference frame of divine redemptive activity – combined with humanist impulses. Many of the animals and plants in his compositions can be identified but he never aims for verisimilitude. The Cuspinian double-portrait is an excellent example: fauna and flora are not fastidiously executed studies from nature but function as a Neo-Platonic riddle. The general aim of these botanical and zoological elements is to invite us to interpret them: it may be an exaggeration to speak of a "hieroglyphic picture puzzle", but, as Dieter Koepplin correctly remarked, the double-portrait is "filled with *figurae* that hide the landscape's higher meaning from the *profanum vulgus*".[18]

As discussed above, Anna Putsch and her husband Johannes Cuspinian are surrounded by nature. They are seated on grassy benches and a wide vista opens up behind them. Grassy benches have been around at least since the descriptions published by the mediaeval theologian and master-gardener Albertus Magnus (c.1200–1280). Albertus suggested installing a "flowering and pleasant raised grassy bench, located approximately in the middle of the garden, and placing there a seat where one can refresh one's senses, and people should sit there to rest in a pleasant way."[19] Such grassy benches are a common feature of classical enclosed pleasure gardens.

But there are, of course, other examples of grassy benches in paintings produced before Cranach's; one of the best-known is Martin Schongauer's *Madonna in a Rose-Bower* (1473; fig. 1). His Virgin's and all the other contemporaneous depictions of grassy benches are placed in an enclosed garden. One exception is Dürer's adaption of the motif in his drawing *Madonna of the Animals* (c.1506; fig. 2): here, the grassy bench is located in an open landscape, and the fauna depicted is similar in many ways to that in the Cuspinian diptych. Even the Bolognese frolicking in the grass at the Virgin's feet is a cousin of the dog in the portrait of Anna Putsch, and here too there is an owl, which has taken shelter in a hollow tree trunk.

Humanist intellectuals from Cuspinian's circle enjoyed spending time in the country, outside the protective walls of the *hortus conclusus*. Joachim Vadian, a pupil of Celtes and Cuspinian, extolled the advantages of spending time outdoors: here, he said, the spirit is prepared for poetry, and pastoral solitude, being far from the madding (urban) crowd, makes one more receptive to poetical inspiration.[20] The Viennese humanists adopted their preference for life in the country and for philosophising out in the open surrounded by "vineyards, orchards, and fishponds"[21] from Italian kindred spirits like Marsilio Ficino and Pomponius Laetus.[22] Of course, humanists did not believe that nature existed solely for recreation and to serve as inspiration; behind a stay in the countryside – and, connected with it, its depiction – lies a pantheistic idea: Nature is divine, and the complete superiority of the Creator God is best experienced through his creation.[23]

In addition to grassy benches, plants play a central role in the diptych, although almost none can be identified. The flower in Anna Putsch's hands is a filled carnation cultivar (Dianthus plumaris), the branches of the tree in the background suggest it may be a weeping willow.[24] None of the other trees or grasses can be identified with certainty; Cranach seems to play with a repertoire of different set pieces. As Dieter Koepplin has pointed out, "all forms are filled with vegetal life. There is no geometric rigor, nothing is lifeless, everywhere and in every detail we see a movement of forms that does not appear chaotic because they are held

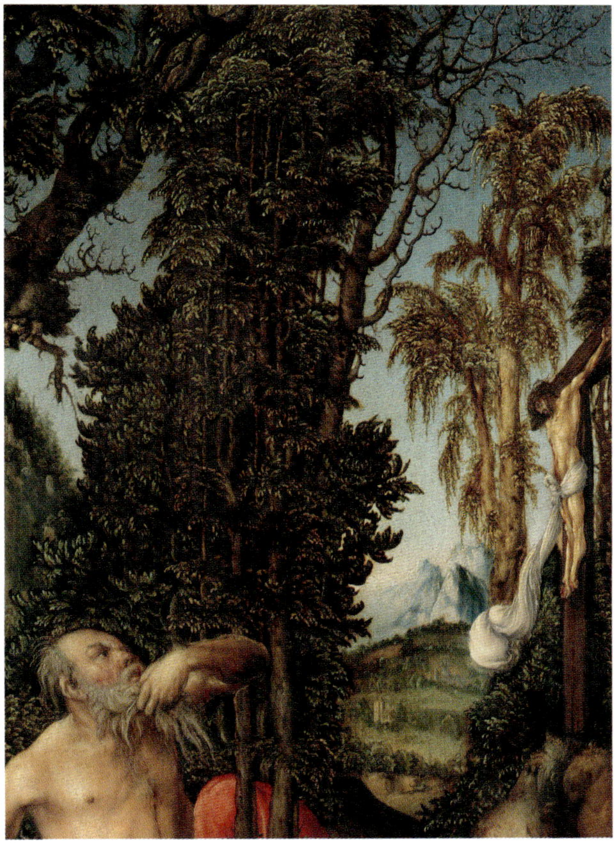

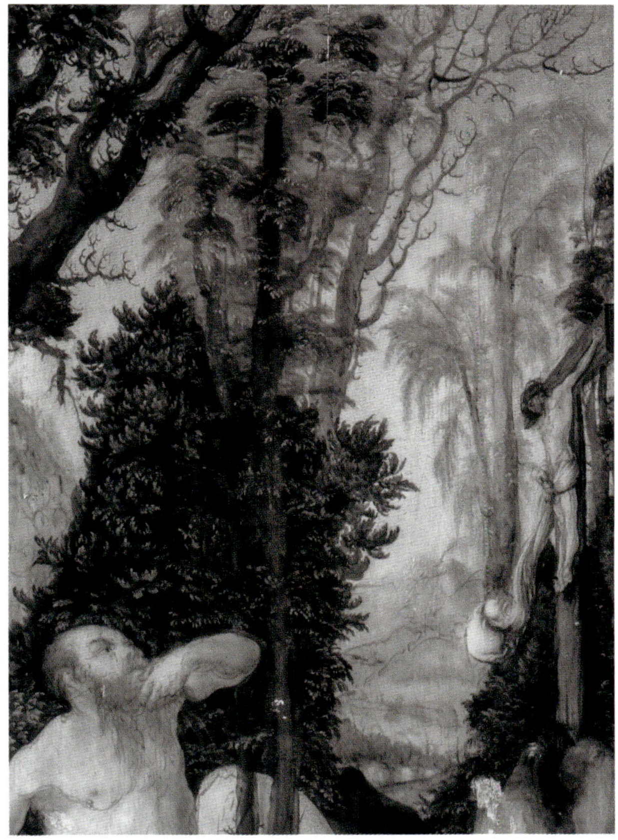

Fig. 3
Lucas Cranach the Elder, *The Penance of St Jerome* (cat. 6, detail)

Fig. 4
Lucas Cranach the Elder, *The Penance of St Jerome* (cat. 6, detail), infrared-reflectograph

together by a clear and subdued composition of colours and large shapes."[25] One inherently vegetal large shape is the foliage, which plays a dominant role in the composition. Koepplin goes so far as to identify the principle behind the leaf configurations in both portraits: just as leaves grow from a dark foil, the botanical décor on the sitters' robes grows from a green ground.[26]

A closer look at handling and technique confirms the impression that the leaves seem to grow from a dark background: the artist applied a bluish-green base for the foliage over the underdrawing. Once it had dried, he executed the contours of the individual leaves with an opaque green paint raised by adding either yellow or white paint. Finally, he applied another layer of highly-diluted dark-green or brown glazes.[27]

We find a similar handling in the *St Jerome*: here, we can also detect modifications in the depiction of nature, executed during the painting process, that enhance the thick woody character of the landscape. Infrared-reflectography (fig. 4) and X-ray analysis have revealed that a tree in the distance was originally conceived as partially dead but was replaced by the flourishing bush-like tree we see now.[28]

Both of these early works already feature the typical "Cranach-foliage" that he used in the majority of his later oeuvre: the foliage is stylised and rendered in a schematic way; the leaves are reminiscent of those of oaks and ash trees but resist unambiguous identification.

The animals, however, are realistically rendered in great detail. The dog in the portrait of Anna Putsch is clearly a Bolognese, then a breed much favoured by members of the aristocracy.

St Jerome's lion has settled down in what appears to be a natural space but which obviously shows that Cranach makes no claim to verisimilitude; instead, different levels of meaning merge in these works. In the *St Jerome*, both lion and dromedary are, of course, motivated by divine redemptive activity. The fauna in the Cuspinian diptych also functions, as mentioned above, as "figurae", opening up room for interpretation.[29] Over the decades, the birds have inspired countless conjectures put forward by art-historians, and the proposed identifications are highly disparate; for the multi-coloured bird in Cuspinian's portrait they run the gamut from parrot to phoenix – and the resulting interpretations differ accordingly.[30] The same is true for the owl included in Cuspinian's portrait, the *St Jerome*, and the calendar dial to identify the dominical letter.[31]

To summarise: in Cranach's Cuspinian portrait-diptych the depiction of nature is accorded a novel – and expanded – amount of space in the composition. This is true also of all the other early works he produced in Vienna: in the *St Francis* (cat. 9) a tree even cuts across the saint; in Cranach's woodcut *Christ on the Mount of Olives* (see essay Heiser, fig. 6) the garden's enclosure is almost invisible and the wilderness accorded an until-then unheard-of prominence. Compared to other contemporary works, Cranach's *Rest on the Flight into Egypt* (see essay Heiser, fig. 4) reveals an exceptional understanding of the natural relationship between figures and space, and the foreground almost functions as an autonomous flower still-life. We can clearly differentiate columbines, thistles, and primroses – and yet they obviously reflect Cranach's unique idiom.[32]

In addition to allowing nature to play a prominent role in his compositions, Cranach gives it a new interpretative scope: humanist ideas born of different tendencies, approaches based on religion, the burgeoning interest in studies from nature and, last but not least, cultural-political motives are conflated in Cranach's image of Nature. And portraits of humanists were a particularly appropriate field for experimentation and innovation for this novel vision of landscape.

1 For Cranach's sojourn in Vienna, see Weniger 2018, and the essays by Guido Messling and Björn Blauensteiner.
2 For Cranach and the Viennese university scene, see also, for example, Heiser 2002, 56–60.
3 Frederick the Wise, Elector of Saxony, later Cranach's patron in Wittenberg, was instrumental in securing this honour for Celtes. Conrad Celtes had already immersed himself in humanist ideas during his studies at the Universities of Erfurt and Ingolstadt, as well as during his sojourn in Italy's humanist strongholds of Ferrara, Bologna, Florence, Padua, Venice, and Rome; see Heiser 2002, 59.
4 See Heiser 2002, 59, and Koepplin 1973, 89. Celtes had founded the first *Sodalitas* at Heidelberg in 1495, an event that Cuspinian may have attended.
5 Koepplin 1973, 88.
6 For more on Cuspinian's career, see Heiser 2002 and Koepplin 1973, and especially Ankwicz-Kleehoven 1959, as well as cat. 12 & 13.
7 See Heiser 2002, 58.
8 For more on this, see the essay by Andreas Fingernagel.
9 For a discussion of the identity of the patron who commissioned the *Filocalus* drawings, see cat. 7.
10 See also the essays by Sabine Heiser and Björn Blauensteiner.
11 See Thun 2018, 10.
12 Ibid., 9.
13 See Pereña 2018, 79; she references Hansjörg Küster, *Geschichte des Waldes. Von der Urzeit bis zur Gegenwart*, Munich 2008, 93–100. For Tacitus's characterisation of the Germanic tribes, see Schama 1996, 111, and Stadlober 2006, 131–132.
14 Pereña 2018, 79.
15 Conrad Celtes, *Libri Odarum Quattuor*, ed. by F. Pindter, Leipzig 1937, Ode 1, 16, quoted in Schama 1996, 114; see also Pereña 2018, 79.
16 Pereña 2018, 79; in this context see also Silver 1983, 4–34.
17 See Luff & Steer 2003, and Heiser 2002, 58.
18 "erfüllt von figurae, die den höheren Sinn der Landschaft vor dem profanum vulgus verbergen"; Koepplin 1973, 88.
19 Albertus Magnus, *De vegetabilibus libri VII* (Seven Books on Plants), *«Von der Anlage der Viridarien»*, translated from the Latin (into German) by Uta Korzeniewski, quoted in Hauschild 2005, 149.
20 See Koepplin 1973, 185–188. He refers to the résumé from Vadian's poetry quoted in Werner Näf, *Vadian und seine Stadt St. Gallen, Bd. 1 bis 1518, Humanist in Wien*, St. Gallen 1944.
21 Cuspinian owned several country estates including one called "Foelicianum", a popular meeting place for his humanist friends and "philosophers"; see Koepplin 1973, 189.
22 Celtes had met them in Italy; Laetus especially proved highly influential: the latter tended a small garden and based his life in the countryside on the classical texts of Cato, Varro and Columella. Cuspinian gave his first lecture on Columella's didactic poem on gardening in 1495, and later had the work published for his students in Vienna. See Koepplin 1973, 190, with a reference to Ankwicz-Kleehoven 1959, 14.
23 Koepplin 1973, 186.
24 Morass & Thalinger 2018, 166.
25 "Sämtliche Formen sind von einem pflanzenhaften Leben erfüllt. Es gibt keine geometrische Härte, nichts Totes, überall sieht man im Kleinen eine Bewegtheit der Formen, die nur darum keineswegs chaotisch wirkt, weil sie von der klaren und ruhigen Komposition der Farben und der Grossformen zusammengehalten wird"; Koepplin 1973, 70.
26 Ibid., 71.
27 Büttner 2018, 143.
28 Exh. cat. Innsbruck 2018, 164; see also https://lucascranach.org/AT_KHM_GG6739/image [retrieved 1 Nov. 2021].
29 Koepplin 1973 has provided the most comprehensive interpretation so far. See also Stadlober 2006, and Borggrefe 2007.
30 In his interpretation, Koepplin identifies the bird as a parrot or macaw, but Endrődi 2018a, 211, writes that "this is not a parrot, as had been suggested until now, but a phoenix, the colours of its plumage correspond to Lactantius's description of the mythical bird". For an ornithological identification, see Morass & Thalinger 2018, 162, and Swen Renner in cat. 6, note, who suggest that this parrot or macaw cannot be identified as a member of a known species.
31 See cat. 6 and 23, and especially Borggrefe 2007.
32 See Weniger 2018, XXXVI–XXXIX.

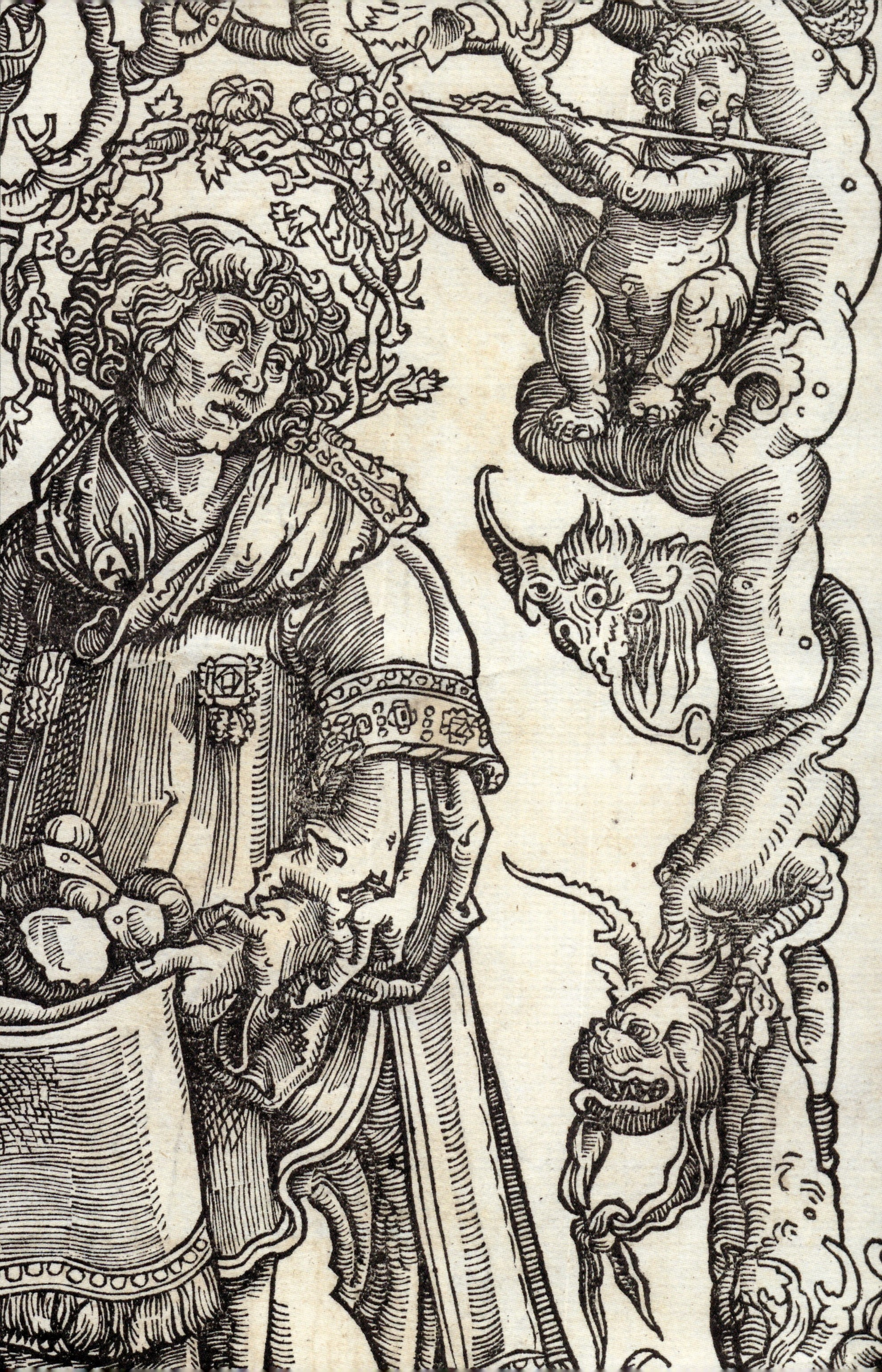

Andreas Fingernagel

Johannes Winterburger and Lucas Cranach

When Lucas Cranach arrived in Vienna around 1500, Johannes Winterburger (c.1460–1519) could already look back on a long and successful career as a publisher.[1] Introduced in the 1480s, publishing was slow to establish itself in the Austrian capital until Winterburger, who had moved to Vienna from the Rhineland in 1482, began to publish large numbers of books (and broadsheets), even holding a monopoly until the end of the first decade of the sixteenth century.[2] By the time he died, Winterburger had published around 200 books;[3] when Cranach arrived in Vienna, he had already published around 80.[4] These early books (incunabula) and broadsheets show the contentual variety typical of the period and include, for instance, (bloodletting) calendars, texts on current politics, medical works (flyers on the plague and syphilis), and letters of indulgence. Later, Winterburger also worked for faculty members of Vienna University, printing textbooks conceived and used as lecture notes. His collaboration with the humanists in Vienna, foremost of them Johannes Cuspinian (1473–1529) and Conrad Celtes (1459–1508), allowed him to publish classical authors, buttressing his prominent position in the city's learned circles; this is also presumably how he met Lucas Cranach.

The *Wiener Heiltumsbuch* (List of Relics in Vienna; fig. 1), which he published in two editions in 1502 and 1514 (i.e. more or less concurrently with the *Missale Pataviense* of 1503) was an important undertaking.[5] Financed by Matthäus Heuperger (d. 1515), a Viennese burgher and city councillor, the elaborate design of this book – together with the reviving trade in liturgical prints – documents Winterburger's prominent and financially secure position.

In this essay I will focus on Winterburger's liturgical books. His first such publication was a *Psalter* dated to "around 1494–1498".[6] The simple design of this liturgical "first edition" produced by the Rhinelander's publishing house uses an alphabet comprising simple, plain initials, augmented by a somewhat more elaborate B(eatus vir)-initial (fol. Ir) embellished with flat spiralling foliage. It has been suggested that the B-initial derives from books published by Erhard Ratdolt at Augsburg, and this is presumably also the case for the missals printed after 1500.[7]

From a publishing point of view, the *Psalter* started a trend. At the onset of the sixteenth century, Winterburger published several missals in quick succession. Missals aligned with Passau continued to be relevant for the local market even after the Diocese of Vienna was canonically established in 1469; they comprise the largest group among Winterburger's liturgical publications. The *Missale Pataviense* of 1503, which forms the focus of this essay and which was illustrated predominantly with woodcuts by Lucas Cranach, was followed by other editions for use in this diocese. In addition, Winterburger produced missals for the dioceses of Olomouc (1505), Salzburg (1506, 1510), and Gran/Esztergom (1508, 1514). Lucas Cranach contributed a stock of woodcuts and initials, some of which were used in these publications (see cat. 22–26)

The woodcut initials in this *Psalter* (c.1494–1498) are typical of the somewhat limited book design characteristic of Winterburger's publications until around 1500. The main reason is that these types of text were not really suitable for elaborate designs. Wherever possible, for example in the family-tree schemata that illustrate Johannes Andreae's popular work on canon law,[8] Winterburger opted for more attractive solutions, most of which were inspired by southern-German templates. The same is true of title-page woodcuts, which Winterburger included in most of his publications from the 1490s onwards.[9] In most cases – for instance, depictions of a scholar in his study[10] – they adapted older models for the to-be-published text, which often resulted in a significant loss of artistic quality and a tendency towards reduction in the logic of the connectivity of shapes.[11] Compared to the designs of Winterburger's other publications, the above-mentioned *Heiltumsbuch* of 1502 is undoubtedly his most sophisticated book.[12] In addition to the detailed illustrated catalogue of the relics (225 objects), the book comprises, among other things, full-page woodcuts of St Stephen's Cathedral (fig. 1) and the Heiltumsstuhl (a building close to St Stephen's from which the relics where displayed); the frontispiece of the 1514 edition is a paraphrase of Cranach's depiction of the saint in the *Missale Pataviense* of 1503 (see cat. 22). Today, most scholars reject earlier suggestions that Cranach was also involved in this enterprise.[13]

THE *MISSALE PATAVIENSE*

Printing missals proved a profitable and safe business at the turn of the sixteenth century, a time when many of the manuscript missals copied in the late Middle Ages were being replaced by printed versions, which generated high sales. However, publishers striving for "mass production" had to take into consideration the liturgical singularities of the different dioceses and religious orders. To print missals, one required an episcopalian permit; in the years between 1500 and 1504 in the Diocese of Vienna, which had been canonically established only in 1469, this presumably meant an application to the administrator Bernhard von Pollheim (1456–1504) or Wiguleus Fröschl, Prince-Bishop of Passau (1445–1517).[14] Vienna's liturgical affiliation to Passau continued in practice after 1469, helping the dissemination of missals aligned to this rite.

Eduard Langer and Walther Dolch, the bibliographers of Johann Winterburger's publications, differentiate between two different editions of the missal of 1503,[15] both dated 25 May 1503. The edition listed as no. 35b is missing the *Missae speciales* (= quire P, fol. 307–312). A different print of the *Canon missae* (no. 36) has survived in a copy now in the Österreichische Nationalbibliothek (22.B.15 Alt-Rara).[16] Despite the presumably large print-run, only fourteen such missals are known today.[17]

The earliest printed *Passau Missal* (after 20 November 1491) was published by Johann Petri in Passau.[18] All other editions published between 1493 and 1512 were printed in Augsburg by Erhard Ratdolt (1494 [two editions], 1498, 1503, 1505 [two editions]) or by Johannes Winterburger in Vienna (1503, 1507, 1509 and 1512).[19] All the missals produced in the Petri workshop featured a woodcut depicting the crucifixion, but otherwise their run-of-the-mill hand-coloured ornamentation was the work of a local (Passau) workshop.[20] Some of the Augsburg printers followed the tradition of more-or-less individually decorated liturgical books, but this played no role in incunabula published by Winterburger and was also omitted in sixteenth-century works. The Viennese publisher – like those of later missals printed in Augsburg – preferred book designs comprising an (initially) limited number of mainly non-figurative woodcut-initials. Ratdolt's *Passau Missals* published between 1494 and 1503 – i.e. slightly before or more

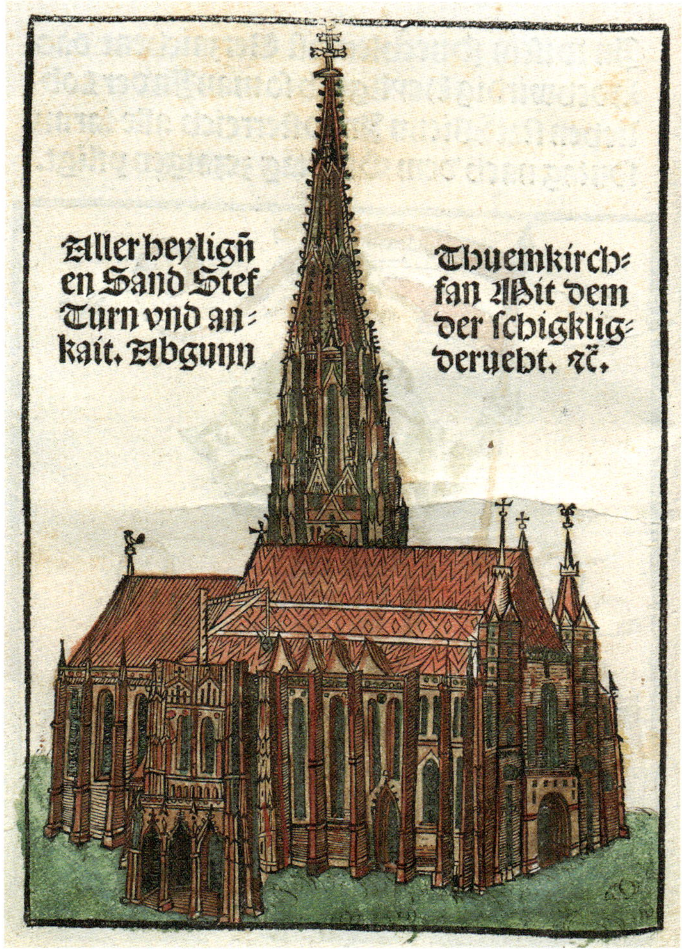

Fig. 1
View of St Stephen's Cathedral, 1502, hand-coloured woodcut. Österreichische Nationalbibliothek, Vienna, CP.2.B.66, fol. 1v (Johannes Winterburger, *Wiener Heiltumsbuch*, 1502)

or less concurrently with the *Viennese Missal* of 1503 – are decorated with unpretentious initials (generally placed at the same passage of the text as in Winterburger's books); we also find woodcuts of the patron saints of the Diocese of Passau (Valentinus, Stephanus and Maximilianus; fig. 2) that function as a frontispiece, a circular diagram for the dominical letter, and a canon with the crucifixion (fig. 3), a Te-igitur-initial, and a "Kussbild".

The reference to Ratdolt's *Passau Missals* is justified for several reasons: his publications already played a prominent role in connection with Winterburger's book designs before the missal of 1503 because the latter imitated Ratdolt's ideal-type model. In the same way, Winterburger modelled his missal of 1503 on the Augsburg template.

CRANACH'S WOODCUTS IN THE *MISSALE PATAVIENSE*

Winterburger's design for the *Missale Pataviense* of 1503 opened a new chapter in the book design of his publications, something his bibliographers Langer and Dolch also recognised when they, somewhat hesitantly, attributed them to Lucas Cranach but classed them as "masterpieces", listing "the woodcuts among the best-ever [...] book illustrations".[21] Once Dodgson (1903) and Dörnhöffer (1904) had expanded Cranach's oeuvre by attributing to him the figurative woodcuts (cat. 22, 23, 25, 26) in the *Passau Missal*, Beth (1907) also identified the artist as the author of most of the initials in the missal (cat. 26). Modern scholarship has mainly accepted these attributions and elaborated on them.

THE *CANON MISSAE*

The crucifixions that precede the Canon of the Mass (see cat. 25) follow a pictorial tradition dating back to the beginnings of book illumination and belong – in Germany since c.1480 – to the standard repertoire also used for printed missals.[22] The contentually seminal role of the Eucharist prayer (*Canon missae*) is reflected in both the frequent use of parchment as support and the choice of a larger and more elaborated typeface.[23] The *Canon missae* was usually printed on a separate quire and integrated into different editions of the missal despite liturgical, diocese-related differences.[24]

Taking this into account, the printers produced – verifiable, for example, for the *Passau Missals* – both missals without a *Canon missae* and separate prints of the Canon of the Mass.[25]

Winterburger's *Missale Pataviense* of 1503 also does this. For example, typeface and design of the *Canon missae* differ in each of the three copies now in the Österreichische Nationalbibliothek (ÖNB). The copy ÖNB 22.B.17 Alt-Rara, which probably once belonged to the Dominican monastery in Vienna and which contains a purely ornamental (vegetal) Te-igitur-initial (the canon illustration [see fig. 3] was cut out), uses a "foreign" Canon of the Mass printed on parchment from a book published by Erhard Ratdolt, which was also included, for example, in the *Passau Missal* of 1494.[26] Winterburger also printed a variation of the Canon of the Mass preserved in, for instance, the copy 22.B.14 Alt-Rara in the Österreichische Nationalbibliothek,[27] which is included in the so-called *Karstner Missal* (ÖNB 22.B.15 Alt-Rara, cat. 25). Normally, the canon illustration faces the Te-igitur initial to produce a diptych-like constellation, which was used contentually to juxtapose the crucifixion with, for example, a Eucharist (depiction of the Mass) or a typological scene:[28] in the missals of 1503 now in Vienna, these are an illustration of the Brazen Serpent (ÖNB 22.B.15 Alt-Rara, fig. 4) and the half-length depictions of a prophet and a king inserted into the initial (ÖNB 22.B.14 Alt-Rara).[29]

In the missal of 1503 we also find variations in the "Kussbilder" that contain, for example, the Lamb of God (ÖNB 22.B.14 Alt-Rara) and Christ's face (Vera icon) in the *Karstner Missal* (ÖNB 22.B.15 Alt-Rara; fig. 5). Dörnhöffer also attributed (not very convincingly) the Brazen Serpent in the Te-igitur-initial (fig. 4) and the "Kussbild" (fig. 5) to Cranach.[30]

SUMMARY

Lucas Cranach's sporadic contributions to the *Passau Missal* of 1503 resulted in a marked improvement in the quality of the book design in Winterburger's publications. By employing Cranach, the Viennese printer was following common practice in the late fifteenth century, commissioning a renowned artist to produce illustrations for his publications.[31] With the *Wiener Heiltumsbuch* (fig. 1), published more or less concurrently (1502), Winterburger also broadened his horizon as a publisher, establishing himself as *the* printer in Vienna for at least a decade. We may assume that Cranach designed his woodcuts expressly for the missal of 1503. The *St Stephen* dated 1502 (cat. 22) and the *Crucifixion* (cat. 25) may be classed as autonomous prints that were adapted for the missal, but the calendar dial for the dominical letter (cat. 23) was clearly produced solely for inclusion in this liturgical book. And the alphabet (cat. 16) chosen for the initials clearly reflects a missal's requirements too.[32]

Winterburger continued to use Cranach's woodcuts – i.e. the initials, the dial for the dominical letter, the *St Stephen,* and the Canon woodcut – in his publications until the early 1510s. The frequently remarked upon innovative character of Cranach's designs also extends to his initials, which evolved from the initially widespread, decorative flat style used in Winterburger's incunabula into a more dynamic, three-dimensional version. Especially compared to southern-German templates, this also applies to the ornamental pendentives in the dial for the dominical letter (see cat. 23). Compared to these templates, the motific "innovation" of placing an

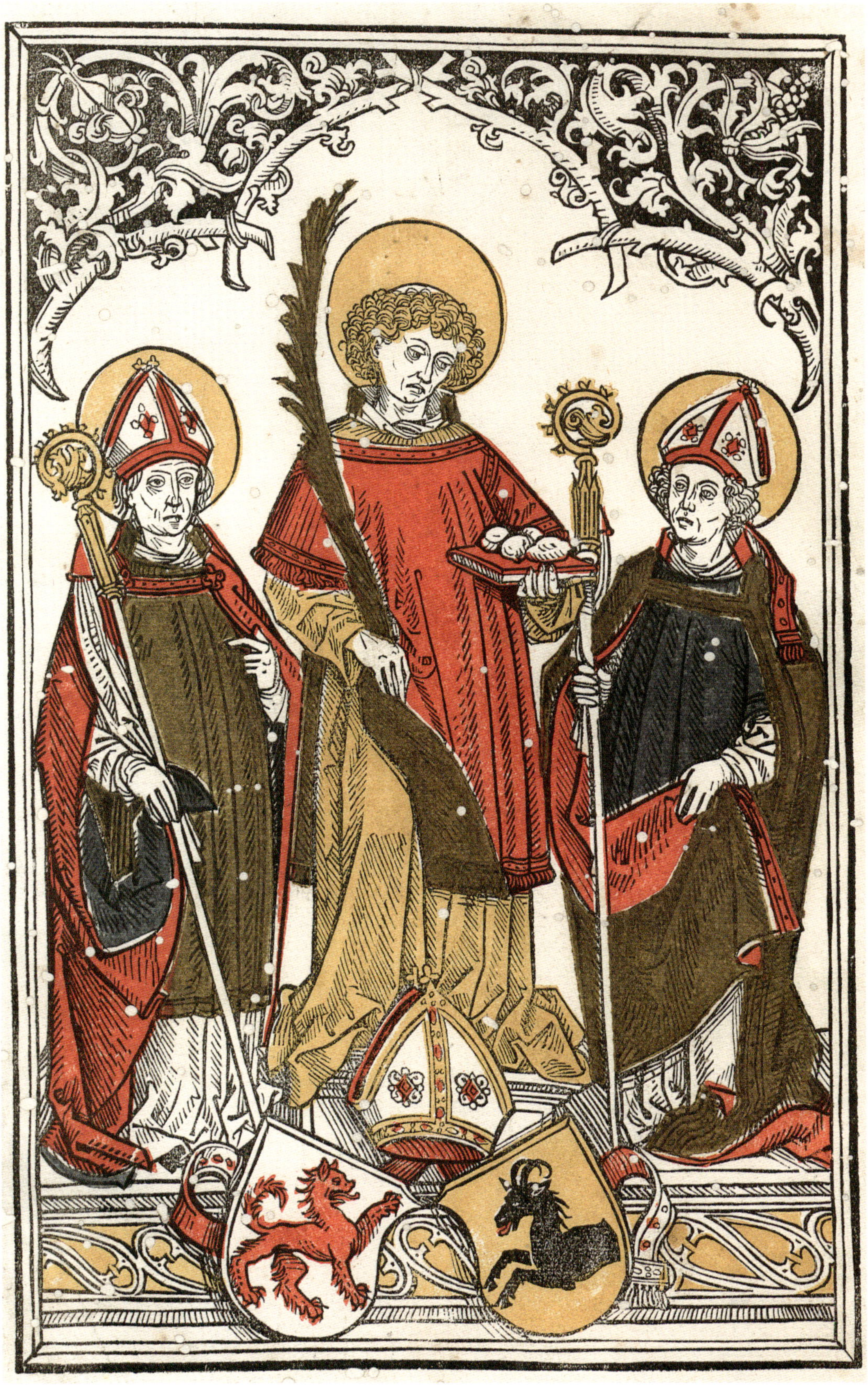

Fig. 2
Hans Burgkmair the Elder, *Saints Valentinus, Stephanus and Maximilianus*, 1494, hand-coloured woodcut. Bayerische Staatsbibliothek, Munich, Rar. 331, frontispiece (Erhard Ratdolt, *Missale Pataviense*, 1494)

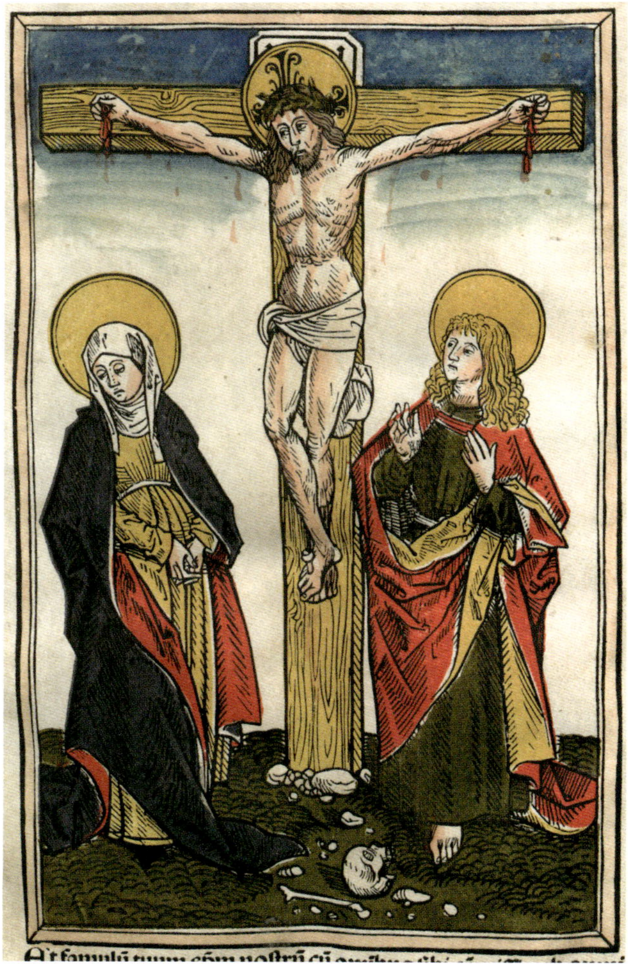

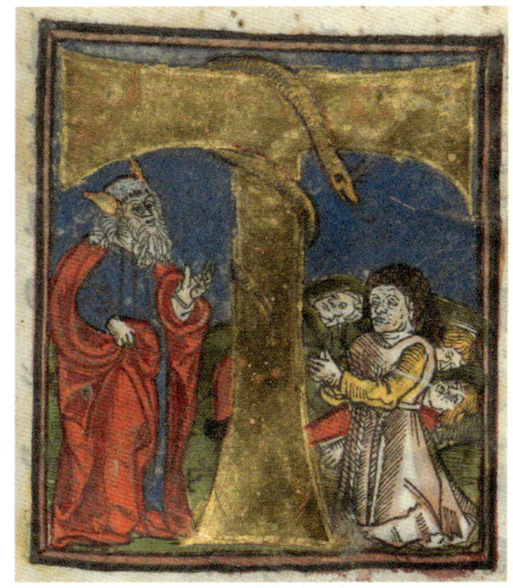

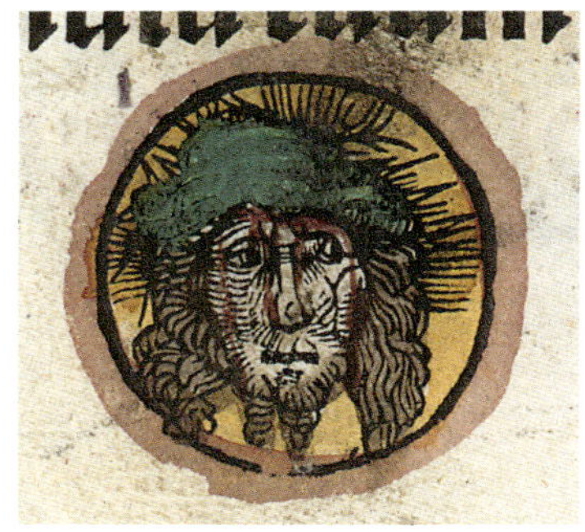

Fig. 3
Hans Burgkmair the Elder, *The Crucifixion* (canon illustration), 1494, hand-coloured woodcut. Bayerische Staatsbibliothek, Munich, Rar. 331, r1b (1/4) (Erhard Ratdolt, *Missale Pataviense,* 1494)

Fig. 4
The Brazen Serpent (Te-igitur-initial), 1502/3, hand-coloured woodcut. Österreichische Nationalbibliothek, Vienna, Ink 22.B.15 Alt-Rara, fol. 146r (Johannes Winterburger, *Missale Pataviense,* 1503)

Fig. 5
The Face of Christ ("Kussbild"), 1502/3, hand-coloured woodcut. Österreichische Nationalbibliothek, Vienna, 22.B.14 Alt-Rara, fol. 150v (Johannes Winterburger, *Missale Pataviense,* 1503)

owl at the centre of the woodcut has already been mentioned. In the *St Stephen* (cat. 22) and the three-figure crucifixion of the canon illustration (cat. 25) note also the "new" relationship between man and nature – in which the latter (in the crucifixion) functions as more than merely a location. We know about Cranach's work for the missal but we do not know much about the graphic arts in Vienna at the turn of the sixteenth century.[33] The rightly-refuted suggestion that Cranach's woodcuts were informed by locally-produced art[34] is confronted with the question whether the relatively large number of woodcuts included in Winterburger's publications even before he began to collaborate with Cranach reflect some kind of "regional" style. The hypothesis that Winterburger also worked as a woodcutter[35] can only cover one aspect of this subject matter.

1 Essential: Langer & Dolch 1913; Heiser 2002, 79–82; Mittendorfer & Fingernagel & Simader 2022.

2 Reske 2005, 123, lists a "Niklas" who worked as a publisher in 1506 in addition to Winterburger; Mittendorfer & Fingernagel & Simader 2022.

3 Langer & Dolch 1913, VI.

4 For the numbers, see Mittendorfer, in: Mittendorfer & Fingernagel & Simader 2022.

5 Exh. cat. Vienna 2015/16, 136–139.

6 GW M36218; ISTC ip01060900; Mittendorfer & Fingernagel & Simader 2022, cat. 13; Copies in the Österreichische Nationalbibliothek, Vienna: Ink 1.C.21 and Ink 25.B.18.

7 Zykan 1965, 11; we should also mention the B(eatus vir)-initial in the *Breviarium Pataviense* (Erhard Ratdolt [c.1490]): GW 5426; ISTC ib011751100; for more on the design of Ratdolt's publications, see exh. cat. Augsburg 2017, 62–73 et passim.

8 Johannes Andreae, *Lectura super arboribus consanguinitatis et affinitatis*, 22 June 1500 (GW 1701; ISTC ia00615000); copy in the Österreichische Nationalbibliothek, Vienna: Ink 22.H.10.

9 Mittendorfer & Fingernagel & Simader 2022.

10 Augustinus Datus, *Elegantie*, 1499 (GW 8120; ISTC id00085700); copy in the Österreichische Nationalbibliothek in Vienna: Ink 23.G.49.

11 In this case the template was the title-page woodcut in Jacobus Wimpheling, *Isidoneus Germanicus de erudienda iuventute*, Strasbourg, Johann (Reinhard) Grüninger, after 22 August 1497 (GW M51653; ISTC iw00038000).

12 Vienna, Österreichische Nationalbibliothek, CP.2.B.64, CP.2.B.65 and CP.2.B.66 (all 1502), CP.2.B.67 (1514).

13 Ankwicz-Kleehoven 1937, 1–6; Ankwicz-Kleehoven 1959, 30; for a dissenting opinion, see Zykan 1965, 29.

14 Oswald 1953, 83.

15 Langer & Dolch 1913, nos. 35a, 35b and 36.

16 Perhaps a variant of the *Missale Pataviense*, printed by Erhard Ratdolt in 1494 in Augsburg, see note 7.

17 vdm 224; we should also include the many extant but apparently cut out woodcuts, which suggest there were other copies, see cat. 24–25 and cat. 22.

18 GW M24626; ISTC im00682000; vdm 1452.

19 For Ratdolt's editions, see Savage 2018, 339–344, 358–361; for Winterburger's, see Oswald 1953, 75–101.

20 Hranitzky 2018; the book's wide dissemination in Austrian libraries (nine of the 17 extant copies) bears witness to the widespread use of missals aligned with this rite in Austria.

21 Langer & Dolch 1913, 23 and 53 (for the initials: L. Cranach?)

22 Heitz 1910.

23 Langer & Dolch 1913, 20.

24 Oswald 1953, 92–94.

25 Oswald 1953, 92. Independent parts of the canon also by Winterburger (after Ratdolt's *Passau Missal* of 1494?) for the *Missale Pataviense* (Langer & Dolch 1913, no. 36) or the *Missale Olomucense* of 1505 (Langer & Dolch 1913, no. *39).

26 GW M 24617; ISTC im00683000; see exh. cat. Augsburg 2017, figs. 39–40; Savage 2018, fig. 3.

27 Without the two lines of text below the crucifixion (erased?), see Langer & Dolch 1913, no. 36.

28 The connection is expressed, for example, by the two angels in the Te-igitur-initial turning to face the crucifixion on the opposite page in a *Missale Constantiense* published in 1505 by Erhard Ratdolt in Augsburg (VD 16 M 5582; vdm 635), see Savage 2018, fig. 2.

29 This too seems to have been modelled on books published by Ratdolt, see Savage 2018, fig. 2.

30 Dörnhöffer 1904, 182. For a dissenting opinion see, for example, Zykan 1965, 31–32 and 47.

31 Compare also the situation in Augsburg, where Hans Burgkmair worked on the book design for Ratdolt's publications, see exh. cat. Augsburg 2017, 72.

32 Compare the identical alphabet in Ratdolt's *Passau Missal* of 1494, see note 7.

33 Koreny 2003, 556–571.

34 Heiser 2002, 82, who rejects the suggestions put forward by Gollob 1926.

35 See Dieter Koepplin in exh. cat. Basel 1974, cat. 66.

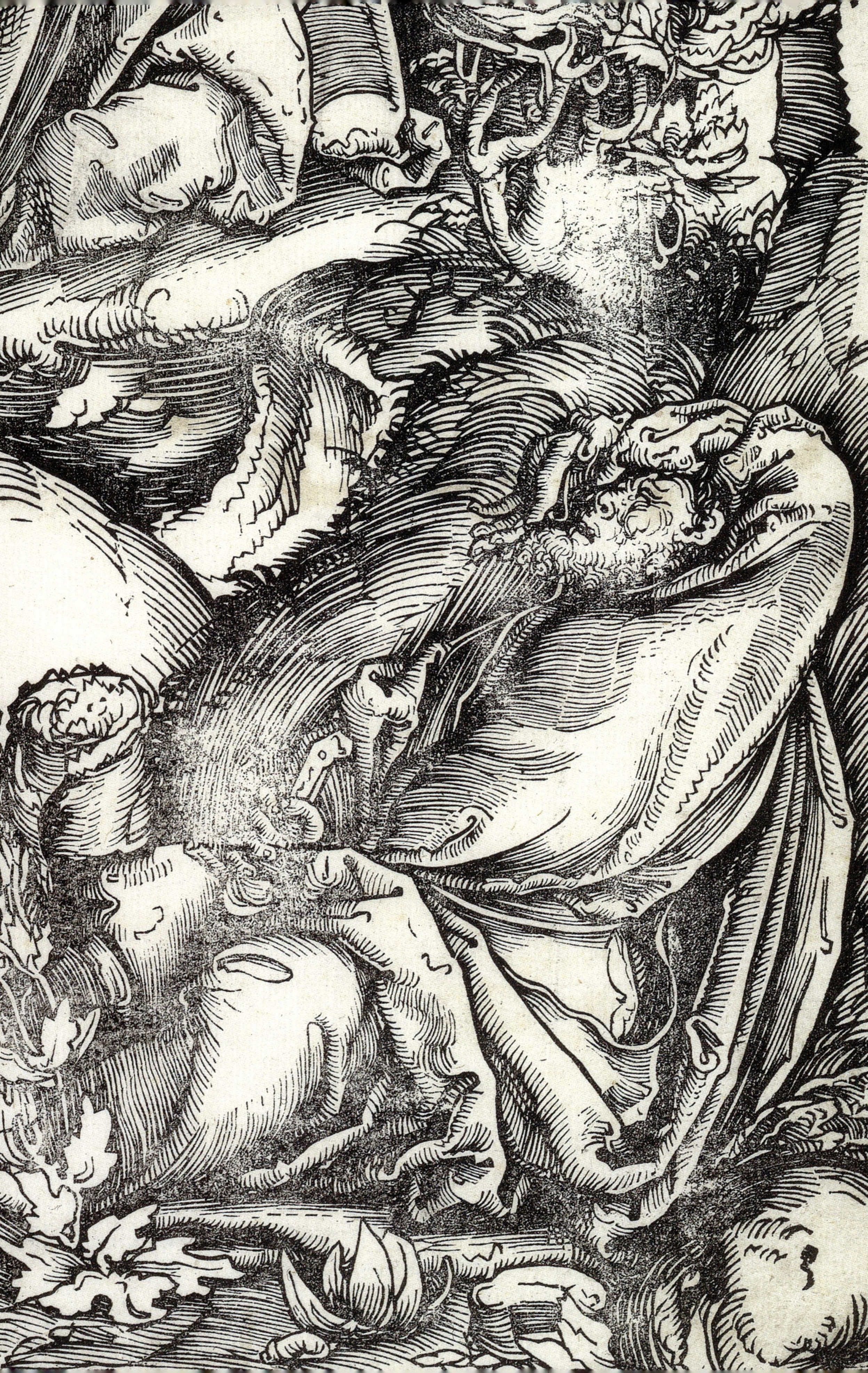

Sabine Heiser

On the Genesis of an Early Oeuvre. Lucas Cranach in Vienna around 1500

At the turn of the twentieth century, a ghost was haunting art history – the "early Cranach". Until then, the artist was known for his portraits of the reformer Martin Luther, gorgeous nudes of Venus, the goddess of love, cheeky Cupids, and dignified likenesses, as well as diverse woodcuts including the *Heiltumsverzeichnisse* (lists of relics) and scenes from the Passion. Art historians knew all about the paintings and prints he had produced in Wittenberg for the court of the Elector of Saxony and wealthy bourgeois patrons.

In this respect, the obstacles baring our access to the early Cranach appear to be of a paradoxical nature. On the one hand, the respected ducal court painter is one of the best-documented artists of his time – both regarding his oeuvre and his life – but on the other hand, next to nothing was known about his life before the age of thirty-two. Cranach's education and training before he appeared in Vienna remain obscure.

We know nothing (so far) about the artists he trained with or who influenced him before 1500. We also do not have any self-reflective remarks or theoretical treatises by him. We can try to gauge information about his friendship with scholars from their few recorded comments on or commissions to Cranach. He left no travel journal or diary, and almost no letters that tell us what he saw or read; compared to Dürer's Netherlandish journal, Cranach's report about what he saw in the Low Countries is decidedly meagre.

But in 1899, the date of an exhibition mounted in Dresden and curated by Karl Woermann, the director of the city's Picture Gallery, the things art historians believed they knew for certain about the court painter of the Elector of Saxony had to be radically augmented and revised. The exhibition – or rather the comprehensive exhibition catalogue – was the initial spark that led to the discovery, listing and appreciation of Lucas Cranach's early oeuvre.[1] This wide-ranging survey functioned as a forum that brought together the various ideas and conjectures about Cranach's art and its evolution that had been printed in disparate publications during the final decades of the nineteenth century, and it kickstarted a major connoisseurship debate. In Dresden in 1899, the various observations and assertions regarding Cranach's works *before* his move to Wittenberg – most published without illustrations – could be verified by assessing and comparing the assembled original works for the first time.[2]

The first dated and signed work listed in the exhibition catalogue was *The Rest on the Flight into Egypt*, then still in a private collection (see fig. 4 and cat. 28). Following a short description, the panel was succinctly described as "Cranach's earliest authenticated and at the same time by general consent most beautiful painting, painted even before he moved to Wittenberg".[3] This panel, dated 1504 and signed with the initials "LC", formed the starting point for all subsequent

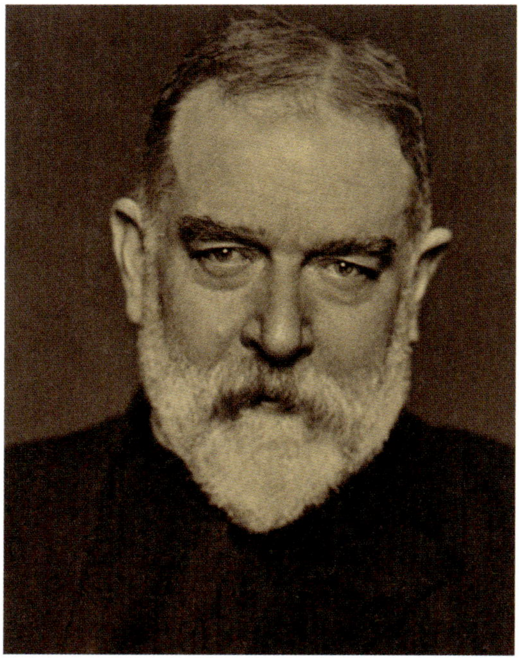

Fig. 1
Hugo Erfurth, *Karl Woermann, director of the Dresden Picture Gallery*, photo taken in 1904. Museum Ludwig, Cologne, inv. FH 01246

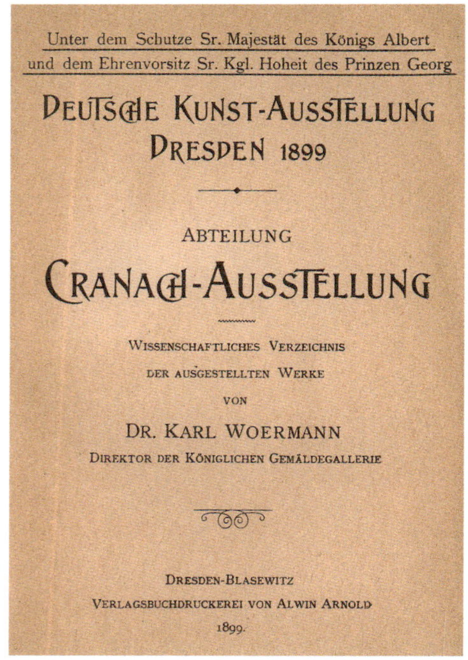

Unter dem Schutze Sr. Majestät des Königs Albert
und dem Ehrenvorsitz Sr. Kgl. Hoheit des Prinzen Georg

DEUTSCHE KUNST-AUSSTELLUNG
DRESDEN 1899

ABTEILUNG
CRANACH-AUSSTELLUNG

WISSENSCHAFTLICHES VERZEICHNIS
DER AUSGESTELLTEN WERKE
VON
DR. KARL WOERMANN
DIREKTOR DER KÖNIGLICHEN GEMÄLDEGALLERIE

DRESDEN-BLASEWITZ
VERLAGSBUCHDRUCKEREI VON ALWIN ARNOLD
1899.

Fig. 2
Title-page of the exh. cat. of the Dresden Cranach Exhibition in 1899. Kunsthistorisches Museum Vienna, Library, inv. 17611

discussions of Cranach's early oeuvre, functioning as the benchmark for the *Schleissheim Crucifixion* of 1503 (fig. 5), and the *Portrait of a Scholar aged Forty-One* (also known as the *Portrait of a Jurist* or of *Johann Stephan Reuss*), also painted in 1503 and also in Nuremberg (cat. 15).[4]

So, in a way, the artist Lucas Cranach was born thrice: for the first time in 1472 in Kronach in Franconia, for the second time in Vienna, where the mature artist appeared around 1500 and created impressive paintings and prints, and for the third time around 1900 in Dresden, when the works he had produced in Vienna were first attributed to him with certainty. Despite much research and scholarship since then, we know next to nothing about the early years of Cranach's life – including his real surname and what conclusions we can draw from the variations of his name.[5]

At the turn of the sixteenth century, Cranach, under remarkable circumstances, stepped into the limelight in Vienna as a painter and graphic artist; a look at the city's coeval guild regulations, which include provisions for foreign artists that Cranach most probably did not fulfill, reveals how little we can take for granted regarding the beginnings of his artistic career.[6]

Today, we should probably accept that, except for the odd more-or-less convincing attempts to attribute new works to Cranach, we will never really know much about the early years of the artist's life and work – but this certainly does not apply to his sojourn in Vienna.

Both the guild-, work- and civil conditions in Vienna and the city's intellectual life, which centred on the imperial court and the university, proved to be vital determinants for Cranach's work – not only in connection with production conditions but also his at times almost revolutionary interpretations of traditional subjects such as the double portrait of the Cuspinians (cat. 12 & 13), or the *Schleissheim Crucifixion* of 1503.

With its three dated paintings – the *Schleissheim Crucifixion, The Rest on the Flight into Egypt,* and the *Portrait of a Scholar Aged Forty-One* – the exhibition mounted in Dresden in 1899 functioned as the point of departure for the discovery of other panels, drawings and woodcuts by Cranach. At the same time, the debates about attributions that consumed scholars during the

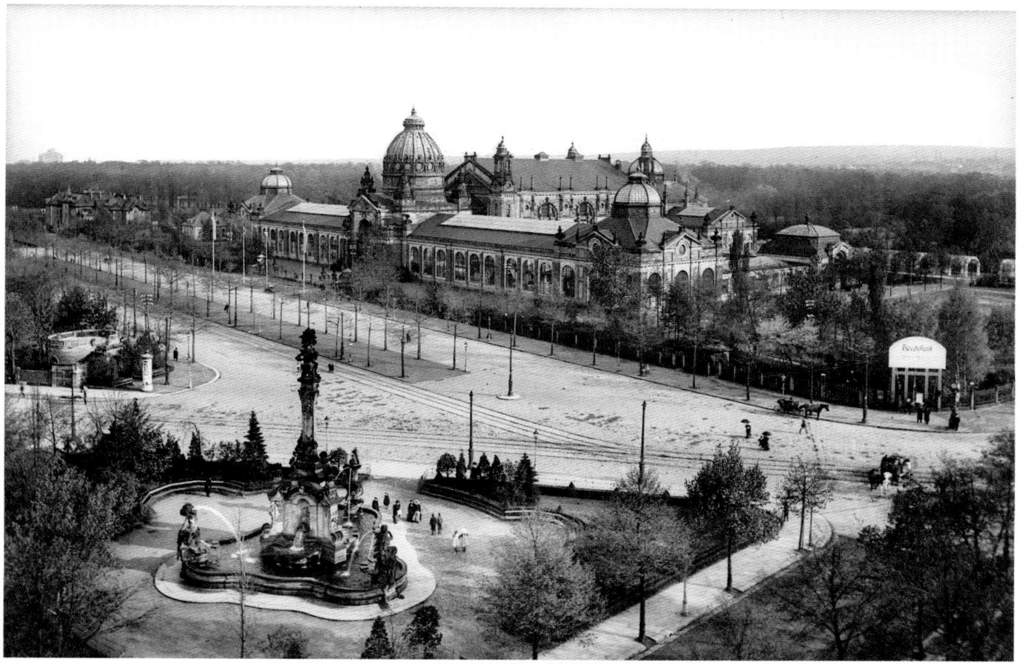

Fig. 3
Municipal Exhibition Palace Dresden (destroyed in 1945), photo taken around 1900

first decades of the twentieth century helped develop central concepts and methods of modern art history and allowed them to be tried out on and discussed in connection with the artworks in question. Of particular importance in this context was the discovery of the "Danube style" or the "Danube School", as whose inventor Cranach has long been (mistakenly) regarded.[7]

At the turn of the twentieth century, art historical research on Early German painting focused on three phenomena: (1) questions regarding the mysterious artist known as "Pseudo-Grünewald", which (2) was related to the discovery of Cranach's early works, and (3) the construction of the "Danube style" or "Danube School". In this context, the 1899 exhibition provided the stage on which were assembled the scattered ideas on the varied questions published since the 1870s, presented them to a wider scholarly audience, and invited the latter to discuss them. One result of these efforts was, of course, that it was no longer possible to doubt the existence of Cranach's early work produced before he took up his post as court painter to the Elector of Saxony in Wittenberg. The art historians who constructed this early oeuvre relied primarily on stylistic criteria – even in cases where content and iconographic peculiarities became the main argument in favour of attributing a work to Cranach. A methodical support for this line of argument, the "Danube style" functioned as a kind of hinge to explain iconographic shifts.

We should see the three sections of the exhibition in Dresden dedicated to Lucas Cranach's early work in the context of these questions. Part of the "Deutsche Kunst-Ausstellung" (Exhibition of German Art) shown at the Municipal Exhibition Palace (fig. 3), the presentation was divided into two main sections – "oil paintings" and "reproductions" – each with additional sub-categories reminiscent of the Chinese encyclopedia referred to by Jorge Luis Borges.[8] Written by Karl Woermann (fig. 1), the director of the Royal Picture Gallery, the exhibition catalogue adopted this classification. An introduction and a short biography of the artist were followed by the third section, which focused on the "Pseudo-Grünewald question"; this was followed by a chapter on "oil paintings", which was in turn divided into nine subdivisions:

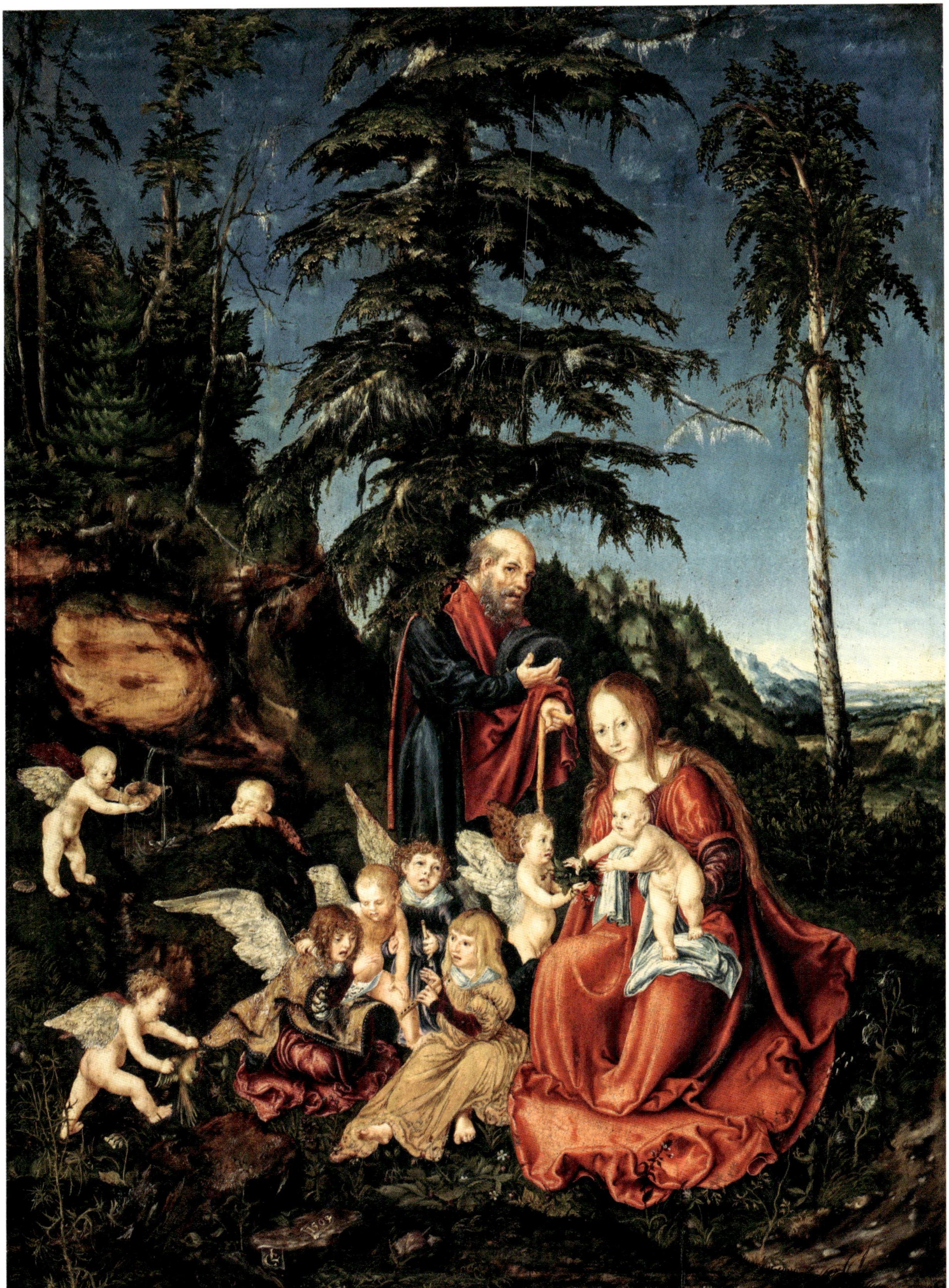

I Signed and dated paintings by Lucas Cranach the Elder
II Signed but not dated paintings by Lucas Cranach the Elder
III Paintings that can be traced back to Lucas Cranach the Elder with the help of old written sources
IV Non-authenticated paintings by Lucas Cranach the Elder or his workshop
V Paintings by the artist called "Pseudo-Grünewald"
VI Paintings attributed by some to various artists, by others to Lucas Cranach the Elder
VII An accepted painting by Matthäus Grünewald
VIII Paintings by Lucas Cranach the Younger
IX Paintings by W. Lukas von Cranach (born 1861)

The section entitled "Reproductions" included and discussed "(I) Facsimile prints after engravings and woodcuts by Lucas Cranach the Elder", and "(II) Photographs of paintings not on show in the exhibition".

The Dresden exhibition catalogue expressly stated that the show's aim was to "celebrate [Cranach] as the leader, or even the founder, of the Saxon School".[9] However, the audience for questions focusing on the works dated before 1504 and the contributions of Cranach's workshop was a "smaller circle of connoisseurs and art historians".[10] Woermann placed the "Pseudo-Grünewald question" at the centre of his research, thereby kickstarting the debate about the phenomenon of the Danube style that began in the early twentieth century and continues to this day.[11]

In the years that followed the Dresden exhibition, art historians identified and assembled Cranach's early oeuvre piece by piece, with Max J. Friedländer playing a seminal role.

When Christian Schuchardt completed his three-volume monograph on Cranach in 1871 he had not been able to examine the original work *The Rest on the Flight into Egypt* (fig. 4).[12] At the time, the painting was still in the Galleria Sciarra, a difficult-to-access private collection in Rome. Nonetheless, Schuchardt decided to include it in his catalogue, but he was not able either to place it in the context of the other early works he did not know or to place it stylistically.

None of the paintings now attributed to the young Lucas Cranach were included in section V of the Dresden catalogue among the works attributed to the "Pseudo-Grünewald"; only in section VI, dedicated to "Paintings attributed by some to various artists, by others to Lucas Cranach the Elder", did art historical research break new ground: the *Schleissheim Crucifixion* is listed as no. 147; it was followed by the Nuremberg portrait of the scholar "Johann Stephan Reuss", which was listed as no. 148. A concurrent exhibition curated by Max Lehrs at the Kupferstichkabinett (Collection of Prints) in Dresden showed drawings and woodcuts by Lucas Cranach, including the two large *Mount of Calvary* woodcuts (cat. 2 & 3).

Reactions to the exhibition in Dresden were varied – the "small circle of experts and connoisseurs" discussed the questions raised by the show in their reviews, trying to identify and add new works to those assembled in the exhibition.[13] A wide-ranging discussion began that mainly focused on the *Schleissheim Crucifixion* and the *Reuss* portrait in Nuremberg, both newly-attributed to Cranach and both included in the show.[14]

Eduard Flechsig proposed two large crucifixion woodcuts (cat. 2 & 3) as Cranach's earliest extant graphic works.[15] He suggested the undated woodcuts were produced "around 1500", thereby pushing back the date until then associated with Cranach's first extant works – 1503 – by three years.[16] The dated woodcut offered proof of a work produced by Cranach in 1502. Flechsig avoided answering the question where exactly the artist was residing at the time by a

Fig. 4
Lucas Cranach the Elder, *Rest on the Fligt into Egypt (The Holy Family in a Landscape)*, 1504. Staatliche Museen zu Berlin, Gemäldegalerie, inv. 564A

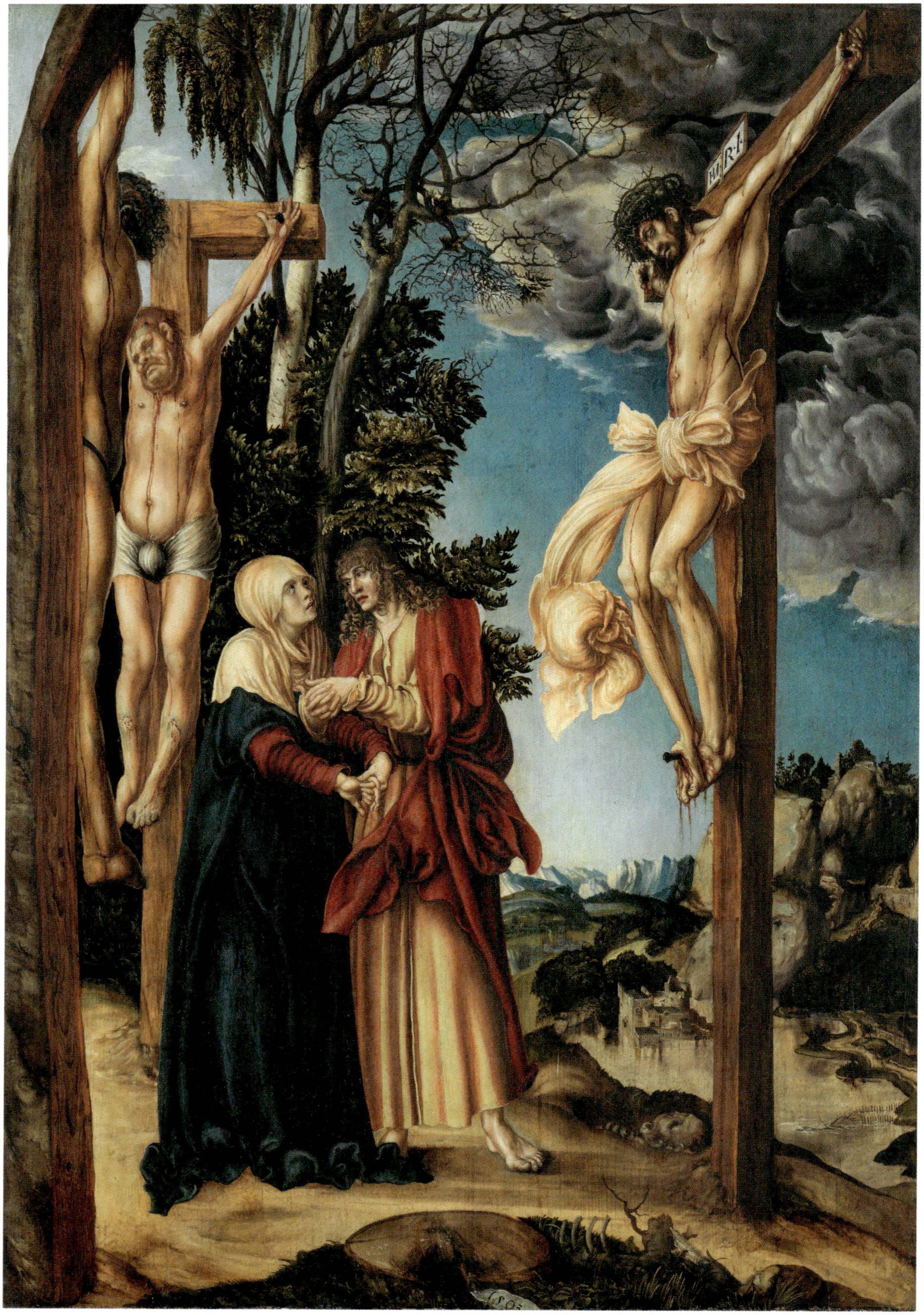

Fig. 5
Lucas Cranach the Elder, *Lamentation at the Foot of the Cross ("Schleissheim Crucifixion")*, 1503. Bayerische Staatsgemäldesammlungen, Alte Pinakothek, Munich, inv. 1416

vague reference to South-Eastern Europe: "the Magyar types clearly indicate where the artist was then living".[17] In Flechsig's timeline the two woodcuts follow the *Schleissheim Crucifixion* and the *Reuss* portrait. Next are the *St Valentine* in the Academy of Fine Arts in Vienna (cat. 10), claimed for Cranach by Ludwig Scheibler, the female *Reuss* portrait now in Berlin (formerly in the collection of Prince Schwarzburg-Rudolfstadt; cat. 16), and the outer wings of an altarpiece in Vienna.[18] *The Rest on the Flight into Egypt* in Berlin (fig. 4) brings up the rear in his list of accepted early works. H. W. Singer, too, begins his review of the exhibition with this painting dated 1504.[19]

Wilhelm Schmidt, the director of the Kupferstichkabinett (Print Room) in Munich, published a summary of reactions and hypotheses after the exhibition had closed.[20] He was the only critic to pay tribute to Lehrs's exhibition at the Kupferstichkabinett in Dresden, and he added two drawings from his collection in Munich to the two crucifixion woodcuts.[21] For the print dated 1502, he also identified the misfits in the crucifixion woodcuts, whom Flechsig had loosely described as "Magyar", as "Janissaries", concluding that Cranach probably lived "in Hungary or Austria, after all" and connecting this with the "as Frimmel called it, Danube style".[22] At this time, Cranach's sojourn in Austria had not yet been established. Schmidt agreed with the attribution of the *Schleissheim Crucifixion* to Cranach, emphasising its closeness to the *Rest on the Flight into Egypt*, and the *St Catherine Altarpiece* of 1506 now in Dresden.

In his report for the Kunstgeschichtliche Gesellschaft (Art Historical Society) published in October 1899, Max J. Friedländer identified positive proof of a "Franconian period" for the artist as the exhibition's most important finding.[23] Like his fellow critics, Friedländer accepted the attribution of *The Rest on the Flight into Egypt* and the *Schleissheim Crucifixion* to Cranach. He also pointed out that both paintings are dated in a similar way, on a scrap of paper. Inspired by the portrait of "*Chancellor Reuss from Constance*" (cat. 15), Friedländer suggested that Cranach may have spent some time in the south-west of Germany.[24] He also explicitly discussed the influence of Dürer on Cranach's early works. Friedländer's review of the exhibition published in the *Repertorium für Kunstwissenschaft* reads like a supplement to the catalogue.[25] Following the Dresden classification, he adds a few comments to some of the catalogue entries, and confirms Cranach as the author of the three early works. He is particularly moved by no. 147, the *Schleissheim Crucifixion*: "The master has not produced anything that compares to the harrowing, dramatic power of this composition."[26]

In his summary of the exhibition he had curated, Karl Woermann lists the findings of the show.[27] He felt the most consequential result was the re-discovery of Cranach's virtuosity. He called *The Rest on the Flight into Egypt* the "starting point for all research on Cranach", identifying only a few traces of the "Franconian School in the widest sense" but possible influences from the "Danube School".[28] But most remarkable is his decisive and unequivocal rejection of the attribution to Cranach of both the *Schleissheim Crucifixion* and the *Reuss* portrait (cat. 15). Woermann refers to "renowned scholars who disagree with this [attribution]. I have to agree with them."[29]

The first two decades of the twentieth century witnessed the second phase of discovery and attribution of works produced by Lucas Cranach during his sojourn in Vienna. In 1903, for example, Campbell Dodgson presented "five uninscribed woodcuts by Lucas Cranach", among them the *St Stephen* dated 1502 from the *Missale Pataviense* (cat. 22).[30] In 1904, Friedrich Dörnhöffer published a summary of the (then) current state of research; he was also able to attribute to Cranach a number of initials (cat. 26), the calendar dial to identify the dominical letter (cat. 23) from the *Missale Pataviense*, and the *St Martin*, a drawing dated 1504 now in Munich (cat. 27).[31] He also proposed the *Schotten Crucifixion* (cat. 1) as a work by Cranach.

Only three years later, Otto Fischer, in his highly-critical review of Hermann Voss's PhD thesis on the "Origins of the Danube Style", drew attention to the *St Jerome*, a panel dated 1502 (cat. 6), and was able to establish Cranach as its author.[32]

And finally, in 1926, Max J. Friedländer published, and identified as works by Cranach, the two *Cuspinian Portraits* (cat. 12 & 13) that had just been acquired by the Reinhart Collection in Winterthur.[33] However, the sitters remained anonymous until Ankwicz-Kleehoven was able to identify them not long afterwards.[34] In the same year, 1927, Max Geisberg added Cranach's large woodcut *Christ on the Mount of Olives* (fig. 6) to the master's graphic oeuvre.[35] Here, too, a change of owners led to its attribution to our artist.[36] In 1935, the Kunsthistorisches Museum Vienna hosted a small exhibition on the "Early Cranach"[37] for a similar reason – to celebrate the acquisition of the *Schotten Crucifixion* and to showcase the "Austrian Cranach".

CRANACH AND THE "DANUBE STYLE"

Unfortunately, one cannot avoid the discussions swirling around the term "Danube style" and the question of Cranach's contribution to this construct when examining the master's earliest extant works.[38]

Albrecht Altdorfer from Regensburg is regarded as the style's best-known and most typical representative. He was the subject of Max J. Friedländer's PhD thesis (1891), the art historian who played such a prominent role in the rediscovery of Cranach's early works.[39]

In 1892, Theodor von Frimmel coined the term "Danube *style*" in his review of Friedländer's thesis,[40] and in 1907 Hermann Voss explored the "Origins of the Danube Style" in his PhD thesis.[41] Franz Rieffel was the first to use the term "Danube style" in connection with Cranach's *Rest on the Flight into Egypt* in his "Kunstwissenschaftliche Controversfragen" (Art Historical Controversies) published in 1895.[42] Since then, most attempts to describe the idiosyncrasies typical of Cranach's early manner cannot refrain from employing the ill-defined term "Danube *School*". However, the bandied-about term is more appropriate for the artists who lived and worked in Austria after Cranach had left for Wittenberg. Trying to identify Cranach as the father of the Danube School is nothing but a stopgap. As early as 1904 Friedrich Dörnhöffer, in his attribution of the *Schotten Crucifixion* (cat. 1) to Cranach, had stated: "in truth it [the painting] precedes the development of the so-called Danube School by quite some time."[43]

In his "Betrachtungen über die Donauschule und den Donaustil" (Reflections on the Danube School and the Danube Style), Herbert Schindler struck out on his own and questioned Cranach's by-then accepted early oeuvre.[44] He not only combined all the genres to create a "Sodalitas Danubia", informed by the similarly-named coeval humanist society founded by faculty members of Vienna University, but identified Cranach's sojourn in Vienna as the catalyst for the entire "Danube style" movement.[45] Schindler only accepted *The Rest on the Fight into Egypt*, the double portraits in, respectively, Nuremberg and Berlin, and the drawing of *St Martin* as authentic works by Cranach produced during his stay in Vienna, rejecting all the others because he discerned stylistic differences between them and the panels Cranach painted when he first moved to Wittenberg.

UNTIL TODAY

In the second half of the twentieth century, it was probably Dieter Koepplin who contributed the most to the research on Lucas Cranach's early oeuvre, first with his PhD thesis on the Cuspinian portraits (submitted to Basel University in 1964, published in 1973), and then with the important Cranach exhibition he and Tilman Frank curated in Basel in 1974.[46] Koepplin explores and discusses both the humanist milieu in Vienna at the turn of the sixteenth century,

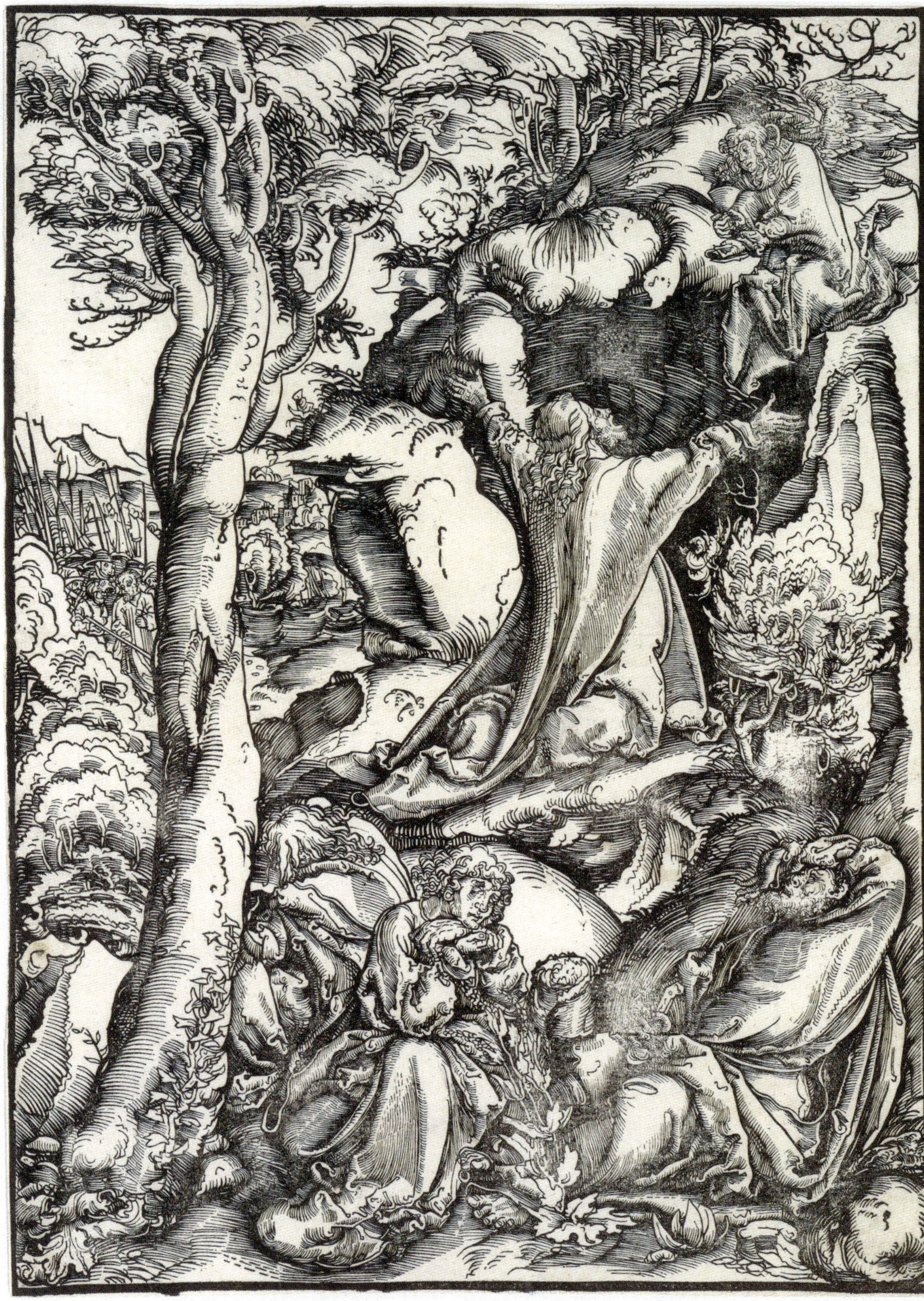

Fig. 6
Lucas Cranach the Elder, *Christ on the Mount of Olives*, woodcut, c.1500. The Metropolitan Museum of Art, New York, inv. 27.54.3

which was dominated by Conrad Celtes and the *Collegium poetarum et mathematicorum*, and Cranach's possible ties to these learned circles. The drawings he produced for Johannes Fuchsmagen's copy of the *Filocalus* calendar (original AD 354; cat. 7) must be seen in this context.[47] Together with his portraits of scholars, they bear witness to Cranach's contacts with the university milieu in Vienna. *The Penance of St Jerome* dated 1502 (cat. 6) may also have been commissioned by Johannes Fuchsmagen.[48]

And, last but not least, this context helps explain Cranach's close ties to the printer Johannes Winterburger.[49]

Dieter Koepplin was also able to show how much Cranach's *Cuspinian Portraits* differ from earlier likenesses; the same is true of the *Schleissheim Crucifixion* (fig. 5).[50] First identified as a work by Cranach by Rieffel in 1895, the panel had been variously attributed to Grünewald, Wolfgang Huber and even Albrecht Altdorfer prior to the Dresden exhibition. Technological analyses carried out at the Alte Pinakothek in Munich at the end of the last century and repeatedly published, provide a new basis for a discussion of the *Schleissheim Crucifixion* dated 1503.[51] The aim of these examinations is both to study Cranach's early manner and to learn more about his drawing technique. Based on the underdrawings revealed in the infrared-reflectographs, Martin Schawe analysed and explained conclusively the evolution of Cranach's compositions. One important finding is that he was able to show that Cranach developed his compositions and the poses of his protagonists while he was painting and did not have a fully worked-out concept or template when he began work on a panel. The traces of the painting's genesis bear witness to its experimental character.

None of the numerous exhibitions and accompanying symposia on the work of Lucas Cranach the Elder held for no commemorative reason since 1994 focused expressly on the artist's early oeuvre, its peculiarities, or the circles in which Cranach moved during his stay in Vienna. On the contrary, even the Cranach-boom at the turn of the twenty-first century was not able to fill the gaps in our understanding of his early oeuvre but made them even more apparent. Most recently, Daniel Görres contributed a short introduction to "Cranach in Vienna" to the catalogue of the Cranach exhibition shown at Düsseldorf in 2017,[52] which included, among other works, *The Penance of St Jerome* (cat. 6), the *Portrait of a Scholar aged Forty-One ("Reuss")*, and a few of the artist's Viennese woodcuts.[53] Tanja Holste had earlier suggested identifying the anonymous jurist as the councillor Jodocus Welling, who had married the widow of Hans Heml, a former mayor of Vienna, and who was elected dean of the Law Faculty in 1503.[54]

The majority of the most recent attributions to Cranach's early oeuvre concerns drawings and woodcuts, such as by Guido Messling in this exhibition catalogue (see essay Messling, fig. 9). Edmund Schilling identified a *Wooded Landscape*, formerly in Dessau but lost since 1945, as a work by Cranach.[55] Rosenberg included the standing *St George* now in Budapest in the appendix to his catalogue raisonné of Cranach's drawings.[56] Koepplin's 1974 attribution of the *Lovers* in Brunswick (cat. 20), until then identified as "Southern German", was generally accepted. Even more unanimous was the welcome extended to the *Martyrdom of St Catherine* now in Budapest when it was proposed by Iván Fenyö, though his dating to before 1505 was rejected.[57] The panel was prominently displayed in the exhibition mounted in Kronach and Leipzig in 1994, featuring on posters and the cover of the exhibition catalogue. In the catalogue Claus Grimm suggested the now generally accepted date "around 1508", which means it was produced after the closely related (both chronologically and compositionally) *St Catherine Altarpiece* in Dresden.[58] These last-named works, and the questions regarding when they were executed and where they belong in the timeline, complete, for the time being, the corpus of Cranach's early oeuvre.

1 Exh. cat Dresden 1899. The exhibition catalogue was revolutionary too: it was one of the first to go beyond merely listing the works on show and include scholarly essays and catalogue entries.
2 One exception is Hubert Janitschek's lavishly-illustrated three-volume publication on the history of German painting (Janitschek 1890); in vol. 3, 490–491, he provides an excellent illustration of *The Rest on the Flight into Egypt* and offers a critical appraisal of the painting.
3 Exh. cat. Dresden 1899, cat. 1 ("das früheste beglaubigte und zugleich anerkanntermassen das schönste Bild Cranach's, noch vor seiner Übersiedelung nach Wittenberg gemalt"); Friedländer & Rosenberg 1979, no. 10.
4 Friedländer & Rosenberg 1979, nos. 5 and 8.
5 Heiser 2002, 44–46.
6 See Heiser, 2002, 6, 50–56, and the essay by Björn Blauensteiner.
7 See Heiser 2002, 34–43, for more on the discussion of Cranach as the founder of this style.
8 The "Celestial Emporium of Benevolent Knowledge", Borges 1952.
9 "Führer, wenn nicht als Begründer, der sächsischen Schule", see exh. cat. Dresden 1899, 1.
10 "engeren Kreis von Kennern und Kunstforschern", ibid.
11 Exh. cat. Dresden 1899, 12–19. See also Tacke 1992, who identifies the painter known as Pseudo-Grünewald as Simon Franck.
12 Schuchardt 1871, 186–192, no. 80.
13 Reviews by, for example, Woermann 1898/1899; Schmidt 1899/1900; Singer 1898/99; Friedländer 1899, and Seidlitz 1899.
14 Rieffel 1895, 424–428, had already identified both as works by Cranach; for a dissenting opinion, see Woermann 1900, and Michaelson 1902, 32–34.
15 Flechsig 1899, col. 337–341.
16 The dating of "*Reuss*" and the "*Schleissheim Crucifixion*".
17 "Wo sich der Künstler damals befand, sagen uns die magyarischen Typen deutlich genug", ibid., col. 337.
18 His attribution of the altarpiece (today in the Belvedere, inv. 5010) to Cranach was rejected.
19 Singer 1899, col. 358–361.
20 Schmidt 1899/1900, col. 145–147.
21 Ibid. col. 145.
22 "in Ungarn oder doch Österreich aufgehalten" and „von Frimmel so genannten ‚Donaustile", ibid. col. 146; Frimmel 1896, 4–6. The term "Danube style": first used in Theodor v. Frimmel's review of Max J. Friedländer's PhD thesis on Altdorfer, in: Repertorium für Kunstwissenschaft 15, 1892, 417.
23 Friedländer 1899.
24 The connections between the supposed Johann Stephan Reuss and Vienna University had not yet been discovered.
25 Friedländer 1899/2, 237–249.
26 "Der Meister hat nichts geschaffen, was an erschütternder dramatischer Wucht dieser Composition nur annähernd gleichkäme"; ibid. 248.
27 Woermann 1900.
28 "fränkischen Schule nur im weitesten Sinne"; ibid., 26–27. Woermann does not elaborate on the term "Danube School".
29 "namhafte Forscher, die ihr [der Zuschreibung, S.H.] durchaus nicht zustimmen können. Diesen muss auch ich mich anschließen"; ibid.
30 Dodgson 1903.
31 Dörnhöffer 1904, col. 175–198.
32 Fischer 1907, 71.
33 Friedländer 1926, 381–383.
34 Ankwicz-Kleehoven 1927, 230–234.
35 Geisberg 1927, 171–173.
36 See Geisberg 1927, 171–173. The woodcut was acquired by the Metropolitan Museum of Art, New York, in 1927.
37 See Cranach Digital Archive (https://lucascranach.org/AT_KHM_GG6905, [retrieved 20 Sept. 2021].
38 See most recently exh. cat. Frankfurt & Vienna 2015. For the highly-problematic instrumentalisation of the term Danube style for ethno-populist and propaganda reasons by the Nazis, see Heiser 2002, 41–42.
39 Friedländer 1891.
40 Frimmel 1892.
41 Voss 1907.
42 Rieffel 1895, 425.
43 "In Wahrheit geht es [das Gemälde, S.H.] der Ausbildung dieser sogenannten Donauschule in ziemlichem Abstande voran"; Dörnhöffer 1904, col. 188.
44 Schindler 1981, 66–73; Schindler 1982, 93–99, and Schindler 1987, 19–29.
45 Schindler 1987, 20. Schindler suggests that a master from Passau from the Kriechbaum workshop produced the rejected works, even tentatively identifying Sebastian Kriechbaum as the artist responsible for them; he also believes that the latter provided important impulses for Cranach's *Rest on the Flight into Egypt*.
46 Koepplin 1973; exh. cat. Basel 1974, esp. Dieter Koepplin, *Cranach bis zum 32. Lebensjahr*, 105–184.
47 Heiser 2002, 61–71, incl. older literature.
48 Angelica Dülberg has recently suggested that the panel may have been a sliding cover for a portrait of Johannes Cuspinian (Dülberg 1990, 164–165, cat. 344). For a dissenting opinion, see Heiser 2002, 73.
49 See the essay by Andreas Fingernagel.
50 See Heiser 2002, 93–111.
51 Sandner & Rietschel 1994, 186–193; Schawe 1995, 11–22; Schawe 1998, 160–166.
52 Exh. cat. Düsseldorf 2017, 100.
53 Ibid., cat. 2–7.
54 See exh. cat. Düsseldorf 2017, cat. 3 (Gunnar Heydenreich).
55 Rosenberg 1960, no. 6 (he mentions Schilling's attribution).
56 Rosenberg 1960, no. A.3 ("by a pupil").
57 Fenyö 1955. Painting: Friedländer & Rosenberg 1979, no. 11.
58 Exh. cat. Kronach & Leipzig 1994, cat. 120.

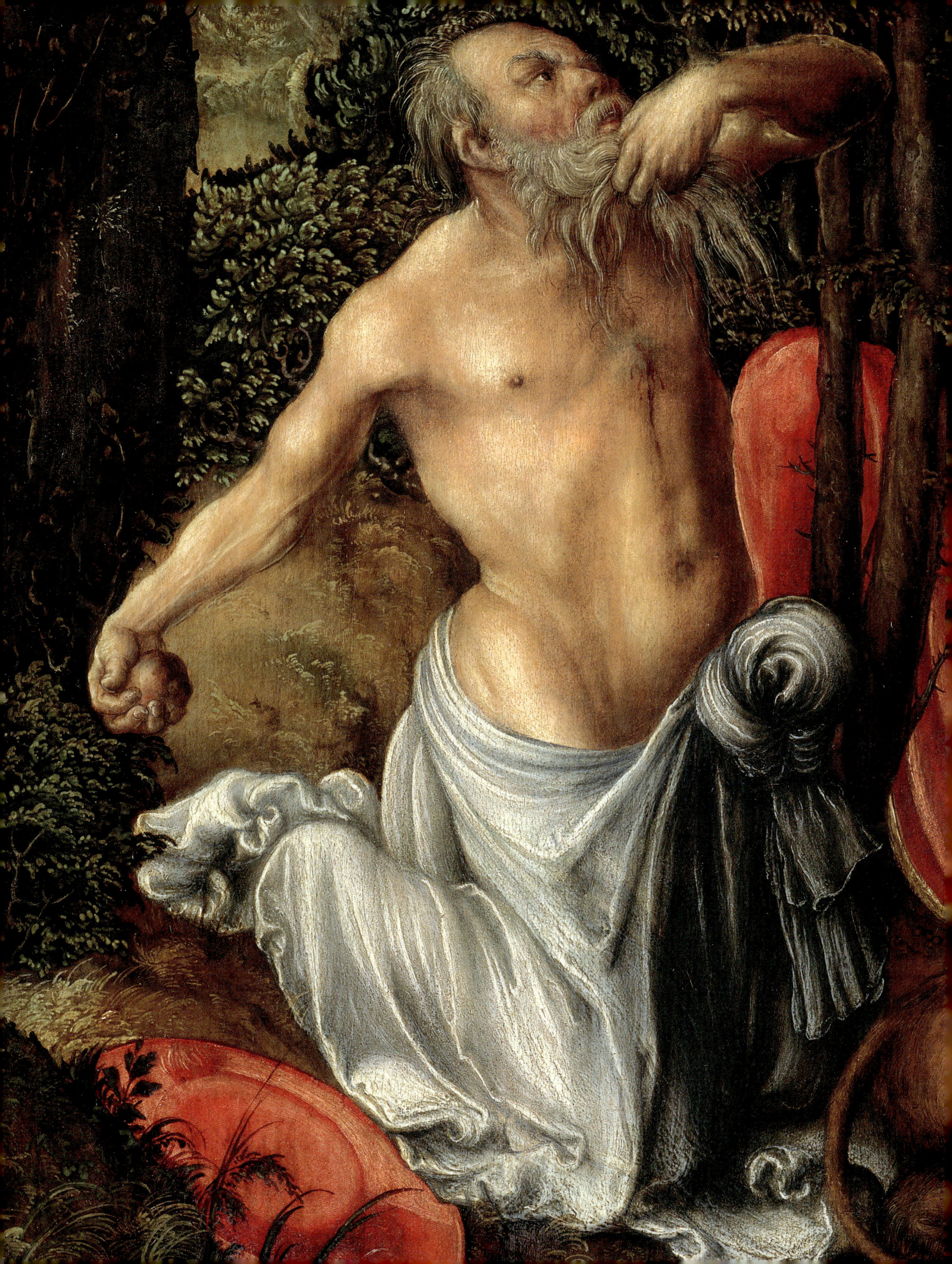

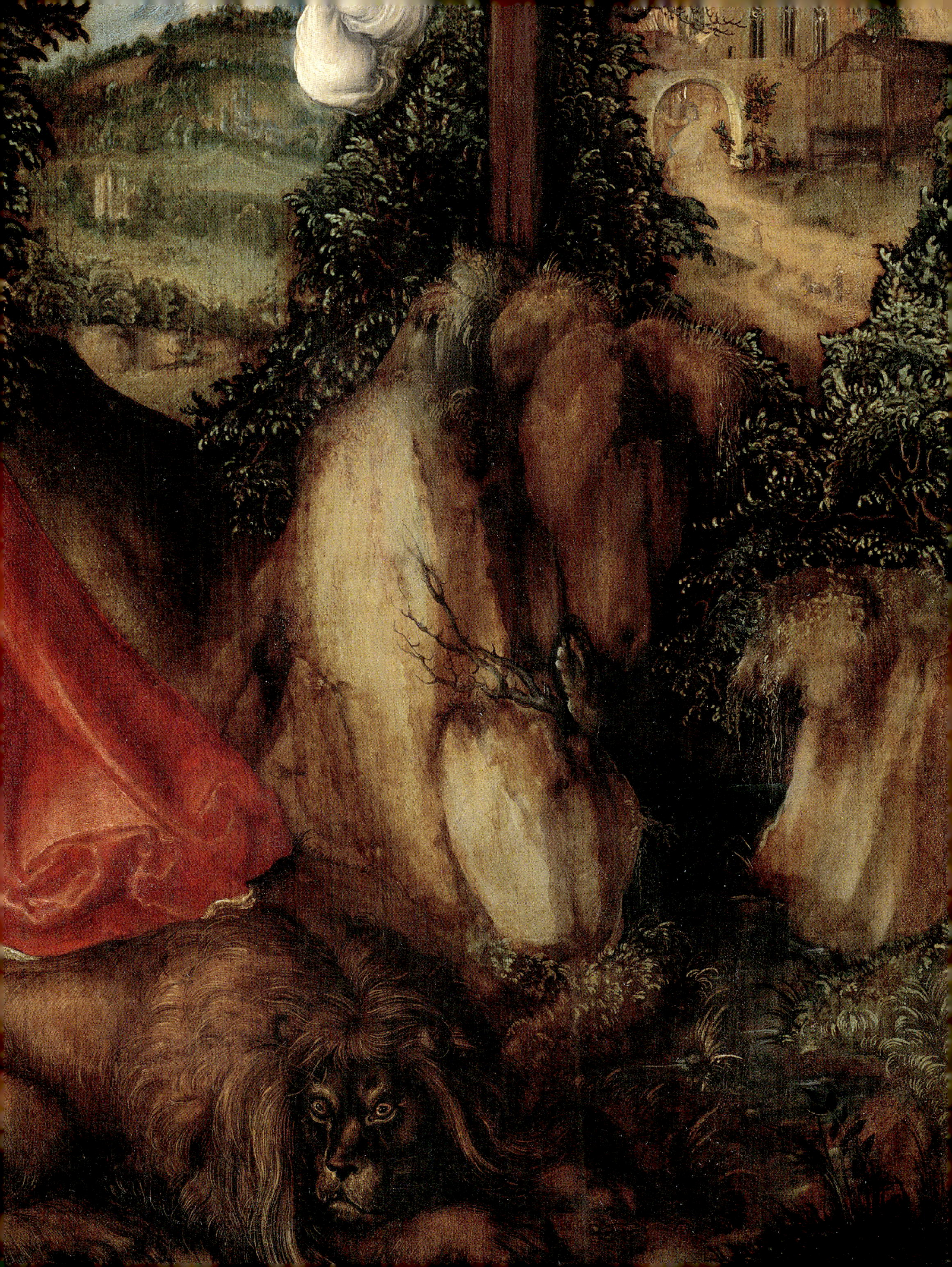

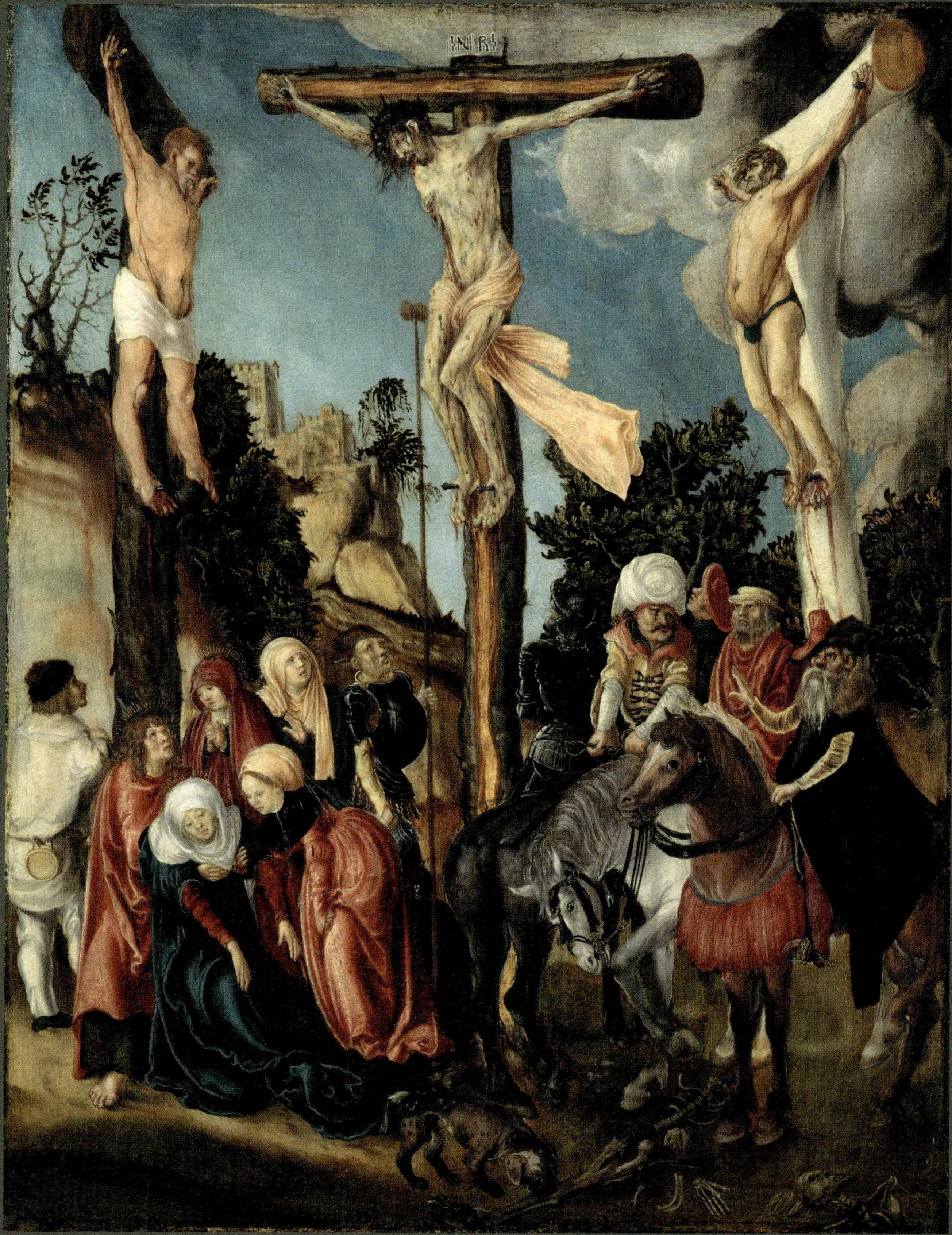
INRI

1

Lucas Cranach the Elder
THE CRUCIFIXION OF CHRIST
("SCHOTTEN CRUCIFIXION")
circa 1500
Kunsthistorisches Museum Vienna

Identified in 1904 as an early work by Cranach by Dörnhöffer, this *Crucifixion* is now unanimously accepted as one of the works that Cranach produced during his sojourn in Vienna. Because of its temperamental, almost coarse character, it is often identified as his earliest work. We will probably never know who commissioned the panel around 1500. Its small size suggests it may have been intended for private devotion in a home. The Kunsthistorisches Museum acquired it from the Schottenstift (Scottish Abbey) in Vienna. The panel probably came into the possession of this Benedictine monastery in the early eighteenth century when it acquired numerous paintings to decorate the new prelature. In 1529, a large part of the monastery's inventory was looted by soldiers billeted there during the first Ottoman siege of Vienna – they would surely have taken this small, movable picture if it had been in the Schottenstift at this point in time.[1]

This means we will probably also never know how much of the iconographic peculiarities that differentiate this composition from other contemporary crucifixions were the artist's decision and how much the result of the patron's specifications – things like the archaic traits in the rendering of Christ, whose feet are nailed to the cross with two nails. Both this solution and Jesus's twisted, sagging body covered all over in bleeding sores are reminiscent of mediaeval depictions, for example fourteenth-century plague-crucifixes. A possibly unique detail is Christ's protruding tongue, with blood dripping from it, which may have been inspired by descriptions of the popular visions of St Bridget of Sweden.[2] Jesus's broken gaze, directed at the viewer, seems to invite us to contemplate his death and sacrifice. The two thieves retreat behind the pathetic image of the martyred Christ. They, too, are nailed to their crosses with four nails each, but their bodies show far fewer signs of having been tortured and their arms and legs appear neither dislocated nor broken, something Cranach exaggerated in his contemporary *Calvary* woodcuts (see cat. 2 & 3). By matching the two thieves and having the crossbeams of their obliquely-placed crosses point towards the centre of the composition, Cranach directs our gaze towards Christ. Despite his brutal humiliation, the majesty of the Son of God is manifested in his prominent position in the composition and his considerable size. The significance of the scene is also reflected in the reactions of the figures assembled at the foot of the cross, which run the gamut from impotent mourning to speechless amazement. Their agitated drapery, together with the dancing branches and the menacing clouds, enhance the painting's expressive, pathos-laden voice.

The cross of the impenitent thief on Christ's left is pale; it was presumably constructed of birchwood, then considered an inferior timber.[3] A parallel for this rare motif can be found in the so-called *Löwenstein Calvary*, painted around 1456 by Hans Pleydenwurff for a church in Bamberg.[4] This is interesting also because Cranach's group of mourners is closely related to the group in this composition, in other depictions of the crucifixion from Franconia, and in a locally widely-adopted *Deposition of Christ* produced around 1450 in the circle of Rogier van der Weyden.[5] For the group of Christ's mounted enemies Cranach seems to have been inspired by something he saw in Austria, because their corrupted, jumbled-together attire is clearly based on Ottoman, Polish and Hungarian models.[6] The knight in armour giving us his back, however, derives from an engraving of the crucifixion attributed to Francesco Rosselli and dated to around 1480/90.[7] GM

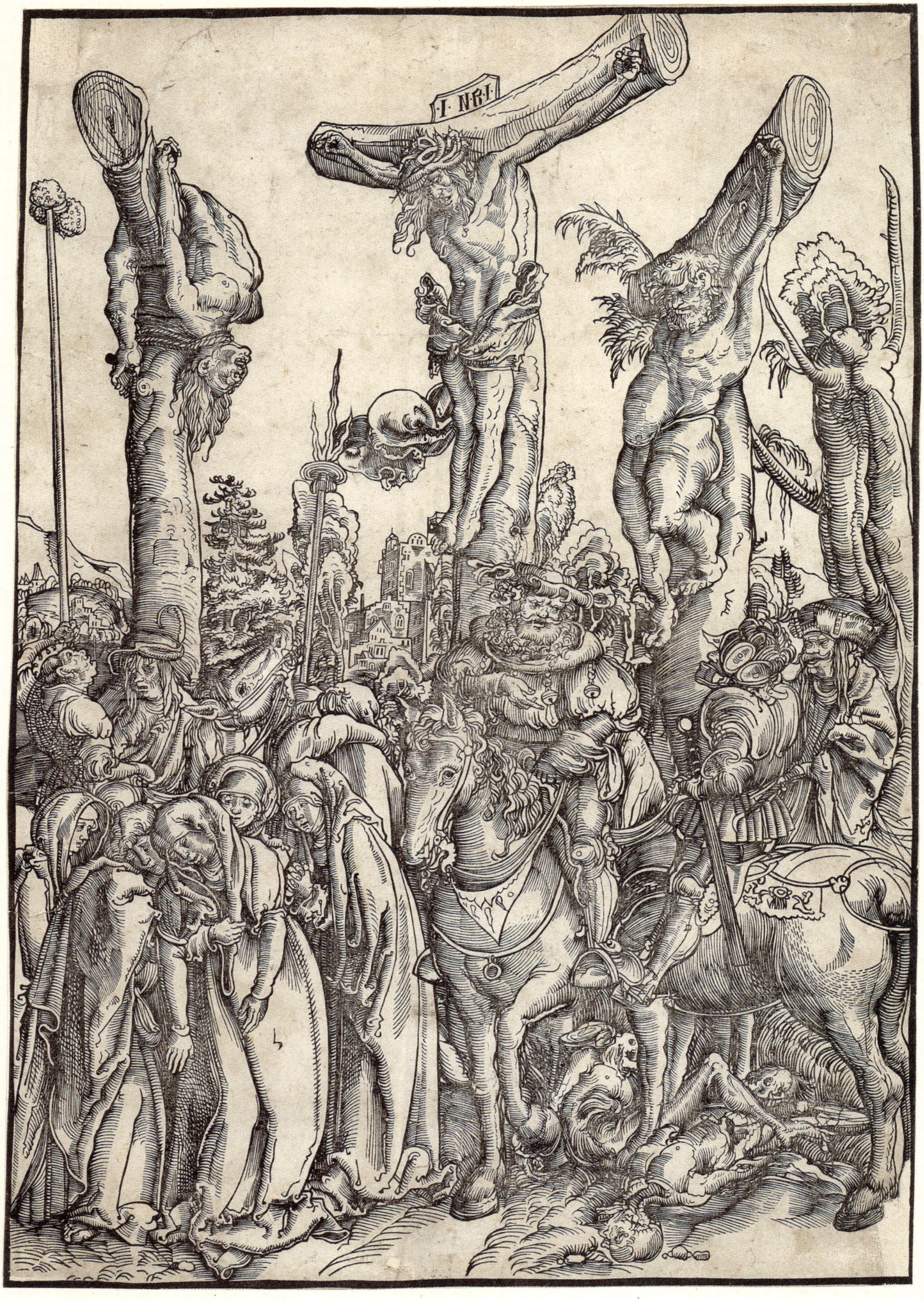

2

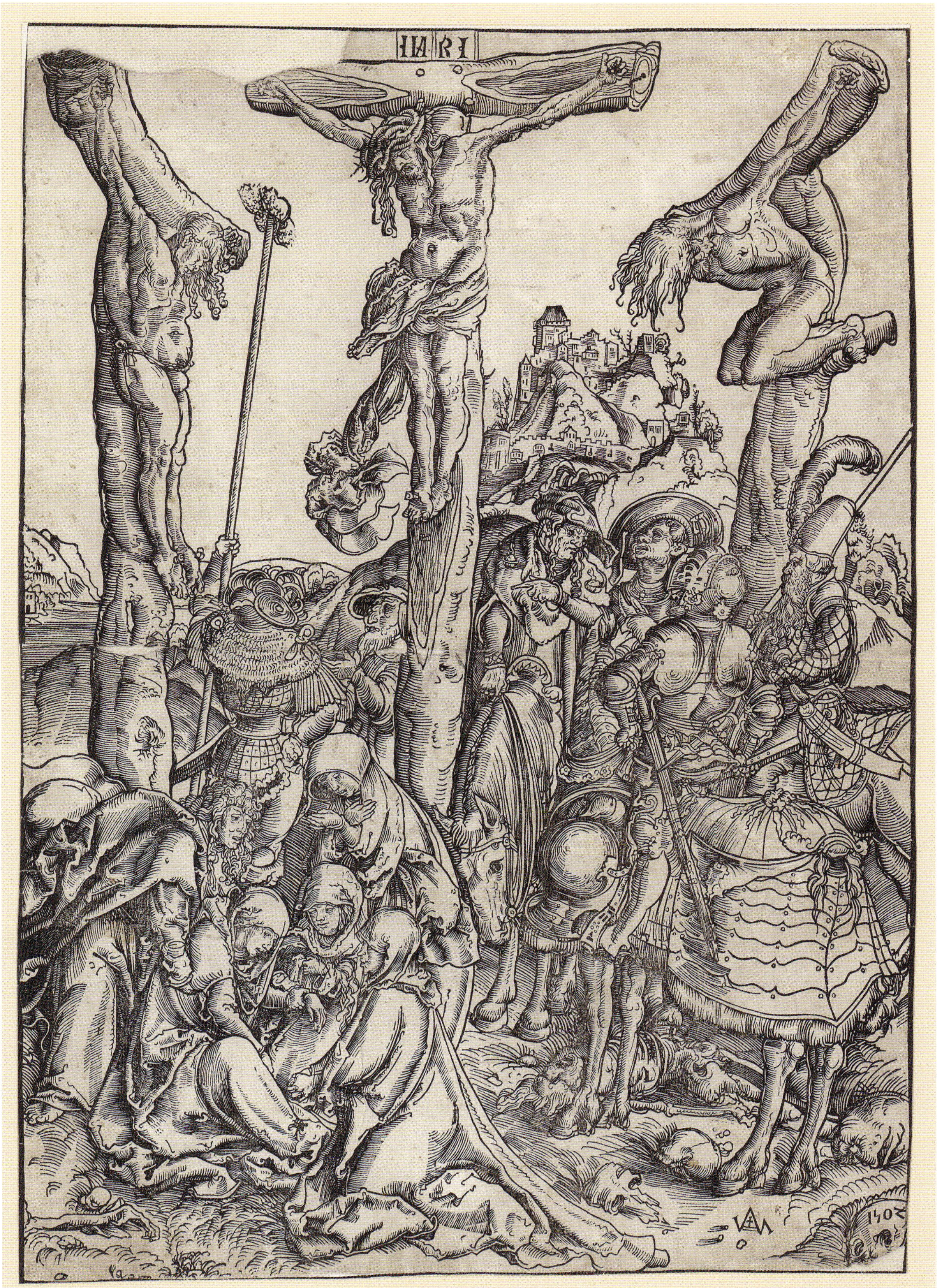

3

2 & 3

Lucas Cranach the Elder
THE MOUNT OF CALVARY
circa 1500
Staatliche Museen zu Berlin, Kupferstichkabinett

THE MOUNT OF CALVARY
1502
Staatliche Museen zu Berlin, Kupferstichkabinett

In some ways both woodcuts, one of which is dated 1502, appear to be some kind of printed versions of the so-called *Schotten Crucifixion* (cat. 1), sharing its format and composition, the number of people assembled at Golgotha, and even striking details like the body parts scattered on the ground. Here, however, Cranach's focus in regards to those condemned to die on the cross is very different, both in the somewhat similar compressed, bulging bodies of Christ and those of the two pairs of thieves. We may assume a preparatory sketch similar to the celebrated charcoal studies now in Berlin (cat. 4 & 5), allowing the artist to create harrowing images of tortured men whose sufferings are chillingly expressed through their in places grotesquely deformed bodies.[1] Cranach refrains from the common differentiation of the two thieves that reflects Luke's identification of the one on the right as the "good thief" who eventually repents and is thus saved (Lk 23:39–43). Despite the shocking verisimilitude of their sufferings, they are thus part of an older tradition of depictions of the crucifixion that dates back to the early fourteenth century. We can, for example, identify several not much older precursors from the Bavarian-Austrian region for the motif of the thief with a broken back tied to his cross in the undated woodcut probably produced shortly before 1502, among them a panel by Rueland Frueauf the Younger painted around 1496 (or 1499) for Klosterneuburg Monastery.[2] The same is true of the pose of the impenitent thief in the 1502 woodcut, with his head lowered and his body slumped forward. This means Cranach not necessarily consulted Jörg Breu's *Aggsbach Crucifixion* (1501, Nuremberg, Germanisches Nationalmuseum), as has repeatedly been suggested. It is just as likely that he was exposed to this unusual motif through an engraving by the Master I.A.M. of Zwolle, because both this print and another depiction of *Mount of Calvary* by this engraver from the northern part of the Low Countries were quite well known in the Bavarian-Austrian region.[3]

During his time in Vienna, Cranach also designed the woodcut *Christ on the Mount of Olives* (see essay Heiser, fig. 6). It seems the artist conceived these prints as autonomous, easy-to-duplicate devotional pictures and not as part of a series of the Passion, something made unlikely by the fact that he executed two crucifixions of Jesus.[4] In much the same way, Dürer had, from 1495/95, produced and disseminated some of the best-known scenes from the Passion as autonomous woodcuts, only completing the full series in 1511. With these exceptionally large prints, Cranach is clearly competing with the revolutionary achievements of the master from Nuremberg, who with his early scenes of the Passion and his series of the *Apocalypse*, published in 1498, had created and was selling woodcuts of a size and quality never seen before. We may read the house mark-like, hard-to-decipher sign on the *Mount of Calvary* dated 1502 as a testament to his self-confidence – this seems to be an early (and never repeated) signet of Cranach's before he began using the first letters of his name. Today, the three monumental prints that Cranach produced during his stay in Vienna are extremely rare – we only have a single impression of both the *Christ on the Mount of Olives* and the undated *Calvary*, and two of the version dated 1502 (The Metropolitan Museum of Art, New York). It seems not many were printed, but they soon began to influence artists far and wide.[5] GM

4 & 5

Lucas Cranach the Elder
THE PENITENT THIEF ON THE CROSS;
THE IMPENITENT THIEF ON THE CROSS
circa 1500
Staatliche Museen zu Berlin, Kupferstichkabinett

In a way, these two studies of the thieves crucified with Jesus allow us to look over Cranach's shoulder because despite their plastic modelling they are quick charcoal sketches that even retain traces of his quest for the most expressive form. The thieves' rough-hewn T-shaped crosses are handled rather cursorily, and the artist's main focus is clearly on the most drastic rendering of the brutal tortures they had to endure when they were crucified with Christ at Golgatha. Cranach treats the bodies of the condemned men like a pliable mass that can be almost randomly deformed, with their overlong arms and legs flailing around ecstatically and their torsos bearing but little resemblance to human anatomy. Unlike in the *Schotten Crucifixion* and the two *Calvary* woodcuts (cat. 1–3), here the thieves are not nailed to their crosses but tied to them, which was the coeval way of depicting this scene. Their related poses appear to be confronted studies in which Cranach tries to visualise being broken by and rising up against the pain as two contradictory reactions to these gruesome tortures. But like in the three above-named depictions of the crucifixion of Christ, here too he refrains from a judgmental characterisation of the two thieves, one of which, according to Luke (Lk 23:39–43), mocked Jesus in his hour of death, while the other repented and asked Christ to remember him in Heaven. Ultimately it is only his bowed head and the fact that he is turning to the right that identifies him as the penitent thief, because he is traditionally depicted to the left of the Son of God, i.e. on the latter's right.

Cranach did not use charcoal in any other extant drawing except the carefully worked portrait of Margrave Albrecht of Brandenburg-Ansbach, which can also be attributed to him.[1] We may assume that at the beginning of his career the artist, in his quest for expressive poses, frequently executed similar figure studies in this medium, something also suggested by the expressive gestures of the protagonists in the works he produced in Vienna. Both the low-quality paper and the corrections also suggest that Cranach saw these two drawings primarily as graphic studies that were not designed to be added to his collection of templates, which is why only they have survived by chance.[2] In addition, the rough surface of the cheap paper he had selected allowed for the charcoal particles to be partly erased or painterly smudged, while the prepared ground mediates between the black of the charcoal and the dappled white highlights. In this, the two male nudes are reminiscent of the almost contemporaneous chiaroscuro drawings of the *Foolish Virgin* (cat. 8) and *St Martin* (cat. 27), although these are highly-detailed pen and brush drawings. Friedländer identified Cranach as the author of the studies; this was recently rejected by Hofbauer though his arguments are not convincing. The attribution is also buttressed by the for Cranach typical wavy contours, and a comparison of the similarly convulsed backs and fronts of the thieves in the two large *Calvary* woodcuts, or *St John the Baptist's* equally flat feet peeking out from under his robe in the chiaroscuro drawing now in Lille (see cat. 27, fig.). The paper used for the two studies was only used in Swabia at the turn of the sixteenth century but that in itself does not necessarily support an attribution to Cranach because this material was as mobile as the artist himself. GM

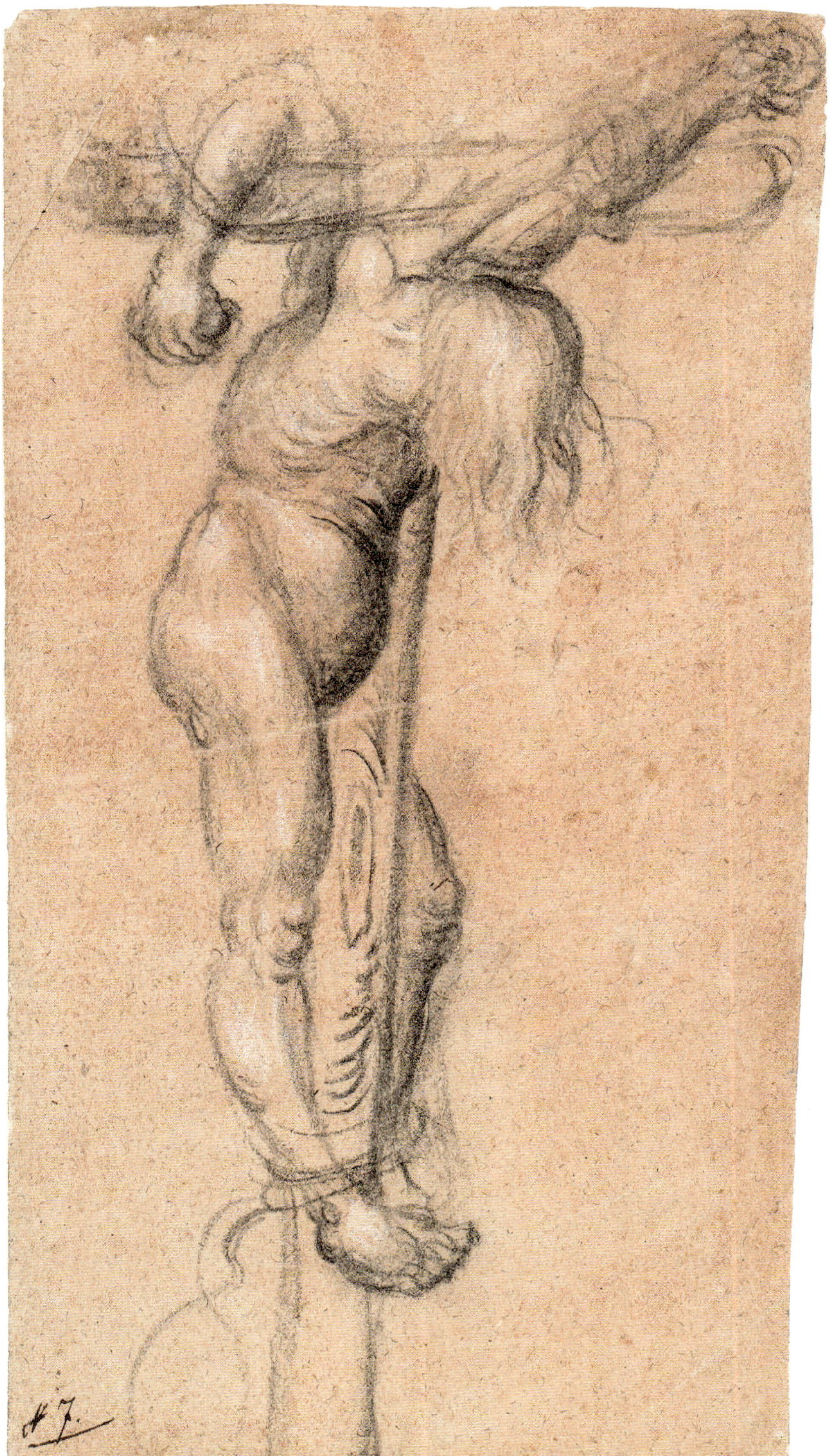

4

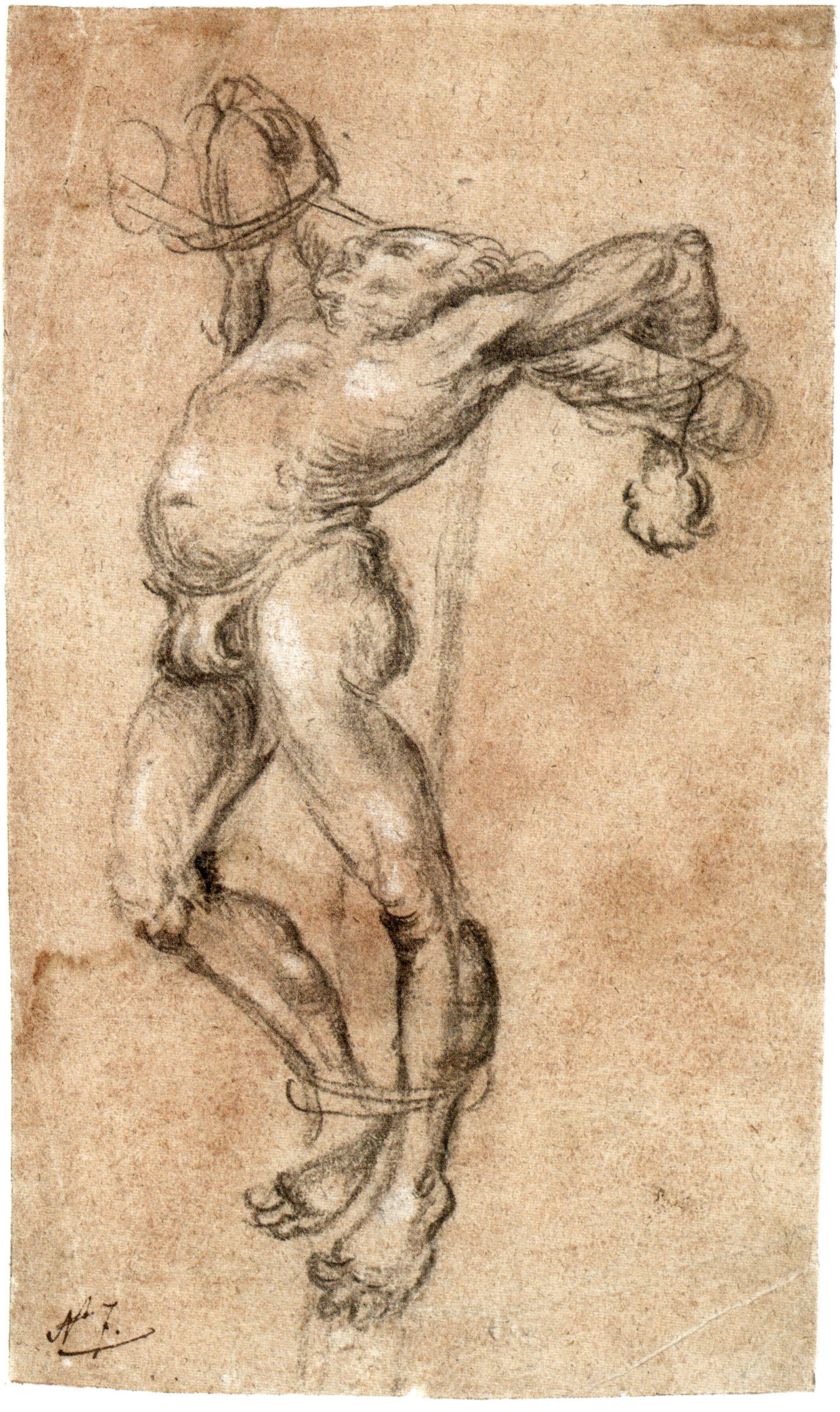

5

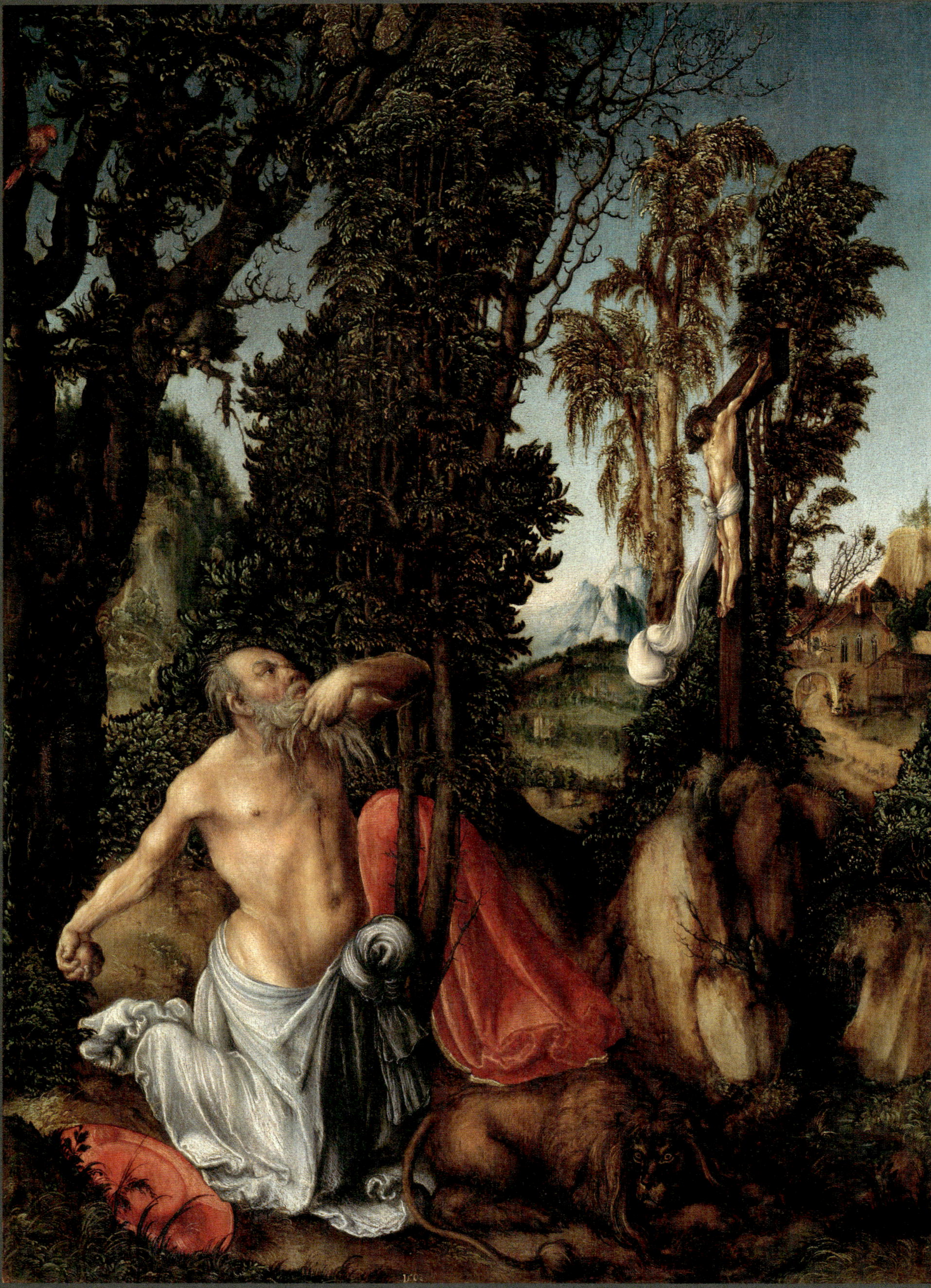

6

Lucas Cranach the Elder

THE PENANCE OF ST JEROME

1502

Kunsthistorisches Museum Vienna

Cranach painted *The Penance of St Jerome* in 1502, which makes it his earliest extant dated painting. Like his other Viennese works, it was only attributed to him in the early twentieth century when Fischer discovered it in Linz. In 1928, shortly after its acquisition by the Kunsthistorisches Museum, Baldass published a comprehensive study of the small panel. Its original location and purpose remain obscure, but he was the first to suggest it was commissioned by Johannes Cuspinian, a humanist who sat with his wife Anna (née Putsch) for their portraits by Cranach around the same time (cat. 12 & 13). Baldass cited the owl killing a small bird and the parrot-like bird in the tree beside the saint – similar to the ones included in the portraits of Cuspinian and his wife and read as references to their respective temperaments (see also cat. 23) – as support for this theory.[1] More plausible though just as difficult to prove is Koepplin's suggestion that it was Johannes Fuchsmagen who commissioned or received the painting because he had chosen Jerome as his patron saint and had commissioned drawings after a late-antique calendar manuscript from Cranach (cat. 23).

Revered as one of the four Latin Fathers of the Church, the erudite St Jerome (c.347–420) was a close confidant of Pope Damasus I who asked him to produce a Latin translation of the Bible, the Vulgate. This is why Jerome is almost always depicted as a cardinal although he was never appointed to this rank. His scarlet vesture is often also included in compositions that depict him in the desert doing penance for the sins he committed during his years in Rome. Cranach's saint has removed his cardinal's hat and cape, beating his bare chest with a stone while kneeling before a Crucifix. The friendly lion – allegedly it became his faithful companion after the saint had removed a thorn from its paw – derives from Dürer's engraving of the penitent Jerome (c.1496).[2] Cranach, however, has the beast fix its beady eye menacingly on the viewer, with the owl doing the same. The ascetic's spiritual agitation is eloquently expressed through the movement of his arm and the way he clasps his flowing beard. In this, Cranach far exceeds Dürer's composition. Jerome's violent agitation is echoed by the restlessly moving leaves and branches, and especially the wild drapery of his robe. This animation of forms manifests itself most dramatically in Jesus's billowing loin cloth, imbuing the depiction of Christ with a heightened degree of reality. Trees and branch-formations too reference Dürer's woodcuts from the turn of the sixteenth century, such as the *Apocalypse*. Cranach, however, discards their clearly legible staggered compositions in favour of a spatially obscure arrangement comprising high tree trunks, and he does not shy away from bold overlappings, placing the figure, as he does in many of his later paintings, in front of a carpet of leaves. GM

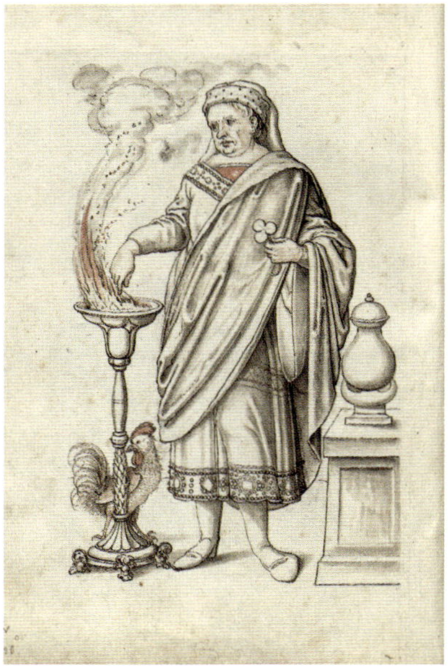

January

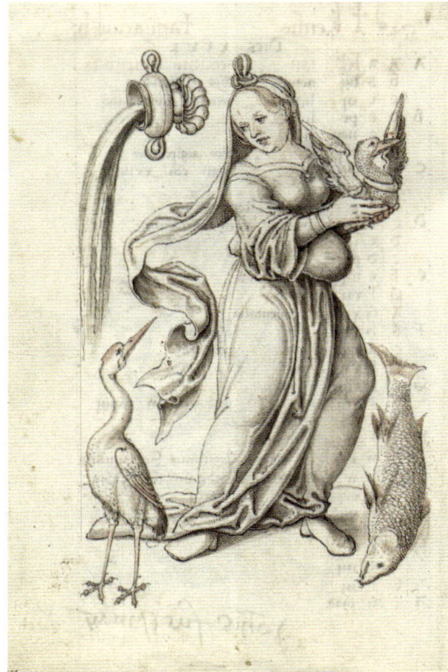

February

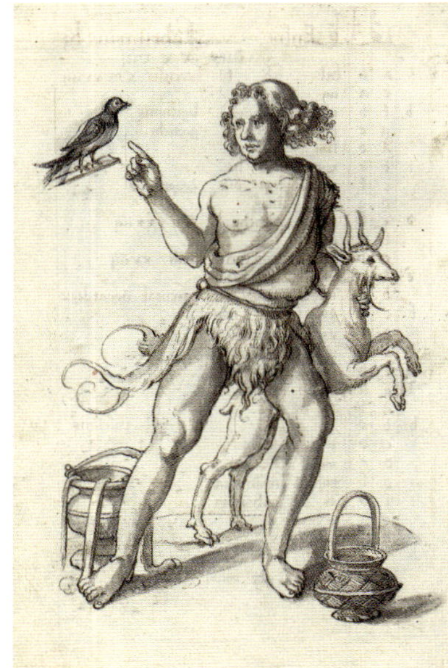

March

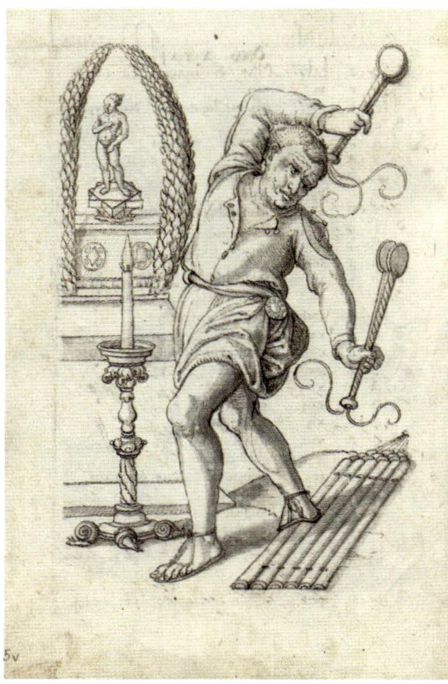

April

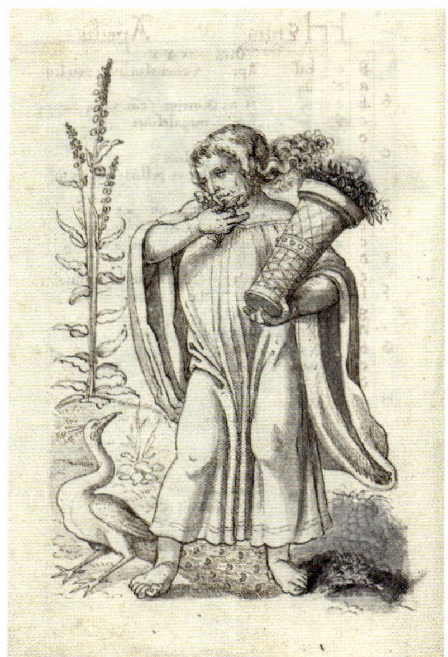

May

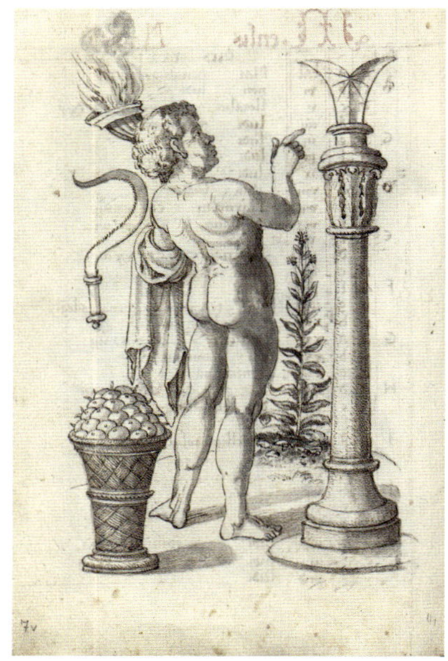

June

7/1–12

Lucas Cranach the Elder

THE TWELVE DRAWINGS OF THE MONTHS IN THE "VIENNA FILOCALUS"

circa 1510

Österreichische Nationalbibliothek, Vienna

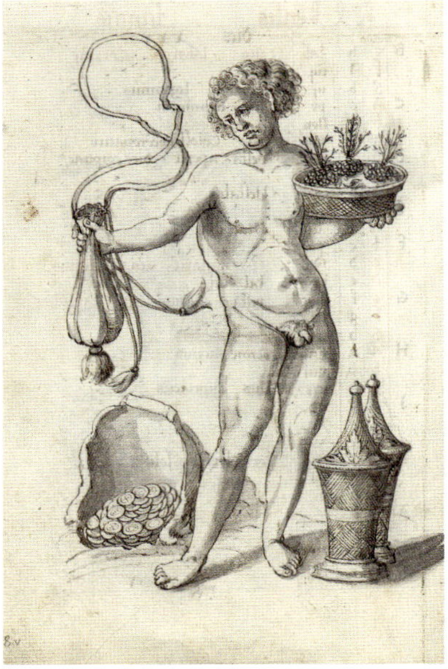

July

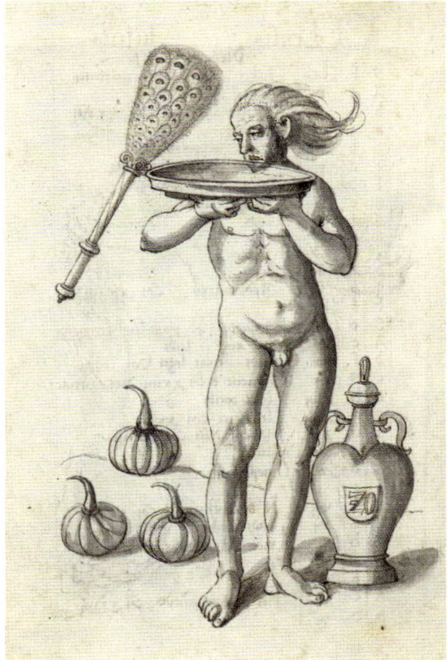

August

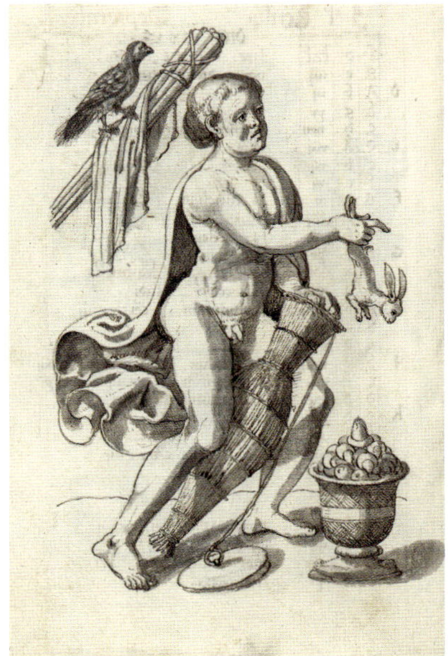

September

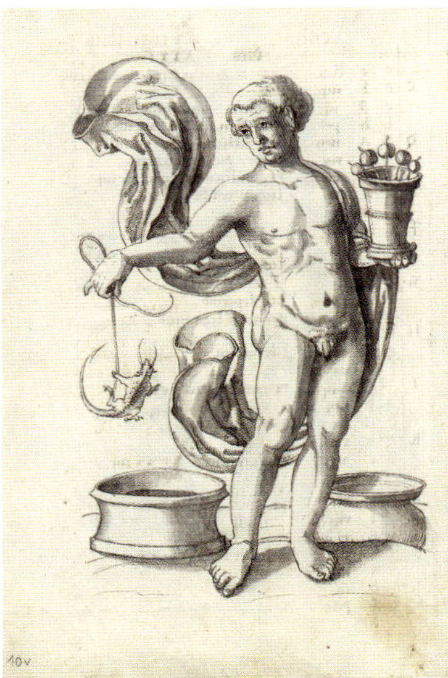

October

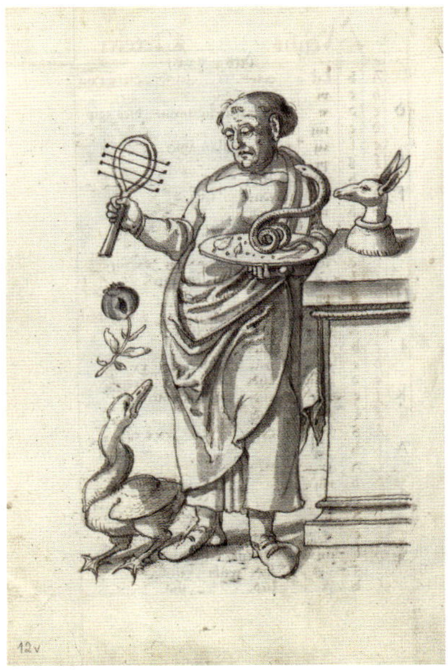

November

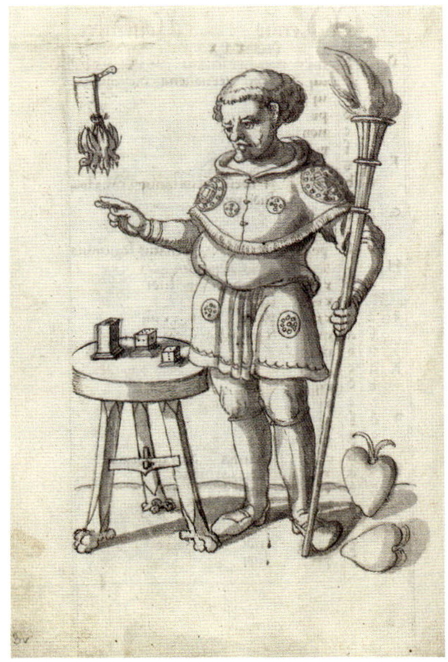

December

The *Vienna Filocalus* is the oldest of several extant copies of a calendar almanac also known as *Chronograph of 354* written by the calligrapher Furius Dionysius Filocalus in AD 354; the original volume has not survived. No single copy contains the entire text, but the *Vienna Filocalus* from the early sixteenth century contains at least all twelve depictions of the months, while the other illustrated manuscripts now in the Vatican, Berlin and Brussels respectively were produced in the seventeenth century and are missing the months from April to August.[1] The draughtsmen of these later copies repeated late-antique depictions without any artistic aspirations of their own, but did it more faithful to the templates.

The *Vienna Filocalus* was commissioned by Johannes Fuchsmagen (c.1450–1510). A humanist and a native of Hall in Tyrol, Fuchsmagen served as royal councillor in Vienna, and as the manuscript's first owner he inscribed his name on the first page (fol 3r): *Joh[ann]is fuchsmag[en] doct[oris]*. When Fuchsmagen died in 1510, the manuscript passed into the possession of Johannes Cuspinian (see cat. 12). It was presumably he who commissioned the text sections on pages 15–70.[2] The manuscript begins with Fuchsmagen's calendar section. The first page – the frontispiece was only added in the seventeenth century[3] – is followed by twelve full-page pictures of the personifications of the months executed on the reverses (fols. 2–13); these pen and ink drawings from the early sixteenth century are confronted (on the opposing page) by lists of the feast- and court days (Latin *fasti*) headed by the name of the relevant month. The first two drawings – *Januarius* and *Februarius* (fols. 2v, 3v) – are more carefully worked than the remainder, most obvious in the fastidious handling of the eyes and facial wrinkles. In addition, these two drawings are washed in delicate hues, while all the others remain monochrome. Presumably, the artist was working under time pressure after the completion of the February image; in some places he even omitted detailing in pen, for instance in some of the outer ears (best seen in the August image, fol. 9v). However, it seems that all the depictions of the months are by the same hand.

But these drawings cannot be considered final artworks, indicated by both the unfinished outer ears and visible corrections (see, for example, the contours of the buttocks in the October picture, fol. 11v).[4] We may assume a change of plans after the completion of the first two drawings, with the initial concept to frame each picture discarded. While February and January fastidiously remain within the "picture frame", the washed shadows and billowing smoke in the other drawings often extend beyond these boundaries. Lines drawn only with a pen continue to respect these invisible borders, see for instance the cropped myrtle frame of the small altar on the left in the April picture (fol. 5v). There are also traces of an erased charcoal drawing of the outline of the originally-planned frame, which would have been congruent with the type area. Perhaps the patron was planning a printed edition, which would also explain the clear linear design of the drawings, suggesting that these illustrations were originally conceived as templates for woodcuts.

A comparison with the copies now in the Vatican, in Berlin, and in Brussels reveals countless differences. A good example is February (fol. 3v): a young woman in a billowing dress clutches a fowl and walks determinedly to the right. Her swirling veil is tied into a stiff bow at the top of her head. At her waist, the dress billows in a way that suggests her belly is hanging over her belt; in the copies in the Vatican etc., however, the draped fabric of her dress imitates the classical kolpos of a chiton. Bottom left we see a heron-like bird, on the right a fish suspended upside down, and top left water flowing down from an overturned kantharos. Fish and kantharos may function as a reference to Pisces and Aquarius, February's zodiac signs,[5] but are here explained by a quatrain (see note 1) that associates the wet month of February with rain and water fowl.[6] In the Brussels version, February is also a woman, while in the copies in the Vatican and Berlin the figure is meant to be a short-haired priest (despite his billowing robe), whose flame-shaped veil-knot also embellishes the head of the god Saturn elsewhere in the Vatican codex,[7] suggesting the templates used for Vienna and Brussels are further removed from the original. A lot of motifs in the Vienna drawings have been reinterpreted while others have been omitted, for instance some of the sea creatures in the February picture.[8] We can no longer determine if they were already missing in the template.

Many of the drawings show traces of subsequent retouching, most of which can be explained by the aforementioned quatrains.[9] See March (fol. 4v) for an example of such a correction executed in opaque white and black ink: a curly-haired young man sporting nothing but a shaggy fur takes a determined step to the right; with his

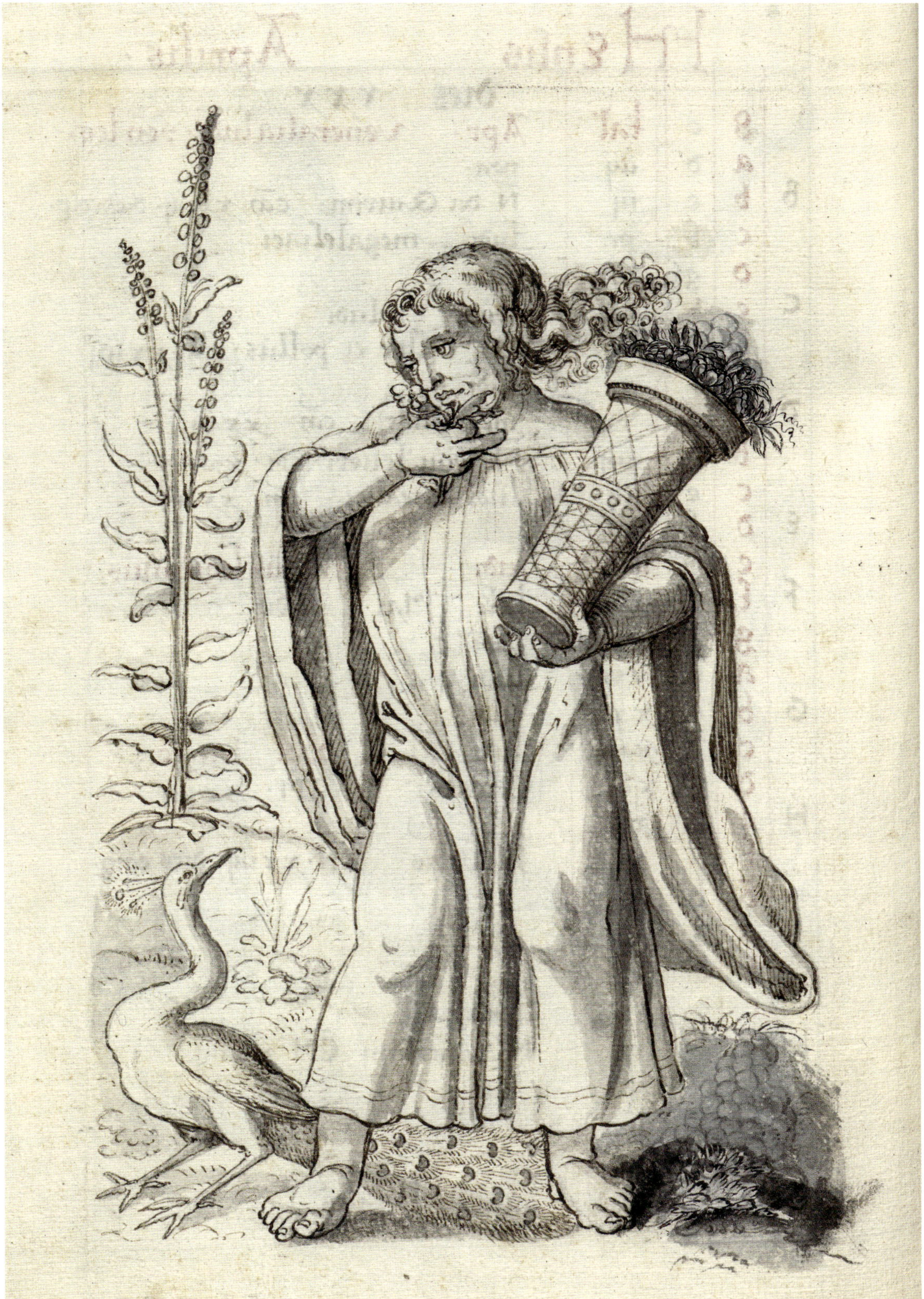

left hand he holds a goat by its neck while he turns around and points with his right hand to a bird sitting on a board. A bucket and a basket stand on the ground beside him. Note the forcefully executed retouching of the bird that ignores the invisible "picture frame" to add a forked tail, turning the bird into a swallow. This presumably reflected the wishes of the patron because the quatrain mentions not only wolfskin, milk bucket, and goat but also a chatty swallow.[10] The same technique was applied in May (fol. 6v) to replace unseasonal grapes with peony-like flowers, because the quatrain speaks of roses. In June (fol. 7v) the flower on the left of the column with the sundial was altered to look like a lily, because the latter appears in the quatrain. The same is true of the basket clutched by the personification of July (fol. 8v), in which the mulberry bush referenced in the quatrain seems to grow.

But not all retouchings relate to the quatrains. In November (fol. 12v) a pomegranate not mentioned in the poem was reworked. In December (fol. 13v) two of the three strange objects placed on a small table were changed into dice which would fit with the Saturnalia mentioned in the quatrain, but one of these objects – a kleroterion? – remains mysterious. We also do not know who ordered the changes. Perhaps Cuspinian commissioned the corrections, perhaps he even commissioned the drawings themselves. It is quite conceivable that in 1510 the reverses of the manuscript pages were still empty. At all events, Cuspinian never mentions the depictions of the months.[11] Philipp Gundel, who added the *Fasti* tables from the *Vienna Filocalus* to a printed version of Ovid's *Fasti* in 1513 without illustrations, never mentions them either.[12] We cannot tell if the drawings met with disapproval or did not exist yet. We can only assume that the obverses were already filled with the Fasti tables when the drawings were added to the reverses. This is indicated by, for example, the traces of an erased charcoal preliminary drawing for July on the page of August (fol. 9v).[13] Before the pages were filled with text and bound, there would have been no reason for this correction.

A date of around 1510, however, contradicts Friedrich Winkler's stylistic attribution of the depictions of the months to the "Viennese Cranach" (Winkler 1936). Most art-historians have accepted this attribution although Winkler himself admits that it is not entirely convincing, and the renowned Cranach experts, Rosenberg and Jahn, too later voiced their doubts.[14] Winkler's hypothetical explanation for these stylistic disparities was that copying the template had caused a corruption of style. At the same time, he recognised that this contradicted the draughtsman's artistic liberty suggested by the many motific disparities between this and the other copies.[15] Winkler countered this incompatibility with a second hypothesis, namely that Cranach copied the drawings in 1501 before the "curly pathos of his drapery" was fully evolved.[16] However, if we compare the mature figure style of the depictions of the months with the expressive figures of the "Viennese Cranach" – think only of the distorted arms and legs, and the physiognomies – then Winkler's early date looks less than convincing. We only find stylistic similarities with Cranach's post-1505 oeuvre, when he was already settled in Wittenberg. Compare, for example, the way he draws fingers and feet, the large eyes, the nasal wings, and the curved upper lips in the drawing *The Promenade* (Stuttgart), whose figure style is close to that of the woodcut *David and Abigail* dated 1509.[17] And, last but not least, we find the same combination of grey wash applied with a brush and delicate, often short pen-strokes in browned iron gall ink in the two *Lucretia* drawings now in Berlin that Cranach produced in 1509.[18] But because other details such as the distinctive drapery are untypical of Cranach, the attribution will never be entirely convincing.

We cannot judge the possible influence of the lost templates because we do not know if they were late-Roman miniatures, Carolingian copies, or contemporary sketches. If a contemporary artist produced the templates with all their contentual changes compared to the original, then all questions regarding artistic freedom become obsolete. It seems that the Vienna depictions of the months were copied from copies, which resulted in this confusing mesh of styles.

We cannot exclude the possibility that a member of Cranach's workshop imitated the master only in some details, but this feels less plausible than stylistic distortions caused by copying. This is why we retain the attribution to Cranach despite the uncertainties discussed above. If this stylistic problem cannot be solved convincingly, we cannot determine the date these drawings were produced. Considering figure style and handling, however, Winkler's early date seems untenable. Cranach's move in 1504/05 to the court of the Elector of Saxony does not preclude this attribution. It would not be unusual for Fuchsmagen or Cuspinian to send the calendar pages together with the templates for the images to Wittenberg.

But we should also not date the drawings too late. Comparisons of depictions of animals like, for example, the heron in the February picture (fol. 3v) with herons and storks in Cranach's marginal drawings in the prayer book of Maximilian I (dated 1515)[19] suggest they were not produced at the same time. Instead, they indicate a gradual evolution of Cranach's naturalism.[20] Together with the above-mentioned drawings Cranach produced around 1509, it seems plausible that the depictions of the months in the *Vienna Filocalus* date from around 1510 rather than 1501. EP

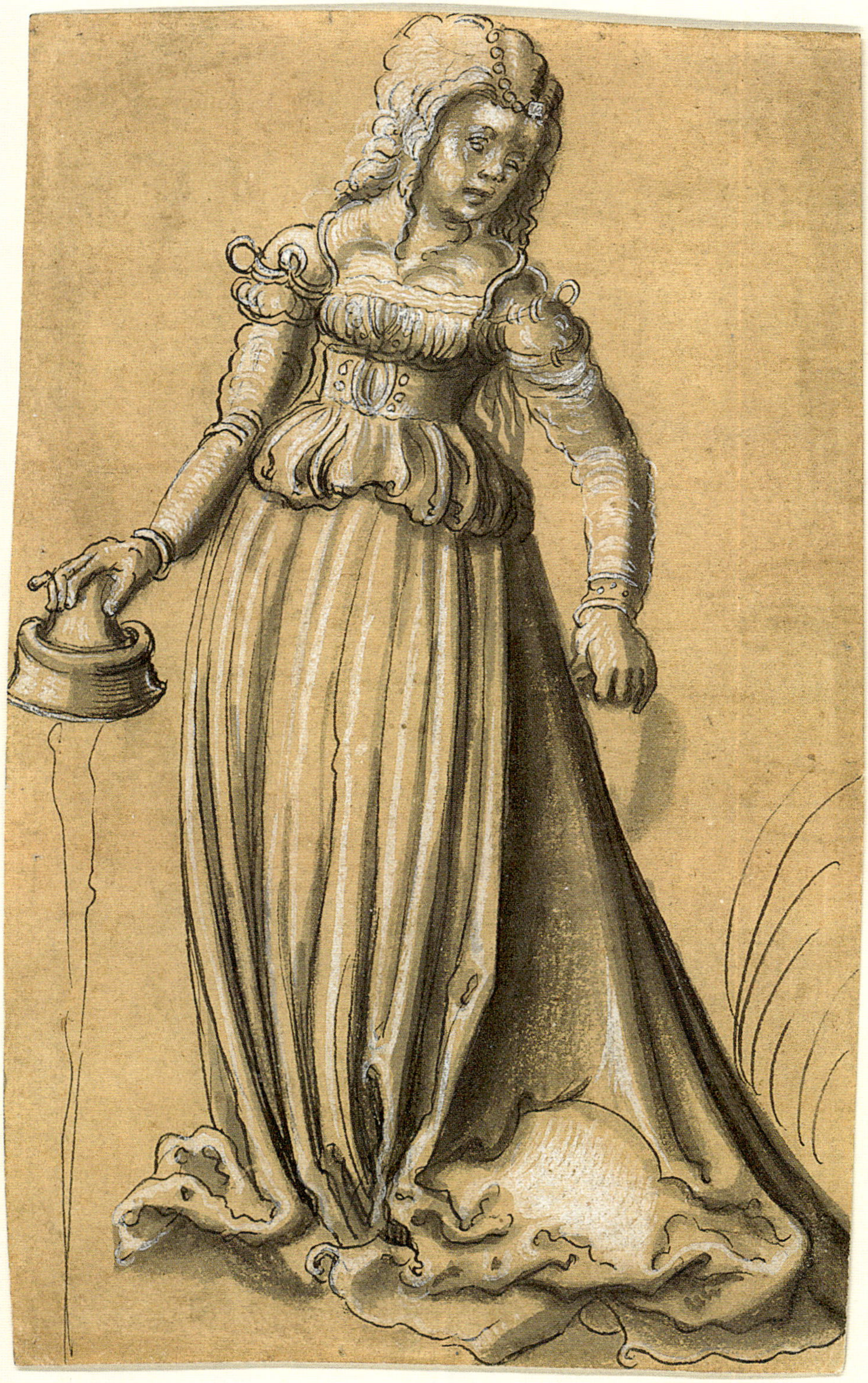

8

Lucas Cranach the Elder
A FOOLISH VIRGIN
circa 1503
Germanisches Nationalmuseum, Nuremberg

This is one of the girls in the Parable of the Wise and Foolish Virgins, one of Jesus's parables. According to Matthew 25:1–3, ten virgins await the arrival of a bridegroom (according to the Vulgate, the arrival of bride and bridegroom). Called to him in the middle of the night, only five were wise enough to bring enough oil for their lamps; the others had to go and buy more oil and so were too late and found themselves locked out of the hall where the wedding was being celebrated. The parable advises forethought and prudence, and to always be prepared for death so as not to be locked out of the kingdom of heaven.

With her décolleté and bare shoulders, the young woman appears neither chaste nor virtuous. This presumably denotes her corrupted morals which are equated with her foolishness. Disappointed, she pours out the lamp oil she had bought too late, her left hand clutching the bridal wreath she has just removed from her head. The draughtsman merely outlined the wreath in quick brushstrokes but did not add more details with a pen, making this a brush drawing with details filled in with a pen. The opposite is true of the handling of the spilt oil: here, he merely intimated the oil with a few strokes of the pen, i.e. he captured a spontaneous idea that only came to him after he had put aside his brush.

The wreath (not executed in pen) and the not-washed pen and ink drawing of the spilt oil suggest this is a study or working template. By using ochre prepared paper and adding opaque-white highlights with a brush, he imitates chiaroscuro drawings, a technique much *en vogue* in the early sixteenth century.

The drawing was first attributed to Cranach in 1929 by Elfried Bock, and this is now generally accepted. The early date is based on comparisons with Cranach's earliest extant works. For example, the dynamically crinkled folds of the young woman's robe on the ground are similar to those in Cranach's early panels and woodcuts, such as his *Lamentation at the Foot of the Cross* in Munich (dated 1503; see essay Heiser, fig. 5), the woodcut of the crucifixion dated 1502 (cat. 3), or the chiaroscuro drawing depicting *St Martin and the Beggar* dated 1504 and also now in Munich (cat. 27). This suggests that Cranach produced the drawing while still in Austria, before he moved to Wittenberg in 1504/05. This is also supported by the watermark, because we know of similar papers used in Transylvania and Moravia around 1504, and in Linz in 1506, and which are therefore more likely to have been available in Vienna than in Wittenberg.[1] EP

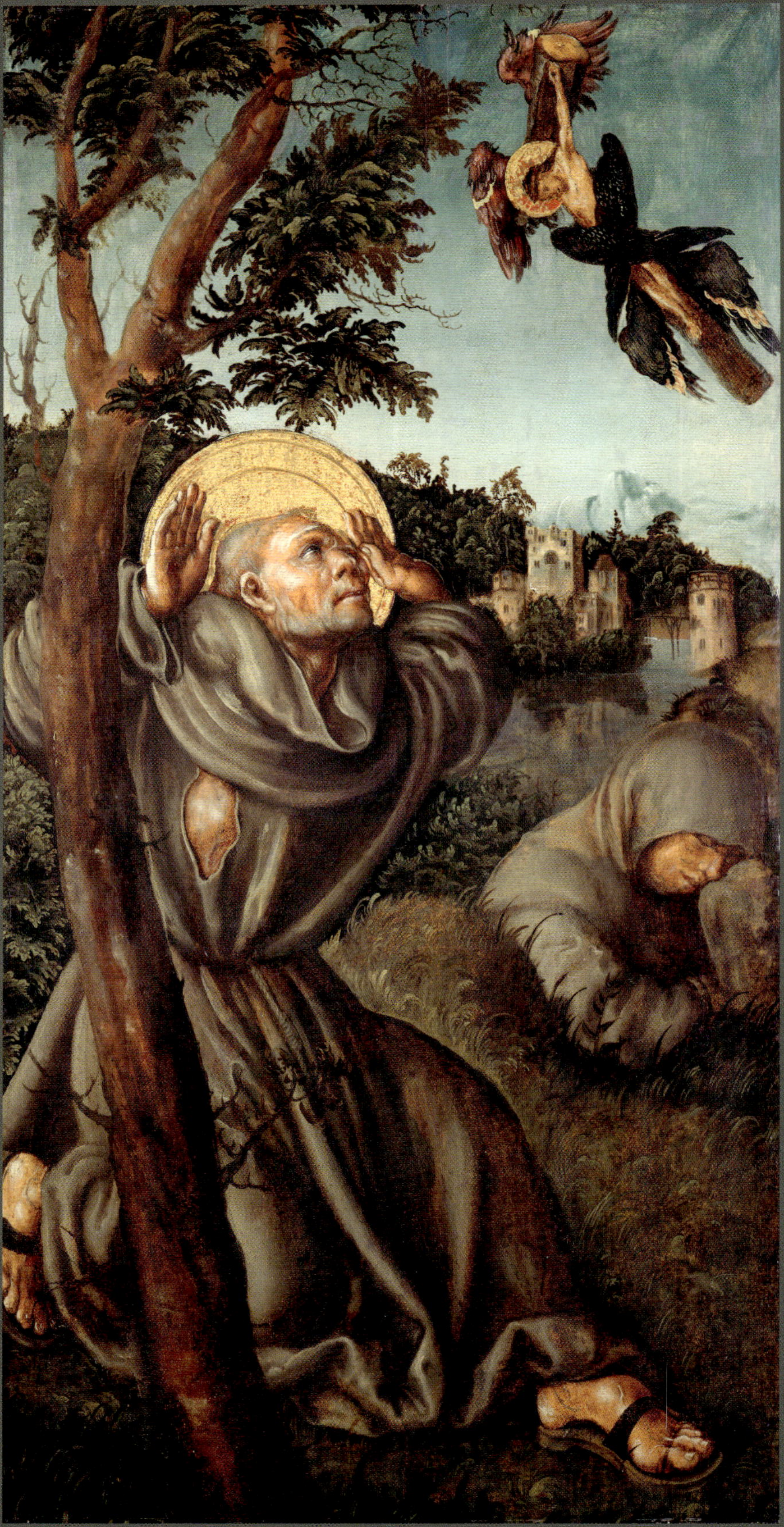

9

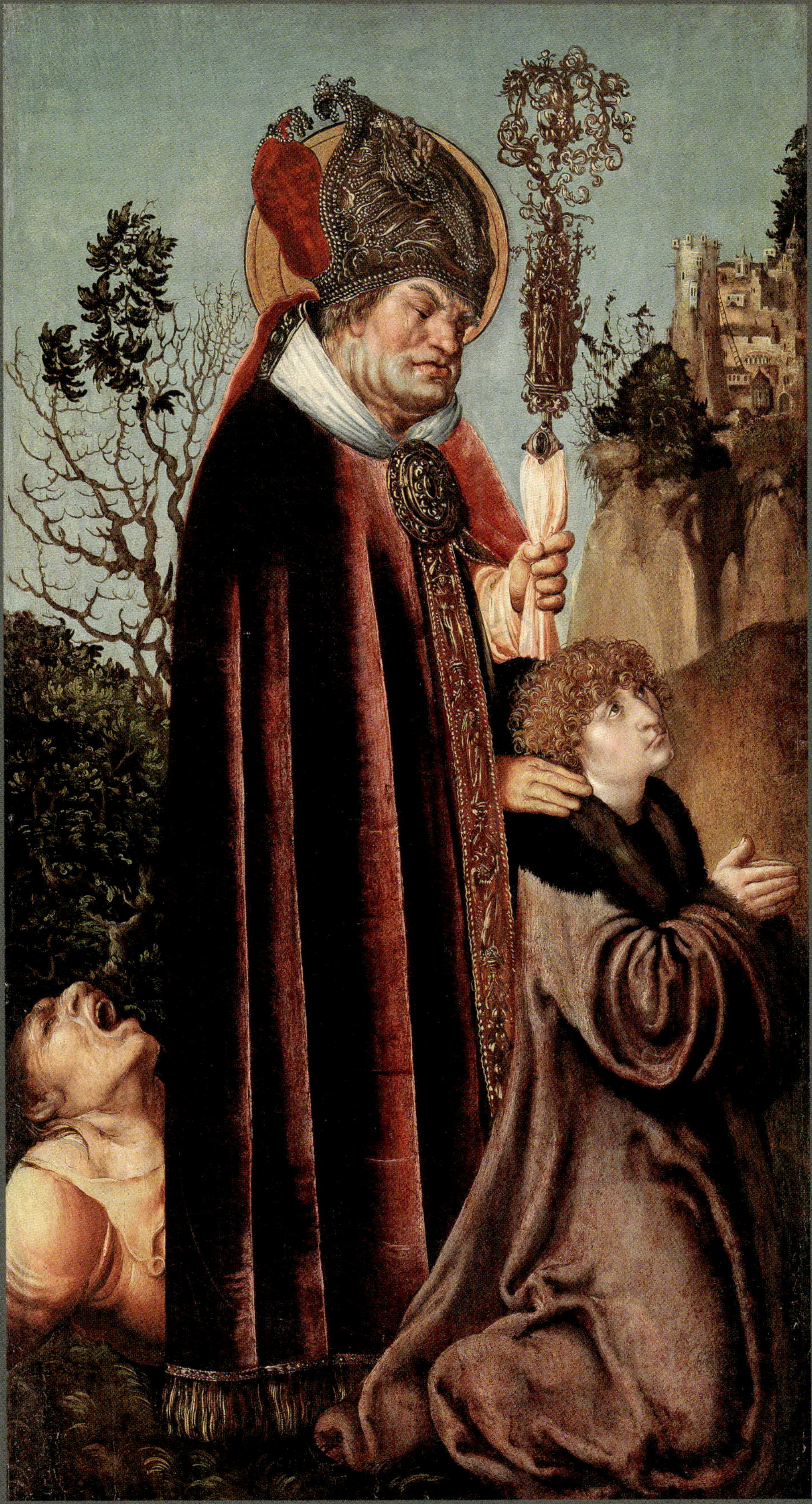

10

9 & 10

Lucas Cranach the Elder

THE STIGMATISATION OF ST FRANCIS

circa 1502/03

Belvedere, Vienna

ST VALENTINE WITH A DONOR

circa 1502/03

Gemäldegalerie der Akademie der bildenden Künste Wien

According to Bonaventura, the Holy Spirit guided St Francis to the mountain of Verna where a Seraph with six wings appeared to him. The angel had brought with him an image of the crucified Christ, and while the saint was musing over the meaning of this divine apparition, he received the stigmata.[1] Like Dürer in his woodcut of this episode, Cranach too moves this pivotal moment in the saint's life from a mountainous desert,[2] which is where Giotto and Pietro Lorenzetti had located it in their iconic frescoes at Assisi (San Francesco),[3] to a valley. Behind his sleeping confrere Leo an atmospheric vista opens up comprising a small castle whose outlines are reflected in the lake. The delicate blues of the silhouetted mountain behind it seem to merge with the sky. St Francis is kneeling in the foreground, his left leg stretched out before him. Startled, his hands raised, he stares up at the apparition. Broad stripes of lead white emphasise the saint's almost cubically-foreshortened face and his hands and feet; the tree on the far left seems to echo his expressive pose.

The saint dressed in the robes of a bishop on the second panel can be identified as St Valentine of Raetia, who was papal missionary bishop to the Roman province of Raetia in the fifth century. Tassilo III, Duke of Bavaria (748–788) decided, presumably for political reasons, to move the saint's remains from Trento to Passau, which greatly encouraged Valentine's veneration in Bavaria.[4] A lack of biographical data led to parts of the vita of the similarly-named St Valentine of Terni, including miraculously healing the sick, being "appropriated". The faithful therefore appeal to St Valentine of Raetia for help against epilepsy, which was also known as falling sickness. Cranach depicts an epileptic behind the saint, already one of his popular attributes around 1500.[5] The unspoilt background landscape is similar to the one in the St Francis panel though this one has less depth. Stadlober noted the landscape's Christian symbolism, emphasising how the castle perched on a steep rock represents a divine place of refuge.[6] Valentine wears sumptuous pontifical robes: a red, gold-trimmed pluvial with a golden clasp, combined with a magnificent mitre and a crozier. Lavishly embroidered with pearls, the obverse of the mitre is decorated with a three-dimensional rendering of the Virgin and Child as the Woman of the Apocalypse. The expressive, almost organic character of the crook of his gold staff reflects the untamed nature of the landscape background. We find a similar expressive power and a tendency to ugliness in the saint's coarse, sallow face and the epileptic's features distorted in pain. This contrasts with the carefully rendered, smooth countenance of the praying patron, whose costly attire – a dark-brown overgown with black fur collar – identifies him as a prominent and prosperous burgher rather than a cleric. The choice of St Valentine may be an indication of the donor's Christian name, suggesting he might be Valentin Kardinger, the only Valentin recorded in coeval local sources who would fit with the sitter in our painting.[7] He was wine tax accountant at Engelhartszell before King (later Emperor) Maximilian I made him *Hansgraf* and *Salzbereiter* (in charge of trade and salt) for Upper and Lower Austria in 1499.[8] In July 1501, however, the king removed him from his posts because Kardinger was said to have discharged his duties so badly and caused such a substantial financial loss that he was even accused of accepting bribes.[9]

Part of the gift presented to the Academy of Fine Arts in Vienna by Anton Franz de Paula, Count Lamberg-Sprinzenstein, the panel depicting *St Valentine* was originally believed to be by Michael Wolgemut. Following various attributions, Scheibler was the first to identify it as an early work by Lucas Cranach the Elder in 1887,[10] but this attribution was only generally accepted after Dörnhöffer supported it in 1904.[11]

The *St Francis* was acquired by the Österreichische Staatsgalerie in Lemberg (now Lwiw/Ukraine) from a private collector in 1912. At the time, it was listed as "Austrian school from the early sixteenth century (similar to the manner of Wolf Huber)".[12] In 1921, Grimschitz finally published it as a work by Lucas Cranach, and he already expressed his belief that it had once formed an ensemble with the *St Valentine*. It is not only their similar formats and closely related compositions that suggest the two panels belong together. The handling of their halos is also identical and unlike any others in Cranach's oeuvre. They are made of polished gold foil comprising concentric equidistant circles[13] drawn with a pair of dividers. Unlike in the *St Valentine*, the puncture is clearly visible in the X-ray of the *St Francis* (fig.). The fact that the reverse of the *St Francis* panel has been planed off and stabilised by inserted bars suggests it was once a fixed wing; the reverse of the *St Valentine* was thinned and cradled, an indication that it was split off from a panel originally painted on both sides.[14] It seems quite probable that the two panels once formed an ensemble, although we also cannot fully exclude the possibility that these 8 mm thick spruce boards once formed something like the front- and back of a wing of an altarpiece. For example, the outer wings of the former retable of the church of the Schottenstift in Vienna comprise separate panels, each c.1 cm thick, conjoined to create the folding altarpiece.[15] In any case, the composition of the two panels suggests Cranach placed them on the left of the original ensemble. *St Valentine* presumably formed the inside of the left wing, so that, when the retable was opened, the praying donor faced the altarpiece's original central zone. BB & CK

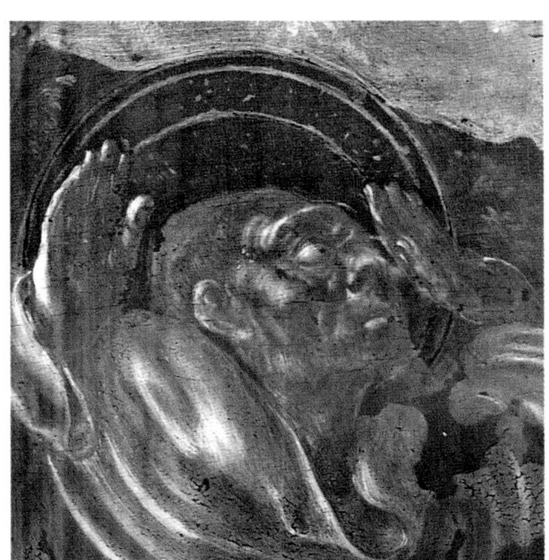

Cat. 9, X-ray, detail

11

Lucas Cranach the Elder (?)
PORTRAIT OF A BEARDLESS YOUNG MAN
before or around 1500
Hessische Hausstiftung, Kronberg

Taking up the entire foreground, the sitter shown in three-quarter view is placed before a landscape background. His obviously squashed left arm frames the pictorial space on two sides, the movement of his body is only discernible in the position of his shoulders and chest. In his right hand is a rosary, and he wears a distinctive signet ring with a red stone on his thumb. The folds of the sleeve of his fur-trimmed overgown are exceptionally thick, and on his chest the white shirt is crossed by four laces; he also wears a black cord around his neck. Modelled in pale hues, the face with its prominent chin and aquiline nose is set off by the sitter's dark clothes. His blue eyes focus on something outside the composition, reminiscent of the portraits of patrons in devotional diptychs, though there is nothing here to suggest a second, now lost panel. Down to the tips of his curly, shoulder-length hair, the portrait evokes strength and determination. White highlights carefully differentiate his blonde locks, their handling similar to that of the fur and the folds of the overgown. This only emphasises the difference between the handling of his face with its prominent cheekbones and the coarser, somewhat sallow hands.

Nothing connects the sitter to the carefully detailed landscape behind him. There is no suggestion of him being in a room, either through a cloth of honour indicating a wall or a window offering a view, making this the first large portrait of this kind in a German-speaking country and placing it in close proximity to Cranach's two early portrait-diptychs.

In the 1470s in the Netherlands this type of portrait was often used by Hans Memling, and it was disseminated throughout Europe via the network of contacts of the international merchants and bankers who frequently sat for Memling in Bruges.

We find almost contemporary local adaptions in Italian portraiture, as well as in Germany in the works of the Master of the Life of the Virgin active in Cologne and of Hermen Rode from Lübeck.[1] With the former, the painting now in Kronberg shares the position of the horizon (at shoulder height), which is also typical of the majority of Memling's works and which increases perspective and depth. The castle on the hill on the left reflects the sitter's face, an effect enhanced by the clouds blowing across the sky. On the left, trees, a rider on a path, and the castle hill feature greens and browns and suggest proximity, but the blues on the right draw our gaze into the mountainous distance. There is neither a connection between the sitter and the landscape nor anything to help localise where he is, but its clarity and energetic charge help to characterise him.

Thanks to a later inscription on the reverse the painting was alternatively identified as a portrait of the young Dürer by an otherwise unknown painter called Neubaurer, or the opposite. Some aspects, like the unusual folds and the somewhat neglected modelling of the hand, have parallels in Cranach's early works.[2] Other things are contrary to his known oeuvre, like the lack of connection between sitter and landscape, the somewhat dry handling, the clearly differentiated trees and leaves, and the absence of a single tree framing the sitter. Today, the painting is attributed to Cranach rather than to Dürer.[3] If it is accepted into Cranach's oeuvre, it must be a very early painting, perhaps informed by the artist's familiarity with Dürer and his works during his stay in Nuremberg. But until we have proof, this remains nothing but a suggestion. KR

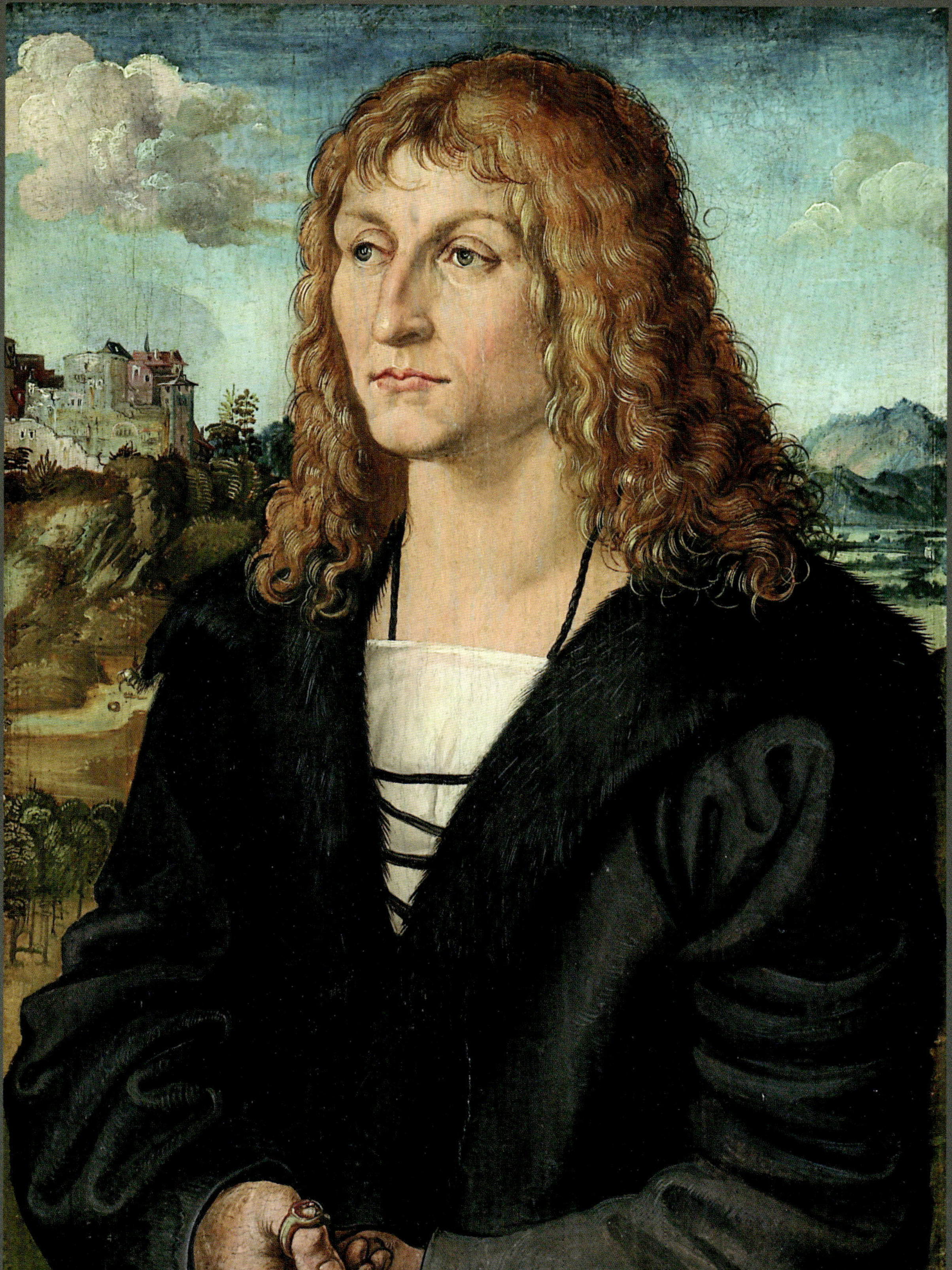

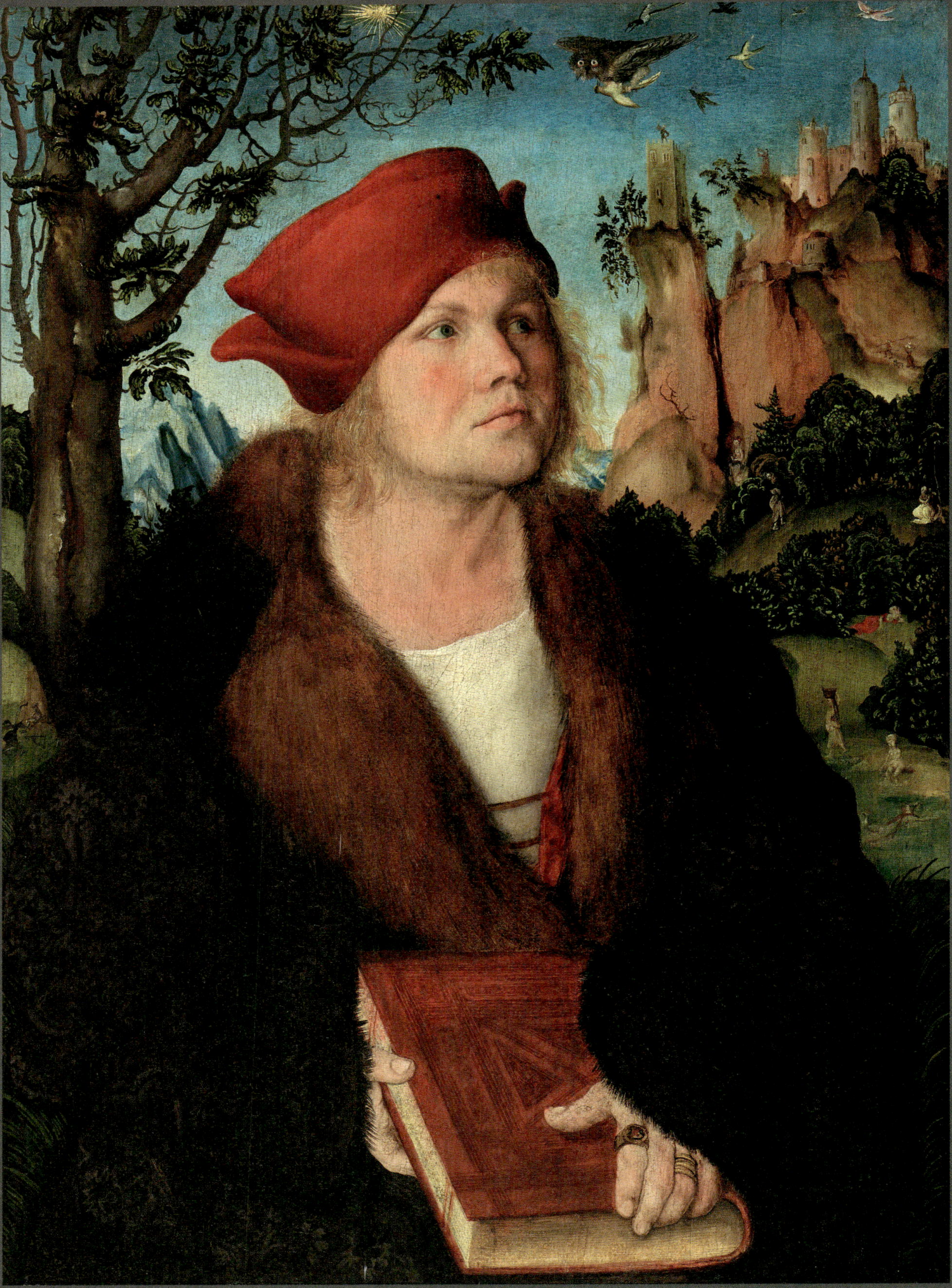

12

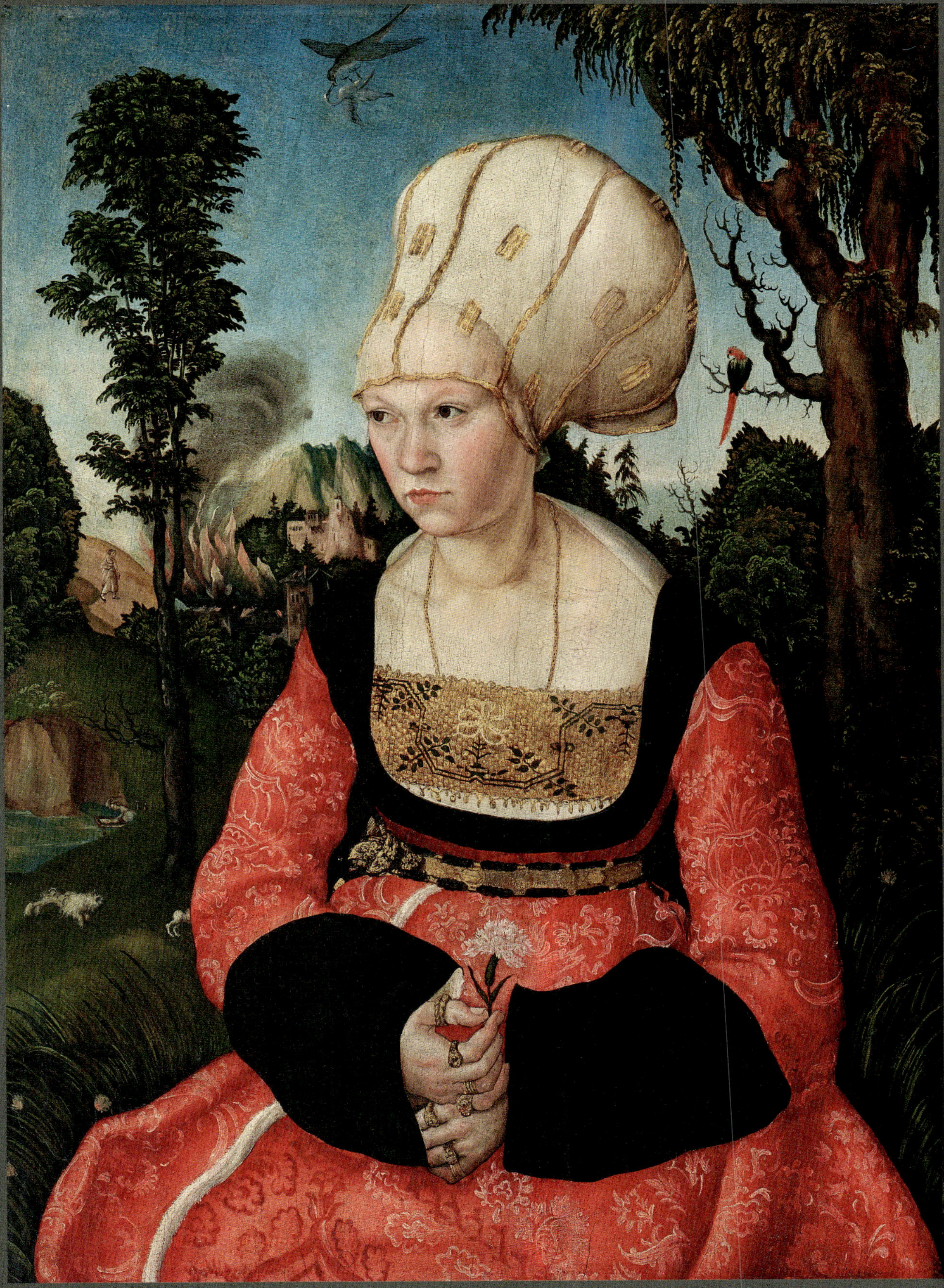

13

12 & 13

Lucas Cranach the Elder

MARRIAGE DIPTYCH OF DR JOHANNES CUSPINIAN AND ANNA CUSPINIAN-PUTSCH

1502/03

Oskar Reinhart Collection "Am Römerholz", Winterthur

This double-portrait of Johannes Cuspinian and his wife is regarded as one of Cranach's most innovative compositions. For the first time, the sitters are not depicted in front of but embedded in the landscape, which is highly charged with symbolism. The two panels also form a physical unit. They could be closed, like a book, and the outside is decorated with their alliance coat of arms (fig.).[1] The panels' unusual format suggests that this is a rare case of the female portrait being fixed to the wall, with the male portrait functioning as the movable part.[2] The two portraits are best viewed together if the diptych is opened less than 180 degrees.

The left, traditionally more prominent side gives us a half-length portrait of Johannes Cuspinian (Schweinfurt 1473–1529 Vienna) facing his spouse. Seated on a grassy bench, he wears a voluminous overgown from which his white shirt peeks out. Its pattern comprising pomegranates and stylised flowers forms a visual link between the sitter and the surrounding landscape. He sports a red cap (*barett*) with upturned brim, which, together with the red lining peeking out from his overgown, may function as a reference to the fact that he was a physician.[3] His blonde hair falls to his shoulders. Cuspinian is clutching a closed, leather-bound folio, but the position of his right hand seems more designed to show off his two rings. He has raised his head and is looking up but there is nothing in the composition to explain the direction of his gaze. It is more an internal gaze, the way an inspired prophet or Evangelist is depicted. The contours of his face are soft, and the main accents of his features are his flushed cheeks, nose and chest. Despite the determined way he turns his head, visible in the tense muscles of his neck, he appears very young.

With her voluminous skirt, his wife too seems to fill almost the entire space of her portrait; she is, however, seated a little further away from us. The paleness of the married woman's face is emphasised by her large, gold-brocaded headdress. Her rose-pink damask gown with a pomegranate pattern edged in black along the décolleté and with large black cuffs carefully repeats the colour-scheme of her husband's attire, but she has added gold to the shared red, black, and white triad by donning a gold chain, a belt, and six rings as well as a gold brocade bodice. In her right hand is a bridal carnation, a motif mirrored in the floral décor of her bodice. Calmly and with her eyes lowered, she is gazing at her husband, best seen if the panels are set at a slight angle. Like a flower, she too is seated on a grassy bench adorned with small blossoms and located in the same continuous landscape as her spouse's. Each sitter is flanked by a single tree, whose crown fills a top corner of the composition – hers heavy and in full leaf, his less so and growing upwards – thus emphasising their different temperaments.

Like Cranach, Johannes Cuspinian (the Latinised version of Spießheimer) was a native of Franconia; he moved to Vienna in 1492, attracted by the patronage of humanist studies by Emperor Frederick III and then his son and successor Maximilian I. Cuspinian quickly made friends, and was crowned "poeta laureatus" when he was only twenty, which allowed him to give lectures on poetry and rhetoric at Vienna University. The prominently displayed ring set with a red stone may have formed part of the coronation insignia. The young scholar began his medical studies in 1494, and in 1499 took up his first post at Klosterneuburg Monastery (just outside Vienna). Soon afterwards he was elected rector of Vienna University and after that he was twice dean of the Faculty of Medicine. In 1501, he was made superintendent, i.e. the ducal supervisor of the university's jurisdiction, a position he retained until the end of his life. His closest friend among the humanists was Conrad Celtes, who had moved to Vienna in 1497 and whose deputy he became both in the newly-founded humanist society *Sodalitas litteraria Danubiana* and in the *Collegium poetarum et mathematicorum*. In his prime and brimming with self-confidence, Cuspinian decided to get married. He probably celebrated his

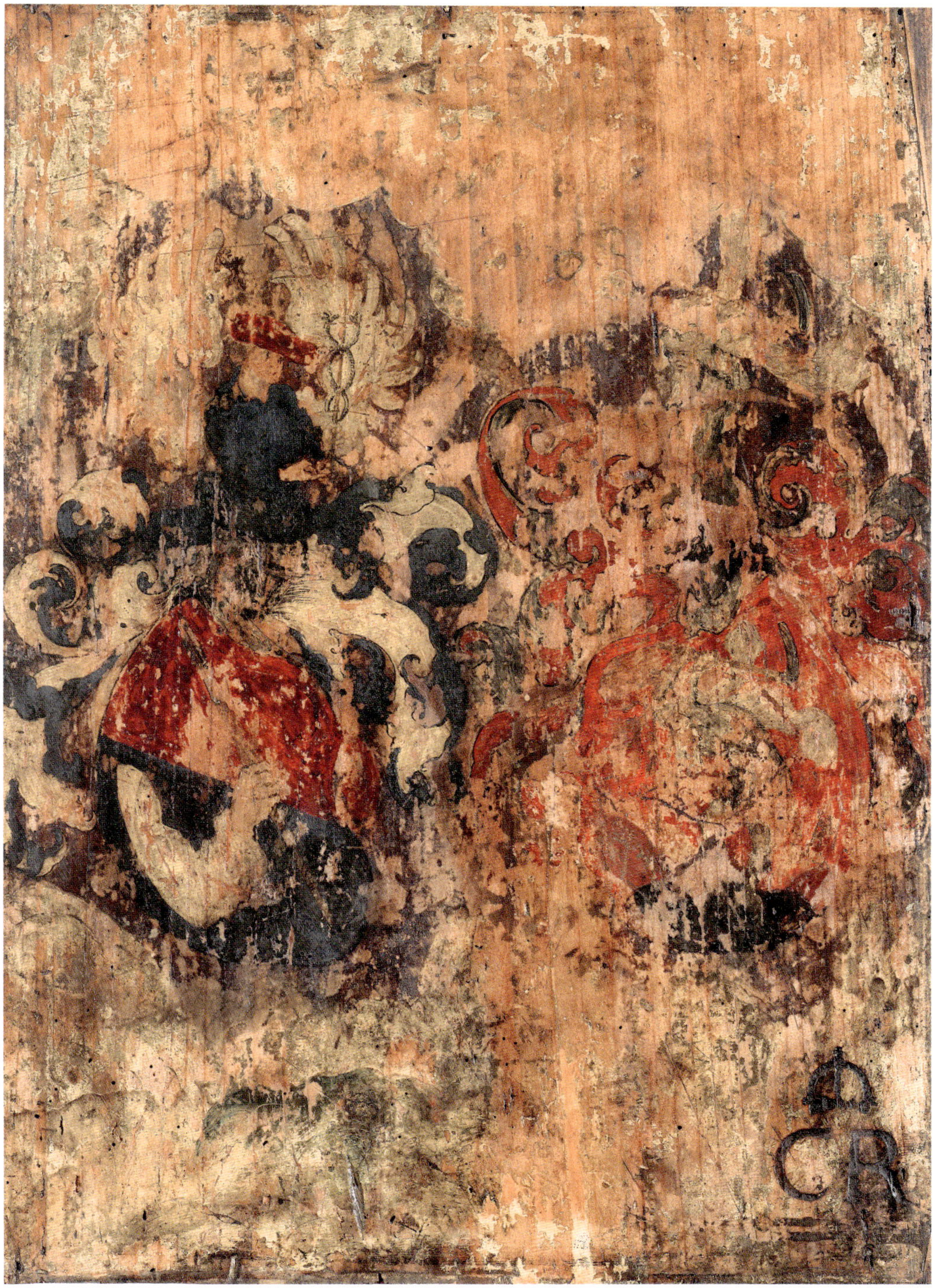

Lucas Cranach the Elder, alliance coat of arms of Johannes Cuspinian and Anna Cuspinian-Putsch, 1502/03; reverse of cat. 12

nuptials with Anna Putsch (1484?–1513), the eighteen-year-old daughter of the imperial chamberlain and sister of a future vice chancellor of Vienna University, in 1502, which allows us to date the two panels.

We may assume that the learned humanist and physician was closely involved in the diptych's composition and content. The continuous landscape is dominated by verdant, partly wooded hills, a lake that connects the two panels, and a castle on a steep rock juxtaposed with a burning, partly ruined farmhouse. Visually, the exposed castle connects the figure of Cuspinian with the framing tree; on the portrait of his wife two trees serve the same purpose. On his side, the pictorial space extends to give us a spiky, blue, somewhat prop-like mountain range far away, on hers the distance is shrouded in mist. This already varied landscape is filled with symbolic elements and figures whose ambiguity has given rise to countless attempts at interpretation. The small figure of Apollo near a spring on the far left suggests the nine female figures frolicking in the landscape represent the nine Muses.[4] Many of his writings confirm that as a physician and a poet Cuspinian felt a deep affinity with Apollo.[5] The Muses' activities enliven the countryside; they are mainly engaged in relaxing (lying on the grass), personal hygiene (combing their hair, bathing) and household activities (washing clothes and putting them away). Only one of them is engaged in an intellectual pursuit, she is reading in a cave. Two of the Muses wear clothes similar to Anna Cuspinian's. One of the Muses is walking towards the ruined farmhouse from which rise up flames and dark plumes of smoke. Many interpretations for this worrying conflagration have been put forward but the juxtaposing of the two elements fire and water – both credited with cleansing powers – seems the most plausible for a marriage portrait.[6] The macaw perched on a branch behind Anna Cuspinian is presumably a Marian symbol of purity as well as a symbol of love: it is either a very early depiction of a bird only discovered in 1500 in Brazil, or a coincidence informed by the choice of the colour triad red, black, and yellow.[7] The suggestion that it is a phoenix opens up a completely new interpretative pathway, but Lactantius's description of this mythical creature has a lot less in common with the bird behind Anna Cuspinian than the much more fantastic one in the *St Jerome* (cat. 6).[8]

In the sky above the wife – thereby emphasising the fourth element – we see a hawk or falcon attacking a heron, a typical occurrence when hunting with falcons. The heron's prone defensive tactics were described in late-mediaeval natural science books and do not lack a certain sexual connotation.[9] In prints and painted portraits, a falcon attack functioned as a warning of excesses and a caricature of false courtly love.[10] Clutching a pheasant in its talons, the much more prominent owl in the male portrait is looking at us while being pursued by six different diurnal birds. During the day, the hunting owl becomes the hunted, which was used to hunt songbirds with owls as lures. Blind and helpless during the day, the owl only becomes a menacing hunter once the sun has set. As a nocturnal creature it represents both the mysterious and the sinister. The many possible interpretations suggest we examine other depictions of owls in Cranach's oeuvre, among them the calendar dial to identify the dominical letter, and the *St Jerome* (cat. 23 and 6). In comparison, the owl may function as either a symbol of the night (taking the place of the moon) or averted calamity, or as a symbol of evil.[11] Interesting in this context is the juxtaposition of owl and star (executed in real gold) at the upper edge of the composition; the latter has been interpreted as both the star of the Magi and the sun, i.e. the second apparition of Phoebus in the painting.[12] We also cannot exclude the possibility that the owl functions as a symbol of melancholy, traditionally the scholar's humour.[13] The spectators on the battlements of the castle are no help, especially as important details have not survived.

However, we do know that Cuspinian gave everyone who saw this novel diptych of a married couple plenty to discuss, and that Cranach congenially transposed these ideas using glowing colours. The learned members of the *Sodalitas* will have appreciated this. In addition, the two panels also bear eloquent witness to the self-assurance and sophistication of Vienna's humanist elite at the turn of the sixteenth century. KR

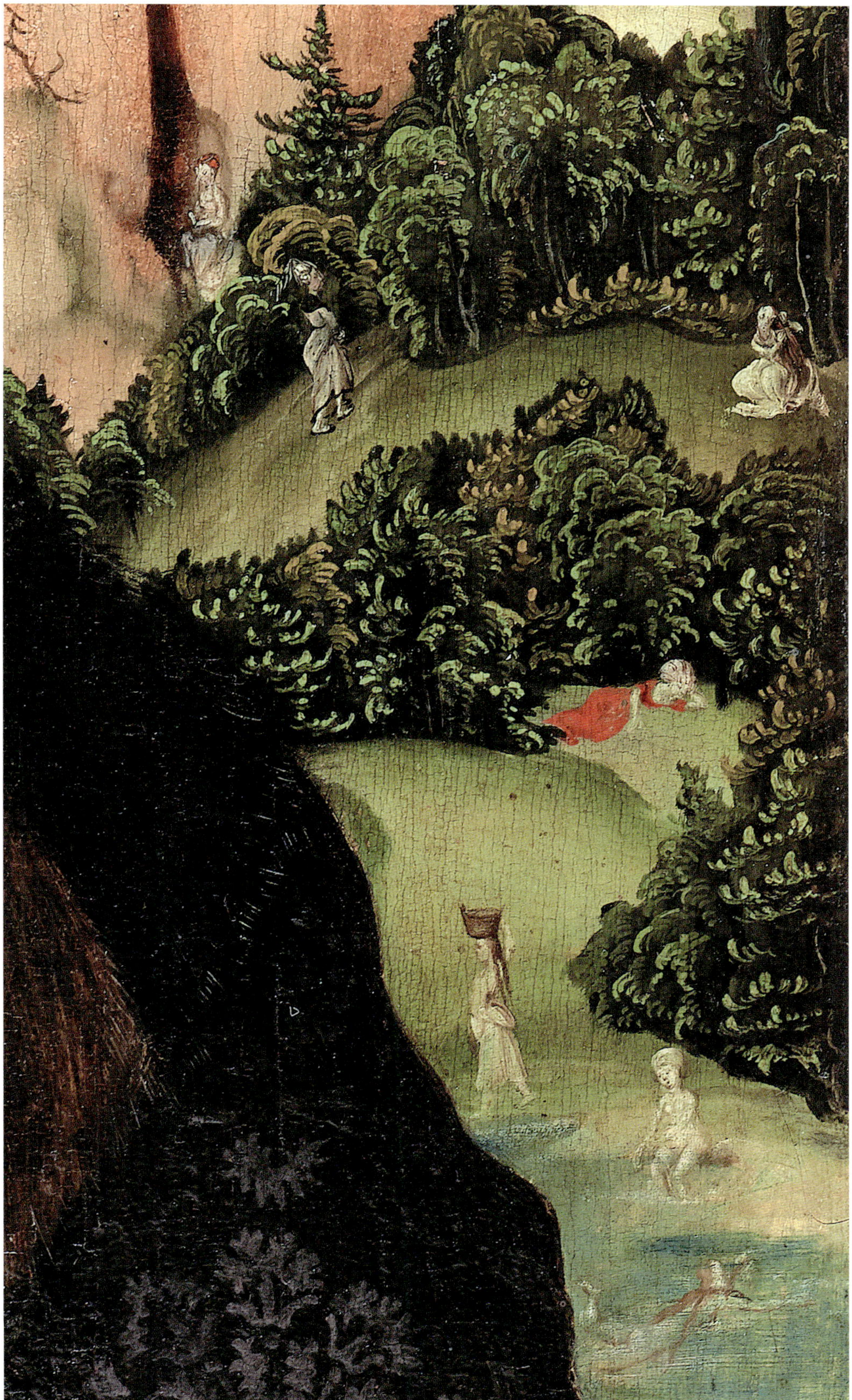

14

Anonymous artist (after Lucas Cranach the Elder)
BOOKPLATE OF JOHANNES CUSPINIAN
circa 1510/15
Österreichische Nationalbibliothek, Vienna

The woodcut shows a half-length portrait of Johannes Cuspinian (Schweinfurt 1473–1529 Vienna) behind a parapet, framed by an elaborate Renaissance aedicula. It is an inverted image of the painting Cranach produced in 1502/03 (cat. 12). The three ungainly figures below the parapet represent the Three Graces as an allegory of the humanist ideal of intellectual give and take. With outstretched arms they are passing a ball and, according to the inscription, calling out to each other: DO / ACCIPIO / REFERO (I give, I receive, I give back).[1] The group is flanked by two shields, the left one bearing Cuspinian's coat of arms (an arm and a pike – a reference to his German family name, Spießheimer), the right one his monogram "CMP" (*Cuspinianus Medicus Poeta*).

Cuspinian used this woodcut as a bookplate, pasting it into his books in order, as the text above the portrait explains, to prevent them from being stolen. The woodcut became more widely known in 1894 when Stiebel discovered it in the Langer Library in Broumov in Bohemia, long famous for its holdings of early prints.[2] Ankwicz-Kleehoven recognised the connection with Cranach's portrait and suggested the woodcut dates from "soon after 1503". Panofsky rejected this early date because the overall composition is influenced by the much better woodcut of Celtes that Hans Burgkmair produced in 1507. Eventually, Lang was able to determine a terminus post quem for Cuspinian's bookplate when he noticed that the typeface used for the text is identical to that used between 1510 and 1518 in the Viennese print shop of Hieronymus Vietor.[3] Lang's suggested date of between 1510 and 1512 fits well with the ornamental frame, because such exuberant festoons flanking a central sphere, with pendant strings of pearls framing the sides, were then just becoming popular in Vienna. We find them, for example, in the stone altarpiece dedicated to St Barbara (1512) in the crypt of St Peter's Church. A coat of arms with handles and the delicate frame of the woodcut were also used in the similarly pedestrian woodcut for the title page of the second edition of Johannes Winterburger's *Heiltumsbuch*, printed in Vienna in 1514, which would also support a slightly later date.[4] EP

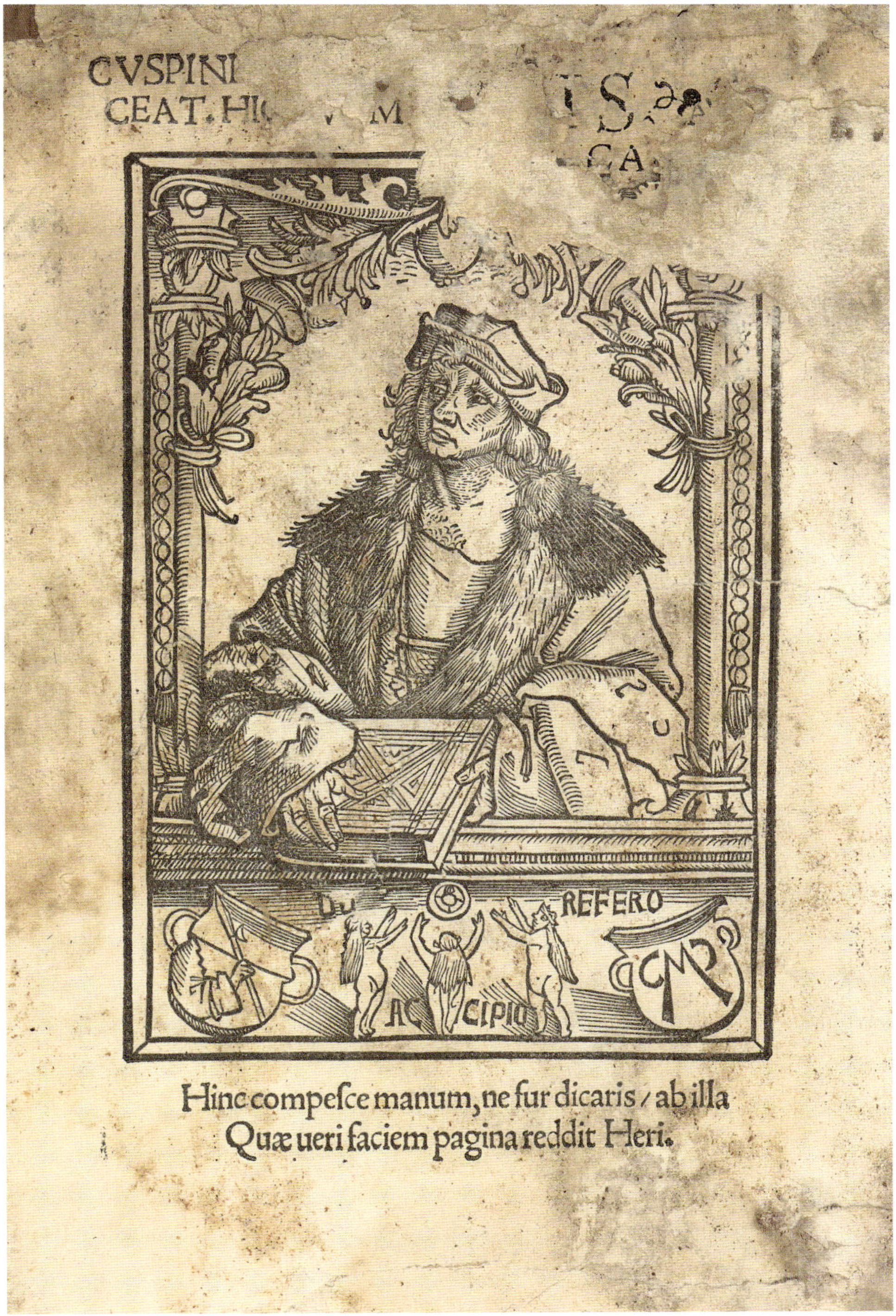

Hinc compesce manum, ne fur dicaris / ab illa
Quæ ueri faciem pagina reddit Heri.

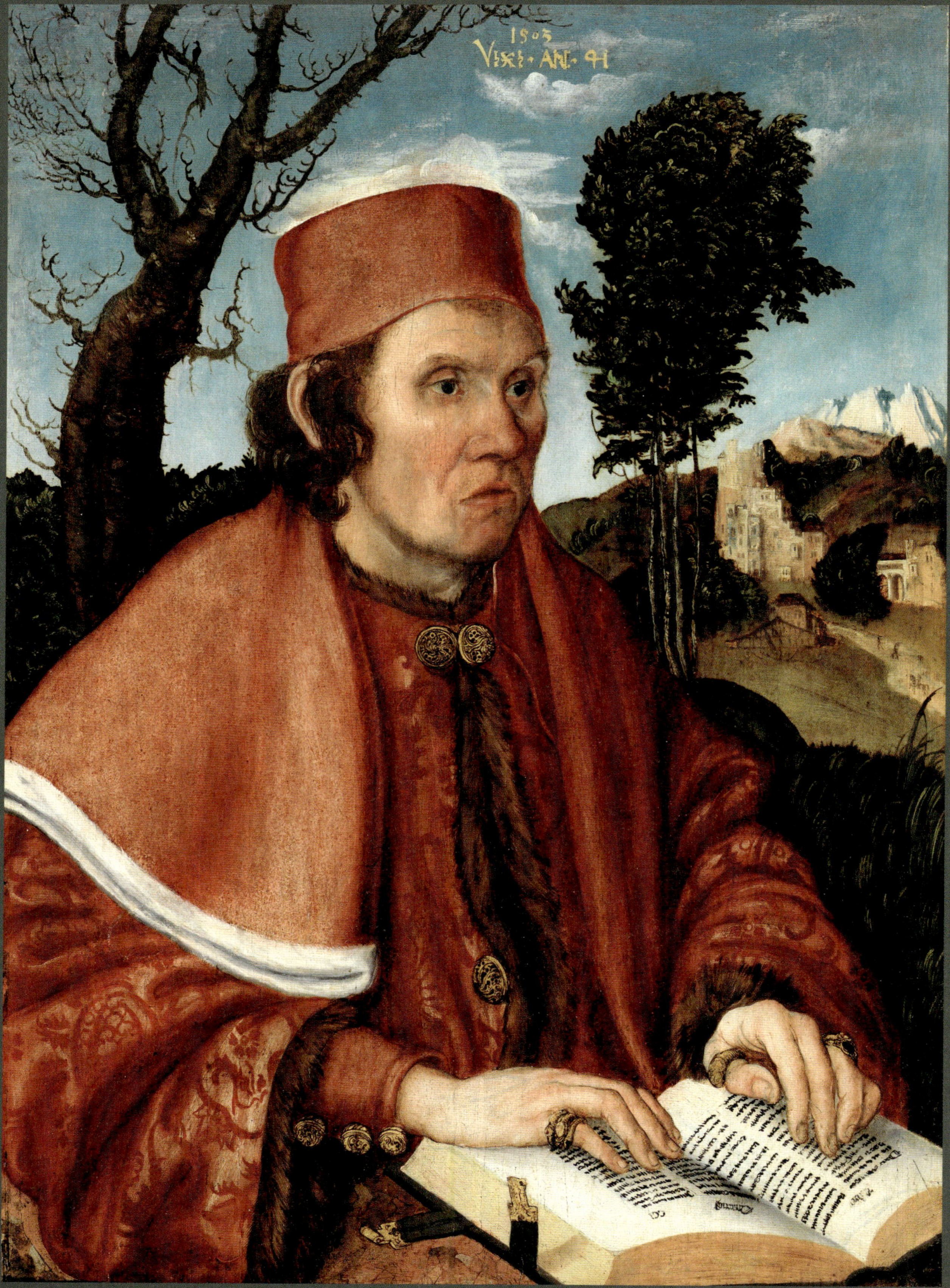
1503
VIXI · AN · 41

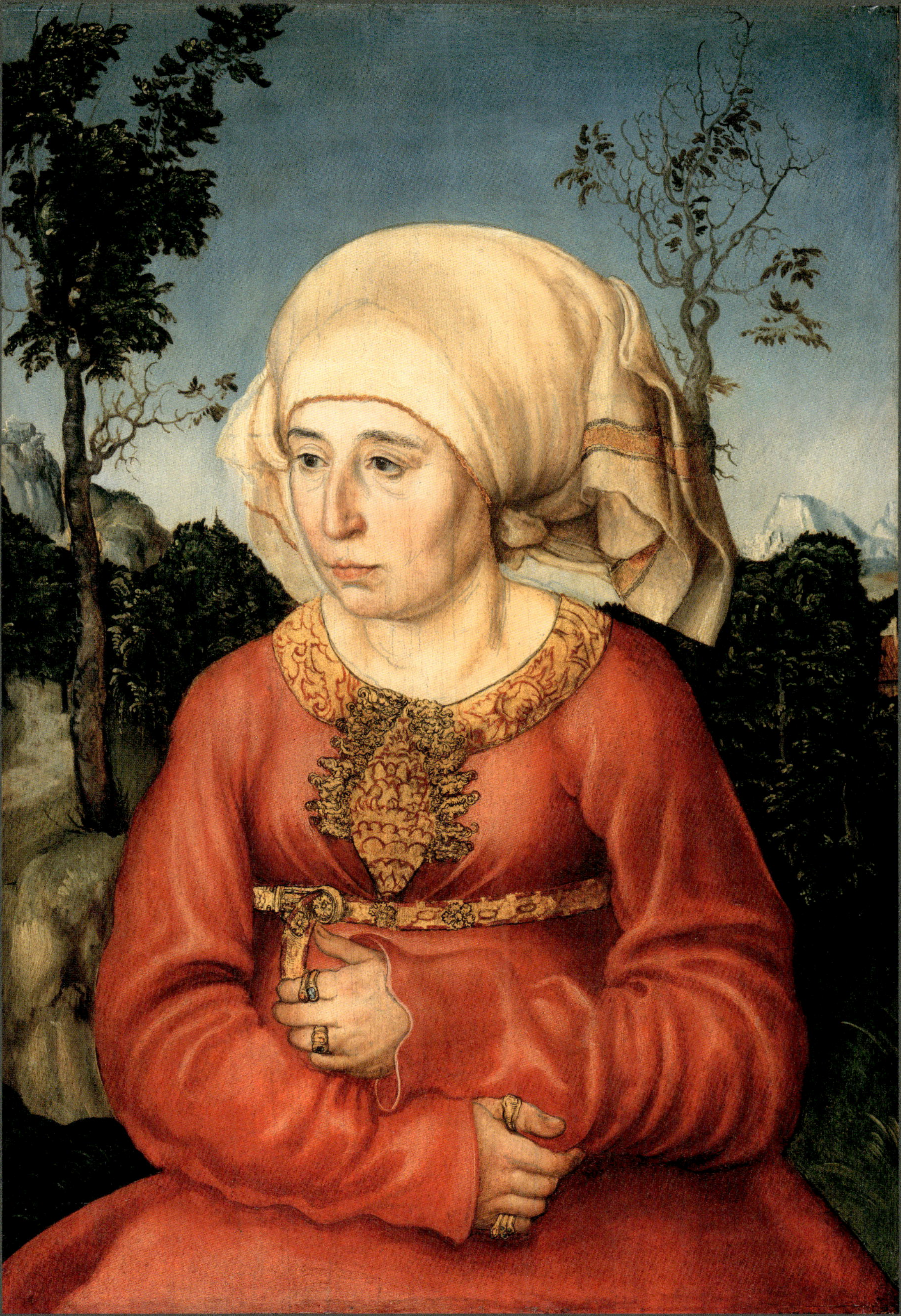

15 & 16

Lucas Cranach the Elder

MARRIAGE-DIPTYCH OF A JURIST AND HIS WIFE

1503

Germanisches Nationalmuseum, Nuremberg

Staatliche Museen zu Berlin, Gemäldegalerie

The second extant portrait diptych that Lucas Cranach painted during his sojourn in Vienna also depicts a married couple embedded in a landscape. Although the two portraits are now housed in two different collections, there is no doubt they once formed a pair: the landscape in one continues in the other, individual details are mirrored, and, despite having been cropped, their sizes also match. Unlike the Cuspinian diptych (cat. 12 & 13), this couple is dated by an inscription on the male portrait; sadly, however, it lacks anything to allow an unambiguous identification of the sitters. A note written in pencil and formerly attached to the back of the male portrait at a later date identifies him as Johann Stephan Reuss (d. 1514); Reuss was elected dean of the Law Faculty of Vienna University for the first time in 1500 and became rector in 1504. However, Dieter Koepplin has put forward convincing arguments that cast doubt on this identification.[1] Tanja Holste then attempted a new identification and suggested that Cranach painted Iodocus Welling, the dean of the Law Faculty in 1503, and his wife Barbara.[2] Most art historians agree that the sitter is most probably a jurist, as indicted by his red cap, the fur-lined gold brocade overgown with gold buttons, and the chaperon ("epomis") draped over his shoulders.[3] His delicate hands rest on an opened two-columned codex with gold-edged pages and precious clasps.[4] We can neither identify nor decipher the text. It lacks the glosses of a legal publication and the illuminated initials of a religious one, which suggests it may function as a scholar's insigne.[5] Analogous to her husband, the wife wears a shimmering scarlet gown, its voluminous skirt taking up almost the entire width of the painting. She has folded her arms across her stomach, which, together with her gold belt, emphasises the horizontal and makes her appear grounded. Both sitters are middle-aged – their features show signs of age, even if this is somewhat amplified by the underdrawing having become visible over time. The jurist's prominent costly buttons, the six rings on his fingers and the ermine trim of his chaperon form focal points of the composition; in his wife's portrait this role is assumed by the gold brocade border of her dress and the adjoining elaborate almond-shaped inset made of the same material and edged in gold lace. The latter features a variation of the main pomegranate motif, which creates yet another connection between the two panels. As a married woman she wears a high headdress enfolded in a piece of cloth with a gold stripe.

Shown in three-quarter view, the spouses are facing each other. When the diptych (the panels were probably originally connected) was opened at an angle of slightly more than 90 degrees, the sitters were presumably looking at each other, something that is somewhat difficult if the paintings are displayed side by side on a wall or a table. Both are seated on a grassy bench placed in an undulating landscape framed by distant snow-capped mountains. Unlike the Cuspinian diptych, the landscape does not abound with symbolic details and figures. The three tiny travellers ascending the path in the male portrait function more as animating props. The path leads past a farmhouse to a village or castle with a bridge clinging to the rockface that recalls southern models. In contrast, nature dominates the background of the female portrait. Both husband and wife are framed by trees, with dead, bare trees juxtaposed with verdant, flourishing ones; this may be read as a symbolic reference to growing and passing away, life and death, and reflects the couple's stage in life. In the two paintings the bare trees are placed at different locations in the composition: the gnarled dying tree in the male portrait is located in the foreground on the left, filling the top left corner – similar to Cuspinian's portrait – while the wife's dying tree is placed further back in the landscape and is juxtaposed with the village in her husband's portrait, which makes the tree look smaller and much less framing. Both connecting middle grounds feature burgeoning trees growing on small hills. Here, too, we note some differences: her single tree has grown to a middle height but in his portrait four birch-like trees grow side by side and their crowns converge. As long as we cannot identify the sitters it is difficult to decipher the meaning of this remarkable pictorial element. In the upper part of the composition the dominant colour chord of red and green-brown is enhanced by the addition of bright blue. Unlike the clear sky in Cuspinian's portrait (cat. 12), here there are some cirrus clouds that appear to form a kind of temporal halo around the jurist's cap. Perhaps this is a reference to his intellectual quest. The sky in the portrait of his wife is cloudless, with the white of her headdress playing a prominent role in the composition.

This second extant double-portrait again documents Cranach's success in Vienna, especially with patrons connected with the university. Innovations like the composition first introduced in the Cuspinian diptych were happily adopted by other sitters and adapted for their own self-display. In this constellation, Cranach was able to modify novel compositions to suit the requirements of different patrons and to vary them without ever copying the template – a concept he would continue to make good use of for the rest of his life. KR

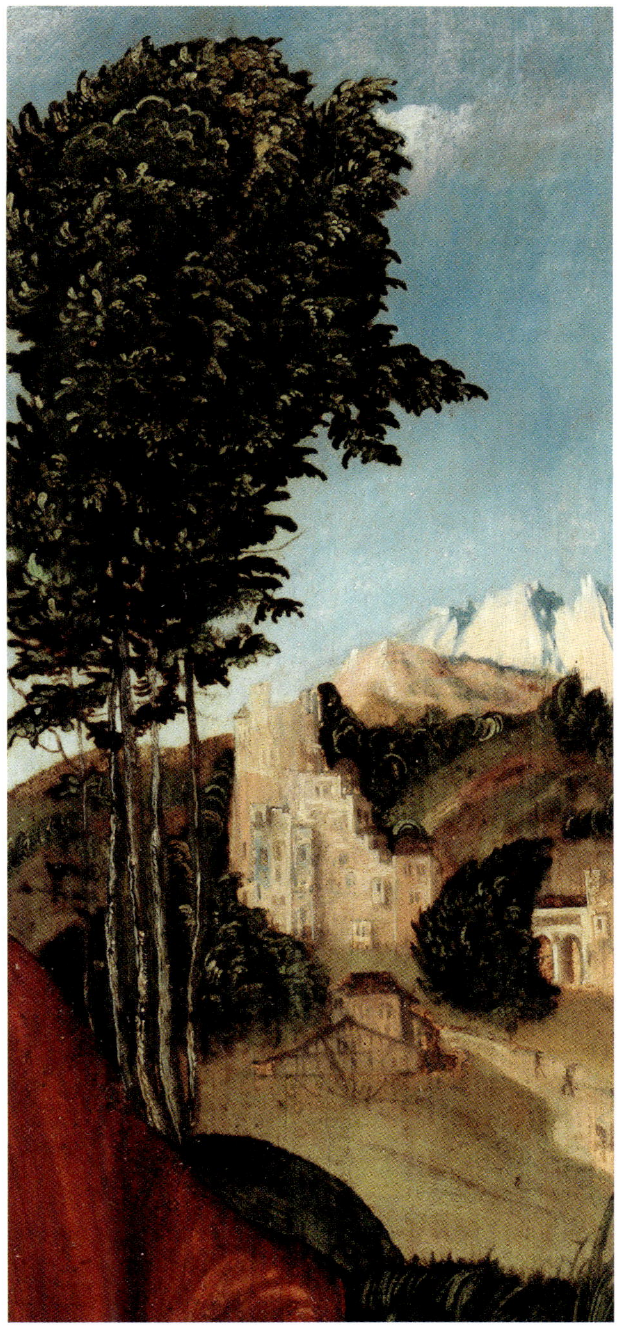

17

Lucas Cranach the Elder (copy)
PORTRAIT OF HIERONYMUS TEDENHAMER (TETTENHAMMER)
first half of the 16th century (after a lost original from 1503)
Kunsthistorisches Museum Vienna

In addition to the two portrait-diptychs of Cuspinian and his spouse (cat. 12 & 13), and the anonymous jurist and his wife (cat. 14 & 15), we have at least copies of some of the other portraits Cranach executed during his stay in Vienna. There are convincing reasons to include this one of Hieronymus Tedenhamer (Tettenhammer), which, in 1950, Max J. Friedländer and William R. Valentiner had regarded as a work by the master himself.[1] The sitter is identified by his family coat of arms (top left) and an inscription top right.[2] The latter also tells us that he commissioned this portrait in 1503 in Vienna. A native of Passau, Tettenhamer enrolled at the university of Ingolstadt in 1493 and was sworn into office there as a ducal councillor in 1517, which suggests he spent only some time in Austria.[3] This at least is indicated by the inscription, because surely otherwise the place where he sat for his portrait would not have been included. This also implies that the inscription was not on the lost original. Arms and inscription are contemporaneous with the handling of the Vienna copy, which may have been produced during the sitter's lifetime and may even have been commissioned by him. We can only speculate about the reasons for his trip to Vienna; perhaps he went there on a political mission. Tettenhammer died in 1543, and on his epitaph by Loy Hering in the Franciscan church in Ingolstadt, which shows him kneeling before the crucified Christ next to his wife Barbara, née Heberkofer, he is identified as a "gewesen firstlicher Ratt zv Ingelstatt" (former princely councillor at Ingolstadt).[4]

In his Vienna portrait he sports a black cap and a black fur-trimmed overgown worn over a white shirt or chemise. Note the gold-coloured bib-like band across his chest decorated with clasped hands (a symbol of fidelity?) and the jewelled agraffe in the form of the letter "M" on his hat. The somewhat lame handling and the hesitant underdrawing in a dry medium exclude Cranach as the author of this portrait, but the conception of a large figure occupying most of the space, the undulating silhouette and, last but not least, the sitter's determined-incommunicative expression show that the copyist must have used an original work by the Franconian artist as his template.[5] The copyist may have been active at Ingolstadt, and he appears to follow his model not only in the way he renders the figure but also in his choice of background, a fawn plane that gradually lightens towards the right. Together with the copies included in the *Portrait Codex of Hieronymus Beck* (cat. 18), this panel suggests that Cranach was already placing some of his sitters before a neutral background, reserving portraits set in a landscape, ideal for including a wealth of meaning, for his humanist patrons. GM

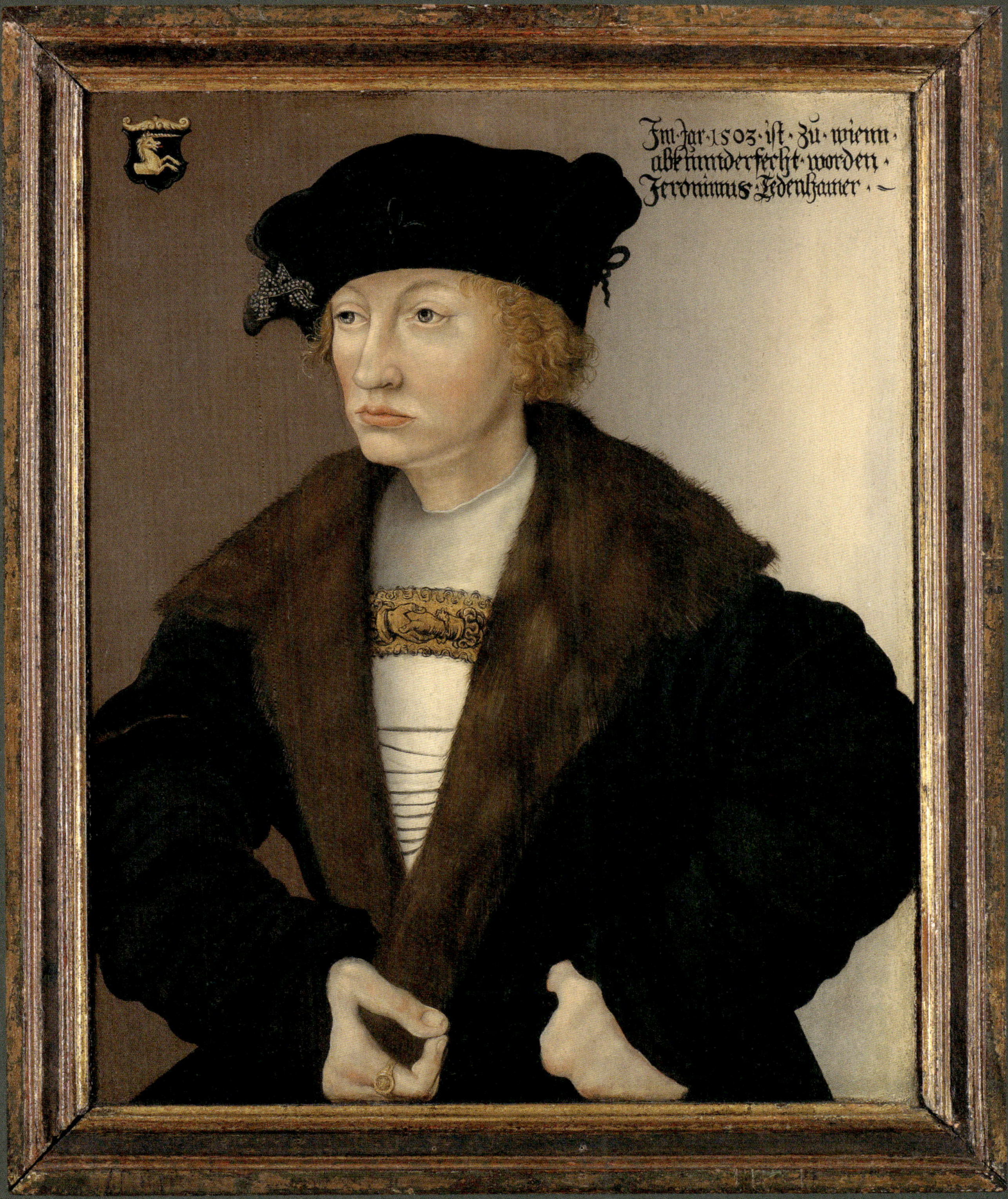
Im · Jar · 1503 · ist · zu · wienn ·
abkunnderfecht · worden ·
Jeronimus · Tedenhamer ·

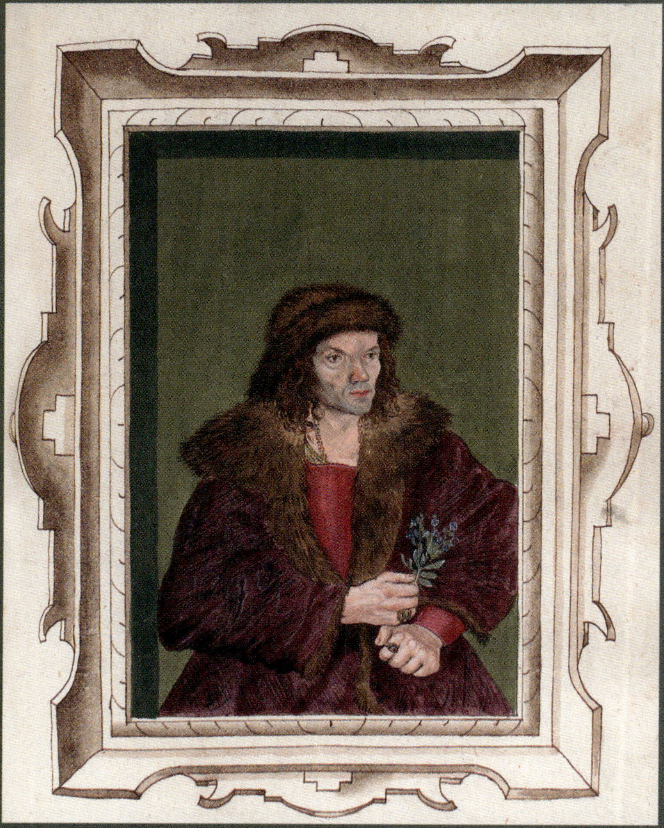

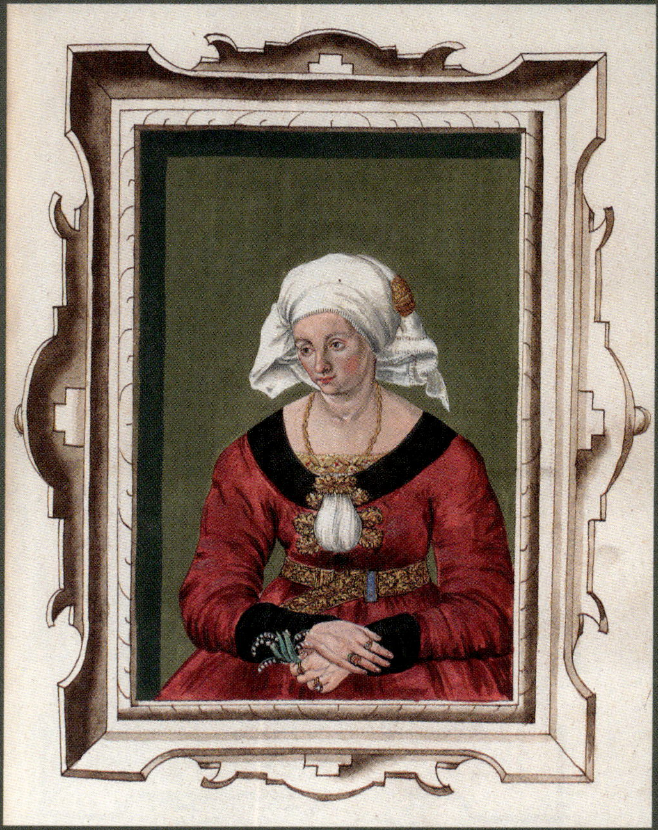

18

PORTRAIT CODEX OF HIERONYMUS BECK VON LEOPOLDSDORF

on display: *Portrait of a Viennese burgher* (p. 489, shown in Vienna),
Portrait of a Viennese burghess (p. 491, shown in Winterthur),
copies after a lost diptych by Lucas Cranach the Elder
circa 1570/80 (originals circa 1503)
Kunsthistorisches Museum Vienna

Around 1570/80, Hieronymus von Beck (1525–1596), a member of the Lower-Austrian aristocracy, commissioned a series of portraits in body colour on paper; they share a common fake frame that reflects contemporary taste and all copy older portraits, most of which date from the early sixteenth century. In this miniature gallery Beck assembled members of the House of Habsburg and other European ruling families as well as members of the Netherlandish and the Lower-Austrian nobility, his own family, and Vienna's bourgeoisie.[1] The latter include a number of remarkable likenesses like these of an anonymous married couple whose now-lost original portraits were obviously painted by Cranach. A comparison between our female portrait and that of the wife of a Viennese jurist (cat. 16) painted in 1503 makes this quite obvious. In both, the sitter leans slightly forward, and both women have a lively, undulating silhouette; similarities in dress reflect local fashion. In 1503, the painter must have produced the now-lost original of the Tettenhammer portrait, whose Viennese copy (cat. 17) again exhibits close stylistic similarities with the anonymous sitter in the Portrait Codex. The man's vigorous features suggest the miniaturist did not deviate far from Cranach's template. The original panels may also have featured a green backdrop; joined by hinges, they presumably formed a lockable married-couple diptych. The well-to-do Viennese burgher and his wife are looking at each other and the flowers in their hands symbolise their pledge of fidelity.

Unfortunately, we do not know the identity of Cranach's patrons. As with many other miniatures, their names may well have been lost when the lower edges were cropped when these originally loose pages were collected in a codex following Beck's death. Beck's selection of sitters reflects his preferences and networks, as well as those of his father Markus Beck (1493–1551). Born in the Allgäu region of southern Bavaria, Markus moved to Vienna in 1510 to study law, becoming a close advisor to King Ferdinand I, who ennobled him in 1530. We may assume that many of the portraits depict friends of Markus Beck's who were, like him, prosperous members of Vienna's bourgeoisie. Almost all of the originals copied in these miniatures are lost, making the Codex an invaluable document of portraiture in Vienna in the early sixteenth century, and bearing witness to Cranach's exceptional role in its development; some examples show that he and his innovative portraits of sitters placed before a landscape inspired local followers.[2] GM

19

Lucas Cranach the Elder

PORTRAIT OF A WOMAN PRAYING

circa 1508

Kunsthaus Zürich (on loan to the Kunstmuseum Basel)

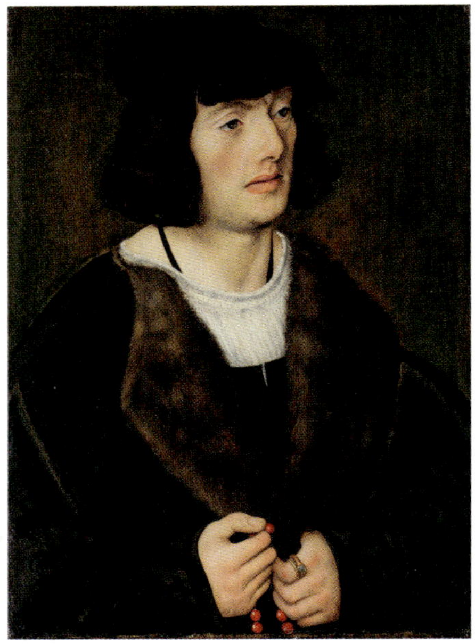

Lucas Cranach the Elder, *Portrait of a Man with a Rosary*, c.1508. The Metropolitan Museum of Art, New York

Initially the praying woman was not alone: the young lady in a white cap depicted in three-quarter view had a counterpart, the *Portrait of a Man with a Rosary* (fig.) now in the Metropolitan Museum of Art in New York. The reverses of both panels each feature the grisaille figure of a saint in a niche. The saint on the reverse of the female portrait is easily identified as St Catherine, but her counterpart on the reverse of the male portrait is so badly damaged that we can only tentatively identify him as the Apostle Peter.

The handling of both portraits is very three-dimensional, delicate, and carefully differentiated. Unlike the double portraits of the Cuspinians (cat. 12 & 13) and of the jurist and his wife (cat. 15 & 16), the sitters are placed before a neutral background; one is now slightly darker than the other, the result of their different states of preservation.

The praying woman wears a black dress edged in white; her hands are folded in prayer. Note the slim ring on her right index finger, her sole piece of jewellery. Her cap, too, is very simple and one typically worn in the Low Countries. Her husband in a fur-trimmed overgown is also clad in sombre colours. He is clutching a rosary – which creates a strong red colour accent. He also sports a signet ring whose coat of arms may be identified as that of the Netherlandish Six de Hillegom family. This and her eye-catching cap are not the only reasons indicating the portraits originated in the Low Countries: the grisailles on the reverses, the rosary, and the hands folded in prayer also suggest the two panels once formed the wings of a triptych whose rectangular central panel presumably depicted a religious scene. At the time these panels were painted, devotional triptychs were very popular in the Netherlands – as was their support: during his stay in Vienna, and especially later in Saxony, Cranach mostly painted on limewood panels, but these two portraits were executed on oak wood – the most commonly used timber in contemporary Netherlandish painting. The wide bevelling on the reverses, a common feature of sixteenth-century Netherlandish panels, also suggests these portraits may have originated in the Low Countries.[1]

Cranach visited the Netherlands in 1508, and there has been much speculation about the reasons for this trip.[2] One of them seems to have been a commission from Margaret of Austria, Governor of the Habsburg Netherlands, to paint a portrait of her nephew Archduke (later Emperor) Charles V. Cranach would have travelled to Malines where Margaret resided and young Charles was being brought up at the court of his aunt. Except for a visit to Antwerp, we know next to nothing about Cranach's travel route and who else he met there. But this portrait with a grisaille on its reverse argues that Cranach may have studied the works of Quentin Massys.

In Antwerp he may also have met Gerard David, whose flourishing atelier perhaps served as a model for Cranach's workshop in Wittenberg.[3] KB

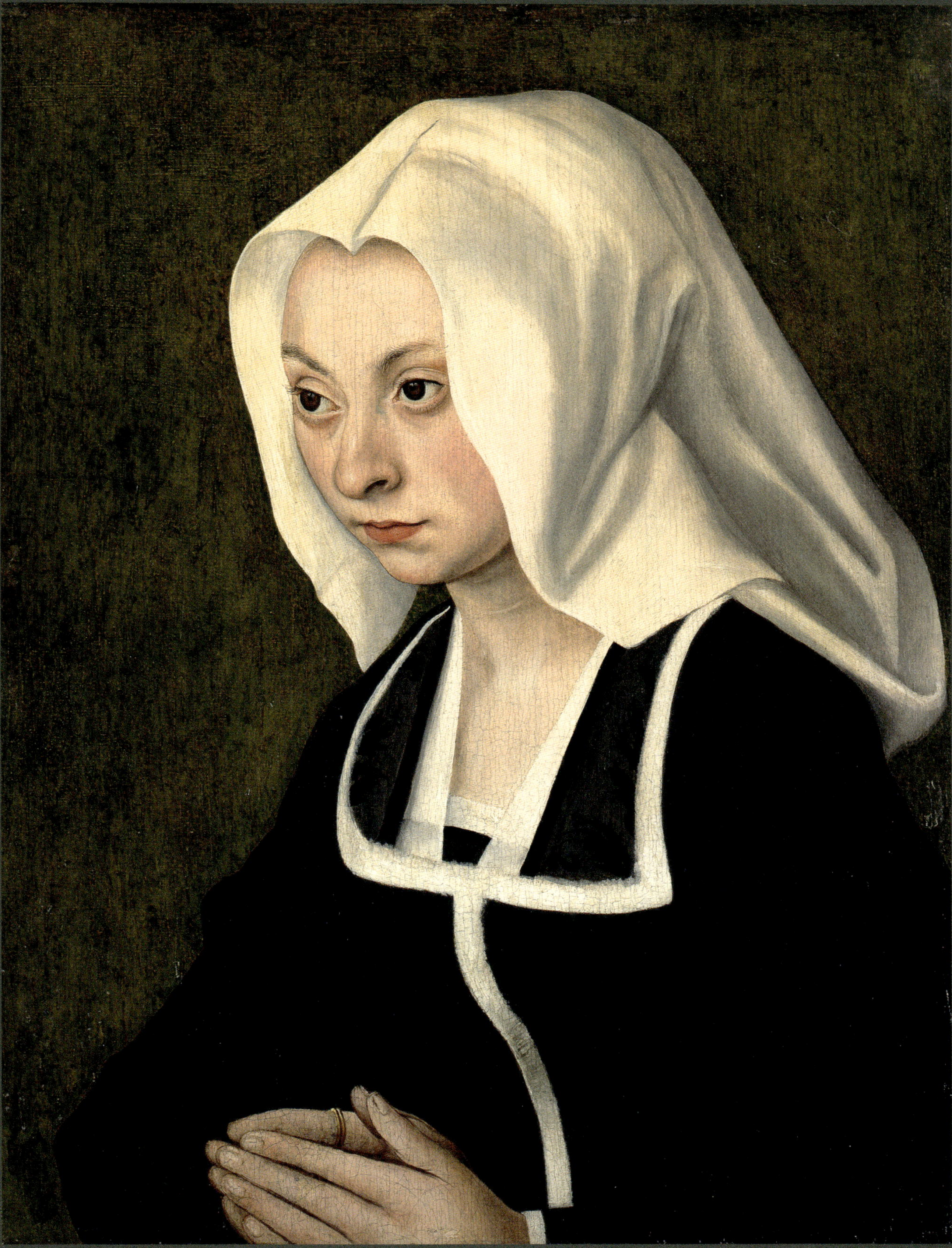

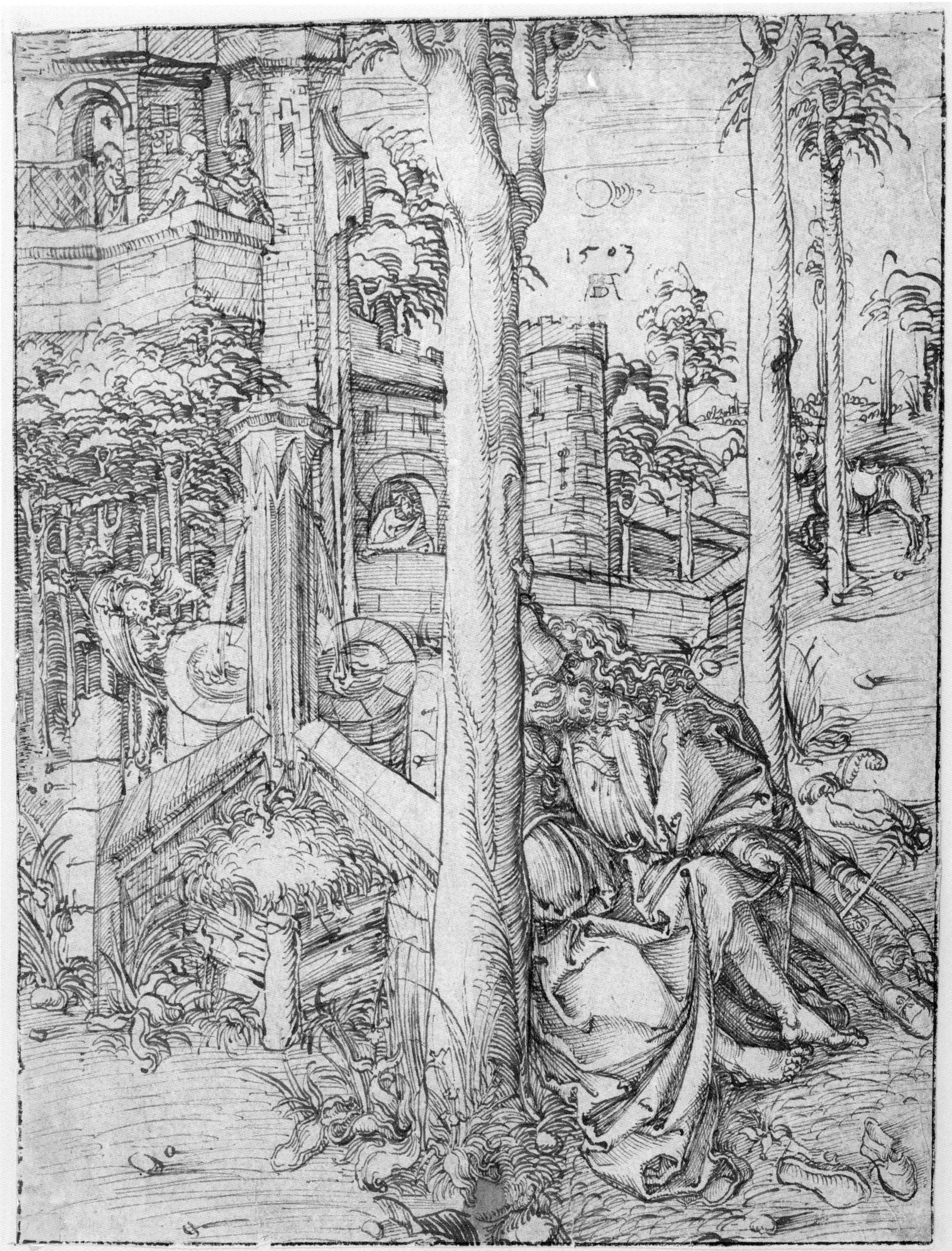
1503

20

Lucas Cranach the Elder (?)

LOVERS AT A FOUNTAIN, IN THE DISTANCE DEATH CLUTCHING A SCYTHE

1503

Herzog Anton Ulrich-Museum, Brunswick

Note the complexity and wealth of detail in this pen and ink drawing of lovers at a fountain, inviting the viewer to slowly discover content and the different elements comprising it. Mistakes in the perspective – in the depiction of the castle but also of the fountain on the right, where side and top views alternate – make it difficult to comprehend the composition.[1]

It requires training and imagination merely to identify and differentiate the eponymous lovers, especially as they are somewhat obscured by a pole-like tree trunk – an element echoed by the line of trees leading into the depth of the painting, helping to map it. The viewer's gaze is invited to linger here until it finally identifies the curly-haired youth who has discarded his sword and his plumed cap and is beginning to lift the skirt of the woman he is kissing. With his right hand he is supporting himself on the tree trunk. It is almost impossible to see the woman's face, but we do see her large headdress which presumably identifies her as a married woman. Her right hand is caressing her lover under his doublet, and she has already discarded her shoes. The young man's horse is tied up in the distance, and, on the left, we see three women standing, unexpectedly close to the amorous couple, on a balcony above the castle walls: one is just approaching while the other two cast their eyes over the surroundings, with one of them pointing at the horse. We do not know if this is meant to symbolise that the about-to-be-committed adultery will soon be discovered, or if it is an attempt to warn the lovers. Because they need to be warned: Death wielding his scythe is rushing towards the unsuspecting couple from behind the fountain. The small figure of the grim reaper is concealed so well among the trees and behind the fountain that he is probably the last thing the viewer notices.

The drawing depicts the lovers' uncontrolled passion while conjoining it with the unexpected appearance of Death – the drastic realism of both is truly innovative.[2] There are links to works by Dürer that also show Death suddenly making an entrance by quitting his hiding place, though Dürer's couples are much better behaved.[3] The handling too is reminiscent of the master from Nuremberg. However, Dürer's monogram has been identified as fake while the date is believed to be correct. The way the numerals are written conforms to Cranach's usual handling. The inconsistencies in the perspective, especially the architectural elements, are irritating but we find a similar additive tendency to combine pictorial elements in other works produced during his stay in Vienna.[4] If we agree with Dieter Koepplin's attribution to Cranach the Elder, then this small work again bears witness to the importance of the subject "lovers in a landscape" that both Cranach and his workshop continue to develop in later compositions.[5] KR

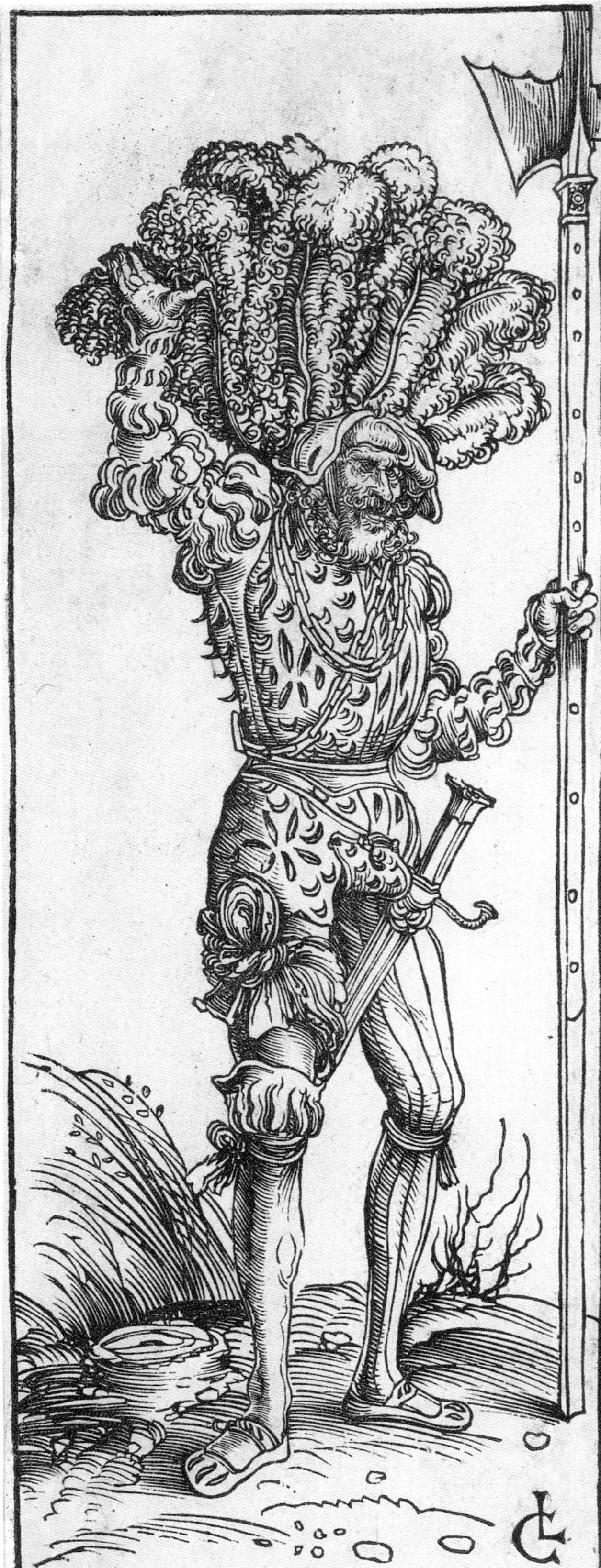

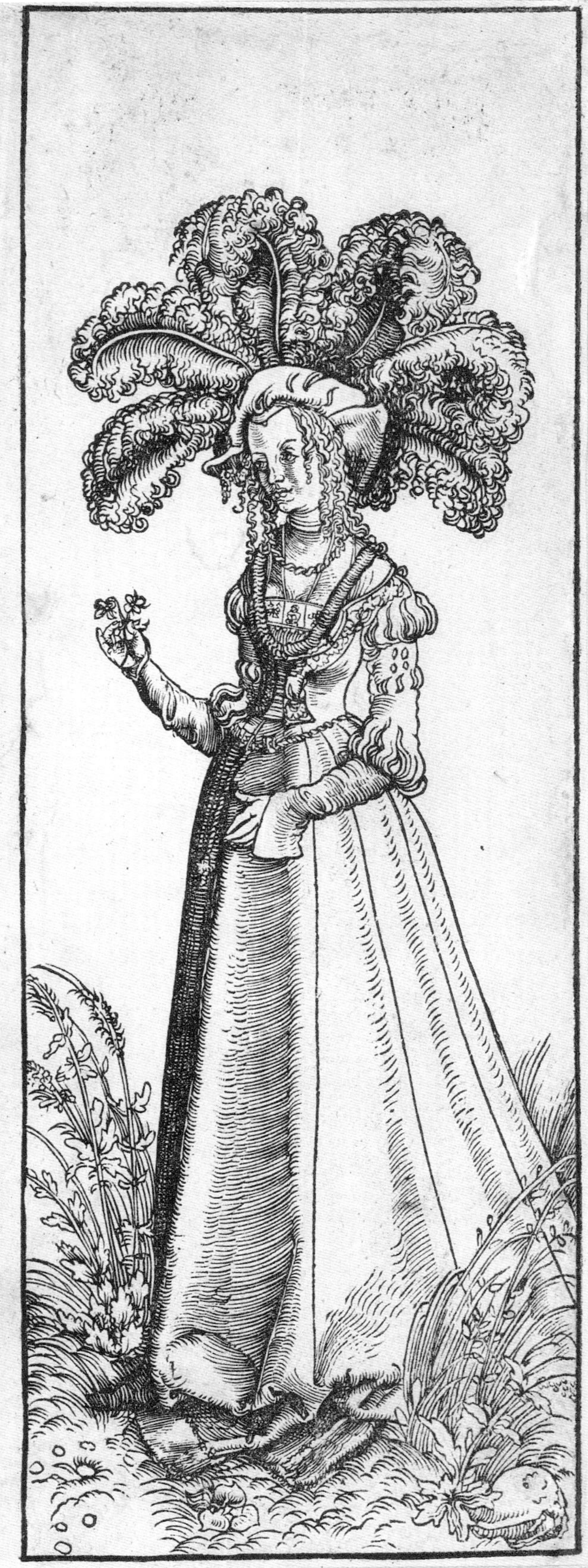

21

Lucas Cranach the Elder

LANDSKNECHT AND YOUNG LADY

circa 1505

Staatliche Museen zu Berlin, Kupferstichkabinett

In this print an ill-matched couple seem to find one another: on the left is an elderly landsknecht or foot soldier, on the right a young lady. They are facing each other but each has their own pictorial space clearly delineated by the frame. Although the backgrounds were left bare, both figures are anchored on clearly differentiated ground adapted to fit them: the landsknecht stands on bare, stony ground next to brambles and a low tree trunk; the gentlewoman is depicted among high grasses and ferns caressing her floor-length gown.[1]

Both figures sport large plumed headdresses; the elegant young lady wears a wide, long skirt and a laced bodice, but the foot soldier, despite his best efforts, clearly tries too hard and looks a little ridiculous. The hose on his right leg is bunched up above the knee, exposing a hairy calve and a naked foot, on which he wears a bear claw shoe. At the time, many landsknechts favoured asymmetrical clothes – they often wore just one striped hose or sleeve and paired this with a monochrome one[2] – but here the contrast appears overdone and is almost a caricature, an impression reinforced by the large sword awkwardly dangling between his legs. He is, however, firmly clutching his halberd with his left hand but it has become an obstacle separating him from the young lady.

His right hand is raised in a greeting, thumb and palm of his hand pointing heavenwards. We find a similar greeting in Cranach's woodcut *A Saxon Prince on Horseback* (1506), and the drawing *The Promenade* (c.1505/09).[3] Here, an elegant gentleman is walking arm in arm with his female companion but, unlike our landsknecht and young lady, they seem to belong to the same social class. Earlier artists like the Master of the Housebook or Albrecht Dürer had also produced such depictions of couples.[4]

The signature near the landsknecht's feet (intertwined initials but without the Saxon arms) is often found in Cranach's early works – see, for example, the drawing *St Martin and the Beggar* (cat. 27), or the panel *Rest on the Flight into Egypt* (see essay Heiser, fig. 4). This is how Cranach, even before he was issued a grant of arms in 1508 (which is when he began to sign his works with a winged serpent), created a kind of "trademark".[5] The intertwined letters are clearly informed by Dürer's signature; he, too, signed even individually sold woodcuts with his monogram.[6] The woodcut probably dates from Cranach's first years in Wittenberg, when he often selected courtly or chivalrous scenes for his graphic works. KB

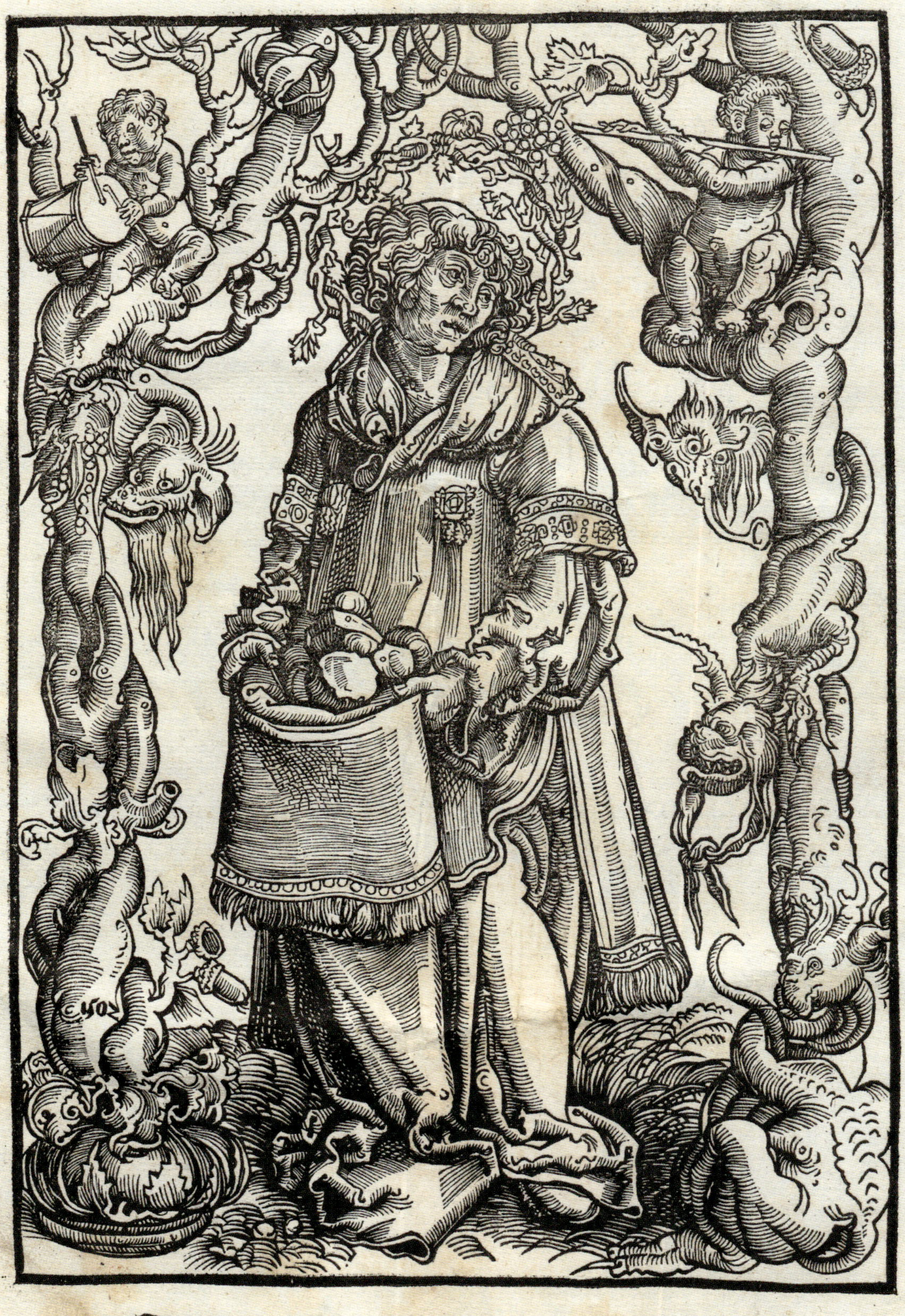

Sanctus Stephanus prothomartyr.

22

Lucas Cranach the Elder

ST STEPHEN

1502

Österreichische Nationalbibliothek, Vienna

Like a frontispiece, this depiction of St Stephen, dated 1502 on the tree trunk bottom left, opens Winterburger's *Missale Pataviense* published in 1503.[1] The woodcut is presumably part of the missal's "standard repertoire" but only a handful of prints have survived *in situ*.[2] The iconographic tradition of adding a picture of the diocese's patron saint to its missals also suggests the woodcut was always part of the missal published in 1503; an earlier example is Erhard Ratdolt's *Passau Missal* printed in 1494,[3] which has a frontispiece by Hans Burgkmair (1471–1531) depicting Passau's three patron saints Valentinus, Stephanus, and Maximilianus (see essay Fingernagel, fig. 2). A comparison with this woodcut and with Albrecht Dürer's print featuring Stephen and Saints Sixtus and Laurence (1504/05)[4] reveals the character of Cranach's idiom: Burgkmair's (and Dürer's) hieratic image of the saint is here contrasted with a more human figure of the first martyr. He is framed by gnarled trees and branches inhabited by dragon-like monsters and putti making music, which play a prominent role in the composition.[5] This vegetal-figurative concept also incorporates the saint's halo formed by verdant branches, creating a mood of man-nature-symbiosis similar to Cranach's more-or-less contemporary woodcut *Christ on the Mount of Olives* (c.1501; see essay Heiser, fig. 6). Interesting from an iconographic viewpoint is a comparison with Ratdolt's frontispiece, which shows that Cranach concentrated on the figure of St Stephen, thus emphasising the strong local connection of this missal printed by Winterburger in Vienna.

Winterburger reused the woodcut in some of the copies of the *Missale Pataviense* printed in 1512, but for the *Missale Pataviense* of 1509 he reverted to the model used in the *Passau Missal* of 1494, and in the *Graduale Pataviense* (1511) he replaced the woodcut with a half-length depiction of the triad Valentinus, Stephanus and Maximilianus.

The small *Missale Pataviense (speciale)* from Passau (printed in 1513) contains a late echo of Cranach's *St Stephen* woodcut.[6] The composition of the frontispiece featuring the diocese's three patron saints is clearly informed by Burgkmair's version in Ratdolt's missal of 1494 but replaces the figure of St Stephen with a copy of Cranach's woodcut for the missal printed in 1503. The second edition of Winterburger's *Wiener Heiltumsbuch* (1514) includes a clearly inferior woodcut with a broad and flat depiction of the saint based on Cranach's image.[7] AF

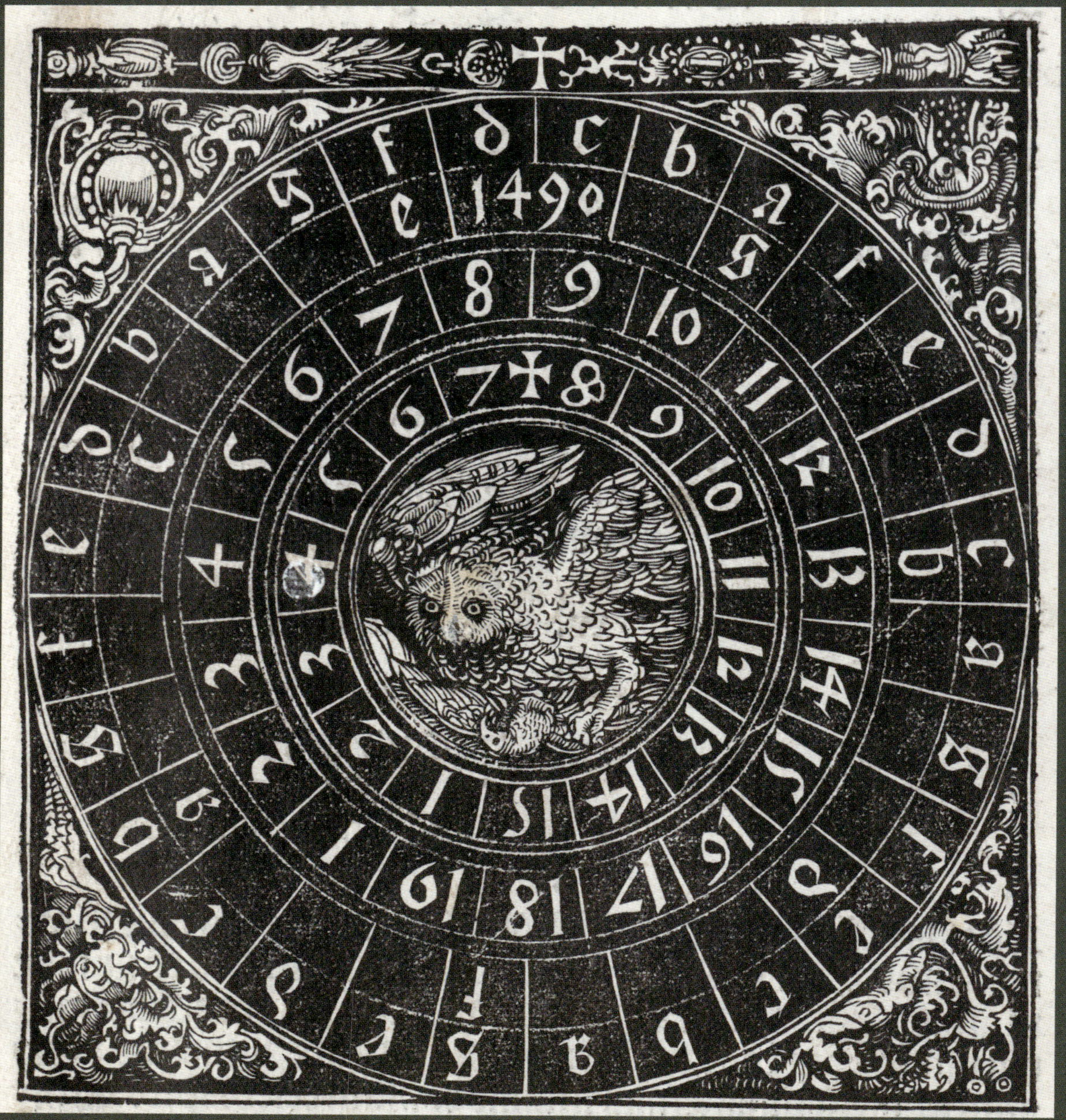
1490

23

Lucas Cranach the Elder

CALENDAR DIAL TO IDENTIFY THE DOMINICAL LETTER

circa 1502/03

Österreichische Nationalbibliothek, Vienna

Always placed after the calendar and filling more than half a page, the dial to identify the dominical letter (*Tabula litterae Dominicalis*) is accompanied by a text explaining the anything-but-trivial use of this diagram. The two outermost circles contain the dominical letters (a–g; note amongst them the date 1490) that indicate which day marks the first Sunday of each year; leap years are given an extra day, which appears in the second circle. The third circle, reflecting the 19-year Metonic cycle, is inscribed with the golden number (1–19). The dominical letter and the golden number are used to calculate the date of Easter. The innermost circle specifies the indication numbers (1–15) used to count the years in a 15-year cycle, originally the periodic assessment of tax in the Roman Empire but in the Middle Ages used primarily to check the calculation of the year.

The image of an owl with outstretched wings and clutching a slain bird forms the centre of the circle. The pendentives between the circle and its almost square frame are filled with vivid sculpted foliage.

Other disks for the same year (1490) included in liturgical texts published in southern Germany have been suggested as templates for this woodcut. The closest to Cranach's vegetal pendentives are the prints produced by Erhard Ratdolt in Augsburg, and a Ratisbon breviary printed in Bamberg in 1495.[1]

A major difference between this dial and the supposed Augsburg template is the fact that the latter's central sun has been replaced by an owl shown in dramatic front view as it kills a smaller bird. It is quite remarkable that the "naïve" sun with a human face of the prints produced in southern Germany has here been replaced by an expressive and, despite its small scale, carefully differentiated owl.

Endrődi has convincingly analyzed the contentual aspect of this image, identifying the owl as a symbol of the moon and the diurnal bird in its clutches as that of the sun. A possible model for the juxtaposition of sun and moon in these computistic tables is a manuscript containing the works of Georg Peuerbach,[2] which in turn is based on the Ratdolt formula of 1490, but with a central image combining the crescent moon *and* the sun with a human face. There are more depictions of owls in Cranach's initials on folio 101v and, confirming the interpretation, on folio 252v (cat. 26), where owl and crescent are confronted.[3]

The motif of an owl killing another bird also appears in the *Penance of St Jerome* (cat. 6).

Cranach's woodcut continued to be used in some of Winterburger's liturgical books issued during the following years, for example the *Missale Olomucense* of 1505, *the Missale Salisburgense* of 1506, and the *Missale Pataviense* of 1509. In the *Missale Salisburgense* of 1510 and the *Missale Pataviense* of 1512, however, Winterburger used a more-or-less plain circular diagram and "updated" it to AD 1507. AF

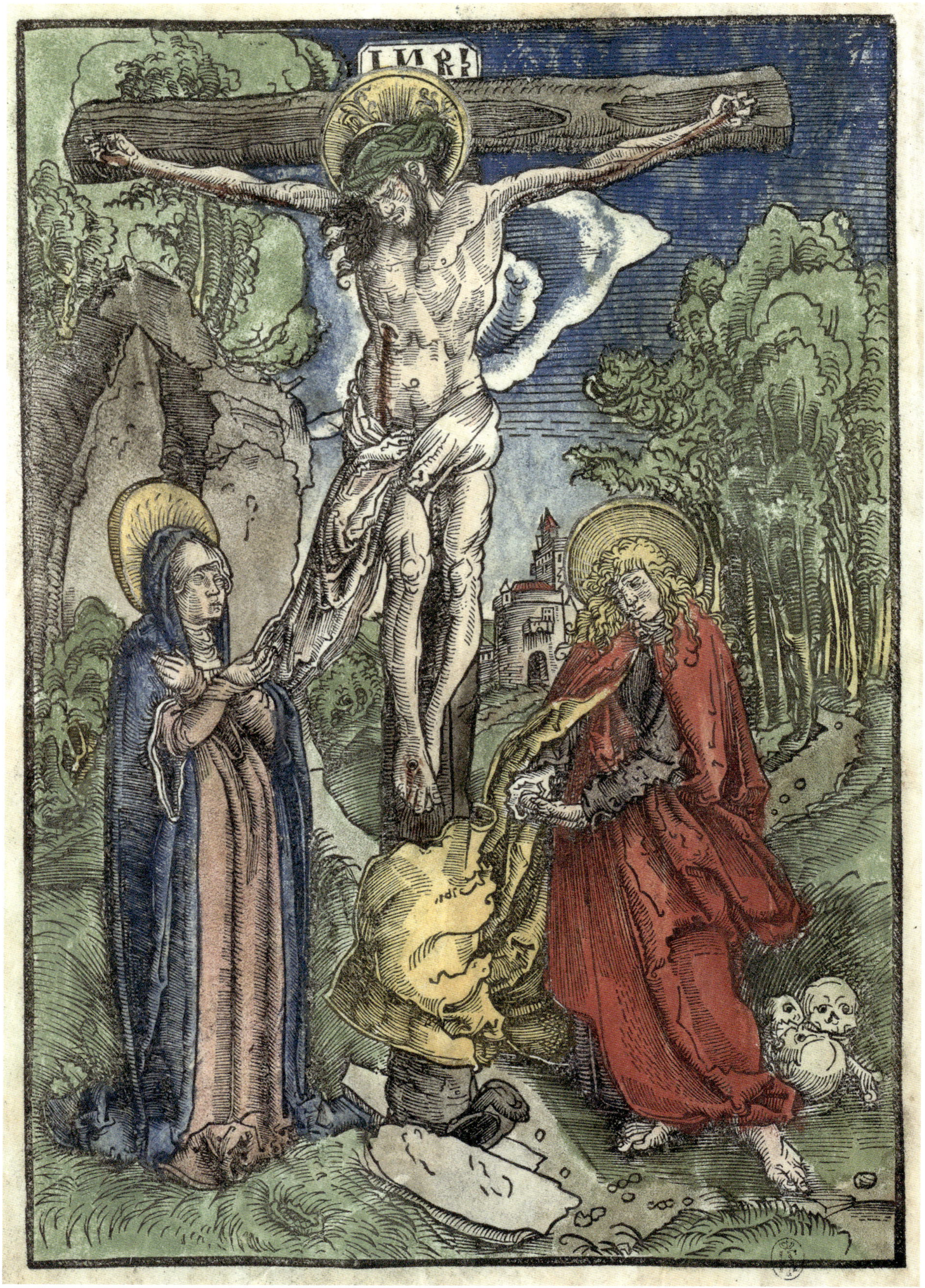

24

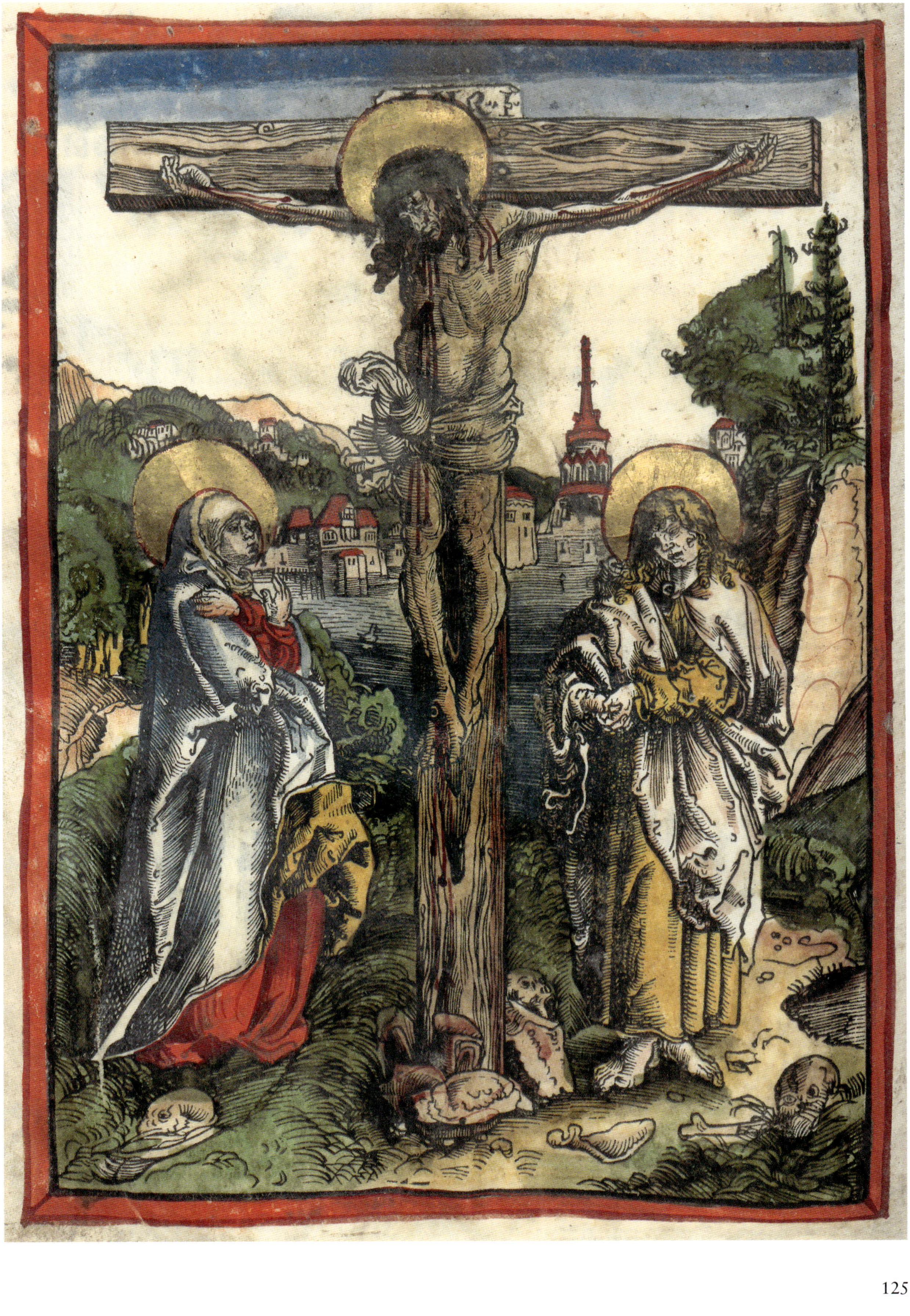

25

24 & 25

Lucas Cranach the Elder

THE CRUCIFIXION OF CHRIST (CANON ILLUSTRATION)
before 1502 (?)
Albertina, Vienna

THE CRUCIFIXION OF CHRIST (CANON ILLUSTRATION)
circa 1502/03
Österreichische Nationalbibliothek, Vienna

In the chronology of Cranach's crucifixion woodcuts the print now in the Albertina is generally dated to before 1502, and it has even been suggested that the artist produced it prior to his sojourn in Vienna.[1] We may assume that this depiction was devised as a canon illustration, probably analogous to the later one included in the *Passau Missal* printed in 1503. However, it has not (yet) been possible to assign this print to a particular missal; all we have is a (loose) connection to a copy of the *Cracow Missal* printed by Georg Stuchs at Nuremberg around 1494, into which an impression of the woodcut was pasted at some point to replace an earlier one.[2]

The crucifixion in Winterburger's *Passau Missal* of 1503 also comprises three figures, and it was printed both on paper and on parchment. The print is generally dated to 1502/03, with the preceding page showing St Stephen dated 1502 (cat. 22) and the date the missal was printed (25 May 1503) providing the timeframe.

In the missal print, Jesus has turned slightly to the left but his body is shown frontally. Her arms crossed, the Virgin turns a little bit to gaze up at her crucified son. St John has turned away from the cross, wringing his hands, his eyes cast to the ground. Behind the cross rammed into the foreground a vista opens up comprising a city on the shore of a lake with a tall tower and distant hills framed by rocks and woods.

The composition in Cranach's earlier crucifixion is similar and the protagonists' poses are also more-or-less identical. There are, however, clear differences in the conception of the two scenes – see, for example, the more solid but elongated figure of St John in the presumably earlier crucifixion, his *contrapposto* is more pronounced and his gestures are more expansive. The altogether more dynamical feel of the canon illustration is also emphasised by the drapery: the saint's billowing cloak theatrically drapes around the base of the cross, Christ's loincloth balloons downwards and touches Mary's hands. Compared to the canon illustration from the missal, the staggered landscape creates less depth and omits the central lake view.

A woodcut produced around 1500 by an artist from Dürer's circle has been identified as the template for both crucifixions, which Cranach transposed "into his own idiom by increasing its expressiveness".[3]

Numerous hand-coloured impressions of both woodcuts by Cranach have survived. The individual handling determines the print's overall appearance and mood.[4] The colouration emphasises (or not) the composition's graphic qualities; the palette selected for the robes differentiates both the various pieces of clothing and transports the scene's emotionalism. The most prominent details accentuated by the colouration are the streams of blood flowing from Christ's wounds (they are not indicated in the print) and the atmospheric clouds above – both elements help determine the woodcuts' mood and emotional charge. The dating of the colouring is problematic, but the canon illustration in the *Karstner Missal*, also on show here, offers a timeframe because the gold halos and the initials of the previous owner Georg Karstner (G K) were clearly executed at the same time: Karstner became provost of the Augustinian monastery St Dorothy in Vienna in 1566, and he died in 1591.[5]

Winterburger repeatedly made use of Cranach's canon illustration, including it in the *Missale Olomucense* (1505), in some copies of the *Missale Salisburgense* (1506) and part of the print run of the *Missale Pataviense* (1512). A simpler version informed by Cranach's woodcut was used for the canon illustration in the *Salzburg Missal* of 1510 and the small Passau *Missale speciale* (1513). From the early 1510s, Cranach's woodcuts competed with a

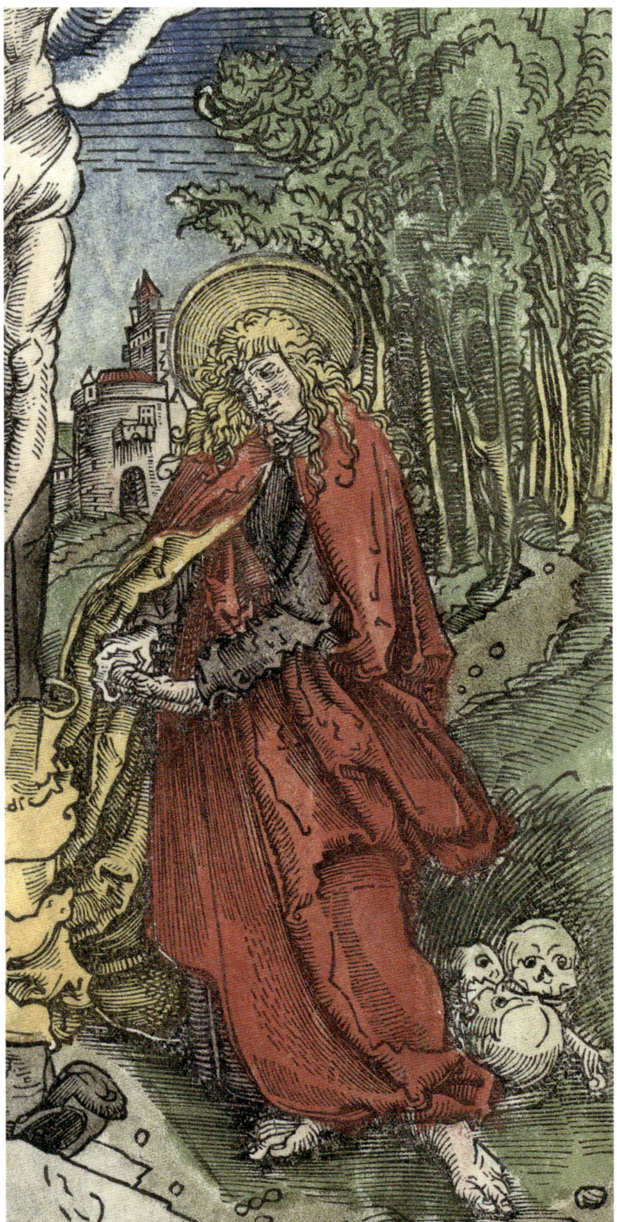

stylistically older canon crucifixion[6] first published by Winterburger in parts of the print run of the *Missale Pataviense* (1512),[7] then in the *Missale Strigoniense* (1514), and the *Missale Defunctorum* published around 1518.[8] It is hard to say if the frequent use of this decorative rather than gloomy-expressive canon-woodcut reflects a "new" taste. AF

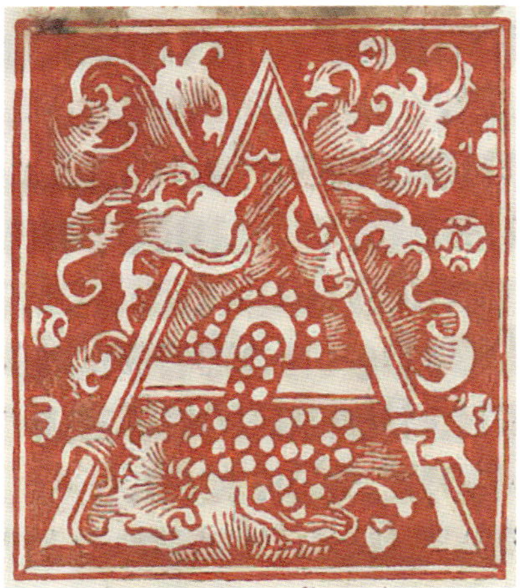
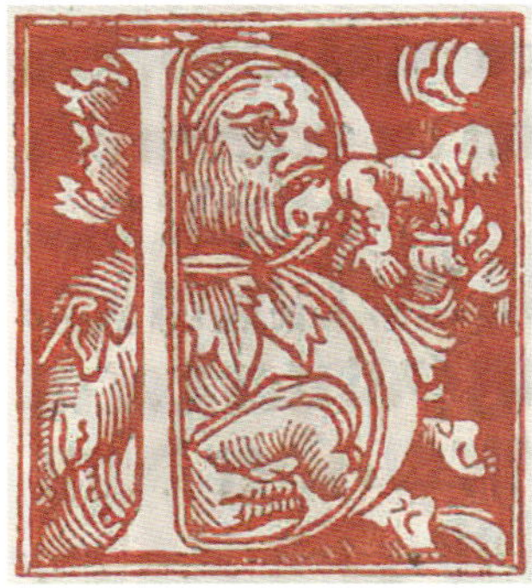

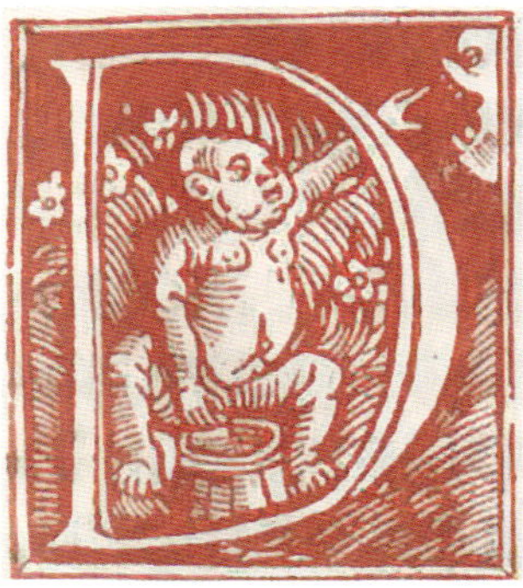
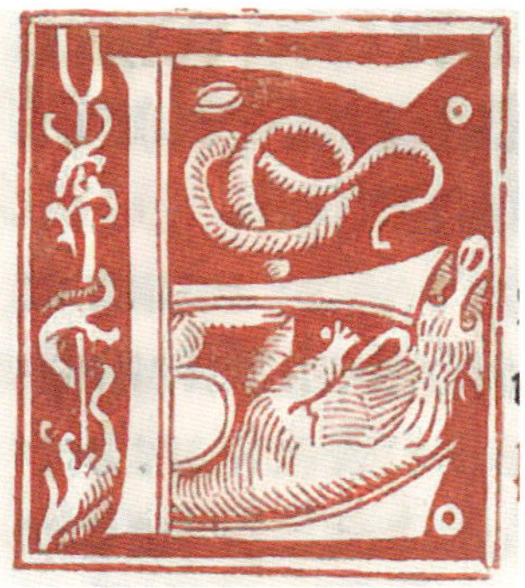
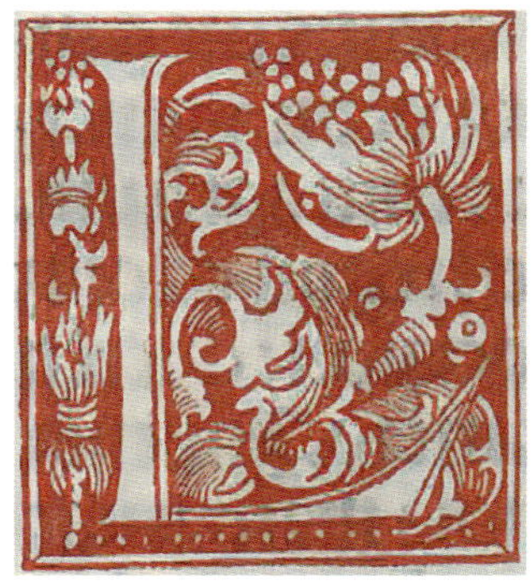
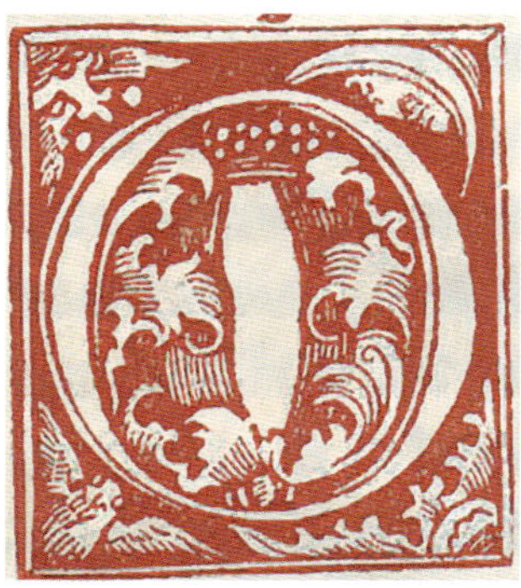
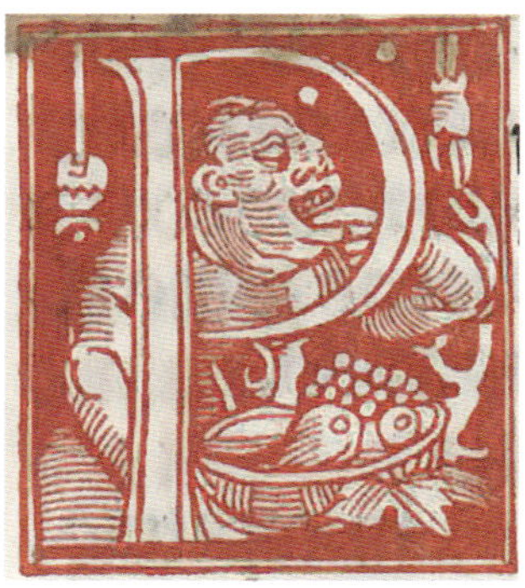
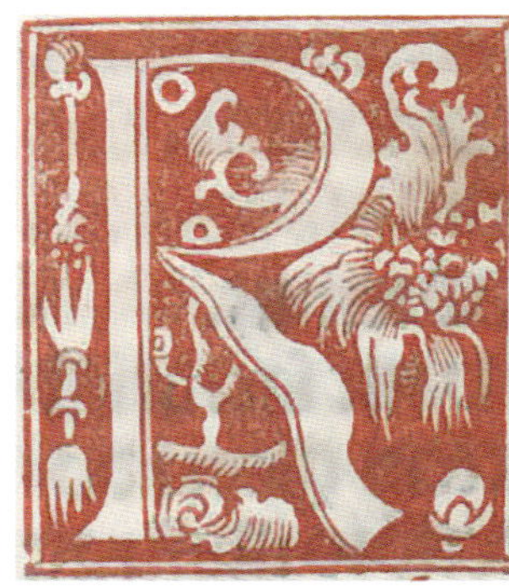
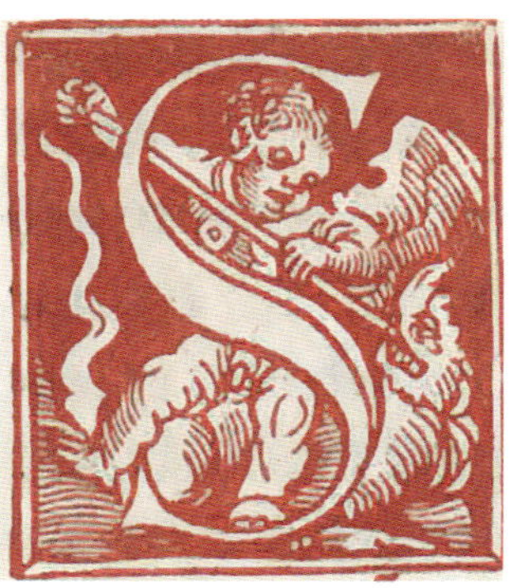
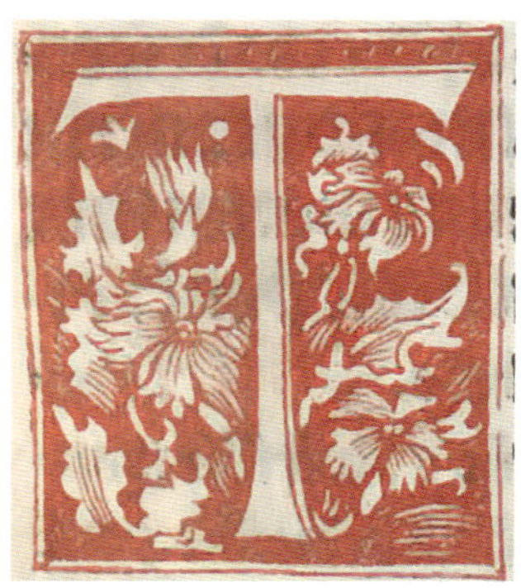

26/1–12

Lucas Cranach the Elder
INITIALS
circa 1502/03
Österreichische Nationalbibliothek, Vienna

This missal contains a total of twelve initials, some of which appear repeatedly. Each initial's body is formed by a clearly legible, sharply defined capital letter: a shape that had already replaced the "mediaeval" bulged Lombard shape in Winterburger's incunabula. The body of the initial, its décor, and the figures were left blank on the red ground, with hatching adding some three-dimensional effects. The vegetal shapes are dominated by composite foliage that includes expansive, flexible tentacle-like leaves, some with claw-like tips.[1] Note the seed heads bursting with pips. The zoomorphic forms include a donkey lying on its back (?) (fol. 17r), and owls in the initials V (fol. 101v) and O (fol. 252v, here confronted with a crescent moon), which motivically connect them with the calendar dial to identify the dominical letter (cat. 23). The content of the anthropomorphic-figurative initials are informed by coarse humour: a wild man gobbling up an infant ("Saturn devouring his children", fol. 112v), a boy urinating into a barrel and pointing to an ugly visage (?; fol. 184v), a fat monk sitting before a full bowl who has put a finger in his mouth (fol. 11v), and a putto fighting a dragon with a lance (e.g. fol. 106v). The contentual relevance of these depictions remains disputed. However, the subsequent use of these initials in different textual contexts suggests they served a primarily decorative purpose. Attempts to connect the initial featuring a depiction of Saturn/Kronos devouring his children with the owl in the calendar dial to identify the dominical letter remain contested.[2]

Winterburger re-used the alphabet from the missal printed in 1503 in his *Olomouc Missal* of 1505.[3] Here, the now increased number of initials are augmented by additional alphabets whose herbaceous, agitated sculpted tendrils are closely related to Cranach's initials and the decorative details in the pendentives of the dominical letter. Comparable stylistic details can also be identified in an alphabet used in the *Missale Salisburgense* (1506),[4] the *Passau Missal* of 1507, and the *Graduale Pataviense* of 1511.[5]

Zykan assumes a motific and stylistic dependance between the pictorial initials and the depiction of the crucifixion of Christ added to the *Passau Missal* of 1509, and the crucifixions in Cranach's panels depicting this scene from the Passion.[6]

The alphabet from the 1503 missal and stylistically-related initials continued to be repeated and reused, which meant that Cranach's handling of the initials remained in use until the end of the 1510s. AF

27

Lucas Cranach the Elder

ST MARTIN AND THE BEGGAR

1504

Staatliche Graphische Sammlung, Munich

From all we know today, this dated and monogramed depiction of St Martin is Cranach's oldest extant signed and dated drawing. He probably produced it during his journey from Vienna via Nuremberg to Wittenberg to take up his new position as court painter to Frederick III, Elector of Saxony: the foreshortened architecture is an inverted quote from Dürer's woodcut *The Visitation of Mary* that he only produced around 1503/04.[1] This suggests the drawing was intended for Prüfening Monastery near Regensburg, which is located along the route Cranach took and from where the drawing eventually found its way to Munich.

Although we need a moment to find our way round this drawing it is much easier to read than, for example, the drawing *Lovers at a Fountain* (cat. 20). A comparison with earlier, much more expressive woodcuts (see cat. 2 & 3), also reveals a certain calming.

St Martin is shown cutting up his cloak: clasping the sword in his right hand, he is forcefully slashing the fabric from the top.

Tellingly, his charger is depicted moving too; it has not stopped but keeps walking, while the beggar remains in one place. He has lost his feet and has tied two boards to the stumps of his legs to crawl about; his mutt has settled down beside him, while the saint's hound also continues on its way. St Martin's retinue is just emerging from a splendid archway and, like him, they are sporting plumed helmets. Their horses are adorned with what appears to be rich tack and caparisons. In contrast, the clothes of the beggar's female companion, leaning against the archway with her child, are cheap and torn. She is clutching three spoons and an almost empty bowl – a clear sign that more than one mouth needs to be fed.

Monogram, date, and the choice of coloured paper ground indicate that Cranach regarded this drawing as an autonomous artwork. The only other early drawing by Cranach to qualify as such is *St John the Baptist in a Landscape* (fig.).

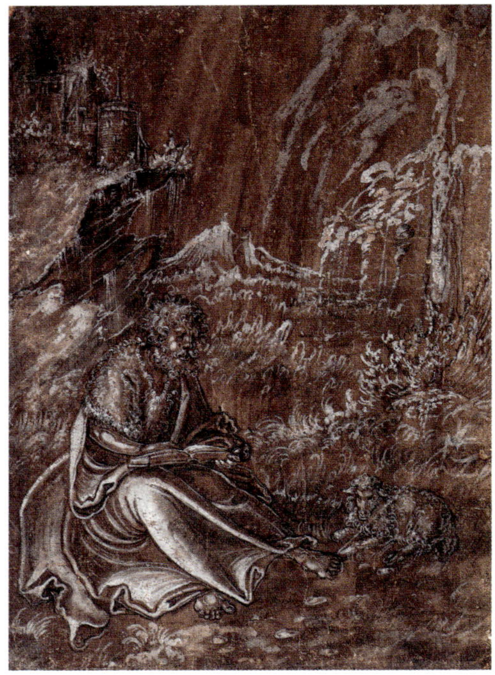

Lucas Cranach the Elder, *St John the Baptist in a Landscape*, c.1504. Musée des Beaux Arts, Lille

Such works were primarily intended for the learned members of Vienna's humanist circles, who prized them as expressions of artistic individuality.[2]

The two *chiaroscuro* drawings, as well as the studies for the two *Thieves* (cat. 4 & 5), and the drawing of the *Foolish Virgin* (cat. 8) were executed on coloured (tinted or grounded) paper. The elaborate technique of dying paper was probably an attempt to soften and enliven the paper's originally hard white, and as early as the fifteenth century artists began to dye their papers using red chalk washes.[3] However, the *chiaroscuro* woodcut was invented soon after the completion of this drawing of *St Martin*, allowing Hans Burgkmair the Elder from Augsburg and Cranach to transpose the popular aesthetics of a coloured ground into prints.[4] KB

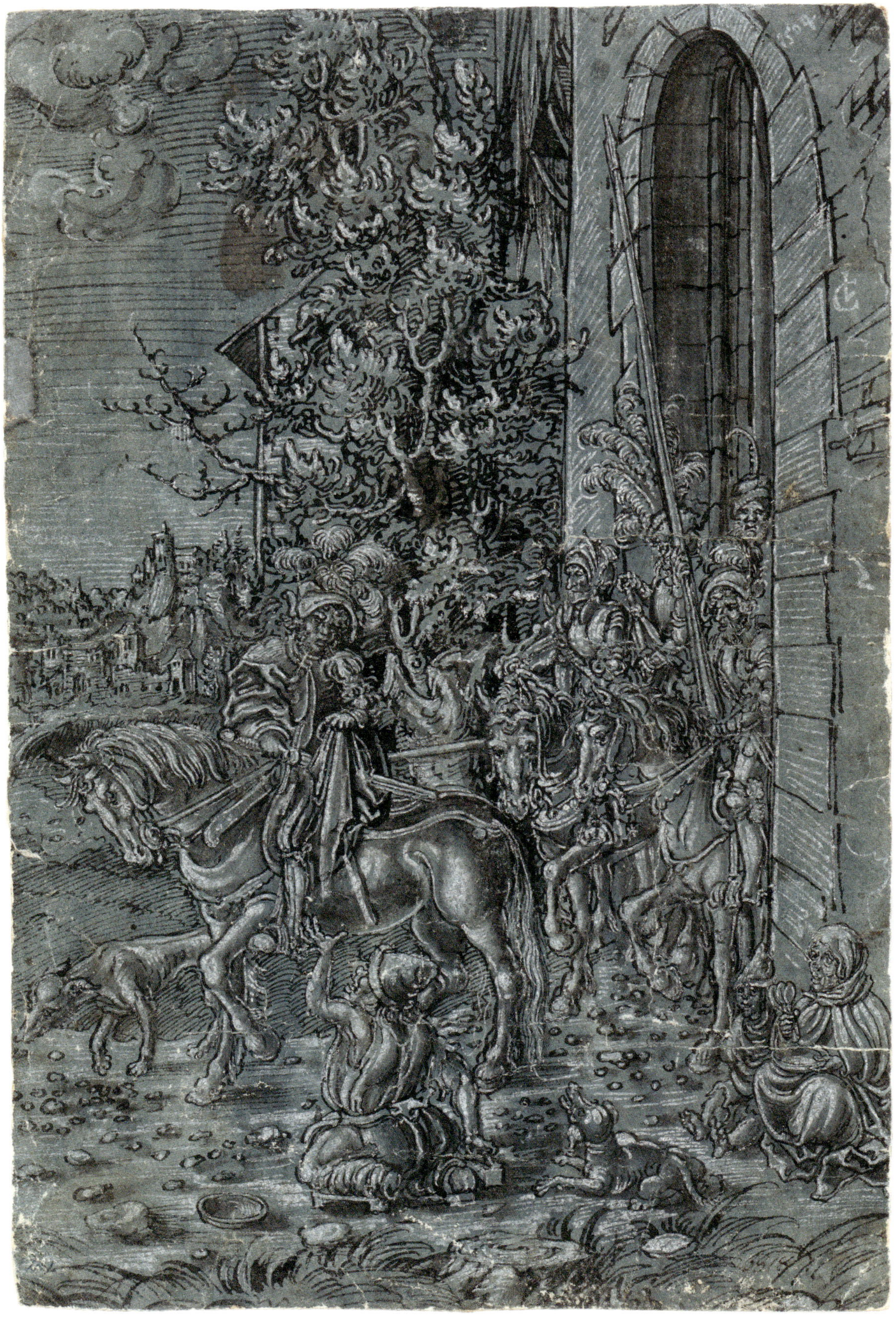

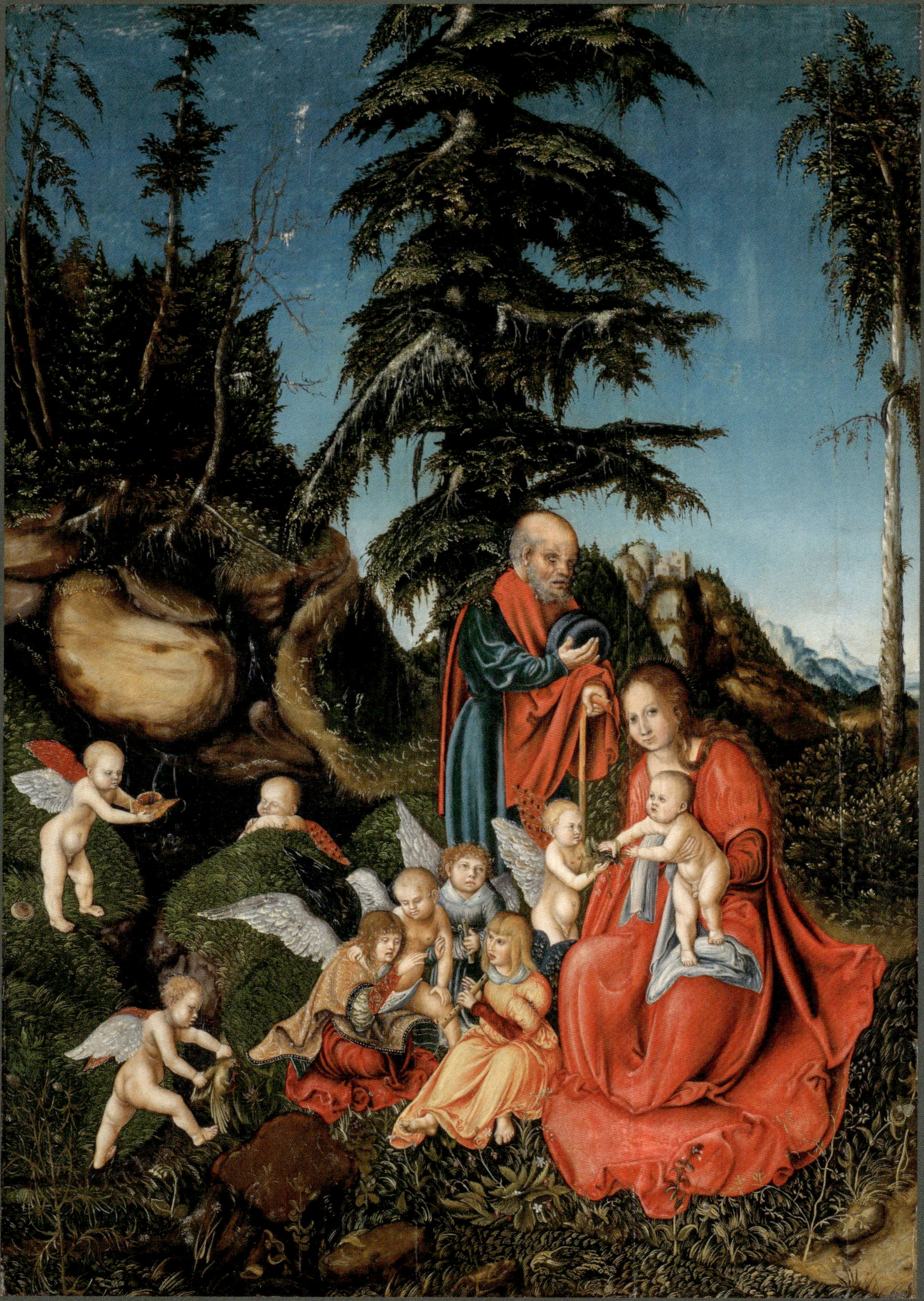

28

Lucas Cranach the Elder (workshop copy)

REST ON THE FLIGHT INTO EGYPT (THE HOLY FAMILY IN A LANDSCAPE)

circa 1515/20 (after the original of 1504 now in Staatliche Museen zu Berlin, Gemäldegalerie)
Kunsthistorisches Museum Vienna

"No other work shows the artist fresher and more fired-up than this one" – most Cranach scholars agreed with Hubert Janitschek's enthusiastic assessment of the master's *Rest on the Flight into Egypt,* painted in 1504, when it became more widely known in the late nineteenth century (fig.; see also essay Heiser, fig. 5):[1] this, Cranach's first dated and monogrammed painting, surprised with its originality and energy, which differentiate it from most of the works Cranach produced at Wittenberg. Only discovered around 1850 in an aristocratic collection in Rome, it was included in the epoch-making exhibition held at Dresden in 1899 and has been in Berlin since 1902; the panel provided the decisive impetus for the discovery of Cranach's Viennese works (see the essay by Sabine Heiser).[2] This faithful copy repeats the original's size, details and palette, and captures the charming mood that characterizes Cranach's invention.

We see the Holy Family in a wooded landscape, attended by bustling child angels and surrounded by countless symbolic references to the Virgin Mary and the Passion. The main impression is one of peaceful happiness, with nothing but the painting's title reminding us that they are not on a cheerful family outing but fleeing King Herod's henchmen.

This little-known copy in Vienna throws new light on the questions where Cranach painted the original dated 1504 now in Berlin, and when exactly he moved to Wittenberg to become court painter to the Elector of Saxony. He is first mentioned in the domains of his new master in early April 1505, shortly after receiving a payment from the ducal treasury at Nuremberg.[3] Clearly, we need to look for the copyist among Cranach's many contemporaries in Wittenberg, because the figures' plumper faces are similar to the workshop-manner that had evolved by, and had become obligatory for all artists employed there, around 1510. The panel's basic, linear underdrawing too is similar to other works produced by the workshop at Wittenberg, while peculiarities regarding its construction and underpainting indicate it dates from around 1515/20.[4] This suggests that the Berlin panel was somewhere in the domains of the Elector of Saxony in the early sixteenth century. Was it perhaps an early commission from Frederick the Wise? We should not forget that Matthias Gunderam, in his 1556 biography of Cranach, writes that Cranach was called to Saxony in 1504, so that this first documented use of a date and his signature/monogram on a painting may reflect his new status.[5] The lively impression of some of Dürer's recent works, manifested in a drawing of *St Martin* also dated 1504 (cat. 27), suggests too that the Berlin painting was not produced in Vienna but later in Nuremberg or during Cranach's journey to Saxony.[6] GM

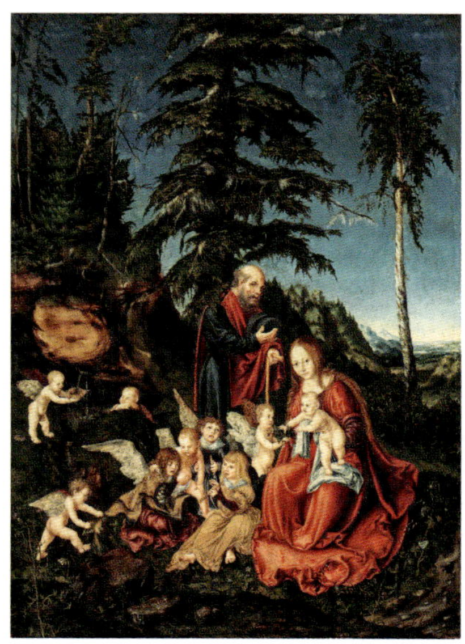

Lucas Cranach the Elder, *Rest on the Flight into Egypt,* 1504. Staatliche Museen zu Berlin, Gemäldegalerie

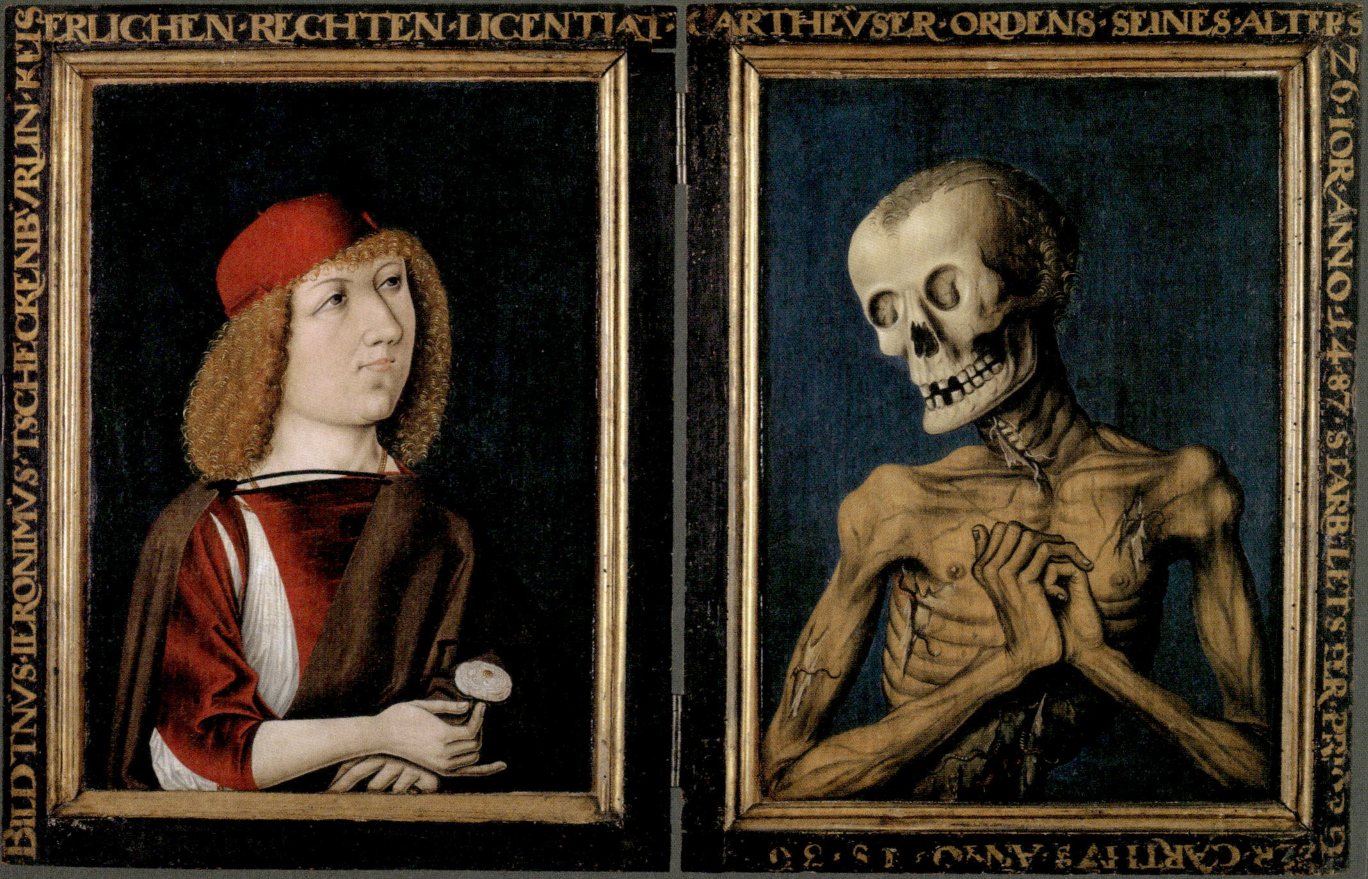
BILDTNVS·IERONIMVS·TSCHECKENBVRLIN·KEIS
ERLICHEN·RECHTEN·LICENTIAT·
CARTHEVSER·ORDENS·SEINES·ALTERS

29

Upper Rhenish master
HIERONYMUS TSCHECKENBÜRLIN AND DEATH (DIPTYCH)
1487
Kunstmuseum Basel

The sitter is unambiguously identified in the posthumous inscriptions on the original frame: "Bildtnus Ieronimus Tscheckenburlin Keiserlichen Rechten Licentiat" (portrait of Jerome Tscheckenburlin imperial law licentate) and "Cartheuser Ordens seines Alters 26 Jor anno 1487, starb letster Prior der Carthus anno 1536" (Carthusian friar aged 26 years in AD 1487, died the last prior of the Charterhouse in AD 1536). When the inscription was added the left frame was also replaced, which resulted in an altered lower moulding of the frame. The two panels of the diptych were connected with hinges and leather straps, and they could be closed and secured using a hook and eye.[1]

The dandy-like young sitter is shown in three-quarter view; the scion of an old and respected Basel family, he was born in 1461. As befits his elevated rank, he sports a purple-grey short cloak over a fashionably slashed velvet doublet from which a carefully pleated shirt peeks out. His fair hair is carefully curled. Turning slightly to the right and clutching a red rose (now faded to white), he is gazing adoringly at his companion. The portrait seems to be one part of a betrothal diptych, in which case we would expect a portrait of the blushing bride to face him in the panel on the right.

But instead of a comely young woman we see the torso of a decomposing cadaver, a *transi*, with leathery skin and rotting intestines crawling with worms. The corpse is wringing its hands in a somewhat *serpentinata*-like pose and turning to face the young man, which almost adds a comic note, especially as it contrasts with the young man's calm and collected demeanour. This strange *mesalliance* is actually based on biographical facts: after completing his law studies in Paris and Orleans, Hieronymus Tscheckenbürlin returned to his native city, where a glittering career awaited him. He, however, decided to abandon it to join the Charterhouse Margarethental, located on the right bank of the Rhine. Before Pentecost he had completed the move, celebrating it with a banquet and a procession to the monastery. The diptych documenting Tscheckenbürlin's decision must have been commissioned at this time, because reflecting on death and rejecting the world's superficial insincerities played a central role for his chosen order. The young aristocrat seems confident in his decision to marry Death. With its stark juxtapositioning of blooming life and the imploring, slightly pained *transi* the composition celebrates overcoming death rather than the triumph of the grim reaper. Not surprisingly, a number of parallels between the *transi's* stance and the Man of Sorrows have been pointed out: its inclined pose and folded arms support this allusion.[2] In the tradition of a *memento mori*, the portrait goes beyond this and the frequent depictions of skulls, skeletons, or *transis* on the reverses or covers of private portraits.[3]

Tscheckenbürlin lived for almost another fifty years. In 1501, he was elected prior of the charterhouse, and he was able to return to his monastery after being forced to flee for a short period of time during riots in the wake of the Reformation. A contemporaneous portrait that copies the composition depicts Tscheckenbürlin in a monk's habit after he had taken his perpetual vows.[4] The second portrait may have served as a template for his confreres. A change in the paintings' function into some kind of epitaph, connected with their installation near his tomb, seems likely.[5] They remained in the possession of the monastery's successor institution, the Bürgerliches Waisenhaus Basel, the city's orphanage. KR

30

Hans Schäufelein

PORTRAIT OF A MAN IN A RED CAP

circa 1505/06

Kunstmuseum Basel

Hans Schäufelein's (Upper Rhine, c.1482/83 – c.1540, Nördlingen) carefully executed half-length portrait of a middle-aged man presents the anonymous sitter in the usual three-quarter view. Despite the turned body, his torso appears flat and little differentiated, but the artist used hatching and subtle colour values to render his fastidiously painted features and emphasise his physiognomic peculiarities. Note the marked asymmetry of sculpted facial elements such as eyes, mouth and nose, and the animated silhouette of the left side of his face. Despite the psychological penetration, the sitter's gaze appears lost and distant.

There are but few hints to the anonymous sitter's personality. The rosary is part of the standard repertoire of props and merely suggests a general piousness. The red headdress from which flows his shoulder-length hair is, however, unusual – a sort of hat or close-fitting cap, similar to the one worn by Johannes Cuspinian in his portrait (cat. 12).

Placing the sitter before a central pier that interrupts the background landscape seen through the two flanking windows is unique in Schäufelein's oeuvre. We glimpse a pre-alpine landscape with tree-lined lake, castles on the shore of the lake and a near-by hill, and a blue-shimmering mountain range in the distance. The only human activity in this idyll is a small, unremarkable boat. The still, almost picturesque landscape reflects the sitter's character and defines his place in the world. Schäufelein employs a type of composition first introduced by Dieric Bouts in 1462 (see essay Richter, fig. 4) and quickly adopted in Franconia and southern Germany: placing the sitter next to an open window. The two views on either side of the pier can also be traced back to Early Netherlandish art.[1] In Schäufelein's portrait this architectural element adds vertical stability to the narrow-shouldered bust. The two windows are not identical – the left one has a straight lintel and a rectangular (if incorrectly foreshortened) opening, the right one a Roman arch.

Dürer used the same (though inverted) composition in his 1498 self-portrait now in Madrid (see essay Richter, fig. 7), but in his painting the Roman arch does not frame a second window. Here too he shows us a wide landscape, a motif typical of his early portraits.[2] Between c.1503 and 1507, Hans Schäufelein was employed in Dürer's workshop, and during this time he adopted many of the elements in his master's compositions. But the artists' psychological understanding of their sitters differs greatly, with Dürer's portraits exuding much more energy and physical presence.[3] This is one of the reasons why this portrait was attributed to Schäufelein as early as 1907.[4] The date was long disputed but 1505/06 is now generally accepted because of the painting's proximity to Dürer's work. KR

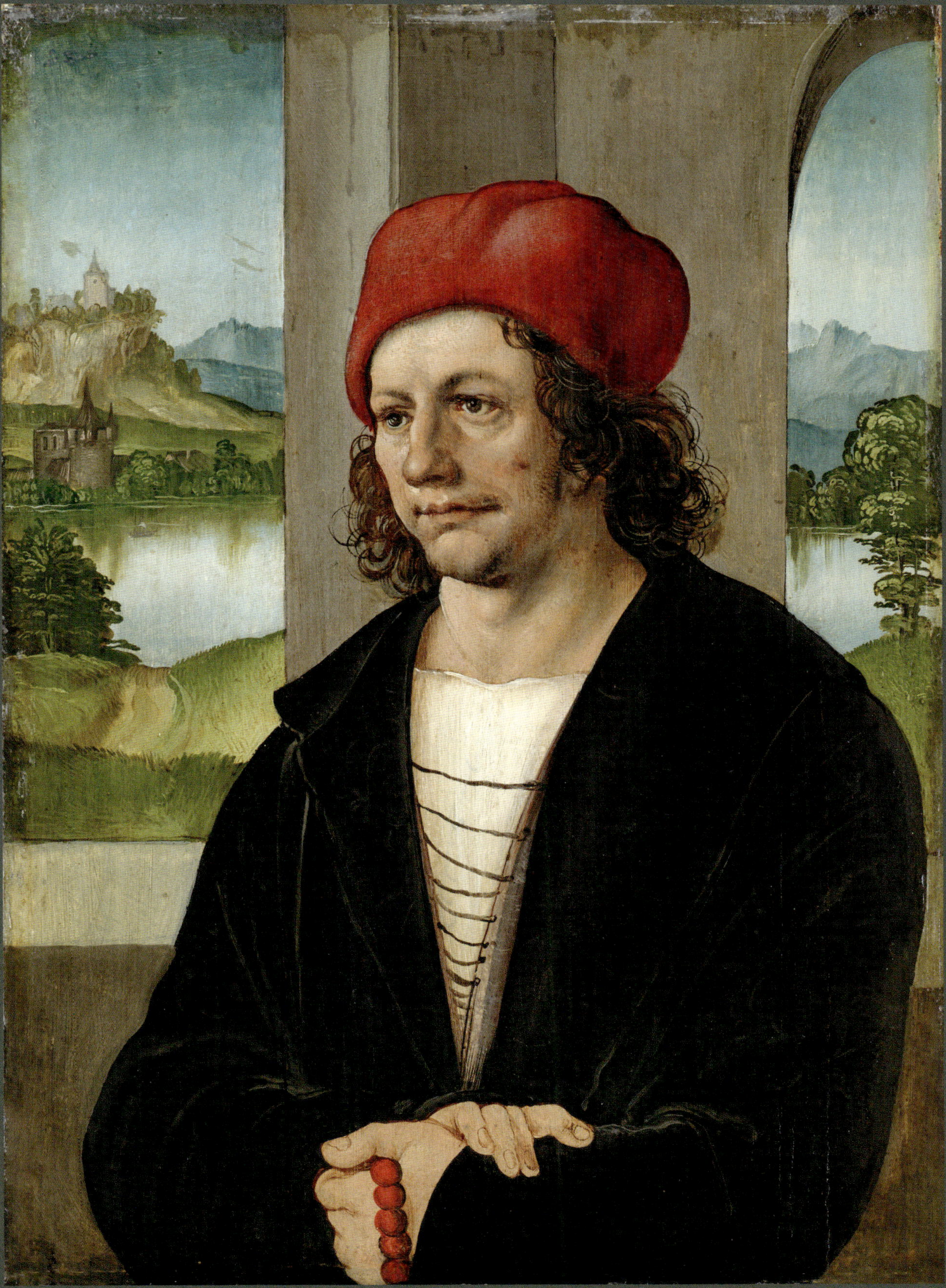

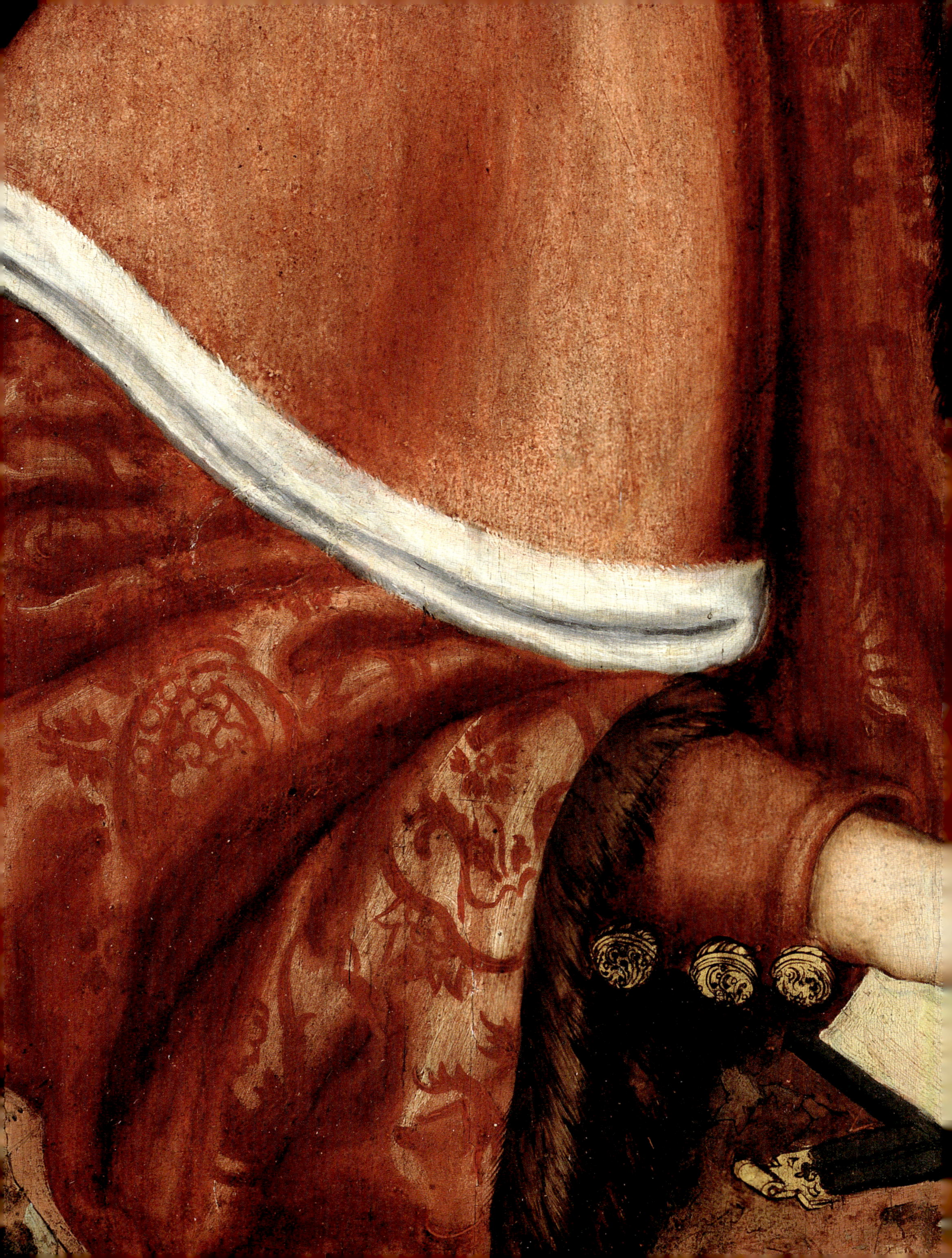

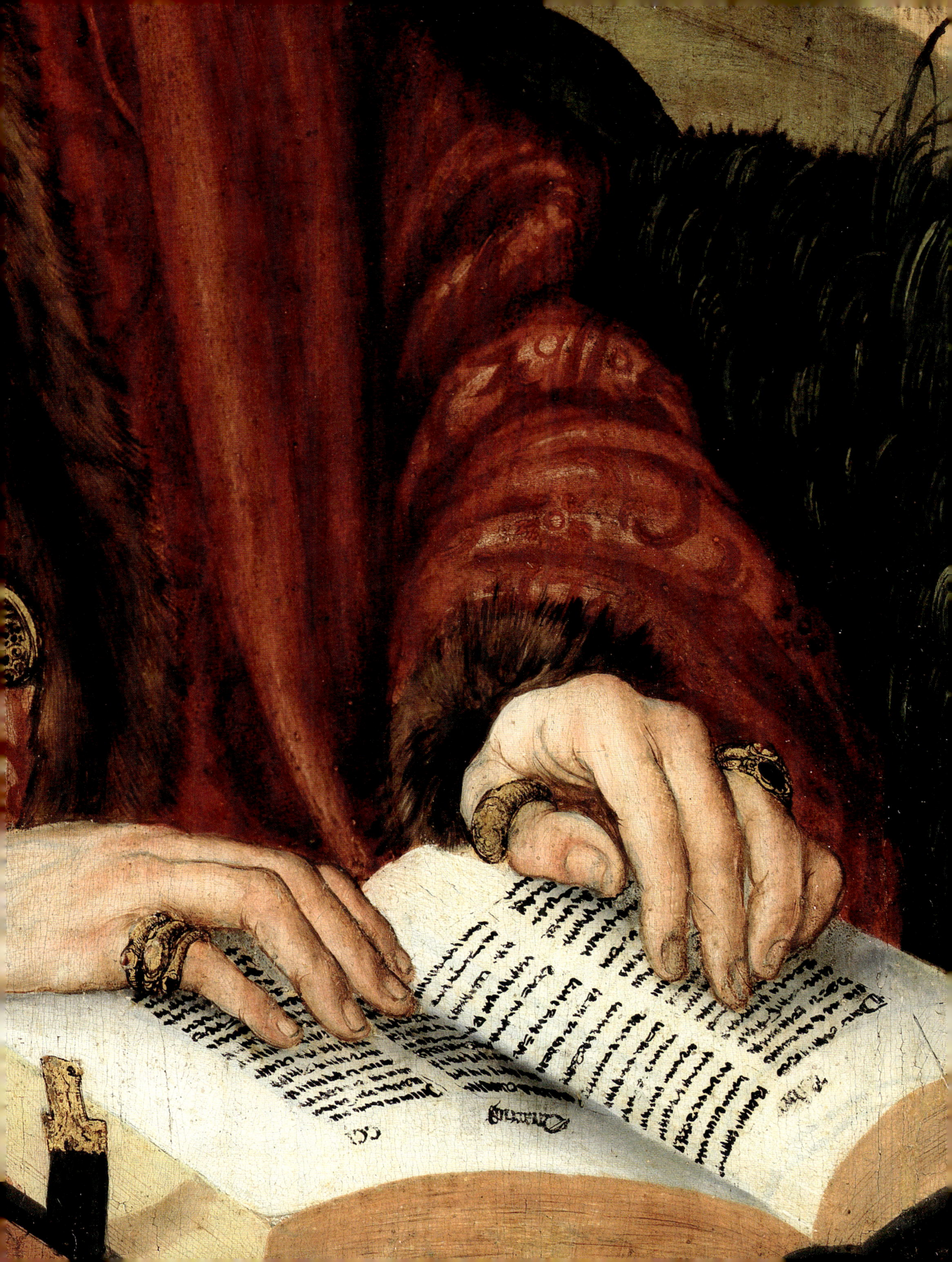

List of Works

1

Lucas Cranach the Elder
The Crucifixion of Christ
("Schotten Crucifixion")

circa 1500
Limewood, 58.2 × 45.9 cm
Kunsthistorisches Museum Vienna, Picture Gallery, inv. 6905

Provenance: Schottenstift, Vienna (first mentioned in a 1791 inventory as a work by "Luca van Leyden"); acquired by the Kunsthistorisches Museum in 1934

Bibl.: Friedländer & Rosenberg 1979, no. 1; Dörnhöffer 1904, col. 188–194, pl. III; Glaser 1921, 18–22, fig.; cat. Vienna 1972, no. 1, fig. 3; exh. cat. Basel 1974, 120, 124, 170, 443, 488; cat. Vienna 1991, 46, pl. 589; Bierende 2002, passim, fig. 1; Heiser 2002, passim, fig. 9; exh. cat. Frankfurt & London 2007/08, cat. 2 (Bodo Brinkmann); Suckale 2009, 91–96, fig. 96; exh. cat. Brussels & Paris 2010–11, cat. 5 (Guido Messling)

1 See the cat. Vienna 1994, nos. 14 (Heinrich Ferenczy) and 39 (Cornelia Reiter).
2 Clarus 1856, vol. 1, 23: "Sein Mund war geöffnet, seine Zunge blutig", (His mouth was open, his tongue bloody); see also vol. 3, 265 and vol. 4, 174. It is no accident that the reed with the sponge soaked in vinegar that Stephaton offers Jesus to sate his thirst points directly to his tongue (I would like to thank Karin Zeleny for drawing my attention to this detail).
3 See Groha 1995, 29.
4 Now Nuremberg, Germanisches Nationalmuseum. Most recently in cat. Nuremberg, vol. 1, no. 25 (Katja von Baum, Dagmar Hirschfelder).
5 Bierende 2002, 42–48; Suckale 2009, vol. 1, 34–53 with fig. 27 (*The Deposition*).
6 For this question see esp. Anzelewsky 1999, 125–134, who wants to trace all foreign-looking elements of the costumes to Polish templates. For a dissenting opinion, see Bierende 2002, 97–98.
7 Hind 1938–1948, vol. 11, no. 10, pl. 182.

2 & 3

Lucas Cranach the Elder
The Mount of Calvary

circa 1500
Woodcut, 399 × 285 mm
Staatliche Museen zu Berlin, Kupferstichkabinett, inv. 86-10

Lucas Cranach the Elder
The Mount of Calvary

Dated 1502 bottom right and marked with a house mark-like sign
Woodcut, 408 × 292 mm
Staatliche Museen zu Berlin, Kupferstichkabinett, inv. 87-10

Provenance: presumably acquired before 1876/77

Bibl.: Hollstein 1959, no. 26 (undated) and 25 (dated 1502); Flechsig 1900, 6–8, ills.; Friedländer 1902, 231–232, ills.; Glaser 1921, 21–24, ills.; exh. cat. Berlin 1973, cat. 64 and 63, ill. 33 (Frank Steigerwald); exh. cat. Basel 1974, cat. 63 and 62, ill. 58 (Dieter Koepplin); exh. cat. Kronach & Leipzig 1994, cat. 128 (Hollstein no. 25, Ursula Timann); Anzelewsky 1999, 125–133, ills. 1 and 2; Merback 1999, 11–15, 172, 176, 238, ills. 1, 2 and 79; Heiser 2002, 30, 32, 34, 85, 93–94, 111, ills. 7 and 8; exh. cat. Frankfurt & London 2007/08, cat. 6 and 7 (Bodo Brinkmann); exh. cat. Karlsruhe 2007/08, cat. 63 (Hollstein no. 25, Dietmar Lüdke); exh. cat. Brussels 2010, cat. 9 (Hollstein no. 25, Armin Kunz)

Cat. 2 exhibited in Vienna only, cat. 3 only in Winterthur

1 The man broken on the wheel in a woodcut with pilgrims at Altötting here attributed to Cranach (essay Messling, fig. 9) could almost be a precursor for this thief, as could the cadaver seen upside down.
2 Most recently exh. cat. Vienna 2017, cat. 16 (Björn Blauensteiner).
3 See Lehrs 1930, nos. 5 and 6. The two thieves in a Bavarian-Austrian crucifixion in Munich (Bayerisches Nationalmuseum) quote both engravings. For a photograph of the painting, see Weniger 2018, fig. 13.
4 See also Armin Kunz in exh. cat. Brussels 2010, cat. 9.
5 See Ursula Timann in exh. cat. Kronach & Leipzig 1994, cat. 128.

4 & 5

Lucas Cranach the Elder
The Penitent Thief on the Cross;
The Impenitent Thief on the Cross

circa 1500
Charcoal, heightened with white, on red prepared paper, 226 × 121 mm and 215 × 218 mm. Watermark (in KdZ 4450): high crown (arch consisting in two lines, bow without pearls, centered on chain line), presumably identical with Piccard-Online nos. 52261 (Bebenhausen 1498) and 52266 (Esslingen 1503, already showing wire losses)
Staatliche Museen zu Berlin, Kupferstichkabinett, invs. KdZ 4450 and 4451

Provenance: Fritz Bamberger Collection, Munich (1814–1873); auctioned at Munich (Montmorillon'sche Kunsthandlung und Auctions-Anstalt), 14 December 1878, lot 337 (as Hans Baldung Grien); Adalbert v. Lanna Collection, Prague; auctioned at Stuttgart (Gutekunst), 6–11 May 1910, lot 36 (as "in the style of Mathias Grünewaldt"), where it was acquired by the Kupferstichkabinett

Bibl.: Rosenberg 1960, cat. 2 & 3; Schönbrunner & Meder no. 1097; Friedländer 1908, 394; cat. Berlin 1921, 19, pl. 23; exh. cat. Berlin 1937, cat. 154 & 155; Girshausen 1937, 7–9, cat. 1 and 2; exh. cat. Berlin 1973, cat. 33 & 34, fig. 13 (KdZ 4450); exh. cat. Kronach & Leipzig 1994; cat. 123 (KdZ 4450, Ursula Timann); Heiser 2002, 26, 94, 102, 110–111, figs. 81 & 82; exh. cat. Frankfurt & London 2007/08, cat. 8 (KdZ 4450, Bodo Brinkmann); Hofbauer 2010, cat. 265 & 266

Exhibited in Vienna only

1 Vienna, Albertina, inv. 3005. Not in Rosenberg 1960, most recently as a Cranach in exh. cat. Düsseldorf 2017, cat. 167 (Christof Metzger).
2 I would like to thank Georg Josef Dietz from the Kupferstichkabinett Berlin for information on the paper and the water mark.

6

Lucas Cranach the Elder
The Penance of St Jerome

dated 1502 bottom centre
Limewood, 56 × 41.4 cm

Kunsthistorisches Museum Vienna, Picture Gallery, inv. 6739

Provenance: Mondsee Monastery, Mondsee; Episcopal Residence, Linz; acquired by the Kunsthistorisches Museum in 1927

Bibl.: Friedländer & Rosenberg 1979, no. 4; Fischer 1907, 71; Baldass 1928; cat. Vienna 1938, no. 1788; cat. Vienna 1958, no. 104, pl. 17; exh. cat. 1972, cat. 2, fig. 2; Koepplin 1973, 39; exh. cat. 1974. 121, 142, 443, 488; Schade 1974, 15, 17, pl. 8; cat. Vienna 1991, 46, pl. 589; Heiser 2002, passim, figs. 36 and 39; Heydenreich 2007, passim, fig. 81; exh. cat. Frankfurt & London 2007/08, cat. 3 (Bodo Brinkmann); exh. cat. Frankfurt & Vienna 2014/15, cat. 10 (Guido Messling); exh. cat. Düsseldorf 2017, cat. 2 (Daniel Görres); exh. cat. Innsbruck 2018; cat. 1; Endrődi 2018

1 Sadly, we cannot determine the species of these parakeets/parrots/macaws. At least the one in the portrait of Anna Putsch has merely changed the colours of its feathers compared to fellow members of its species (Ara tricolor), while the one in the *St Jerome* combines the body of a crow or a medium-sized bird of prey with a fantastic plumage. I would like to thank Swen Renner (Vienna, Natural History Museum) for information about these avian creatures. Endrődi 2018 identifies the two birds in the St Jerome panel as a phoenix and an owl and interprets them as symbols of day and night.
2 Schoch & Mende & Scherbaum, vol. 1, no. 6.

7/1–12

Lucas Cranach the Elder
The Twelve Depictions of the Months in the "Vienna Filocalus" (after unknown templates)

circa 1510
Pen and black and iron gall ink, grey wash (the first two drawings also delicately hand-coloured in red and green watercolour), on paper, 285 × 215 mm; later corrections executed with a brush in black ink and opaque white
The most important lines were traced with a graphite pen probably by Tobias Sadeler for his engravings included in Peter Lambeck's *Commentarii* published in 1671
Watermarks: Two slightly varying versions of a crown with high arch and cross. They appear 35 times in the first 70 sheets of the codex: version A (134 × 53 mm) 19 times (fol. 1, 3, 6, 14, 19, 20, 22, 24, 27, 28, 30, 33, 44, 47, 48, 59, 61, 66, 69), version B (134 × 56 mm) 16 times (fol. 4, 9, 13, 16, 31, 35, 37, 39, 40, 42, 52, 57, 58, 62, 68, 70). This mark is nearly identical with the Piccard-Online nos. 53421 and 53422 and can therefore also be found in papers used in Innsbruck in 1503. This conformity suggests Fuchsmagen only commissioned the texts on the calendar sheets after 1503.
Österreichische Nationalbibliothek, Vienna, Codex 3416 (fols. 2–13, each verso)

Provenance: Johannes Fuchsmagen (d. 1510); Johannes Cuspinian (d. 1529); Johann Fabri (d. 1541); Collegium apud Sanctum Nicolaum (1540); University Library; Imperial Library

Bibl.: Strzygowski 1888, 44–88, 100, 103; Herrmann 1923, 2–5; Nordenfalk 1936, 6–7; Winkler 1936; Byvanck 1940, 180; Stern 1953, 342–343; Rosenberg 1960, nos. A, A1a–f; exh. cat. Linz 1965, cat. 416; Jahn 1972, 170–183; exh. cat. Basel 1974, cat. 69, figs. 64 and 65 (Dieter Koepplin); Salzmann 1984, 43–50; Salzmann 1990, 71–72, 260–261; Heiser 2002, 61–73; Divjak 2002, 19–38; Koreny 2003, 558; Wood 2008, 85; Hofbauer 2010, 306–311, nos. 145–156; Burgess 2013, 359; Divjak & Wischmeyer 2014, 7–10, 61–64, 157–184; Fingernagel 2015, 129–133; Weidemann & Weidemann 2016, 29–30; Divjak 2020, 99

Exhibited in Vienna only

1 Divjak & Wischmeyer 2014, 157–185. The copy in the Vatican is the only one to include the architectural frame of the pictures, as well as the verses (*tetrasticha*) ascribed to the poet Ausonius (AD 310–395) that explain some of the content of the paintings. The January picture in the Vatican Codex is regarded as an invented "reconstruction" (Divjak & Wischmeyer 2014, 68–69, 157), which may, at least partially, also be true of the exceptional selection of motifs in the January picture in the copy now in Vienna.
2 Divjak & Wischmeyer 2014, 8.
3 It copies a woodcut which added an archway to the wall hangings in the Brussels copy of the *Filocalus* (Divjak & Wischmeyer 2014, 76–77, figs. 8–10). The woodcut was published together with the seven depictions of the months preserved in the Brussels copy in: Gilles Bouchier (Aegidius Bucherius), *In Victorii Aquitani Canonem Paschalem […]*, Antwerp 1633/34 (275, 279–280), URL: https://onb.digital/result/10486968 [retrieved on 30 August 2021]. Perhaps the frontispiece of the Vienna Filocalus was only produced after 1671, because, unlike the depictions of the months, it was not traced.
4 The outline of the buttocks was altered again in 1670/71 when it was traced with a stylus in preparation for producing an engraved copy.
5 See the zodiac sign Aquarius in the *Filocalus* copy Codex Vat. lat. 9135 (which lacks the depictions of the months), fol. 232r (Divjak & Wischmeyer 2014, 187, fig. 82).
6 Divjak & Wischmeyer 2014, 335. The quatrain (Tetrastichon) also mentions a knotted cloak and a purification sacrifice.
7 Codex Barberini lat. 2154, fol. 8r; Divjak & Wischmeyer 2014, 110, fig. 33.
8 The other copies feature three triton's horns (left) and three other marine creatures (right) – in Brussels it is an octopus, in Berlin and in the Vatican it resembles a jellyfish. A second marine creature can be identified as a squid, a third as an eyed electric ray. The latter can only be identified in the Vatican copy by its typical five points; in Berlin the five points are missing. In Brussels, the draughtsman – clearly not familiar with this fish – added the head of a fowl. See Divjak & Wischmeyer 2014, 140 (fig. 50a), 142 (fig. 52–53), 143 (fig. 54).
9 Divjak & Wischmeyer 2014, 332–340.
10 Ibid., 335.
11 Ibid., 8.
12 *Publii Ovidii Nasonis Fastorum libri Sex diligentissime recogniti; Addito Calendario Romano, venerandae vetustatis, nunquam antea impresso*, Vienna 1513 (Österreichische Nationalbibliothek, Vienna, Sign. 44.R.63). The same printer produced Cuspinian's bookplate (cat. 14).
13 We are planning a comprehensive publication outlining the results, presented here for the first time, of the analyses carried out in connection with a research project led by Martin Wagendorfer and financed by the FWF, in which the scientific analyses will be discussed in detail. These analyses were carried out by Katja Sterflinger, Federica Cappa, Dubravka Jembrih-Simbürger (Akademie der bildenden Künste), Christa Hofmann (Österreichische Nationalbibliothek), and Simon Brenner (Technical University Vienna).
14 Rosenberg 1960, 34; Jahn 1972, 170–171. Non-art historical scholarship

generally places the draughtsman in Nuremberg, see Burgess 2012, 359; Divjak & Wischmeyer 2014, 51; Divjak 2020, 99.
15 Winkler 1936, 155.
16 Ibid., 146, 155.
17 For this drawing, see Rosenberg 1960, no. 19, and Hofbauer 2010, no. 12; for the woodcut, see Hollstein 1959, no. 3.
18 Rosenberg 1960, nos. 15 and 16; Hofbauer 2010, nos. 15 and 16.
19 Munich, Bayerische Staatsbibliothek, 2 L.impr.membr. 64, fols. 57v and 61v.
20 Other examples are the unnatural goat's head in March (fol. 4v), and the hare in October (fol. 11v). The latter is still informed by the type of hares in Albrecht Dürer's woodcut *The Holy Family with three Hares* produced around 1497 (Schoch & Mende & Scherbaum, vol. 2, no. 108).

8

Lucas Cranach the Elder
A Foolish Virgin

circa 1503
Brush and pen in black ink, with grey wash, heightened with white, on ochre prepared paper, 191 × 121 mm.
Watermark: fragment of a pair of scales in a circle; the diameter of the circle (39.5 mm) and the distance between the chain lines (29 mm) could be identical to Briquet no. 2485 (Sibiu 1503–06; Brno 1504–05) or Piccard-Online no. 117412 (Linz 1506).
The back features collectors' notes and the stamps Lugt no. 5084 (Aufseß), and Lugt no. 1076 (Germanisches Nationalmuseum), and traces of a charcoal sketch of a figure of which only the outlines of their head with curly hair, a hand, and fragments of the drapery can be distinguished.
Germanisches Nationalmuseum, Nuremberg, Department of Prints and Drawings, inv. Hz 56

Provenance: Hans Freiherr von und zu Aufseß (1801–1872), founder of the Germanisches Nationalmuseum

Bibl.: Rosenberg 1960, 15, no. 1; Bock 1929/30, 71; Benesch 1936, 51; exh. cat. Berlin 1937, cat. 156; Girshausen 1937, 61–62, no. 3; Thöne 1939, 8; cat. Nuremberg 1968, no. 116; Jahn 1972, 6, 32; exh. cat. Basel 1974, 131–132, cat. 70 (Dieter Koepplin); exh. cat. Nuremberg 1992, cat. 30; exh. cat. Kronach & Leipzig 1994, cat. 122 (Ursula Timann); Heiser 2002, 114–115, fig. 86; exh. cat. Brussels 2010, cat. 10 (Guido Messling); Hofbauer 2010, 86–87, no. 9

Exhibited in Vienna only

1 I would like to thank Roland Damm (Germanisches Nationalmuseum, Nuremberg) for the photograph of the watermark and for pointing out the mark Briquet no. 2485, and Erwin Frauenknecht (Hauptstaatsarchiv Stuttgart) for drawing my attention to the mark Piccard-Online no. 117412.

9 & 10

Lucas Cranach the Elder
The Stigmatisation of St Francis

circa 1502/03
Spruce wood, 86.5 × 47.5 cm
Dendrochronological analysis of the support established it dates from after 1475 (age and type of wood determined by Michael Grabner, Universität für Bodenkultur Vienna, Department of Materials Sciences and Process Engineering, analysis carried out on 28 September 2021).
Belvedere, Vienna, inv. 1273

Provenance: acquired in 1912 in Lemberg (Lwiw) (from Ladislaus Ritter von Wiktor)

Bibl.: Friedländer & Rosenberg 1979, no. 3; Grimschitz 1921; Eigenberger 1927, 89–90; Benesch 1928, 94–95; exh. cat. Berlin 1937, cat. 3; exh. cat. Munich 1938, cat. 390; exh. cat. Vienna 1939, cat. 183; exh. cat. St. Florian & Linz 1965, cat. 27; Hutter 1972, 4–6; exh. cat. Basel 1974, cat. 86, pl. 4 (Dieter Koepplin); Heydenreich 1998, 185–186; Rosenauer 2003, no. 248; Stadlober 2006, 175–177; exh. cat. Frankfurt & London 2007/08, cat. 5 (Bodo Brinkmann); Heydenreich 2007, 47, 52, 55–58, 95–97, 99, 102, 117–118, 195f., 298; Messling 2021, 124 (cat. 27)

Lucas Cranach the Elder
St Valentine with a Donor

circa 1502/03
Spruce wood, 91.5 × 49.5 cm
Gemäldegalerie der Akademie bildenden Künste Wien, inv. GG-549

Provenance: Bequest of Count Lamberg-Sprinzenstein, 1822 (as a Wolgemut)

Bibl.: Friedländer & Rosenberg 1979, no. 2; Scheibler 1887, 296, note 1; Dörnhöffer 1904, 180, fig. pl. IV; Eigenberger 1927, 88.89; exh. cat. Berlin 1937, 13, cat. 2; exh. cat. Basel 1974, cat. 85, pl. 3 (Dieter Koepplin); Hutter 1972, 4–5, fig. 2; Trnek 1997, 64; Rosenauer 2003a, no. 248; exh. cat. Frankfurt & London 2007/08, cat. 4 (Bodo Brinkmann); Heydenreich 2007, 47, 52, 55–59, 95–97, 99, 102, 110, 117–118, 195–196; Stadlober 2006, 173–175; Messling 2021, 124

Exhibited in Vienna only

1 Bonaventura 1874, 114–116 (chapter 13/1–3).
2 Schoch & Mende & Scherbaum 2001–2004, vol. 2, no. 134.
3 Another example of this tradition of canonical depictions is the tympanum relief over the south-west entrance of the Minoritenkirche in Vienna from the mid-fourteenth century; see Ginhart 1955, 72–73.
4 Valentine is the first of the three patron saints of the Diocese of Passau; his feast day in 7 January, see https://www.bistum-passau.de/bistum-pfarreien/bistumspatrone [retrieved on 24 Oct. 2021].
5 LCI, vol. 8, col. 529–530.
6 Stadlober 2006, 175.
7 Perger 1988, 175 (no. 74).
8 Wiesflecker 1996, 125 (no. 9588), 128 (no. 9606).
9 Wiesflecker 1996, 487 (no. 12207).
10 Scheibler 1887, 296, note 1.
11 Dörnhöffer 1904, 180.
12 "Österreichische Schule aus dem Beginn des XVI. Jahrhunderts (der Kunst Wolfgang Hubers nahestehend)"; historical archive of the Belvedere, file no. 1912/0384.
13 Heydenreich 2007, 95, 110, 117–118.
14 Heydenreich 1998, 185–186; Heydenreich 2007, 57.
15 Koller 1994, 193. For the ensemble dated 1469 on one of the panels, see the essay by Björn Blauensteiner, 29, fig. 3.

11

Lucas Cranach the Elder (?)
Portrait of a Beardless Young Man

before or around 1500
Reverse: 16th cent. inscription: "Ant°[n] Neypaurer handt / soll Albrecht dürer sein / wie er Jung ist gewest" (Anton Neypaurer hand / said to be Albrecht Dürer / as a young man); 17th cent. inscription: "die Handt

vom Newpauer" (the hand of Newpauer)
Spruce wood, 46 × 33 cm
Hessische Hausstiftung, Kronberg

Provenance: Nuremberg, Praun'sches Kabinett; Prince Wilhelm of Prussia (after 1801); inherited by his daughter Princess Elisabeth of Prussia (after 1851); Louis IV, Grand Duke of Hesse and by Rhine; Ernest Louis, Grand Duke of Hesse and by Rhine (after 1937); Margaret, Princess of Hesse and by Rhine (after 1968); Hessische Hausstiftung Kronberg (after 1997)

Bibl.: Buchner 1953, 146–147, 213, no. 167, fig. 168; exh. cat. Nuremberg 1971, cat. 75 (Peter Strieder); exh. cat. Basel 1974, 164–166, cat. 91, fig. 81 (Dieter Koepplin); Anzelewsky 1999, 134–137; Heiser 2002, 121; Koepplin 2003, 127–130; exh. cat. Frankfurt & London 2007/08, cat. 10 (Bodo Brinkmann); exh. cat. Vienna & Munich 2011, cat. 58 (Thomas Kuster)

Exhibited in Winterthur only

1 Master of the Life of the Virgin, *Portrait of a Scholar*, c.1480, Karlsruhe, Staatliche Kunsthalle; Hermen Rode, *Portrait of a Praying Man*, c.1485–90, Milan, Pinacoteca di Brera. See Buchner 1953, nos. 9 and 27.
2 For a similar handling of hands, see *Portrait of the Wife of a Jurist*, 1503 (cat. 16). For the folds of the drapery, see the *Stigmatisation of St Francis*, 1502/03 (cat. 9).
3 First suggested by Strieder (in exh. cat. Nuremberg 1971), and Anzelewsky 1999. In a similar vein, Brinkmann (in exh. cat. Frankfurt & London 2007/08), and Kuster (in exh. cat. Vienna & Munich 2011). For a dissenting viewpoint, see Buchner 1953, and Koepplin 1974 and 2003.

12 & 13

Lucas Cranach the Elder
Marriage Diptych of Dr Johannes Cuspinian and Anna Cuspinian-Putsch

1502/03
Pine wood, each 60 × 45 cm
Oskar Reinhart Collection "Am Römerholz", Winterthur, inv. 1925.1

Provenance: collection of Charles I, King of England; the Locker-Lampson family, England; Baron of Sandys, England; art dealers A.-G., Lucerne; Julius W. Böhler; Oskar Reinhart (from 1925); Oskar Reinhart Collection "Am Römerholz" (from 1965)

Bibl.: Friedländer & Rosenberg 1979, nos. 6–7; Friedländer 1926; Buchner 1953, 165–167, 218, nos. 189–190, fig. 190 and 191; Ankwicz-Kleehoven 1959, 30–34; Koepplin 1973; exh. cat. Basel 1974, 121, 130, 142, 160–168 (Dieter Koepplin); Schade 1974, 15, 17–18.; Dülberg 1990, cat. 39, figs. 445–449; Hinz 1993, 9–11; Heiser 2002, 119–122 et passim, figs. 16 and 17; cat. Winterthur 2003, no. 6 (Dieter Koepplin); Stadlober 2006, 180–197, figs. 36 and 37; Borggrefe 2007; Endrődi 2018a

1 The badly-damaged alliance coat of arms is a dimidiated shield party per pale on the left an arm clutching a pike, a crest with the torso of a beardless man in a red cap (*barett*) with a caduceus, and on the right a wild man clutching a miner's pick with both hands, which is also an element of the crest.
2 Dülberg 1990, 62–63.
3 Koepplin 1973, 129–130.
4 Koepplin 1973, 121.
5 See, for instance, the poem addressed to Blasius Hölzel, in which he claims to have received both gifts – the ability to compose poems and to heal the sick – from Apollo: "Ne vatem medicumque tuum, rogo, Cuspinianum / Spernas, cui Phoebus munus utrumque dedit", quoted in Koepplin 1973, 128.
6 Ankwicz-Kleehoven reads the fire as the influence of Mars on Anna Cuspinian's horoscope; Borggrefe identifies the scene as both cleansing and as the conflagration of Troy with Creusa. For Koepplin the cleansing influence of fire dominates the interpretation, as it does for Stadlober. Schade identified all four elements, as does Endrődi. See Ankwicz-Kleehoven, 1959, 33; Borggrefe, 2007, 30–31; Koepplin 1973, 117–118, 198–202; Stadlober 2006, 185; Schade 1974, 18; Endrődi 2018, 210–211.
7 According to Sick 1984, it is most likely a scarlet macaw (*Ara macaw*), which has yellow upper wing coverts. Other ornithologists have suggested it is a now extinct Ara tricolor (see note 1 in cat. 6).
8 In his contribution on the *St Jerome* in Vienna, Endrődi 2018, 92, refers to Lactantius's elegy *De ave Phoenice* and believes the birds are identical.
9 Thomas von Cantimpré, *De natura rerum* 5, 6, written 1225–1241, ed. by Boese 1973, 180; Konrad von Megenberg, *Buch der Natur*, III, vol. 3, written 1348–1350, ed. by Luff & Steer 2003, 196.
10 See, for example, the Master E.S., *The Garden of Love (Large Plate)*, engraving, second third of the fifteenth century, or Michael Wolgemut's *Portrait of Levinus Memminger*, c.1485, now in Madrid (it depicts a fight between falcons, without a heron).
11 Koepplin 1973, 219–246, refers to the ambivalence inherent in depictions of owls, which can function as symbols of persecuted wisdom, the melancholic temperament with both positive and negative properties, and the personification of evil. Endrődi 2018a, 216, emphasises the superiority of the pursuing diurnal birds.
12 For an interpretation of the star as that of the Magi, see Koepplin 1973, 154–163; he references the hymns of Aurelius Prudentius, who emphasised Christ's importance as the bringer of light and the star of Bethlehem, which Cuspinian edited and published in 1494. For an interpretation of the second appearance of Apollo in the shape of the sun, see Endrődi 2018a, 221–225, who refers to the odes of Celtes and an illustration of *Carmen elegiacum de Apolline et novem Musis* (1503).
13 Ankwicz-Kleehoven 1959, 32–33, combines this interpretation with a reading of both paintings as the sitters' horoscopes, with the melancholic Cuspinian under the influence of Saturn. The star is here interpreted as Saturn himself. A similar interpretation in Stadlober 2006, 191–192, who identifies all seven planets in the painting, and references Celtes's *Carmen saeculare* of 1500 as a seminal source for the motifs.

14

Anonymous artist (after Lucas Cranach the Elder)
Bookplate of Johannes Cuspinian

circa 1510/15
Woodcut, image 131 × 94 mm, top and below typographic text; size of the stained sheet with a large central tear and a large loss top right: 200 × 138 mm
Above the woodcut: "CVSPINIANVS, VT FVRES SI POSSET, AR / CEAT. HIC SVAM IMAGINEM LOCAVIT." (Cuspinian has, in order to discourage thieves, if possible, placed his portrait here); below the woodcut: "Hinc compesce manum, ne fur dicaris, ab illa / Quae ueri faciem pagina reddit Heri" (remove your hand if you do

not want to be called a thief, from this page, which shows the face of the real owner)
Österreichische Nationalbibliothek, Vienna, in: Cod. Suppl. gr. 45

Provenance: Johannes Cuspinian; Johannes Alexander Brassicanus; Johann Fabri; Collegium Nicolai (Fabri Foundation Collegium trilingue); University Library; Imperial Library

Bibl.: Stiebel 1894, 112; Ankwicz-Kleehoven 1927, 230, note 4; Rathe 1940, 54; Panofsky 1942, 382–383; Benzing 1959/60, 180–181; Burger 1969, 7–8; Koepplin 1973, 142–143, 183; Lang 1971, 33–34; Treier 1986, 20–22; Mertens 1994, 76–77; Mossakowski 2007, 111–112

Unfortunately, we were not able to obtain this work for the exhibition.

1 The Graces' allegorical ballgame can be traced back to Seneca (*De beneficiis*, I, 3). See Mertens 1994, 76–77.
2 Today, this copy is believed lost; it was sold at auction together with the Striebel Collection in 1910. See auction catalogue Boerner 1910, 7, lot 56.
3 In 1513, Vietor also printed the lists of the feast and court days from the *Vienna Filocalus* (cat. 7).
4 VD 16, H 3283. The coarse handling may be compared to a woodcut that Winterburger began to use for title pages in 1509, and that copies Cranach's *St Stephen* woodcut of 1502 (cat. 22), e.g. in the *Missale Pataviense* of 1509; VD 16, M 5610.

15 & 16

Lucas Cranach the Elder
Marriage-Diptych of a Jurist and his Wife

1503
Inscription at the top of the male portrait: "1503 | VIXI·AN[NNOS]·41 [1503. I have lived for 41 years]"
Pinewood, 54,1 × 39 cm, 52,6 × 36,7 cm
Germanisches Nationalmuseum Nuremberg, inv. Gm207
Staatliche Museen zu Berlin, Gemäldegalerie, inv. 1907

Provenance:
Male portrait: Prince Sulkowski Collection, Feistritz near Vienna; acquired by the Germanisches Nationalmuseum Nuremberg in 1889
Female portrait: Collection of the Princes of Schwarzburg-Rudolstadt, Heidecksburg Palace in Rudolstadt; art market, Berlin; acquired by the Gemäldegalerie Berlin in 1923

Bibl.: Friedländer & Rosenberg 1979, nos. 8 and 9; Buchner 1953, 164–165, 217–218, nos. 187 and 188, figs. 188 and 189; Koepplin 1973, 266–277; exh. cat. Basel 1974, 164, cat. 88 (male portrait, Dieter Koepplin); Rebel 1994, 131–132; exh. cat. Nuremberg 1997, 123–126; Heiser 2002, 123–127 et passim, figs. 3 & 4; exh. cat. Frankfurt & London 2007/08, cat. 9 (male portrait, Bodo Brinkmann); Heydenreich 2007, 190–192, 213, 227; exh. cat. Düsseldorf 2017, cat. 3 (male portrait, Gunnar Heydenreich)

Unfortunately, we were not able to obtain either of these two paintings for the exhibition.

1 Koepplin 1973, 270. Until 1534, only unmarried men could become rector of Vienna University.
2 Holste 2004, 50.
3 Cranach used the "sgraffito" technique for the brocade pattern, i.e. he scratched the design into the still-wet paint (Heydenreich 2007, 192).
4 X-ray images show that the book initially rested on his lap; the marble parapet was subsequently painted over parts of his overgown (Heydenreich 2007, 213).
5 Heiser 2002, 124–125.

17

Lucas Cranach the Elder (copy)
Portrait of Hieronymus Tedenhamer (Tettenhammer)

first half of the 16th century (after a lost original from 1503)
Top left the Tettenhammer family coat of arms, to right inscribed: "Im Jar 1503 ist zu wienn / abkunnderfecht worden / Ieronimus Tedenhamer" (AD 1503 at Vienna, / was portrayed / Hieronymus Tedenhamer)
Limewood, 55.2 × 57 cm (incl. frame) or 47.2 × 38.8 cm (painted panel)
Kunsthistorisches Museum Vienna, Picture Gallery, inv. 9107

Provenance: acquired by the Kunsthistorisches Museum from Frederick Mont, New York, in 1951, together with two paintings by Jan Siberechts (inv. 9106) and Rubens's workshop (inv. GG 9108), in exchange for a painting by Paolo Veronese (formerly inv. GG 3674, now National Gallery, Washington, D.C.)

Bibl.: Schaffran 1957, 206, fig. p. 205; cat. Vienna 1958, 35, no. 105; Stange 1966, 24, fig. 13; Koepplin 1973, 33–34; exh. cat. Basel 1974, 168, cat. 94, fig. 85; Koepplin 1977b, 14; Stievermann 1994, 66, fig. A 37; Heiser 2002, 128–129, fig. 102; Heydenreich 2007, 337 (note 1), 363 (note 92), 405

1 Written opinions, excerpts in the files of the Picture Gallery of the Kunsthistorisches Museum Vienna.
2 For the coat of arms, see Siebmacher 1873, 34, pl. 57 (as "Teltenhammer", 1560 in Regensburg).
3 Biographical information in Pölnitz 1940, col. 222; Lanzinner 1980, 322.
4 Reindl 1977, cat. A 104 (reproduced).
5 Only Stange identified it as a work by Jörg Breu the Elder, but the painter had already left Austria in 1502 to return to Augsburg.

18

Portrait Codex of Hieronymus Beck von Leopoldsdorf

circa 1570/80
Codex comprising 320 sheets of paper with 240 body colour miniatures measuring ca. 275 × 183 mm; dimensions of the codex: 52.7 × 38.5 cm (incl. leather cover when closed)
Kunsthistorisches Museum Vienna, Picture Gallery, inv. 9691

Provenance: acquired around 1600 by Archduke (later Emperor) Matthias (1557–1619) and incorporated into the imperial library; entered Count Lamberg's collection housed at Ottenstein Castle in Bratislava before 1900; acquired by the Kunsthistorisches Museum Vienna in 1973

Bibl.: Heinz 1975 (on the Portrait Codex), for the two miniatures, see 178, 296–298, cat. 216 and 217, figs. 189, 428 and 429; Koepplin 1977b; Löcher 1979, 20–22, fig. 9; Heiser 2002, 129–131; exh. cat. Vienna 2003, cat. 3.31 (Karl Schütz)

1 At an early date, a number of portraits of Oriental personages were separated from the rest of the collection and are now bound with Codex 8615 in the

Österreichische Nationalbibliothek, Vienna, see Stichel 1999.
2 See Löcher 1979, 20, figs. 10 and 11.

19

Lucas Cranach the Elder
Portrait of a Woman Praying
reverse: *St Catherine*

circa 1508
Oak wood, 43 × 33 cm
Kunsthaus Zürich, inv. 1643 (on loan to the Kunstmuseum Basel)

Provenance: Rudolf Chillingworth Collection, Nuremberg; sold at auction in Lucerne (Galerie Fischer), 5 Sept. 1922, lot 42, acquired by August Abegg (1861–1924); Abegg's heirs donated it to the Zürcher Kunstgesellschaft (i.e. the Kunsthaus Zürich) in 1925

Bibl: Friedländer & Rosenberg 1979, no. 27; Schade 1974, 54, fig. 62; exh. cat. Basel 1974, cat. 595, figs. 334 and 336 (Dieter Koepplin); Heydenreich 2007, 48–49, figs. 24 and 332, note 49; exh. cat. Frankfurt & London 2007/08, cat. 13 (Bodo Brinkmann); exh. cat. Brussels & Paris 2010/11, cat. 61 (Guido Messling); exh. cat. Düsseldorf, cat. 69 (Benjamin D. Spira)

Exhibited in Winterthur only

1 See Heydenreich 2007, 332, note 49, and Guido Messling in exh. cat. Brussels 2010, cat. 60–61.
2 For more on Cranach's journey to the Netherlands, see Koepplin 2003, 58–69, and Borchert 2010.
3 Borchert 2010, 28.

20

Lucas Cranach the Elder (?)
Lovers at a Fountain, in the Distance Death Clutching a Scythe

1503
Pen and brown ink, with a hand-drawn frame executed in brown ink, on paper, 274 × 207 mm
Top right in the sky dated in brown ink: "1503"; below in lighter-brown ink: "AD" (later false Dürer monogram)
Herzog Anton Ulrich-Museum, Brunswick, Kupferstichkabinett, inv. Z 59

Provenance: old holdings, entered the collection before 1878

Bibl.: cat. Brunswick 1922, pl. 10; cat. Brunswick 1955, no. 59; Koepplin 1972, 347–348; exh. cat. Basel 1974, 149–156, cat. 78, fig. 73 (Dieter Koepplin); exh. cat. Berlin & Regensburg 1988, cat. 215; cat. Brunswick 1992/1997, vol. 1, pl. 42, vol. 2, 275–276; Heiser 2002, 34, fig. 5

Exhibited in Winterthur only

1 For more details on the fountain, see Mielke in exh. cat. Berlin & Regensburg 1988, 330.
2 This is why Koepplin (in exh. cat. Basel 1974, 150) talks of an "anti-garden of love" compared to earlier depictions of lovers.
3 See, for instance, Dürer's engraving *The Promenade* (c.1498). He also employed a similar composition in his engraving *The Ill-Matched Couple* (c.1495), but without the presence of Death.
4 Koepplin (exh. cat. Basel 1974, 152) references, for instance, the "*Schleissheim Crucifixion*" of 1503.
5 Dieter Koepplin in exh. cat. Basel 1974, 149–156. Before this, the work was regarded as "southern German".

21

Lucas Cranach the Elder
Landsknecht and Young Lady

circa 1505
Woodcuts, each 242 × 89 mm, printed on a single sheet of paper
signed bottom centre: "LC"
Staatliche Museen zu Berlin, Kupferstichkabinett, inv. 748-2

Bibl.: Hollstein 1959, no. 109; Jahn 1972, no. 81, 378; exh. cat. Basel 1974, cat. 21, fig. 20 (Dieter Koepplin); Heiser 2002, 83; exh. cat. Brussels & Paris 2010/11, 132, see cat. 48 (Guido Messling)

Exhibited in Winterthur only

1 In his *Naturalis Historia* (27, 55), Pliny writes that ferns can cause stillbirths and make women infertile; this is also included in the *Hortus Sanitatis*, of which several editions were published from 1491 onwards. This is why ferns were commonly used as a form of contraceptive (in the German vernacular they were called "hurenwurz", i.e. whores' roots); Aigremont 1909, 20. I would like to thank Karin Zeleny for this information.
2 Compare, for example, Cranach's painting *The Martyrdom of St Catherine* (c.1508/09, Friedländer & Rosenberg 1979, no. 11).
3 Woodcut: Hollstein 1959, no. 110; drawing: Rosenberg 1960, no. 19.
4 See exh. cat. Brussels & Paris 2010/11, cat. 48 (Guido Messling).
5 Heiser 2002, 83.
6 Heiser 2002, 83, she also references Wood 1993, 71.

22

Lucas Cranach the Elder
St Stephen

1502 (dated bottom left in the tree-like frame)
Woodcut, image 218 × 148 mm, sheet 330 × 250 mm
Österreichische Nationalbibliothek, Vienna, in: 22.B.17 Alt-Rara (*Missale Pataviense*, Vienna, Johannes Winterburger 1503), fol. Iv

Provenance: Vienna, entered the imperial library from a monastery, presumably the Dominican monastery St Maria Rotunda (ownership remark on fol. 298v)

Bibl.: Hollstein 1959, no. 89; Dodgson 1903, 284–285, figs.; Koepplin 1973, 231–232, note 680; exh. cat. Basel 1974, cat. 50 (Dieter Koepplin); Zykan 1975, 3–5; Koreny 2003, 561–562 (cat. 299); exh. cat. Brussels 2010, cat. 11 (Armin Kunz); exh. cat. Frankfurt & Vienna 2014/15, 172, cat. 90 (Christof Metzger)

Substituted exhibit on show in Winterthur: Österreichische Nationalbibliothek, Vienna, in: 229552-D. Alt-Rara (Missale Pataviense, Vienna, Johannes Winterburger 1512), fol. Iv

1 See the relevant remarks in my essay.
2 See, for instance, the hand-coloured copies in Munich, Bayerische Staatsbibliothek, and Amsterdam, Rijksmuseum (see exh. cat. Brussels 2010, cat. 11 [Armin Kunz]). Koepplin 1973 and others consider the possibility that the woodcut was (also) sold individually or as a single print, like, for example, the impression in Vienna, Albertina (not hand-coloured); see exh. cat. Frankfurt & Vienna 2014/15, cat. 90 (Christof Metzger).

3 GW M 24617; ISTC im00683000.
4 Schoch & Mende & Scherbaum 2001–2004, vol. 2, no. 140 (Bernd Mayer).
5 Armin Kunz (in exh. cat. Brussels 2010, cat. 11) suggests a possible connection between these monsters and St Stephen, to whom Catholics appealed to ward off evil spirits.
6 Oswald 1953, 83–84.
7 VD 16 H 3284. The 1502 edition (VD 16 H 3282) contains a scene depicting the saint's martyrdom.

23

Lucas Cranach the Elder
Calendar Disk to Calculate the Dominical Letter

circa 1502/03
Woodcut, image 160 × 150 mm
Österreichische Nationalbibliothek, Vienna, in: 22.D 23 Alt-Rara (*Missale Olomucense*, Vienna, Johannes Winterburger 1505), fol. [7v]

Bibl.: not mentioned in Hollstein 1959 – Dörnhöffer 1904, 182; Langer & Dolch 1913, 27; Gollob 1936, 84–85; Zykan 1965, 45–46; Koepplin 1973, 234–235.; exh. cat. Basel 1974, cat. 65 (Dieter Koepplin); Heiser 2002, 80–81, fig. 42; Endrődi 2018

Exhibited in Winterthur only

1 In, for example, the *Breviarium Pataviense* for 27 November 1490 (GW 5426; ISTC ib01175100), or in the *Breviarium Augustanum* for January 1493 (GW 5266; ISTC ib01146950), see exh. cat. Augsburg 2017, cat. 55 (Helmut Zäh). For the *Ratisbon Breviary* see GW 5435; ISTC ib01177000 (I would like to thank Guido Messling for drawing my attention to this).
2 See Endrődi in exh. cat. Innsbruck 2018, 88–91 incl. a picture of the manuscript.
3 For more on a possible contentual connection with the initial *Saturn devouring his children,* see cat. 26.

24 & 25

Lucas Cranach the Elder
The Crucifixion of Christ (canon illustration)

before 1502 (?)
Woodcut, hand-coloured, image 215 × 153 mm, sheet 268 × 177 mm
Albertina, Vienna, inv. DG 1927/128

Lucas Cranach the Elder
The Crucifixion of Christ (canon illustration)

circa 1502/03
Woodcut, hand-coloured, image 215 × 150 mm, sheet 310 × 200 mm
Vienna, Österreichische Nationalbibliothek, in: 22.B.15 Alt-Rara (*Missale Pataviense*, Johannes Winterburger, Vienna 1503), so-called *Karstner Missal,* fol. [145v]

Bibl.: Hollstein 1959, nos. 28 (only known as individual prints) and 29 (in the *Missale Pataviense* 1503); Dodgson 1903, fig.; Beth 1907; Gollob 1926, 16–17; exh. cat. Basel 1974, cat. 64 (Hollstein no. 29, Dieter Koepplin); Heiser 2002, 52, 80–82 and 94–95, figs. 13, 14, 62 and 63; exh. cat. Brussels 2010, cat. 12 (Hollstein no. 29, Armin Kunz); exh. cat. Düsseldorf 2017, cat. 7 (Hollstein no. 26, Daniel Görres)

Exhibit substituted for cat. 25 in Winterthur: Österreichische Nationalbibliothek, Vienna, in: 14861-C.Alt-Rara (Missale Salisburgense, Vienna, Johannes Winterburger 1506), fol. [157v]

1 For the dating, see Heiser 2002, 94–95.
2 Cracow, Jagiellonian Library, Ink. 2850 (GW M 24359; ISTC im00658100). See Schade 1974, 14; Heiser 2002, notes 605 and 607.
3 Daniel Görres in exh. cat. Düsseldorf 2017, cat. 7.
4 For more on this, see Heiser 2002, 95; exh. cat. Brussels 2010, cat. 12 (Armin Kunz). A monochrome print is in the Kupferstichkabinett Berlin (inv. 84-1929).
5 Stelzhammer 1836, 98–99. For example, we can precisely date the colouring of the crucifixion woodcut in the Kupferstichkabinett Basel (1508); see exh. cat. Basel 1974, cat. 64, fig. 59 (Dieter Koepplin).
6 Heitz 1910, no. 40; Schreiber VIII 1930, no. *398c.
7 Langer & Dolch 1913, no. 70, list a second canon illustration included in this missal, a woodcut dated 1514 that has survived, for instance, in London, British Library, 3395.ee.16.
8 The dating of the *Missale defunctorum* to around 1500 by, for example, Schreiber 1930, VIII, no. *398c, is now generally rejected; there are certain similarities between Cranach's crucifixion in the 1503 missal and this print in the way the landscape background is handled.

26

Lucas Cranach the Elder
Initials

circa 1502/1503
Woodcuts (printed in red), 60 × 52 mm (f1r), the remainder 45 × 40 mm
Österreichische Nationalbibliothek, Vienna, in: 22.B.14 Alt Rara (*Missale Pataviense*, Vienna, Johannes Winterburger 1503), fols. 1r, 11v, 17r, 87v, 101v, 106v, 112v, 113v, 114v, 184v, 252v, 271v

Bibl.: Beth 1907, 510–512; Langer & Dolch 1913, 22–25; Gollob 1941; Gollob 1964; Zykan 1965, 46–47; Zykan 1967; Koepplin 1973, 231–236; exh. cat. Basel 1974, cat. 66, fig. 168a (Dieter Koepplin); Heiser 2002, 80–83, figs. 43–54; Endrődi 2018

Not exhibited

1 Heiser 2002, 81, conflates the initials as a "second series of vegetative initials".
2 Koepplin 1973, 233–235; for more on the connection between chronologies and depictions of Saturn, see Schramm 1935, fig. 409; for a contrary view, see Endrődi 2018, 94, see note 13.
3 Zykan 1967, 39–41, fig. 11 among others; Heiser 2002, 80–81, 95.
4 Zykan 1967, figs. 10, 17 among others.
5 Exh. cat. Linz 1965, cat. 431–436; Zykan 1967.
6 Zykan 1967, 43–44, fig. 37; see also Heiser 2002, 82, figs. 56 and 57.

27

Lucas Cranach the Elder
St Martin and the Beggar

1504
Pen and black ink, greyish-brown wash and heightened with white, on bluish-green prepared paper, 155 mm × 125 mm monogram "LC" and date 1504 to the right of the archway, both executed with a white brush
Staatliche Graphische Sammlung Munich, inv. 36 Z

Provenance: from Prüfening Monastery/Regensburg; entered the Königliches Zeichnungs- und Kupferstichkabinett in Munich in 1807

Bibl.: Rosenberg 1960, no. 5; Dörnhöffer 1904, col. 185–186; exh. cat. Berlin 1937, cat. 157; exh. cat. Munich 1938, cat. 394; exh. cat. Basel 1974, 112–114, cat. 53, fig. 48 (Dieter Koepplin); Schade 1974, 50, pl. 23; exh. cat. Berlin & Regensburg 1988, cat. 217; exh. cat. Kronach & Leipzig 1994, cat. 124 (Ursula Timann); exh. cat. Brussels & Paris 2010/11, cat. 13 (Guido Messling); Dietz & Messling 2017, 69, fig. 1 (detail)

Exhibited in Winterthur only

1 Schoch & Mende & Scherbaum, vol. 2, no. 174.
2 See Dietz & Messling 2017, 69.
3 See Hans Mielke in exh. cat. Berlin & Regensburg 1988, 19.
4 See also Kunz 2010, 84–85, and Savage & Stijnman 2017.

28

Lucas Cranach the Elder (workshop copy)
Rest on the Flight into Egypt (The Holy Family in a Landscape)

circa 1515/20 (after the original of 1504 now in Berlin, Staatliche Museen, Gemäldegalerie)
Limewood, 71.9 × 50.9 cm
Kunsthistorisches Museum Vienna, Picture Gallery, inv. 3561

Provenance: possibly identical with the painting "Maria mit dem Kindl, dorbey viel Engl" (Mary and Child, with many angels) listed in the Prague Inventory A of 1648 (Dudík 1867, XXXVIII, no. 77); first verifiably mentioned in the Prague inventory of 1718 as "Maniera Luca Cranich: Unsere Liebe Frau sambt dem Kind, sanct Joseph und etliche engeln" (in the manner of Lucas Cranach: Our Lady and Child, with Joseph and many angels; Köpl 1889, CXXXVII, no. 379); removed from Prague to Vienna in 1890

Bibl.: cat. Vienna 1896, gallery no. 1463; Frimmel 1899, 596; exh. cat. Vienna 1972, cat. 33; exh. cat. Berlin 1973, see cat. 1 (Wilhelm Köhler); Heydenreich 2007/08, 40

Exhibited in Vienna only

1 Janitschek 1890, vol. 3, 491, folding pl. between 490 and 491. For the painting (Staatliche Museen zu Berlin, Gemäldegalerie, inv. 564 A, limewood, 70.9 × 53 cm), see Friedländer & Rosenberg 1979, no. 10; Heiser 2002, 32 and 111–119, figs. 1, 83–85.
2 Exh. cat. Dresden 1899, cat. 1.
3 Lang & Neugebauer 2015, document no. 1; Gurlitt 1895, 113 (without a date).
4 This date is suggested by Ute Tüchler's technological analyses of the panel; the results of her analyses will be published in the forthcoming catalogue raisonné of German Painting before c.1540 in the Kunsthistorisches Museum Vienna.
5 Facsimile of the biography in exh. cat. Wittenberg 2011, 58–61, here: 59.
6 First suggested by Flechsig 1900, 252, with reference to the payment Cranach received from Nuremberg. Without knowing about its older Prague provenance, Köhler saw the copy in Vienna as confirmation that Cranach painted the panel now in Berlin during his sojourn in Vienna (see exh. cat. Berlin 1973, see cat. 1).

29

Upper Rhenish master
Hieronymus Tscheckenbürlin and Death (diptych)

1487
Inscriptions on the frames, left: "BILDTNVS·IERONIMVS·TSCHECKENBVRLIN·KEISERLICHEN·RECHTEN·LICENTIAT"; right: "CARTHEVSER·ORDENS·SEINES·ALTERS·26·IOR·ANNO·14.87·STARB·LETSTER·PRIOR·DER·CARTHVS·ANNO·15·36"
Limewood, left panel: 40 × 28.5 cm (incl. frame: 48.5 × 38 cm), right panel: 40.5 × 29 cm (incl. frame: 48.5 × 37.5 cm)
Kunstmuseum Basel, Depositum of the Bürgerliches Waisenhaus 1907, inv. 33

Provenance: Charterhouse Margarethental Basel, Bürgerliches Waisenhaus Basel; 1907 Depositum of the Bürgerliches Waisenhaus in the Kunstmuseum Basel

Bibl.: Buchner 1953, 20, 59–60, 193, no. 49, fig. 8; Ringbom 1965, 47; cat. Basel 1966, 36, ill.; Dülberg 1990, 70, 90, 121, 250–251, no. 214, fig. 270; Geelhaar 1992, figs. 10, 37; exh. cat. Basel 2006, cat. 4

Exhibited in Winterthur only

1 See Dülberg,1990, 250.
2 Ringbom 1965, 47.
3 A particularly poignant coeval example is the *Bridal Couple*, painted around 1470 by a southern German master (The Cleveland Museum of Art) and its reverse which features two *transis* (Strasbourg, Musée de l'Oeuvre Notre-Dame), see Buchner 1953, no. 197.
4 Upper-Rhenish master, *Diptych of Hieronymus Tscheckenbürlin*, shortly before 1487, Basel, Historisches Museum. The reverse also depicts a skull, with a serpent wriggling though its cheekbones.
5 Reference in Dülberg 1990, 70.

30

Hans Schäufelein
Portrait of a Man in a Red Cap

circa 1505/06
Limewood, 42,5 × 31,5 cm (cropped left, right, and top)
Kunstmuseum Basel, inv. 1243

Provenance: Helbing Auctioneers, Munich or Frankfurt; Bachofen Collection, Basel; incorporated into the Öffentliche Kunstsammlung Basel in 1920, together with the J.J. Bachofen-Burckhardt Foundation

Bibl.: Burckhardt 1907, 19, no. 15, pl. 15; cat. Basel 1966, 63; exh. cat. Basel 1974, 166, cat. 92 (Dieter Koepplin); Weih-Krüger 1986, 60–63; Metzger 2002, 71–72, 105-106, 225–227, no. 6, fig. 159; exh. cat. Basel 2019, 250, fig. p. 31

Exhibited in Winterthur only

1 Petrus Christus, *Portrait of a Young Man*, 1460, London, The National Gallery, and Master of the Legend of Saint Ursula (Bruges), *Portrait of Ludovico Portinari*, c.1470, Philadelphia Museum of Art.
2 Examples are, for instance, the *Portrait of Elsbeth Tucher*, 1499, Kassel, Staatliche Kunstsammlungen, the diptych of *Hans and Felicitas Tucher*, 1499, Kunstsammlungen Weimar (vista seen through a cloth of honour), and the *Portrait of a Young Woman with Pinned-up Hair*, 1497, Berlin, Gemäldegalerie (vista seen through a side window).
3 This is especially true of the *Portrait of Oswolt Krel*, 1499, Munich, Alte Pinakothek.
4 Burckhardt 1907, 19, no. 15, pl. 15.

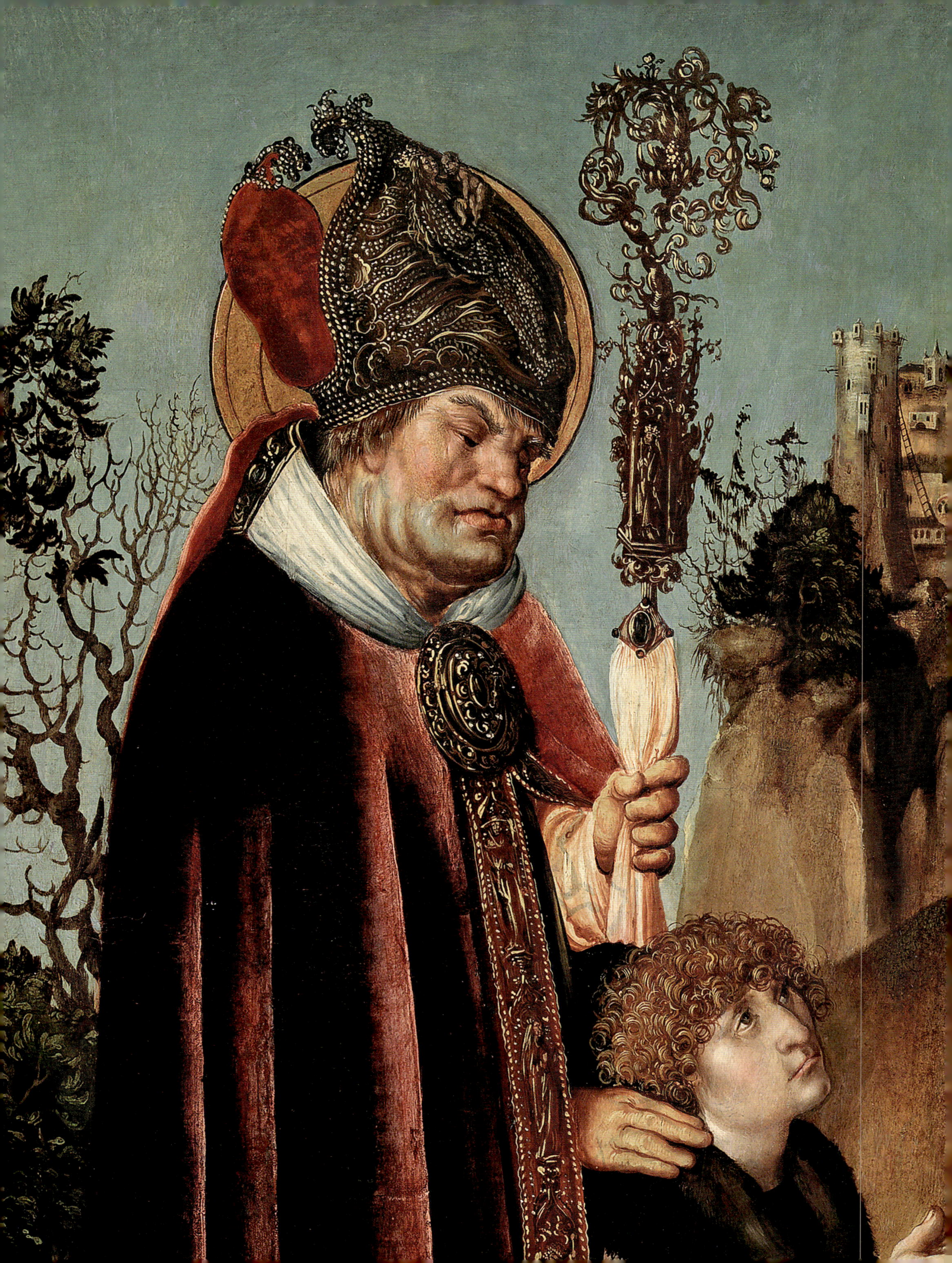

Bibliography

Aigremont 1909
Dr. Aigremont [= Siegmar von Schultze-Galléra], *Volkserotik und Pflanzenwelt*, vol. 2, Halle n.y. [1909]

Alberti 1435/2000
Leon Battista Alberti, *De Pittura* (1435), in: Bätschmann & Schäublin 2000

Alberti 1540
Leon Battista Alberti, *De Pictura Praestantissima, et Nunquam satis laudata arte libri tres absolutissimi*, Basel (Thomas Gechauff) 1540

Albrecht 1997
Claudia F. Albrecht, *Stilkritische Studien zum mittleren Werk des Veit Stoß, unter besonderer Berücksichtigung der Volckamer-Stiftung*, Würzburg 1997

Ankwicz-Kleehoven 1922
Hans Ankwicz-Kleehoven, *Lucas Cranach in Wien*, in: Alt-Wiener Kalender, 1922, 58–65

Ankwicz-Kleehoven 1927
Hans Ankwicz-Kleehoven, *Cranachs Bildnisse des Dr. Cuspinian und seiner Frau*, in: Jahrbuch der Preußischen Kunstsammlungen 48, 1927, 230–234

Ankwicz-Kleehoven 1937
Hans Ankwicz-Kleehoven, *Das Exlibris des Matthäus Heuperger*, in: Österreichisches Jahrbuch für Exlibris und Gebrauchsgraphik 32, 1937, 1–6

Ankwicz-Kleehoven 1959
Hans Ankwicz-Kleehoven, *Der Wiener Humanist Johannes Cuspinian, Gelehrter und Diplomat zur Zeit Maximilians*, Graz & Cologne 1959

Anzelewsky 1971
Fedja Anzelewsky, *Albrecht Dürer. Das malerische Werk*, Berlin 1971

Anzelewsky 1999
Fedja Anzelewsky, *Studien zur Frühzeit Lukas Cranachs d.Ä.*, in: Städel-Jahrbuch N.F. 17, 1999, 125–144

Auction catalogue Boerner 1910
C. G. Boerner, *Auktions-Katalog der Sammlungen des in Frankfurt a/M. verstorbenen Herrn Heinrich Eduard Stiebel: Exlibris, alter Buchschmuck, Druckerzeichen, Buntpapiere, Gelegenheitsdrucke, Wunsch- und Besuchskarten, Handbibliothek für Exlibris- und Bücherkunde, kostbare Einbände, Bibliothek, Buchkunst des XV.–XX. Jahrhunderts, z.T. aus dem Besitz eines Berliner Bibliophilen; Versteigerung: Montag bis Sonnabend, den 21.–26. November 1910 (Katalog Nr. 101)*, Leipzig 1910

Bätschmann & Schäublin 2000
Oskar Bätschmann & Christoph Schäublin (eds.), *Das Standbild. Die Malkunst. Grundlagen der Malerei*, Darmstadt 2000

Baldass 1928
Ludwig von Baldass, *Cranachs büßender Hieronymus von 1502*, in: Jahrbuch der Preußischen Kunstsammlungen 19, 1928, 76–81

Bauer 1964/65
Robert Bauer, *Das Büchlein der Zuflucht zu Maria. Altöttinger Mirakelberichte von Jacobus Issickemer*, in: Ostbairische Grenzmarken, vol. 1964/65, 206–236

Baumgärtel-Fleischmann 1968
Renate Baumgärtel-Fleischmann, *Bamberger Plastik von 1470 bis 1520*, in: Bericht des Historischen Vereins für die Pflege der Geschichte des ehemaligen Fürstbistums Bamberg 104, 1968, 5–353

Belting 2013
Hans Belting, *Faces. Eine Geschichte des Gesichts*, Munich 2013

Belting & Kruse 1994
Hans Belting & Christiane Kruse, *Die Erfindung des Gemäldes. Das erste Jahrhundert der Malerei*, Munich 1994

Benesch 1928
Otto Benesch, *Zur Altösterreichischen Tafelmalerei. I: der Meister der Linzer Kreuzigung; II: die Anfänge Lucas Cranachs*, in: Jahrbuch der Kunsthistorischen Sammlungen in Wien 2, 1928, 63–118

Benesch 1930/32
Otto Benesch, *Der Meister des Krainburger Altars*, in: Wiener Jahrbuch für Kunstgeschichte 7, 1930, 120–200; 8, 1932, 17–68

Benesch 1936
Otto Benesch, *Österreichische Handzeichnungen des 15. und 16. Jahrhunderts*, Freiburg i.Br. 1936

Benzing 1959/60
Josef Benzing, *Das Exlibris Cuspinians, ein Werk des Hans Sueß von Kulmbach?*, in: Das Antiquariat. Zeitschrift für alle Fachgebiete des Buch- und Kunstantiquariats 15, 1960, no. 9/10, 180–181

Beth 1907
Ignaz Beth, *Zu Cranachs Missalien-Holzschnitten*, in: Repertorium für Kunstwissenschaft 30, 1907, 501–513

Beyer 2002
Andreas Beyer, *Das Porträt in der Malerei*, Munich 2002

Bierende 2002
Edgar Bierende, *Lucas Cranach d.Ä. und der deutsche Humanismus. Tafelmalerei im Kontext von Rhetorik, Chroniken und Fürstenspiegeln*, Munich & Berlin 2002

Blauensteiner 2021
Björn Blauensteiner, *Die Kunst der Dürerzeit in Österreich. Zu den Anfängen der Renaissance in der österreichischen Kunst*, in: exh. cat. Vienna 2021/22, 26–49

Bock 1929/30
Elfried Bock, *A Foolish Virgin*, in: Old Master Drawings 4, 1929/30, 71

Boehm 1985
Gottfried Boehm, *Bildnis und Individuum. Über den Ursprung der Porträtmalerei in der italienischen Renaissance*, Munich 1985

Boese 1973
Helmut Boese (ed.), *Thomas Cantipratensis: De natura rerum*, Berlin & New York 1973

Bonaventura 1874
Chrysostomus Johannes Bonaventura, *Leben des hl. Franziskus von Assisi. Aus dem Lateinischen übersetzt*, Regensburg et al. 1874

Borchert 2010
Till-Holger Borchert, *Cranach der Ältere in den Niederlanden*, in: exh. cat. Brussels & Paris 2010/11, 26–29

Borges 1952
Jorge Luis Borges, *El idioma analítico de John Wilkins*, in: *Otras Inquisiciones (1937–1952)*, Buenos Aires 1952, engl. translation by Lilia Graciela Vázquez, URL:https://ccrma.stanford.edu/courses/155/assignment/ex1/Borges.pdf [retrieved: 10 Feb. 2022]

Borggrefe 2007
Heiner Borggrefe, *Cranachs Cuspinian-Bildnisse neu interpretiert*, in: Tacke 2007, 15–41

Bredekamp 2008
Horst Bredekamp, *Der Künstler als Verbrecher. Ein Element der frühmodernen Rechts- und Staatstheorie*, Munich 2008

Brilliant 1991
Richard Brilliant, *Portraiture*, London 1991

Buchner 1953
Ernst Buchner, *Das deutsche Bildnis der Spätgotik und der frühen Dürerzeit*, Berlin 1953

Buck & Messling 2009
Stephanie Buck & Guido Messling, *Zeichnen vor Dürer – Eine Einführung*, in: Dickel 2011, XI–XX

Büttner 2018
Nils Büttner, *Die Kunst aus der Natur reißen. Natur und Landschaft bei Lucas Cranach d.Ä.*, in: exh. cat. Innsbruck 2018, 143–151

Burckhardt 1907
Rudolf F. Burckhardt, *Katalog der Gemäldesammlung von Frau Prof. J.J. Bachofen-Burckhardt*, Basel 1907

Burger 1969
Heinz Otto Burger, *Renaissance, Humanismus, Reformation. Deutsche Literatur im europäischen Kontext*, Bad Homburg & Berlin & Zurich 1969

Burgess 2013
Richard W. Burgess, *The Chronograph of 354: Its Manuscripts, Contents, and History*, in: Journal of Late Antiquity 5/2, 2013, 345–396

Byvanck 1940
Alexander Willem Byvanck, *Antike Buchmalerei III. Der Kalender vom Jahre 354 und die Notitia dignitatum*, in: Mnemosyne 8/3, 1940, 17–198

Campbell 2005
Lorne Campbell, *Memling und die Tradition der altniederländischen Malerei*, in: exh. cat. Madrid & Bruges & New York 2005, 48–67

Cárdenas 2021
Livia Cárdenas, *The Texture of Images. The Printed Relic-Book within the Context of Late Medieval Religiosity*, Boston 2021

Celtis 1937
Konrad Celtis, *Libri Odarum Quattuor*, ed. by F. Pindter, Leipzig 1937

Clarus 1856
Ludwig Clarus (ed.), *Leben und Offenbarungen der heiligen Brigitta*, 4 vols., Regensburg 1856

Csendes 2001
Peter Csendes, *Geschichte Wiens im Mittelalter. Vom späten 14. Jahrhundert bis zur Ersten Wiener Türkenbelagerung (1529)*, in: Csendes & Opll 2001, 145–198

Csendes & Opll 2001
Peter Csendes & Ferdinand Opll (eds.), *Wien. Geschichte einer Stadt*, vol. 1, Vienna et al. 2001

Csendes & Opll 2021
Peter Csendes & Ferdinand Opll (eds.), *Wien im Mittelalter. Zeitzeugnisse und Analysen*, Vienna & Cologne 2021

Dickel 2011
Hans Dickel (ed.), *Zeichnen vor Dürer. Die Zeichnungen des 14. und 15. Jahrhunderts in der Universitätsbibliothek Erlangen*, Petersberg 2011

Dickel 2018
Hans Dickel (ed.), *Zeichnen in Cranachs Werkstatt. Die sächsischen Zeichnungen der Renaissance in der Universitätsbibliothek Erlangen*, Petersberg 2018

Didi-Huberman 1999
Georges Didi-Huberman, *Für eine Anthropologie der formalen Eigenheiten. Bemerkungen zu Warburgs Erfindung*, in: Ilsebill Barta-Fliedl & Christoph Geissmar-Brandi & Naoki Sato (eds.), exh. cat. *Rhetorik der Leidenschaft. Zur Bildsprache der Kunst im Abendland. Meisterwerke aus der Graphischen Sammlung Albertina und aus der Portraitsammlung der Österreichischen Nationalbibliothek*, Tokyo (National Museum of Western Art) & Hamburg (Museum für Kunst und Gewerbe), Hamburg 1999, 240–249

Dietz & Messling 2017
Georg Josef Dietz & Guido Messling, *Cranach der Ältere als Zeichner*, in: exh. cat. Düsseldorf 2017, 67–71

Divjak 2002
Johannes Divjak, *Der sogenannte Kalender des Filocalus*, in: Adolf Primmer & Kurt Smolak & Dorothea Weber (eds.), *Textsorten und Textkritik*, Tagungsbeiträge, Österreichische Akademie der Wissenschaften, Sitzungsberichte der philosophisch-historischen Klasse, vol. 693 (Veröffentlichungen der Kommission zur Herausgabe des Corpus der Lateinischen Kirchenväter 21), Vienna 2002, 19–38

Divjak 2020
Johannes Divjak, *Review of:* Konrad Weidemann & Margarete Weidemann, *Römische Staatskalender aus der Spätantike. Die von Furius Dionisius Filocalus und Polemius Silvius überlieferten römischen Staatskalender und deren historische Einordnung*, Mainz 2016, in: Plekos 22, 2020, 95–107 (URL: http://www.plekos.unimuenchen.de/2020/r-weidemann.pdf)

Divjak & Wischmeyer 2014
Johannes Divjak & Wolfgang Wischmeyer, *Das Kalenderhandbuch von 354. Der Chronograph des Filocalus, Teil 1. Der Bildteil des Chronographen*, Vienna 2014

Dodgson 1903
Campbell Dodgson, *Fünf unbeschriebene Holzschnitte Lucas Cranachs*, in: Jahrbuch der Königlich Preußischen Kunstsammlungen 24, 1903, 284–290

Dodgson 1911
Campbell Dodgson, *Catalogue of Early German and Flemish Woodcuts Preserved in the Department of Prints and Drawings in the British Museum*, London 1911, vol. II

Dörnhöffer 1904
Friedrich Dörnhöffer, *Ein Jugendwerk Lucas Cranachs*, in: Jahrbuch der K. K. Zentral-Kommission für Erforschung und Erhaltung der Kunst- und Historischen Denkmale, N.F. 2, 1904, col. 175–198

Dudík 1867
Bela Dudík, *Die Rudolphinische Kunst- und Raritätenkammer in Prag*, in: Mittheilungen der k.k. Centralkommission zur Erforschung und Erhaltung der Baudenkmale 12, 1867, XXXIII–XLIV

Dülberg 1990
Angelica Dülberg, *Privatporträts. Geschichte und Ikonologie einer Gattung im 15. und 16. Jahrhundert*, Berlin 1990

Dürer 1508/09
Albrecht Dürer, *Entwurf für ein Lehrbuch der Malerei* (1508/09), in: Rupprich, vol. 2, 1966

Dürigl 1975/76
Günter Dürigl, *Wien vom Hochmittelalter bis zum Beginn der Neuzeit – ein historischer Abriß*, in: exh. cat. Vienna 1975/76, 15–20

Dyballa 2014/15
Katrin Dyballa, *Landschaft als Ausdrucksträger*, in: exh. cat. Frankfurt & Vienna 2014/15, 115–117

Eigenberger 1927
Robert Eigenberger, *Die Gemäldegalerie der Akademie der Bildenden Künste in Wien*, Vienna et al. 1927

Endrődi 2018
Gábor Endrődi, *„Nach ständigem Aufblick zum Himmel": Die Vögel auf Cranachs Wiener Hieronymusbild*, in: exh. cat. Innsbruck 2018, 87–95

Endrődi 2018a
Gábor Endrődi, *Die heilige Zweifaltigkeit Apolls. Ein Versuch über Cranachs Cuspinian-Bildnisse*, in: Johana Lomová & Jindřich Vybíral (eds.), *Umění a revoluce. Pro Milenu Bartlovou*, Prague 2018, 198–227

Erichsen 1994
Johannes Erichsen, *Cranach und Dürer*, in: exh. cat. Kronach & Leipzig 1994, 293

Fenyö 1955
Ivan Fenyö, *An Unknown Early Cranach*, in: Burlington Magazine 97, 1955, 68–71

Fingernagel 2015
Andreas Fingernagel (ed.), *Goldene Zeiten. Meisterwerke der Buchkunst von der Gotik bis zur Renaissance. Katalogband zur Ausstellung der Österreichischen Nationalbibliothek vom 20. November 2015 bis 21. Februar 2016*, Lucerne 2015

Fischer 1907
Otto Fischer, *Review of:* Hermann Voss, *Der Ursprung des Donaustils*, Leipzig 1907, in: Kunstgeschichtliche Anzeigen, vol. 1907, 66–76

Flechsig 1898/99
Eduard Flechsig, *Die Lösung der Pseudogrünewald-Frage* (Zur Eröffnung der Cranach-Ausstellung in Dresden), in: Kunstchronik, N.F. X, 1898/1899, col. 337–341

Flechsig 1900
Eduard Flechsig, *Cranachstudien*, vol. 1, Leipzig 1900

Flood 2006
John L. Flood, *Poets Laureate in the Holy Roman Empire. A Bio-Bibliographical Handbook*, 4 vols., Berlin et al. 2006

Franz-Duhme 1994
Helga Nora Franz-Duhme, *Auftraggeber und Maler im Bistum Bamberg*, in: exh. cat. Kronach & Leipzig 1994, 89–95

Friedländer 1891
Max J. Friedländer, *Albrecht Altdorfer, der Maler von Regensburg*, Leipzig 1891 (= Beiträge zur Kunstgeschichte, N.F. XIII)

Friedländer 1899
Max J. Friedländer, *Ueber Lucas Cranach*, in: Sitzungsberichte der Kunstgeschichtlichen Gesellschaft zu Berlin, 1899, 31–34

Friedländer 1899a
Max J. Friedländer, *Die Cranach-Ausstellung in Dresden*, in: Repertorium für Kunstwissenschaft 22, 1899, 237–249

Friedländer 1902
Max J. Friedländer, *Die frühesten Werke Cranachs*, in: Jahrbuch der Königlich Preußischen Kunstsammlungen 23, 1902, 228–234

Friedländer 1908
Max J. Friedländer, *Review of:* Hermann Voss, *Der Ursprung des Donaustils*, Leipzig 1907, in: Repertorium für Kunstwissenschaft 31, 1908, 392–394

Friedländer 1926
Max J. Friedländer, *Zwei Bildnisse von Lucas Cranach*, in: Kunst und Künstler 24, 1926, 381–383

Friedländer & Rosenberg 1979
Max J. Friedländer & Jakob Rosenberg, *Die Gemälde von Lucas Cranach*, 2nd ed., Basel & Boston & Stuttgart 1979 (1st ed. Berlin 1932)

Friesen 1989
Ilse Friesen, *Die Humanisten-Epitaphien im Dom von St. Stephan und die Anfänge der Renaissance-Skulptur in Wien*, in: Wiener Geschichtsblätter 44, 1989, 53–77

Frimmel 1892
Theodor von Frimmel, *Review of:* Max J. Friedländer, *Albrecht Altdorfer, der Maler von Regensburg*, PhD thesis, Leipzig 1891, in: Repertorium für Kunstwissenschaft 15, 1892, 417–421

Frimmel 1896
Theodor von Frimmel, *Aus den Gemäldeslg. in Olmütz und Kremsier*, in: Zeitschrift für Bildende Kunst, Kunstchronik 31, N.F. 7, 1896, 4–6

Frimmel 1899
Theodor von Frimmel, *Geschichte der Wiener Gemäldesammlungen, vol. 1, 1: Einleitung und Geschichte der kaiserlichen Gemäldegalerie*, Leipzig 1899

Gall & Szaivert 1967
Franz Gall & Willy Szaivert (eds.), *Die Matrikel der Universität Wien, II. vol.: 1451–1518, 1. Lieferung* (Publikationen des Instituts für österreichische Geschichtsforschung, VI. Reihe: Quellen zur Geschichte der Universität Wien, 1. Abt.), Graz & Vienna & Cologne 1967

Gastgeber & Klecker 2013
Christian Gastgeber & Elisabeth Klecker (eds.), *Iohannes Cuspinianus (1473–1529). Ein Wiener Humanist und sein Werk im Kontext* (Singularia Vindobonensia 2), Vienna 2013

Geelhaar 1992
Christian Geelhaar, *Kunstmuseum Basel. Die Geschichte der Gemäldesammlung und eine Auswahl von 250 Meisterwerken*, Basel 1992

Geisberg 1923–1930
Max Geisberg (ed.), *Der Deutsche Einblatt-Holzschnitt in der ersten Hälfte des 16. Jahrhunderts*, Munich 1923–1930

Geisberg 1929
Max Geisberg (ed.), *Die 111 Einblatt-Holzschnitte Lukas Cranachs des Älteren, mit einem Vorwort von M. Geisberg* (Der deutsche Einblatt-Holzschnitt in der ersten Hälfte des 16. Jahrhunderts 3, 11), Munich 1929

Geisberg 1939
Max Geisberg, *Geschichte der deutschen Graphik vor Dürer* (Forschungen zur deutschen Kunstgeschichte 32), Berlin 1939

Geldner 1964
Ferdinand Geldner, *Die Buchdruckerkunst im alten Bamberg, 1458/59 bis 1519*, Bamberg 1964

Ginhart 1955
Karl Ginhart, *Die gotische Plastik in Wien*, in: Verein für Geschichte der Stadt Wien (ed.), *Geschichte der bildenden Kunst in Wien. Zweiter Band: Gotik*, Vienna 1955, 68–181

Girshausen 1937
Theo Ludwig Girshausen, *Die Handzeichnungen Lucas Cranachs d.Ä.*, PhD thesis, Frankfurt 1937

Glaser 1921
Curt Glaser, *Lukas Cranach*, Leipzig 1921

Gneiß 2017
Markus Gneiß, *Das Wiener Handwerksordnungsbuch (1364–1555). Edition und Kommentar*, Vienna 2017

Goldberg & Heimberg & Schawe 1998
Gisela Goldberg & Bruno Heimberg & Martin Schawe, *Albrecht Dürer. Die Gemälde der Alten Pinakothek*, Heidelberg 1998

Gollob 1925
Hedwig Gollob, *Systematisches beschreibendes Verzeichnis der mit Wiener Holzschnitten illustrierten Wiener Drucke vom Jahre 1482–1550*, Strasbourg et al. 1925

Gollob 1926
Hedwig Gollob, *Der Wiener Holzschnitt in den Jahren 1490 bis 1550. Seine Bedeutung für die nordische Kunst, seine Entwicklung, seine Blüte und seine Meister*, Vienna 1926

Gollob 1929
Hedwig Gollob, *F. Altmann. Ein Wiener Maler des XV. Jahrhunderts*, Strasbourg et al. 1929

Gollob 1936
Hedwig Gollob, *Winterburgers buchkünstlerische Beziehungen zu Oberitalien*, in: Gutenberg-Jahrbuch 11, 1936, 82–87

Gollob 1941
Hedwig Gollob, *Die Initialserien aus Wiener Incunabeln und Frühdrucken*, Strasbourg 1941

Gollob 1964
Hedwig Gollob, *Johann Winterburgers Missale-Initialen*, in: Gutenberg-Jahrbuch 39, 1964, 299–304

Grimschitz 1921
Bruno Grimschitz, *Ein unbekanntes Frühwerk Lukas Cranachs*, in: Die bildenden Künste 4, 1921, 148–150

Groha 1995
Ulla Katharina Groha, *Der Kreuzaltar der St. Justinuskirche in Frankfurt-Höchst und seine Stellung in der spätgotischen Tafelmalerei*, PhD thesis, Mainz 1995

Gurlitt 1895
Cornelius Gurlitt, *Zur Lebensgeschichte Albrecht Dürer's*, in: Repertorium für Kunstwissenschaft 18, 1895, 112–113

GW
Gesamtkatalog der Wiegendrucke, URL: https://www.gesamtkatalogderwiegendrucke.de/ [retrieved 28 Sept. 2021]

Hambrecht 1995
Rainer Hambrecht, *Lukas Cranach d. Ältere und Coburg. Revision des Forschungsstandes und neue Erkenntnisse*, in: Stefan Oehmig (ed.), *700 Jahre Wittenberg. Stadt – Universität – Reformation*, Weimar 1995, 349–364

Haupt 2007
Herbert Haupt, *Das Hof- und hofbefreite Handwerk im barocken Wien 1620 bis 1770. Ein Handbuch*, Vienna et al. 2007

Hauschild 2005
Stephanie Hauschild, *Die sinnlichen Gärten des Albertus Magnus*, Ostfildern 2005

Heinz 1975
Günther Heinz, *Das Porträtbuch des Hieronymus Beck von Leopoldsdorf*, in: Jahrbuch der kunsthistorischen Sammlungen in Wien 71, 1975, 165–310

Heiser 2002
Sabine Heiser, *Das Frühwerk Lucas Cranachs des Älteren. Wien um 1500 – Dresden um 1900*, Berlin 2002

Heitz 1910
Paul Heitz, *Christus am Kreuz. Kanonbilder der in Deutschland gedruckten Meßbücher des fünfzehnten Jahrhunderts*, Strasbourg 1910

Hengelhaupt 1994
Uta Hengelhaupt, *Bamberger Buchillustration um 1500*, in: exh. cat. Kronach & Leipzig 1994, 111–115

Hermann 1923
Hermann Julius Hermann, *Die frühmittelalterlichen Handschriften des Abendlandes* (Beschreibendes Verzeichnis der illuminierten Handschriften in Österreich, I. Band: Die illuminierten Handschriften und Inkunabeln der Nationalbibliothek in Wien), Leipzig 1923

Heydenreich 1998
Gunnar Heydenreich, *Herstellung, Grundierung und Rahmung der Holzbildträger in den Werkstätten Lucas Cranachs d.Ä.*, in: exh. cat. Eisenach 1998, 181–200

Heydenreich 2007
Gunnar Heydenreich, *Lucas Cranach the Elder. Painting Materials, Techniques and Workshop Practice*, Amsterdam 2007

Heydenreich 2007/08
Gunnar Heydenreich, *„…dass Du mit wunderbarer Schnelligkeit malest.“ Virtuosität und Effizienz in der künstlerischen Praxis Lucas Cranachs d.Ä.*, in: exh. cat. Frankfurt & London 2007/08, 29–47

Hind 1938–1948
Arthur M. Hind, *Early Italian Engraving, a Critical Catalogue*, 7 vols., London 1938–1948

Hinz 1974
Berthold Hinz, *Studien zur Geschichte des Ehepaarbildnisses*, in: Marburger Jahrbuch für Kunstwissenschaft 19, 1974, 139–218

Hinz 1993
Berthold Hinz, *Lucas Cranach d.Ä.*, Reinbek 1993

Hirschfelder 2012
Dagmar Hirschfelder, *Die Bildnisse der Familie Tucher*, in: exh. cat. Nuremberg 2012, 346–348 & cat. 64 & 65

Hörsch 1994
Markus Hörsch, *Zur Bamberger Malerei in der Jugendzeit Cranachs*, in: exh. cat. Kronach & Leipzig 1994, 96–110

Hofbauer 2010
Michael Hofbauer, *Cranach – Die Zeichnungen*, Berlin 2010

Hollnsteiner 1937
Pauline Hollnsteiner, *Das Lehrlings- und Gesellenwesen Österreichs im 15. Jahrhundert*, unpublished PhD thesis, Vienna 1937

Hollstein 1959
Hollstein's German Engravings, Etchings and Woodcuts, ca. 1400–1700, vol. 6, Amsterdam 1959

Holste 2004
Tanja Holste, *Die Porträtkunst Lucas Cranachs d.Ä.*, PhD thesis, Kiel 2004, http://e-diss.uni-kiel.de/diss_1383/d1383.pdf [retrieved 15 Dec. 2021]

Holter & Wutzel 1967
Kurt Holter & Otto Wutzel (eds.), *Werden und Wandlung. Studien zur Kunst der Donauschule*, Linz 1967

Hranitzky 2018
Katharina Hranitzky, *Das erste gedruckte Passauer Missale und sein Buchschmuck*, in: Jeffrey F. Hamburger, *Unter Druck. Mitteleuropäische Buchmalerei im 15. Jahrhundert*, Petersberg 2018, 196–208

Hutter 1972
Herbert Hutter, *Lucas Cranach der Ältere in der Akademie der bildenden Künste in Wien*, Vienna 1972

ISTC
Incunabula Short Title Catalogue, URL: https://data.cerl.org/istc/_search?lang=de [retrieved 28 Sept. 2021]

Jan & Mayhoff 1967–2002
Ludwig von Jan & Karl Mayhoff (eds.), *C. Plinii Secundi naturalis historiae libri XXXVII*, Stuttgart 1967–2002

Jahn 1972
Johannes Jahn, *Lucas Cranach d.Ä. Das gesamte graphische Werk*, Munich 1972

Janitschek 1890
Hubert Janitschek, *Geschichte der deutschen Malerei*, 3 vols., Berlin 1890

Klebel 1925
Ernst Klebel, *Das alte Chorgestühl zu St. Stefan in Wien*, Vienna 1925

Klecker 2013
Elisabeth Klecker, *Texte und Kontexte des Humanisten. Cuspinian-Forschung nach Ankwicz-Kleehoven*, in: Gastgeber & Klecker 2013, 5–18

Köpl 1889
Karl Köpl (ed.), *Urkunden, Acten, Regesten und Inventare aus dem k.k. Statthalterei-Archiv in Prag*, in: Jahrbuch der kunsthistorischen Sammlungen des Allerhöchsten Kaiserhauses 10, 1889, LXIII–CC

Koepplin 1967
Dieter Koepplin, *Das Sonnengestirn der Donaumeister. Zur Herkunft und Bedeutung eines Motivs*, in: Holter & Wutzel 1967, 78–114

Koepplin 1972
Dieter Koepplin, *Zu Cranach als Zeichner. Addenda zu Rosenbergs Katalog*, in: Kunstchronik 25, 1972, 345–348

Koepplin 1973
Dieter Koepplin, *Cranachs Ehebildnis des Johannes Cuspinian von 1502: seine christlich-humanistische Bedeutung*, unpublished PhD thesis, Basel 1973

Koepplin 1977a
Dieter Koepplin, *Erwägungen zu den Anfängen Lucas Cranachs d.Ae.*, in: *Akten des Kolloquiums zur Basler Cranach-Ausstellung 1974*, Basel 1977, 8–9

Koepplin 1977b
Dieter Koepplin, *Nachtrag*, in: *Akten des Kolloquiums zur Basler Cranach-Ausstellung 1974*, Basel 1977, 14

Koepplin 2003
Dieter Koepplin, *Neue Werke von Lucas Cranach und ein altes Bild einer polnischen Schlacht – von Hans Krell?*, Basel 2003

Koller 1994
Manfred Koller, *Der Wiener Schottenaltar. Befund und Restaurierung*, in: Museum im Schottenstift (ed.), *Museum im Schottenstift. Kunstsammlungen der Benediktinerabtei zu den Schotten in Wien*, Vienna 1994, 190–199

Koreny 2003
Fritz Koreny, *Handzeichnung und Druckgraphik*, in: Artur Rosenauer (ed.), *Geschichte der bildenden Kunst in Österreich, vol. 3: Spätmittelalter und Renaissance*, Munich et al. 2003, 556–571

Küster 2008
Hansjörg Küster, *Geschichte des Waldes. Von der Urzeit bis zur Gegenwart*, Munich 2008

Kunz 1996
Armin Kunz, *Die Jerusalemfahrt Lucas Cranachs d.Ä. Quellenkritische Untersuchung der Überlieferungsgeschichte eines (kunst)historischen Topos*, in: Archiv für Kulturgeschichte 78, 1996, 87–114

Kunz 2010
Armin Kunz, *Anmerkungen zu Cranach als Graphiker*, in: exh. cat. Brussels & Paris 2010/11, 80–93

Lanc 1983
Elga Lanc, *Die mittelalterlichen Wandmalereien in Wien und Niederösterreich* (Corpus der mittelalterlichen Wandmalereien Österreichs 1), Vienna 1983

Lang 1971
Helmut W. Lang, *Das Exlibris Cuspinians. Ein Druck aus der Wiener Offizin Vietor & Singriener*, in: Mitteilungen der deutschen Exlibris-Gesellschaft 5, 1971, 33–34

Lang & Neugebauer 2015
Thomas Lang & Anke Neugebauer, *Kommentierter Quellenanhang*, in: Heiner Lück et al. (eds.), *Das ernestinische Wittenberg: Spuren Cranachs in Schloss und Stadt* (Wittenberg-Forschungen 3), Petersberg 2015, 139–293

Langer & Dolch 1913
Eduard Langer (ed.), *Bibliographie der österreichischen Drucke des XV. und XVI. Jahrhunderts, 1. Band, 1. Heft, bearbeitet von Walther Dolch*, Vienna 1913

Lantz-Della Casa 2013
Johanna Lantz-Della Casa, *„Instar phoenicis rarissimi“ (Austria, cap. VI): Cuspinians Klage über den Gelehrtenmangel in Österreichs Klöstern und Schulen seiner Zeit*, in: Gastgeber & Klecker 2013, 378–392

Lanzinner 1980
Maximilian Lanzinner, *Fürst, Räte und Stände*, Göttingen 1980

LCI
Wolfgang Braunfels (ed.), *Lexikon der christlichen Ikonographie*, 8 vols., Freiburg i.Br. 1968–1976

Lenz 1972
Angelika Lenz, *Der Meister MZ, ein Münchner Kupferstecher der frühen Dürerzeit*, unpublished PhD thesis, Munich 1972, Gießen 1972

Lehrs 1930
Max Lehrs, *Geschichte und kritischer Katalog des deutschen, niederländischen und französischen Kupferstichs im XV. Jahrhundert*, vol. 7, Vienna 1930

Löcher 1979
Kurt Löcher, *Auf den Spuren verlorener Porträts. Kopien altdeutscher Meisterwerke aus der Dürerzeit*, in: Kunst und Antiquitäten. Zeitschrift für Kunstfreunde, Sammler und Museen 3, 1979, 16–22

Löw 1907
Alois Löw, *Die St. Lukas-Zeche in Wien. Beiträge zur Geschichte der Glasmalerei in Wien*, in: Berichte und Mittheilungen des Alterthums-Vereines zu Wien 40, 1907, 165–189

Lüdecke 1953
Heinz Lüdecke, *Lucas Cranach der Ältere im Spiegel seiner Zeit. Aus Urkunden, Chroniken, Briefen, Reden und Gedichten*, Berlin 1953

Luff & Steer 2003
Konrad von Megenberg, *Das «Buch der Natur», Kritischer Text nach den Handschriften*, ed. by Robert Luff & Georg Steer, Tübingen 2003

Madersbacher 2003
Lukas Madersbacher, *Malerei und Bild 1430 bis 1520. Wien und Niederösterreich*, in: Artur Rosenauer (ed.), *Spätmittelalter und Renaissance* (Geschichte der bildenden Kunst in Österreich 3), Munich et al. 2003, 411–425

Marx 1997
Harald Marx, *Dresden – eine Cranach-Stadt?*, in: Dresdner Hefte, vol. 15, no. 52,4, ed. by Dresdner Geschichtsverein, Themenheft „Kurfürst Moritz und die Renaissance“, 1997, 64–72

Menz 1982
Cäsar Menz, *Das Frühwerk Jörg Breus des Älteren*, Augsburg 1982

Merback 1999
Mitchell B. Merback, *The Thief, the Cross and the Wheel. Pain and Spectacle of Punishment in Medieval and Renaissance Europe*, London 1999

Mertens 1994
Veronika Mertens, *Die drei Grazien. Studien zu einem Bildmotiv in der Kunst der frühen Neuzeit*, Wiesbaden 1994

Mertens 1996
Dieter Mertens, *Zur Sozialgeschichte und Funktion des poeta laureatus im Zeitalter Maximilians I.*, in: Rainer Christoph Schwinges (ed.), *Gelehrte im Reich. Zur Sozial- und Wirkungsgeschichte akademischer Eliten des 14. bis 16. Jahrhunderts* (Zeitschrift für historische Forschung, Beiheft 18), Berlin 1996, 327–348

Messling 2021
Guido Messling, *Nicht gerade linientreu. Expressives in der österreichischen Kunst der Dürerzeit*, in: exh. cat. Vienna 2021/22, 122–131

Metzger 2002
Christof Metzger, *Hans Schäufelin als Maler*, Berlin 2002

Michaelson 1902
Hedwig Michaelson, *Lukas Cranach der Ältere. Untersuchungen über die stilistische Entwickelung seiner Kunst*, PhD thesis, Heidelberg 1902, Leipzig 1902 (= Beiträge zur Kunstgeschichte, N.F. 28)

Mittendorfer & Fingernagel & Simader 2022
Konstanze Mittendorfer & Andreas Fingernagel & Friedrich Simader, *Johannes Winterburger (um 1460 [?] bis 1519), Teil 1: Die Inkunabeln der Österreichischen Nationalbibliothek*, in: Codices manuscripti & impressi (to be published in 2022)

Morass & Thalinger 2018
Peter Morass & Michael Thalinger, *Cranach im Fokus der Naturwissenschaft, Ausgewählte botanische und zoologische Identifikationen*, in: exh. cat. Innsbruck 2018, 163–203

Mossakowski 2007
Stanislaw Mossakowski, *The Latin Inscriptions in the Royal Palace on the Wawel Hill in Cracow*, in: Anna Skolimowska (ed.), *Respublica litteraria in action. Letters – speeches – poems – inscriptions*, Warsaw & Cracow 2007, 105–114

Mühlberger 2001
Kurt Mühlberger, *Die Gemeinde der Lehrer und Schüler – Alma Mater Rudolphina*, in: Csendes & Opll 2001, 319–410

Näf 1944
Werner Näf, *Vadian und seine Stadt St. Gallen, vol. 1: bis 1518, Humanist in Wien*, St Gallen 1944

Niederstätter 1996
Alois Niederstätter, Österreichische *Geschichte 1400–1522 – Das Jahrhundert der Mitte. An der Wende vom Mittelalter zur Neuzeit*, Vienna 1996

Nordenfalk 1936
Carl Nordenfalk, *Der Kalender von 354 und die lateinische Buchmalerei des IV. Jahrhunderts* (Göteborgs Kungliga Vetenskaps- och Vitterhets-Samhälles handlingar, Ser. A, Humanistiska skrifter, vol. 5, no. 2), Gothenburg 1936

Oettinger 1949
Karl Oettinger, *Das Taufwerk von St. Stephan in Wien*, Vienna 1949

Ogesser 1779
Joseph Ogesser, *Beschreibung der Metropolitankirche zu St. Stephan in Wien*, Vienna 1779

Olorovsky 1997
Elsa Olorovsky, *Kranich und Schlange, Phoenix und Drache. Zur Rezeption persischer und chinesischer Fabelmotive im Parzival mit einem Ausblick auf weitere Epen des Artuskreises*, in: Komparatistische Studien 21, 1997, 57–89

Oswald 1953
Josef Oswald, *Das Missale Passaviense*, in: *Passauer Studien, Festschrift für Bischof Dr. Dr. Simon Konrad Landersdorfer OSB*, Passau 1953, 75–101

Pächt 1929
Otto Pächt, Österreichische Tafelmalerei der Gotik, Augsburg 1929

Panofsky 1942
Erwin Panofsky, *Letter to the Editor*, in: The Art Bulletin 24, no. 4, 1942, 182–183

Panofsky 1997
Erwin Panofsky, *Studies in Iconology. Humanistic Themes in the Art of the Renaissance*, New York 1972 (1st ed. Oxford 1939), German: *Studien zur Ikonologie der Renaissance. Mit einem Vorwort von Jan Bialostocki und einem Nachwort von Andreas Beyer*, Cologne 1997

Passavant 1860–1864
Johann David Passavant, *Le Peintre Graveur*, 6 vols., Leipzig 1860–1864

Pereña 2018
Helena Pereña, *Von der Einöde ins Paradies, die Wüste als Wald bei Cranach*, in: exh. cat. Innsbruck 2018, 71–85

Perger 1973
Richard Perger, *Zur Herkunft der Votivtafel des Jodok Hauser († 1478)*, in: Mitteilungen der Österreichischen Galerie 17, 1973, 7–14

Perger 1980
Richard Perger, *Hans Siebenbürger. Meister des Hauser-Epitaphs und Stifter des Ölbergs zu St. Michael in Wien*, in: Österreichische Zeitschrift für Kunst und Denkmalpflege 34, 1980, 147–150

Perger 1988
Richard Perger, *Die Wiener Ratsbürger 1396–1526. Ein Handbuch*, Vienna 1988

Perger 2001
Richard Perger, *Der organisatorische und wirtschaftliche Rahmen*, in: Csendes & Opll 2001, 199–246

Perger 2005
Richard Perger, *Wiener Künstler des Mittelalters und der beginnenden Neuzeit. Regesten*, Vienna 2005

Pfändtner 2011
Karl-Georg Pfändtner, *Die Handschriften des Lehrbüchermeisters. In memoriam Gerhard Schmidt (1924–2010)*, Purkersdorf 2011

Plieger 2009
Cornelia Plieger, *Die Passionsreliefs – Werke aus dem Umkreis Michael Tichters. Überlegungen zur Autorschaft*, in: Agnes Husslein-Arco et al. (eds.), *Die Passionsreliefs vom Wiener Stephansdom*, Vienna (Belvedere) 2009

Plieger 2018
Cornelia Plieger, *Lukas Cranach d.Ä. und die Plastik des frühen 16. Jahrhunderts in Wien*, in: Jiří Fajt & Susanne Jaeger (eds.), *Das Expressive in der Kunst 1500–1550. Albrecht Altdorfer und seine Zeitgenossen*, Berlin et al. 2018, 237–253

Pölnitz 1937
Götz von Pölnitz, *Die Matrikel der Universität Ingolstadt-Landshut-München, Teil 1: Ingolstadt, vol. 1: 1472–1600, 1. Halbvol.: 1472–WS 1554*, Schöpping 1937

Rathe 1942
Kurt Rathe, *Die Impresa eines Wiener Humanisten*, in: La Bibliofilia 42, 1940, 54–65

Rebel 1994
Ernst Rebel, *Lucas Cranachs Porträtkunst. Personendarstellungen zwischen Vitalität und Formel*, in: exh. cat. Kronach & Leipzig 1994, 131–138

Reindl 1977
Peter Reindl, *Loy Hering. Zur Rezeption der Renaissance in Süddeutschland*, Basel 1977

Reiter 1994
Cornelia Reiter, *Der Wiener Schottenaltar. Geschichte, Stil und Charakteristika seiner Bildsprache*, in: Museum im Schottenstift (ed.), *Museum im Schottenstift. Kunstsammlungen der Benediktinerabtei zu den Schotten in Wien*, Vienna 1994, 172–189

Reske 2005
Richard Reske, *Wiener Künstler des Mittelalters und der beginnenden Neuzeit – Regesten*, Vienna 2005

Reudenbach 1996
Bruno Reudenbach, *Individuum ohne Bildnis? Zum Problem künstlerischer Ausdrucksformen von Individualität im Mittelalter*, in: Jan A. Aertsen & Andreas Speer (eds.), *Individuum und Individualität im Mittelalter* (Miscellanea mediaevalia 24), Berlin & New York 1996, 807–818

Rieffel 1895
Franz Rieffel, *Kleine kunstwissenschaftliche Controversfragen. II.*, in: Repertorium für Kunstwissenschaft 18, 1895, 424–428

Ringbom 1965
Sixten Ringbom, *Icon to Narrative. The Rise of the Dramatic Close-Up in Fifteenth Century Devotional Painting*, Åbo 1965

Röhrig 1981
Floridus Röhrig, *Geschichte und Thematik des Albrechtsaltars*, in: Floridus Röhrig (ed.), *Der Albrechtsaltar und sein Meister*, Vienna 1981, 21–91

Rosenauer 1981
Artur Rosenauer, *Zum Stil des Albrechtsmeisters*, in: Floridus Röhrig (ed.), *Der Albrechtsaltar und sein Meister*, Vienna 1981, 97–122

Rosenauer 2003
Artur Rosenauer (ed.), *Geschichte der bildenden Kunst in Österreich, Bd 3: Spätmittelalter und Renaissance*, Munich et al. 2003

Rosenauer 2003a
Artur Rosenauer, *Malerei der Donauschule*, in: *Spätmittelalter und Renaissance* (Geschichte der bildenden Kunst in Österreich 3), Munich et al. 2003, 477–493

Rosenauer 2017
Artur Rosenauer, *Zur kunsthistorischen Stellung der Grabplatte des Kaisers*, in: Renate Kohn (ed.), *Der Kaiser und sein Grabmal. 1517–2017*, Vienna 2017, 81–88

Rosenberg 1960
Jakob Rosenberg, *Die Zeichnungen Lucas Cranachs des Älteren*, Berlin 1960

Rupprich 1966–1969
Hans Rupprich (ed.), *Dürer. Schriftlicher Nachlaß*, 3 vols., Berlin 1956–1969

Salzman 1990
Michele Renee Salzman, *On Roman Time. The Codex-Calendar of 354 and the Rhythms of Urban Life in Late Antiquity*, Berkeley & Los Angeles & Oxford 1990

Salzman 1984
Michele Renee Salzman, *The Representation of April in the Calendar of 354*, in: American Journal of Archaeology 88/1, 1984, 43–45

Sandner & Rietschel 1994
Ingo Sandner & Iris Rietschel, *Arbeitsweise und Maltechnik Lucas Cranachs und seiner Werkstatt*, in: exh. cat. Kronach 1994, 186–193

Savage 2018
Elizabeth Savage, *Hans Burgkmair's Colour Woodcuts: An Overview*, in: Wolfgang Augustyn & Manuel Teget-Welz (eds.), *Hans Burgkmair. Neue Forschungen* (Veröffentlichungen des Zentralinstituts für Kunstgeschichte in München 44), Passau 2018, 333–366

Savage & Stijnman 2017
Elizabeth Savage & Ad Stijnman, *Die Farbholzschnitte von Lucas Cranach dem Älteren*, in: exh. cat. Düsseldorf 2017, 59–65

Schade 1974
Werner Schade, *Die Malerfamilie Cranach*, Dresden 1974

Schaffran 1957
Emerich Schaffran, *Neuerwerbungen der Gemäldegalerie im Kunsthistorischen Museum zu Wien*, in: Die Kunst und das schöne Heim 55, 1957, 205–207

Schama 1996
Simon Schama, *Der Traum von der Wildnis. Natur als Imagination*, Munich 1996

Schawe 1995
Martin Schawe, *Die Kreuzigung Christi von Lucas Cranach d.Ä. aus dem Jahre 1503*, in: Bayerische Staatsgemäldesammlungen, Jahresbericht 1995, 11–22 (incl. an additional review by Werner Schade, in: Frankfurter Allgemeine Zeitung, 19 June 1996, p. N6)

Schawe 1998
Martin Schawe, *Das Tafelgemälde „Kreuzigung Christi" Lucas Cranachs des Älteren von 1503*, in: exh. cat. Eisenach 1998, 160–166

Schedel 1493
Hartmann Schedel, *Buch der Croniken und geschichten mit Figuren und Pildnussen von Anbeginn der Welt bis auf dise unnsere Zeit*, Nuremberg 1493

Scheibler 1887
Ludwig Scheibler, *Über altdeutsche Gemälde in der kaiserlichen Galerie zu Wien*, in: Repertorium für Kunstwissenschaft 10, 1887, 271–305

Schepers 1994
Elisabeth Schepers, *Die Maler von Kronach*, in: exh. cat. Kronach & Leipzig 1994, 44–51

Schindler 1981
Herbert Schindler, *Albrecht Altdorfer und die Anfänge des Donaustils*, in: Ostbairische Grenzmarken. Passauer Jahrbuch für Geschichte, Kunst und Volkskunde 23, 1981, 66–73

Schindler 1982
Herbert Schindler, *Die „Wilden Maler" von der Donau*, in: *Donaubairisches. Vorträge zur Kunstgeschichte*, Passau 1982, 93–99

Schindler 1987
Herbert Schindler, *Sodalitas Danubia. Betrachtungen über die Donauschule und den Donaustil*, in: Oberösterreich 37, 1987, 19–29

Schlosser 1925
Ignaz Schlosser, *Die Kanzel und der Orgelfuß zu St. Stefan in Wien*, Vienna 1925

Schmidt 1899/1900
Wilhelm Schmidt, *Zur Cranach-Ausstellung*, in: Kunstchronik N.F. XI, 1899/1900, col. 145–147

Schoch & Mende & Scherbaum 2001–2004
Rainer Schoch & Matthias Mende & Anna Scherbaum, *Albrecht Dürer. Das druckgraphische Werk*, 3 vols., Munich & London & New York 2001–2004

Schönbrunner & Meder 1896–1908
Josef Schönbrunner & Josef Meder, *Handzeichnungen alter Meister aus der Albertina und anderen Sammlungen*, 12 vols., Vienna 1896–1908

Scholz 2009
Hartmut Scholz, *„Sind überauß schöne Stückh gewiß AD Invention, wie auch das Leben Benedicti uff solche arth im Creutzgang, ao. 1501 gemahlt". Zur Überlieferung des Benediktzyklus in den Kreuzgangsfenstern des Nürnberger Egidienklosters*, in: Ulrich Großmann (ed.), *Buchmalerei der Dürerzeit*, Nuremberg 2009, 193–226

Schramm 1934
Albert Schramm, *Der Bilderschmuck der Frühdrucke*, vol. XVII, Leipzig 1934

Schramm 1935
Albert Schramm, *Der Bilderschmuck der Frühdrucke*, vol. XVIII, Leipzig 1935

Schuchardt 1851–1871
Christian Schuchardt, *Lucas Cranach des Älteren Leben und Werke*, Leipzig 1851–1871

Seidl 1987
Christina Seidl, *Beiträge zur Wiener und Niederösterreichischen Tafelmalerei der zweiten Hälfte des 15. Jahrhunderts*, 3 vols., unpublished PhD thesis, Vienna 1987

Seidlitz 1899
Woldemar von Seidlitz, *L'exposition Cranach à Dresde*, in: Gazette des Beaux Arts 41, 1899, 191–207

Siebmacher 1873
Siebmacher's großes und allgemeines Wappenbuch, Bd. 5 (Bürgerliche Geschlechter Deutschlands und der Schweiz), 2. Abt.: Zweitausend bürgerliche Wappen, Nuremberg 1873

Sick 1984
Helmut Sick, *Brasilianischer Ara 1502/03 in Europa gemalt*, in: Journal für Ornithologie 125/4, 1984, 479–481

Signori 1999
Gabriela Signori, *Wallfahrt, Wunder und Buchdruck um 1500. Jakobus Issickemers „buchlein der zuflucht zu Maria der muter gottes in alten Oding" (Kaspar Hochfeder: Nürnberg 1497)*, in: exh. cat. *Maria Allerorten. Die Muttergottes mit dem geneigten Haupt, 1699–1999. Das Gnadenbild der Ursulinen zu Landshut – Altbayerische Marienfrömmigkeit im 18. Jahrhundert*, Landshut (Museen der Stadt) 1999, 53–66

Silver 1983
Larry Silver, *Forest Primeval: Albrecht Altdorfer and the German Wilderness Landscape*, in: Simiolus 13/1, 1983, 4–34

Singer 1898/99
H. W. Singer, *Die Dresdener Cranach-Ausstellung*, in: Kunstchronik, N.F. X, 1898/1899, col. 358–361

Stadler 1913
Franz J. Stadler, *Michael Wolgemut und der Nürnberger Holzschnitt im letzten Drittel des XV. Jahrhunderts* (Studien zur deutschen Kunstgeschichte 161), Strasbourg 1913

Stadlober 1998
Margit Stadlober, *Das Frühwerk Lucas Cranachs d.Ä. und Österreich. Ein Entwicklungsweg*, in: Österreichische Zeitschrift für Kunst und Denkmalpflege 52, 1998, 414–423

Stadlober 2006
Margit Stadlober, *Der Wald in der Malerei und der Graphik des Donaustils*, Vienna & Cologne & Weimar 2006

Stange 1966
Alfred Stange, *Gedanken über Jörg Breus Werke und Wege*, in: Jahrbuch der Staatlichen Kunstsammlungen in Baden-Württemberg 4, 1967, 19–30

Stern 1953
Henri Stern, *Le calendrier de 354. Étude sur son texte et ses illustrations* (Bibliothèque archéologique et historique 55), Paris 1953

Stichel 1999
Rudolf H. W. Stichel, *Ein Nachtrag zum Porträtbuch des Hieronymus Beck von Leopoldsdorf. Bildnisse orientalischer Herrscher und Würdenträger in Cod. Vindob. 8615*, in: Jahrbuch des Kunsthistorischen Museums Wien 1, 1999, 189–207

Stiebel 1894
Heinrich Eduard Stiebel, *Bücherzeichen des Johann Cuspinianus aus Schweinfurt*, in: Zeitschrift für Bücherzeichen-, Bibliothekenkunde und Gelehrtengeschichte 4, 1894, 112

Stievermann 1994
Dieter Stievermann, *Lucas Cranach und der kursächsische Hof*, in: exh. cat. Kronach & Leipzig 1994, 66–77

Strohmer 1955
Erich V. Strohmer, *Die Malerei der Gotik in Wien*, in: Verein für Geschichte der Stadt Wien (ed.), *Geschichte der bildenden Kunst in Wien. Zweiter Band*, Vienna 1955, 182–200

Strzygowski 1888
Josef Strzygowski, *Die Calenderbilder des Chronographen vom Jahre 354* (Jahrbuch des Deutschen Archäologischen Instituts. Erstes Ergänzungsheft), Berlin 1888

Suckale 2004
Robert Suckale, *Der Maler Johannes Siebenbürger (um 1440–1483) als Vermittler Nürnberger Kunst nach Osteuropa*, in: Evelin Wetter (ed.), *Die Länder der Böhmischen Krone und ihre Nachbarn zur Zeit der Jagiellonenkönige (1471–1526). Kunst – Kultur – Geschichte* (Studia Jagellonica Lipsiensia 2), Ostfildern 2004, 363–384

Suckale 2009
Robert Suckale, *Die Erneuerung der Malkunst vor Dürer*, 2 vols., Petersberg 2009

Tacke 1992
Andreas Tacke, *Der katholische Cranach. Zu zwei Großaufträgen von Lucas Cranach d.Ä., Simon Franck und der Cranach-Werkstatt* (Berliner Schriften zur Kunst 2), Berlin 1992

Tacke 2007
Andreas Tacke (ed.), *Lucas Cranach 1553/2003. Wittenberger Tagungsbeiträge anlässlich des 450. Todesjahres Lucas Cranachs des Älteren*, Leipzig 2007

Teget-Welz 2018
Manuel Teget-Welz, *Cranach trifft Dürer. Facetten einer Künstlerbegegnung*, in: Dickel 2018, LI–LXX

Thöne 1939
Friedrich Thöne, *Lucas Cranachs des Älteren Meisterzeichnungen*, Burg 1939

Thun 2018
Agnes Thun, *Cranachs Hieronymusbilder und die Natur*, in: exh. cat. Innsbruck 2018, 7–19

Tietze 1931
Hans Tietze, *Geschichte und Beschreibung des St. Stephansdomes in Wien* (Österreichische Kunsttopographie 23), Vienna 1931

Treier 1986
Albert Treier, *Redende Exlibris. Geschichte und Kunstform des deutschen Bücherzeichens*, Wiesbaden 1968

Trnek 1997
Renate Trnek, *Die Gemäldegalerie der Akademie der bildenden Künste in Wien. Die Sammlung im Überblick*, Vienna et al. 1997

Uhlirz 1896
Karl Uhlirz, *Urkunden und Regesten aus dem Archive der k. k. Reichshaupt- und Residenzstadt Wien (1440–1619)*, in: Jahrbuch der Kunsthistorischen Sammlungen des Allerhöchsten Kaiserhauses 17, 1896, CIX–CCXXXIV

Vaisse 2019
Pierre Vaisse, *Quand Cranach est-il né?*, in: Revue de l'Art 203, 2019, 69–82

Van der Vekene 1974
Emil van der Vekene, *Kaspar Hochfeder. Ein europäischer Drucker des 15. und 16. Jahrhunderts*, Baden-Baden 1974

VD 16
Verzeichnis der im deutschen Sprachbereich erschienenen Drucke des 16. Jahrhunderts, URL: https://www.bsb-muenchen.de/sammlungen/historische-drucke/recherche/vd-16/ [retrieved 28 Sept. 2021]

vdm
Verzeichnis deutscher Musikfrühdrucke, URL: http://www.vdm16.sbg.ac.at/db/music_prints.php?content=project_introduction&menu=0 [retrieved 28 Sept. 2021]

Vogel 1909
Julius Vogel, *Lucas Cranach in Wien*, in: Monatshefte für Kunstwissenschaft 2, 1909, 545

Voss 1907
Hermann Voss, *Der Ursprung des Donaustiles – Ein Stück Entwickelungsgeschichte deutscher Malerei*, Leipzig 1907

Weidemann & Weidemann 2016
Konrad Weidemann & Margarete Weidemann, *Römische Staatskalender aus der Spätantike. Die von Furius Dionisius Filocalus und Polemius Silvius überlieferten römischen Staatskalender und deren historische Einordnung*, Mainz 2016

Weih-Krüger 1986
Sonja Weih-Krüger, *Hans Schäufelein. Ein Beitrag zur künstlerischen Entwicklung des jungen Hans Schäufelein bis zu seiner Niederlassung in Nördlingen 1515 unter besonderer Berücksichtigung des malerischen Werkes*, Nuremberg 1986

Weniger 2018
Matthias Weniger, *Cranach und Kronach. Das Dilemma des Frühwerks und die Bestände in der Fränkischen Galerie*, in: Dickel 2018, XXIX–XLIX

Wiesflecker 1996
Hermann Wiesflecker, *Regesta imperii. Ausgewählte Regesten des Kaiserreiches unter Maximilian I., 1493–1519. Band 3, Teil 1: Maximilian I., 1499–1501*, Vienna et al. 1996

Wiesner 1985
Felix Wiesner, *Die Erfindung der Zweiten Natur beim Wiener Cranach*, Munich 1985

Winkler 1936
Friedrich Winkler, *Die Bilder des Wiener Filocalus*, in: Jahrbuch der Preußischen Kunstsammlungen 57, 1936, 141–155

Woermann 1898/99
Karl Woermann, *Die Cranach-Ausstellung (Dresden 1899) und die Pseudogrünewald-Frage*, in: Kunstchronik, N.F. X, 1898/1899, col. 145–154

Woermann 1900
Karl Woermann, *Die Dresdener Cranach-Ausstellung*, in: Zeitschrift für bildende Kunst 35, N.F. 11, 1900, 25–33, 55–66, 78–88 (with revised notes reprinted in Karl Woermann, *Von Apelles zu Boecklin und weiter*, Esslingen 1912, vol. 1, 217–247)

Wood 1993
Christopher S. Wood, *Albrecht Altdorfer and the Origins of Landscape*, London 1993

Wood 2008
Christopher S. Wood, *Forgery, Replica, Fiction: Temporalities of German Renaissance Art*, Chicago & London 2008

Worringer 1908
Wilhelm Worringer, *Lukas Cranach*, Munich & Leipzig 1908

Zykan 1965
Maria Magdalena Zykan, *Die Holzschnitte in den Werken des Wiener Druckers Johann Winterburger (1492–1519)*, examination essay submitted to the Institut für Österreichische Geschichtsforschung in Wien, 1965 (typescript)

Zykan 1967
Maria Magdalena Zykan, *Der Buchschmuck Johann Winterburgers und der Donaustil*, in: Holter & Wutzel 1967, 37–53

Zykan 1975
Marlene Zykan, *Ein früher Nürnberger Missaldruck und der Wiener Buchholzschnitt*, in: Kunstjahrbuch der Stadt Linz, 1974/75, 3–14

EXHIBITION CATALOGUES

exh. cat. Augsburg 2017
Günter Hägele & Melanie Thierbach (eds.), *Augsburg macht Druck. Die Anfänge des Buchdrucks in einer Metropole des 15. Jahrhunderts*, Augsburg (Diözesanmuseum St. Afra) 2017

exh. cat. Basel 1974
Dieter Koepplin & Tilman Falk, *Lukas Cranach. Gemälde, Zeichnungen, Druckgraphik*, 2 vols., Basel (Kunstmuseum), Basel & Stuttgart 1974

exh. cat. Basel 2006
Stephan Kemperdick, *Das frühe Porträt. Aus den Sammlungen des Fürsten von und zu Liechtenstein und dem Kunstmuseum Basel*, Basel (Kunstmuseum Basel), Munich 2006

exh. cat. Basel 2019
Kunstmuseum Basel & Bodo Brinkmann (eds.), *Bilderlust. Louise Bachofen-Burckhardt: Sammeln und Stiften in Basel*, Lindenberg im Allgäu 2019

exh. cat. Basel & Berlin 1997/98
Gerhard Brunner (ed.), *Dürer Holbein Grünewald. Meisterzeichnungen der deutschen Renaissance aus Berlin und Basel*, Basel (Öffentliche Kunstsammlung, Kupferstichkabinett) & Berlin (Staatliche Museen, Kupferstichkabinett), Ostfildern 1997

exh. cat. Berlin 1937
Lucas Cranach d.Ä. und Lucas Cranach d.J., Berlin (Deutsches Museum) 1937

exh. cat. Berlin 1973
Lucas Cranach. Gemälde – Zeichnungen – Druckgraphik, Berlin (Museum Dahlem) 1973

exh. cat. Berlin & Regensburg 1988
Hans Mielke, *Albrecht Altdorfer. Zeichnungen, Deckfarbenmalerei, Druckgraphik*, Berlin (Staatliche Museen, Kupferstichkabinett) & Regensburg (Museen der Stadt), Berlin 1988

exh. cat. Bruges 2010
Till-Holger Borchert (ed.), *Van Eyck bis Dürer. Altniederländische Meister und die Malerei in Mitteleuropa*, Bruges (Groeningemuseum), Stuttgart 2010

exh. cat. Brussels & Paris 2010/11
Guido Messling (ed.), *Die Welt des Lucas Cranach. Ein Künstler im Zeitalter von Dürer, Tizian und Metsys*, Brussels (BOZAR) & Paris (Musée du Luxembourg) 2010/11

exh. cat. Chemnitz 2005
Harald Marx & Ingrid Mössinger (eds.), *Cranach. Mit einem Bestandskatalog der Gemälde in den Staatlichen Kunstsammlungen Dresden*, with Karin Kolb, Staatliche Kunstsammlungen Dresden, Chemnitz & Cologne 2005

exh. cat. Dresden 1899
Karl Woermann (ed.), *Deutsche Kunstausstellung Dresden 1899. Abteilung Cranach-Ausstellung. Wissenschaftliches Verzeichnis der ausgestellten Werke*, Dresden (Ausstellungspalast), Dresden 1899

exh. cat. Düsseldorf 2017
Gunnar Heydenreich & Daniel Görres & Beat Wismer (eds.), *Lucas Cranach der Ältere. Meister – Marke – Moderne,* Düsseldorf (Museum Kunstpalast), Munich 2017

exh. cat. Eisenach & Torgau 1994
Wartburg-Stiftung Eisenach (ed.), *Gesetz und Gnade. Cranach, Luther und die Bilder*, edited by Günter Schuchardt, Eisenach 1994

exh. cat. Eisenach 1998
Ingo Sandner & Wartburg-Stiftung Eisenach (eds.), *Unsichtbare Meisterzeichnungen auf dem Malgrund – Cranach und seine Zeitgenossen. Unterzeichnungen auf Gemälden Cranachs, seiner Werkstatt und seiner Zeitgenossen*, Wartburg in Eisenach, Regensburg 1998

exh. cat. Erlangen 1994/95
Andreas Tacke (ed.), *Cranach. Meisterwerke auf Vorrat. Die Erlanger Handzeichnungen der Universitätsbibliothek,* cat. raisonné and exh. cat., Nuremberg, Halle, Augsburg 1994/95 (= Schriften der Universitätsbibliothek Erlangen-Nürnberg, ed. by Konrad Wickert, vol. 25), Munich 1994

exh. cat. Frankfurt & London 2007/08
Bodo Brinkmann (ed.), *Cranach der Ältere 1473–1973,* Frankfurt (Städel Museum) & London (Royal Academy of Arts), Ostfildern 2007

exh. cat. Frankfurt & Strasbourg 2011/12
Stefan Roller (ed.), *Niclaus Gerhaert. Der Bildhauer des späten Mittelalters*, Frankfurt (Liebieghaus Skulpturensammlung) & Strasbourg (Musée de l'Oeuvre Notre-Dame), Petersberg 2011

exh. cat. Frankfurt & Vienna 2014/15
Sabine Haag et al. (eds.), *Fantastische Welten. Albrecht Altdorfer und das Expressive in der Kunst um 1500,* Frankfurt (Städel Museum) & Vienna (Kunsthistorisches Museum), Munich 2014

exh. cat. Gotha 1994
Almuth Schuttwolf (ed.), *Gotteswort und Menschenbild. Werke von Cranach und seinen Zeitgenossen*, Schlossmuseum Gotha, Forschungs- und Landesbibliothek Gotha Schloss Friedenstein, Gotha 1994

exh. cat. Innsbruck 2018
Wolfgang Meighörner (ed.), *Cranach Natürlich. Hieronymus in der Wildnis*, Innsbruck (Tiroler Landesmuseum Ferdinandeum), Innsbruck 2018

exh. cat. Karlsruhe 2007/08
Dietmar Lüdke (ed.), *Grünewald und seine Zeit*, Karlsruhe (Staatliche Kunsthalle) 2007/08

exh. cat. Kronach & Leipzig 1994
Claus Grimm et al. (eds.), *Lucas Cranach. Ein Maler-Unternehmer aus Franken*, Kronach (Festung Rosenberg) & Leipzig (Museum der bildenden Künste) 1994

exh. cat. Linz 1965
Fritz Dworschak & Brigitte Heinzl & Kurt Holter & Otto Wutzel (eds.), *Die Kunst der Donauschule 1490–1540. Malerei, Graphik, Plastik, Architektur*, Linz (Stift St. Florian & Schlossmuseum), Linz 1965

exh. cat. Madrid & Bruges & New York 2005
Till-Holger Borchert (ed.), *Hans Memling Portraits*, Madrid (Museo Thyssen-Bornemisza) & Bruges (Groeningemuseum) & New York (The Frick Collection), Stuttgart 2005

exh. cat. Munich 1938
Ernst Buchner (ed.), *Albrecht Altdorfer und sein Kreis*, Munich (Bayerische Staatsgemäldesammlungen) 1938

exh. cat. Munich 2011
Martin Schawe (ed.), *Cranach in Bayern*, Bayerische Staatsgemäldesammlungen, Munich 2011

exh. cat. Nuremberg 1971
Albrecht Dürer 1471/1971, Nuremberg (Germanisches Nationalmuseum), Nuremberg 1971

exh. cat. Nuremberg 1992
Rainer Schoch, *Meister der Zeichnung. Zeichnungen und Aquarelle aus der Graphischen Sammlung des Germanischen Nationalmuseums,* Nuremberg (Germanisches Nationalmuseum) 1992

exh. cat. Nuremberg 2012
Daniel Hess & Thomas Eser (eds.), *Der Frühe Dürer*, Nuremberg (Germanisches Nationalmuseum), Nuremberg 2012

exh. cat. St. Florian & Linz 1965
Otto Wutzel (ed.), *Die Kunst der Donauschule. 1490–1540*, Stift Sankt Florian & Linz (Schlossmuseum) 1965

exh. cat. Tokyo & Osaka 2016
Guido Messling & Atsushi Shinfuji (eds.), *Lucas Cranach the Elder. 500 Years of the Power of Temptation*, Tokyo (The National Museum of Western Art) & Osaka (The National Museum of Art), Vienna & Tokyo 2016

exh. cat. Vienna 1896
Kunsthistorische Sammlungen des Allerhöchsten Kaiserhauses. Die Gemälde-Galerie. Alte Meister, Vienna 1896

exh. cat. Vienna 1939
Altdeutsche Kunst im Donauland, Vienna (Staatliches Kunstgewerbemuseum) 1939

exh. cat. Vienna 1972
Karl Schütz, *Lucas Cranach der Ältere und seine Werkstatt. Jubiläumsausstellung museumseigener Werke 1472–1972*, Vienna (Kunsthistorisches Museum) 1972

exh. cat. Vienna 1975/76
Historisches Museum der Stadt Wien (ed.), *Wien im Mittelalter,* Vienna (Historisches Museum der Stadt Wien) 1975/76

exh. cat. Vienna 2003
Kaiser Ferdinand I. – Das Werden der Habsburgermonarchie, Vienna (Kunsthistorisches Museum) 2003

exh. cat. Vienna 2015/16
Andreas Fingernagel (ed.), *Goldene Zeiten – Meisterwerke der Buchkunst von der Gotik bis zur Renaissance,* Vienna (Österreichische Nationalbibliothek) 2015/16

exh. cat. Vienna 2017
Björn Blauensteiner & Stella Rollig (eds.), *Rueland Frueauf d.Ä. und sein Kreis*, Vienna (Belvedere) 2017

exh. cat. Vienna 2021/22
Björn Blauensteiner & Stella Rollig (eds.), *Dürerzeit. Österreich am Tor zur Renaissance*, Vienna (Belvedere) 2021/22

exh. cat. Vienna & Munich 2011
Sabine Haag et al. (eds.), *Dürer Cranach Holbein. Die Entdeckung des Menschen: Das deutsche Porträt um 1500*, Vienna (Kunsthistorisches Museum) & Munich (Kunsthalle der Hypo-Kulturstiftung), Munich 2011

exh. cat. Wittenberg 1998
Jutta Strehle & Armin Kunz, *Druckgraphiken Lucas Cranachs d.Ä. im Dienst von Macht und Glauben. Bestandskatalog der Druckgraphiken Lucas Cranachs d.Ä. anläßlich der Ausstellung Im Dienst von Macht und Glauben in der Lutherhalle Wittenberg*, ed. by Stiftung Luthergedenkstätten in Sachsen-Anhalt, Wittenberg 1998

exh. cat. Wittenberg 2011
Marlies Schmidt (ed.), *Maler Lucas aus Kronach. Lucas Cranachs frühe Jahre*, Wittenberg (Cranach Foundation) 2011

COLLECTION CATALOGUES

cat. Basel 1966
Öffentliche Kunstsammlung Basel. Katalog. 1. Teil. Die Kunst bis 1800. Sämtliche ausgestellten Werke, Basel 1966

cat. Berlin 1921
Elfried Bock, *Die deutschen Meister: beschreibendes Verzeichnis sämtlicher Zeichnungen* (Staatliche Museen zu Berlin, Die Zeichnungen alter Meister im Kupferstichkabinett), 2 vols., Berlin 1921

cat. Brunswick 1922
Eduard Flechsig (ed.), *Zeichnungen alter Meister im Landesmuseum zu Braunschweig, Teil 1: Deutsche*, Frankfurt a.M. 1922

cat. Brunswick 1955
Hans Werner Schmidt, *Die deutschen Handzeichnungen bis zur Mitte des 16. Jahrhunderts* (Kunsthefte des Herzog Anton Ulrich-Museums, no. 9), Brunswick 1955

cat. Brunswick 1992/1997
Christian von Heusinger, *Herzog Anton Ulrich-Museum Braunschweig. Die Handzeichnungssammlung*, 2 vols., Brunswick 1992/1997

cat. Nuremberg 1968
Fritz Zink, *Die deutschen Handzeichnungen, Band I* (Kataloge des Germanischen Nationalmuseums Nürnberg: Die Handzeichnungen bis zur Mitte des 16. Jahrhunderts), Nuremberg 1968

cat. Nuremberg 1997
Kurt Löcher, *Die Gemälde des 16. Jahrhunderts, Germanisches Nationalmuseum Nürnberg*, Stuttgart 1997

cat. Nuremberg 2019
Daniel Hess et al. (eds.), *Die Gemälde des Spätmittelalters im Germanischen Nationalmuseum, Franken* (2 vols.), Regensburg 2019

cat. Vienna 1938
Katalog der Gemäldegalerie (Führer durch das Kunsthistorische Museum Nr. 8), Vienna 1938

cat. Vienna 1958
Kunsthistorisches Museum, Wien. Katalog der Gemäldegalerie. II. Teil: Vlamen, Holländer, Deutsche, Franzosen, Vienna 1958

cat. Vienna 1971
Elfriede Baum, *Katalog des Museums Mittelalterlicher Österreichischer Kunst*, Vienna et al. 1971

cat. Vienna 1972
Karl Schütz, *Lucas Cranach der Ältere und seine Werkstatt. Jubiläumsausstellung museumseigener Werke 1472–1972*, Kunsthistorisches Museum, Vienna 1972

cat. Vienna 1984
Robert Waissenberger, *Schausammlung historisches Museum der Stadt Wien*, Vienna 1984

cat. Vienna 1987
Waltraut Kuba-Hauk & Arthur Saliger, *Dom- und Diözesanmuseum Wien*, Vienna 1987

cat. Vienna 1991
Sylvia Ferino-Pagden & Wolfgang Prohaska & Karl Schütz, *Die Gemäldegalerie des Kunsthistorischen Museums in Wien. Verzeichnis der Gemälde*, Vienna 1991

cat. Vienna 1994
Cornelia Reiter, *Museum im Schottenstift. Kunstsammlungen der Benediktinerabtei zu den Schotten in Wien*, Vienna 1994

cat. Winterthur 2003
Mariantonia Reinhard-Felice (ed.), *Sammlung Oskar Reinhart "Am Römerholz", Gesamtkatalog*, Basel 2003

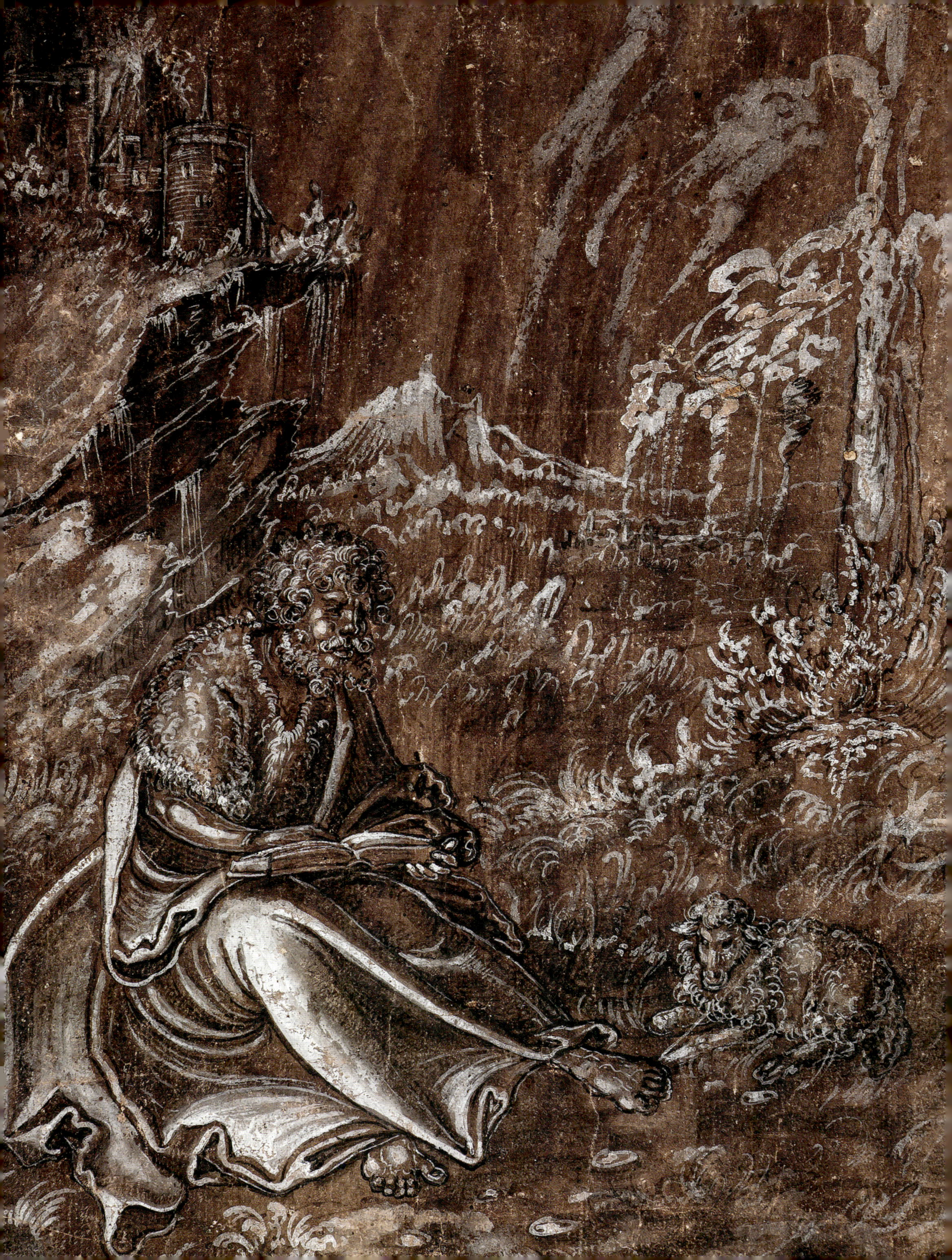

Authors

Katja Baumhoff

read English and Art History at Düsseldorf, Naples and Reading (UK). PhD thesis on Early American Modernism at the Heinrich Heine University in Düsseldorf. Visiting scholar at the Department of Art History at Yale University, New Haven. Independent curator for numerous international projects, and artistic head of Shed in Frauenfeld. Since 2018, deputy head of the director of the Oskar Reinhart Collection "Am Römerholz" in Winterthur.

Björn Blauensteiner

read Law and Art History in Vienna, Utrecht, Berlin and Frankfurt. 2008–2010 scholarship at the Internationales Forschungszentrum für Kulturwissenschaften (IFK; International Research Centre for Cultural Studies), 2010–2015 research assistant and curator at the Picture Gallery of the Kunsthistorisches Museum Vienna. Since 2016, curator of the Mediaeval Collection at the Belvedere in Vienna. His main research focus is on fifteenth- and sixteenth-century art north of the Alps.

Andreas Fingernagel

read Art History and Classical Archaeology at the Universities of Salzburg and Vienna, where he graduated (PhD) in 1985. 1983–1985 research assistant at the Art History Institute of Vienna University. 1985–1989 research assistant at a DFG project at the Staatsbibliothek Berlin, Preußischer Kulturbesitz. 1989–1994 researcher at the Österreichische Akademie der Wissenschaften. Since 1995 researcher at the Österreichische Nationalbibliothek (Collection of Manuscripts, Autographs and Estates); since 2008 director of its newly-founded Collection of Manuscripts and Old Prints.

Sabine Heiser

read Art History, Classical Archaeology and Religious Studies at the Freie Universität Berlin, where she graduated (PhD) in 2000. 1995–2002 research assistant at the University of Paderborn, 2003–2007 at the Justus-Liebig-Universität Gießen, 2007/2008 visiting professor at the HBK Brunswick, 2009–2014 visiting professor of Art History at the TU Darmstadt.

Claudia Koch

read Art History at the Universities of Vienna, Graz and Utrecht. Since 1999, curator of the Gemäldegalerie der Akademie der bildenden Künste Wien, and since 2008 lecturer at its Institute of Conservation and Restoration. Her main research focus is on fifteenth- to seventeenth-century painting north of the Alps and the history of the collection. She has written numerous contributions to guide books and exhibition catalogues and has curated exhibitions shown as part of the "In Focus" series.

Guido Messling

read Art History, Modern History and Media Studies/Museum Management at the Freie Universität Berlin, where he graduated (PhD) in 2002. 2001–2005 intern and interim head of the education dept. of the Staatsgalerie Stuttgart. Then compiler for the series *New Hollstein German*, wrote several cat. raisonnés of Early German drawings, and worked as an independent curator. Since 2011, curator of German Painting at the Kunsthistorisches Museum Vienna.

Erwin Pokorny

read art History and History at the University of Vienna, where he graduated (PhD) in 1990. Worked as an independent art historian, specialising in research and exhibition projects on Netherlandish drawings, prints, and the iconography of the early modern era. External lecturer at the Akademie der bildenden Künste in Vienna and the Leopolds-Franzens University Innsbruck; one focus of his research is Hieronymus Bosch and Albrecht Dürer and their contemporaries.

Kerstin Richter

graduated in Rehabilitation from the Pedagogical University of St Petersburg, then read Art History and Mediaeval History at the University of Basel, where she graduated (PhD) in 2007. Worked as an independent curator on various exhibition projects in museums and exhibition spaces in and around Basel. Worked in museum education at, for example, the Fondation Beyeler/Riehen and the Kunstmuseum Basel, interned in the old masters dept. at the Kunstmuseum Basel. 2009–2016 research assistant at the Oskar Reinhart Collection "Am Römerholz"/Bundesamt für Kultur. Its director since 2016.

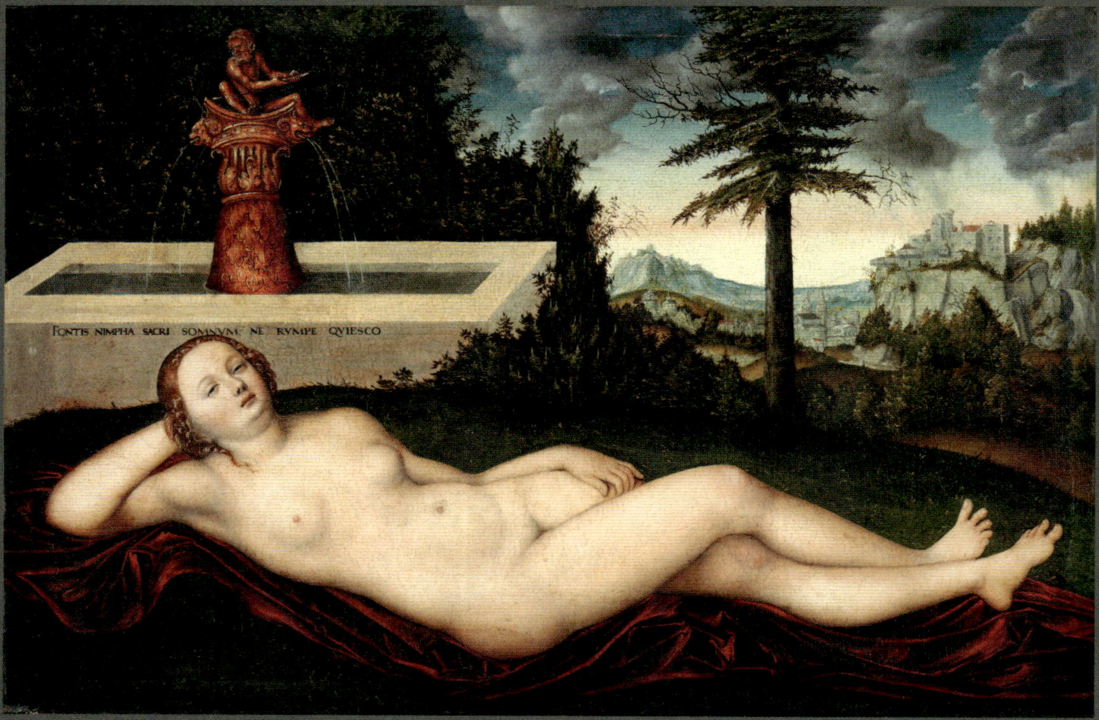
FONTIS NIMPHA SACRI SOMNVM NE RVMPE QVIESCO

Quomodo in Vindobonensi Silva Serpentis Signum Grus Obtinuerit
Chloridis Epigramma

FONTIS NIMPHA SACRI SOMNVM NE RVMPE QUIESCO
custodit pacem grus uigil absque metu
olim hic dormiuit serpentum rex modo pransus
destituit lassum digna corona caput
aduolat en plumis teneris niueisque superba
noctua quae uarios candida temnit aues
urget caeca fames: regis sub uentre plicatas
alas turgenti non uidet inde nefas
nam rex serpentum sacer est auibusque canoris
alatus colitur nobilis instar auis
aggreditur: uigilat sed grus teretemque lapillum
ut solet et bolum sustinet ungue luti
quos iacit et bolo lutescens noctua cedit
sanguine perfusae lutea pluma rubet
psittacus et phoenix pauo cirisque cachinnant
lucus quotquot aues uindobonensis habet
tergere mox frustra uelit inuisum illa colorem
uenari pictam post nisi nocte pudet
rex seruatorem commendat cumque corona
serpentis merito signa tenere iubet
inde uiator abi: satis est spectasse puellam
pictor quod faciat grus tibi caute caue

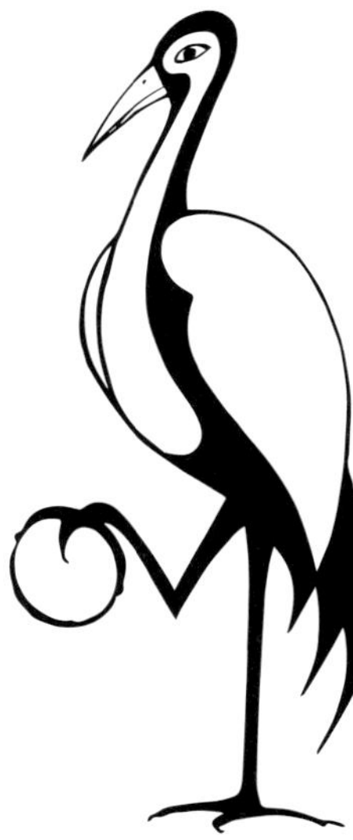

How the Crane in the Vienna Woods received the Sign of the Serpent
an epigram by Chloris

I, THE NYMPH OF THIS SACRED SPRING, AM RESTING:
DO NOT DISTURB MY SLUMBER!
The watchful and fearless crane guards the peace.
Once the serpent king rested here after his dinner;
his worthy crown had rolled off his tired head.
See, the white owl approaches, so proud of its fragile and snowy plumage,
who despises the colourful birds.
Blind hunger propels it forward: it sees not the folded wings
hidden by the king's bloated stomach and thus not the sacrilege,
for the serpent king is sacred and revered like a noble bird by the singing multitude,
because he too is winged.
The owl attacks him, but the crane is keeping watch and, as always, clasps
a smooth pebble and a piece of mud in its claw,
which it throws, and the owl, turning yellow from the earthy pigment, retreats.
Where blood drips from the wound its yellow plumage turns red.
Parrot and phoenix, peacock and kingfisher snigger,
joined by all the birds who live in the Vienna Woods.
The owl would love to wipe off the hated colour at once – but to no avail:
dyed and coloured, henceforth it is too ashamed to hunt but at night.
The king praises his saviour and bestows on the crane the well-deserved privilege
to bear the sign of the crowned serpent as its own.
So be warned, wanderer, and move on: it is enough to have set eyes on the maiden!
Beware of what the painter Crane could do to you.

(English translation: Agnes Stillfried & Karin Zeleny)

Fig. left: Lucas Cranach the Elder, *Water Nymph at a Fountain*, 1518. Museum der bildenden Künste, Leipzig, inv. 757 (inscribed "FONTIS NIMPHA SACRI SOMNVM NE RVMPE QUIESCO" on the rim of the fountain)

Photograph Credits

Basel
© Kunstmuseum Basel / Martin P. Bühler, pp. 39, 134, 137

Berlin
© bpk Berlin / Gemäldegalerie, SMB / Volker-H. Schneider, pp. 64, 107, 133

© bpk Berlin / Gemäldegalerie, SMB / Jörg P. Anders, p. 37

© bpk Berlin / Kupferstichkabinett, SMB / Jörg P. Anders, pp. 80, 81

© bpk Berlin / Kupferstichkabinett, SMB / Volker-H. Schneider, pp. 76, 77

© bpk Berlin / Kupferstichkabinett, SMB, pp. 118

Boston
© Bridgeman Images / Isabella Stewart Gardner Museum, Boston, MA, USA, p. 46

Brunswick
© Herzog Anton Ulrich-Museum, Brunswick, Kunstmuseum des Landes Niedersachsen, p. 116

Cologne
© bpk / Rheinisches Bildarchiv Köln / Erfurth / Hugo, p. 62

Dresden
© bpk / Staatliche Kunstsammlungen Dresden / Elke Estel / Hans-Peter Klut, p. 17

© bpk / Staatliche Kunstsammlungen Dresden / Herbert Boswank, p. 21

© SLUB / Deutsche Fotothek, p. 63

Klosterneuburg
Stift Klosterneuburg, Stiftsmuseum, © Peter Böttcher, Institut für Realienkunde, Salzburg University, p. 24, 27, 30

Kronberg
© Hessische Hausstiftung, Kronberg im Taunus, p. 97

Leipzig
© bpk / Museum der bildenden Künste, Leipzig / Bertram Kober (Punctum Leipzig), p. 162

Lille
© Musée des Beaux-Arts Lille, Fonds photographique et iconothèque / Jean-Marie Dautel, pp. 130, 160

London
© The National Gallery, pp. 38, 39

Madrid
© Photographic Archive Museo Nacional del Prado, p. 41

© Museo Thyssen-Bornemisza, Madrid, pp. 34, 41

Munich
© Bayerisches Nationalmuseum München; photo: Bastian Krack, p. 15

© Bayerische Staatsbibliothek München, pp. 16, 20, 57, 58

© bpk / Bayerische Staatsgemälde-sammlungen, Alte Pinakothek, Munich, pp. 12, 17, 66

© Staatliche Graphische Sammlung, Munich, p. 131

New York
© bpk / The Metropolitan Museum of Art, p. 114

The Metropolitan Museum of Art / © Harris Brisbane Dick Fund, 1927, pp. 18, 60, 69

Nuremberg
Germanisches Nationalmuseum, © photo: Dirk Meßberger, pp. 90, 106, 109, 138, 139

Kirche St. Sebald, © photo: Thomas Bachmann, p. 18

Vienna
© Albertina, Vienna, pp. 46, 124, 127

© Dom Museum Wien / Domkirche St. Stephan / photo: Leni Deinhardstein / Lisa Rastl, pp. 36

© Dom Museum Wien / Erzbistum / photo: Leni Deinhardstein / Lisa Rastl, pp. 31

© Gemäldegalerie der Akademie der bildenden Künste Wien, pp. 93, 95, 148

© KHM-Museumsverband / photo: Andreas Uldrich, pp. 49, 62, 72, 73, 74, 82, 111, 112, 132, 166, 167

© Österreichische Galerie Belvedere Wien / Johannes Stoll, pp. 28, 92

© Österreichische Nationalbibliothek Wien, pp. 19, 52, 55, 58, 84, 85, 87, 105, 120, 122, 125, 128

© Schottenstift Museum, Vienna / photo: P. Christoph Merth, p. 27

© Wien Museum, p. 26

Weimar
© Klassik Stiftung Weimar, Bestand Museen, p. 42

Winterthur
© Sammlung Oskar Reinhart "Am Römerholz", Winterthur / P. Schälchli, Zurich, pp. 2, 3, 10, 11, 44, 98, 99, 101, 103

Zurich
© Kunsthaus Zürich, donated by August Abegg 1925, p. 115

If you believe any material has been included in this publication improperly, despite all due care taken, please contact us.

Imprint

Published by the Swiss Confederation, represented by the Federal Office of Buildings and Logistics, on behalf of the Federal Office of Culture, Bern, and the KHM-Museumsverband, Vienna, in connection with the exhibitions

Cranach – The Early Years in Vienna
Oskar Reinhart Collection "Am Römerholz", Winterthur (SOR)
12 March to 12 June 2022
&
Cranach the Untamed – The Early Years in Vienna
Kunsthistorisches Museum Vienna (KHM)
21 June to 16 October 2022

Federal Department of Home Affairs of the Swiss Confederation, Federal Office of Culture
The Oskar Reinhart Collection "Am Römerholz" is an institution of the Federal Office of Culture, Bern
Haldenstrasse 95, 8400 Winterthur, Switzerland
www.roemerholz.ch

Director
Carine Bachmann

Deputy Director
Yves Fischer

Head of Museums and Collections Section
Benno Widmer

Director SOR
Kerstin Richter

KHM-Museumsverband
Burgring 5, 1010 Vienna, Austria
www.khm.at

Director General
Sabine Haag

Hirmer Verlag GmbH
Bayerstraße 57–59, 80335 Munich, Germany
www.hirmerverlag.de

ISBN 978-3-7774-3926-6
Printed in Italy

EXHIBITION SOR

Curators
Kerstin Richter
Katja Baumhoff

Registrar
Florence Le Bègue

Press and Publicity
Valentina Zingg

Exhibition design
Holzer Kobler Architekturen GmbH, Zurich

Exhibition set-up / technicians
Bertalan Bozsanyi
Martin Lanz
Andreas Fürst

Conservation
Hanspeter Marty
Olivier Masson

EXHIBITION KHM

Curator
Guido Messling

Exhibition management
Julia Neudorfer

Exhibition design
Gerhard Veigel

Conservation
Elke Oberthaler (head)
Monika Strolz
Ingrid Hopfner

General sponsor
OMV

Partner
UNIQA

EXHIBITION CATALOGUE

Edited by
Guido Messling
Kerstin Richter

Authors of the catalogue entries
Katja Baumhoff (KB)
Björn Blauensteiner (BB)
Andreas Fingernagel (AF)
Claudia Koch (CK)
Guido Messling (GM)
Erwin Pokorny (EP)
Kerstin Richter (KR)

Image rights
Florence Le Bègue, SOR

Publication management
Benjamin Mayr, KHM

Copy editor
Karin Zeleny, KHM

English translations and copy-editing
Agnes Stillfried, KHM

French translations and copy-editing
Martine Passelaigue

Creative direction
Stefan Zeisler, KHM

Graphic design
Michaela Noll, KHM
Johanna Kopp, KHM (cover)

Typesetting
Clemens Wihlidal

Image editing
Thomas Ritter, KHM

Project editor (publisher)
Jürgen Kleidt, Hirmer

Printing and binding
Printer Trento S.r.l., Trento

Typeface
Sabon Next

Paper
Gardamatt Ultra 170g

German National Library has archived this publication in the German National Bibliography; detailed bibliographical data is available at http://dnb.de

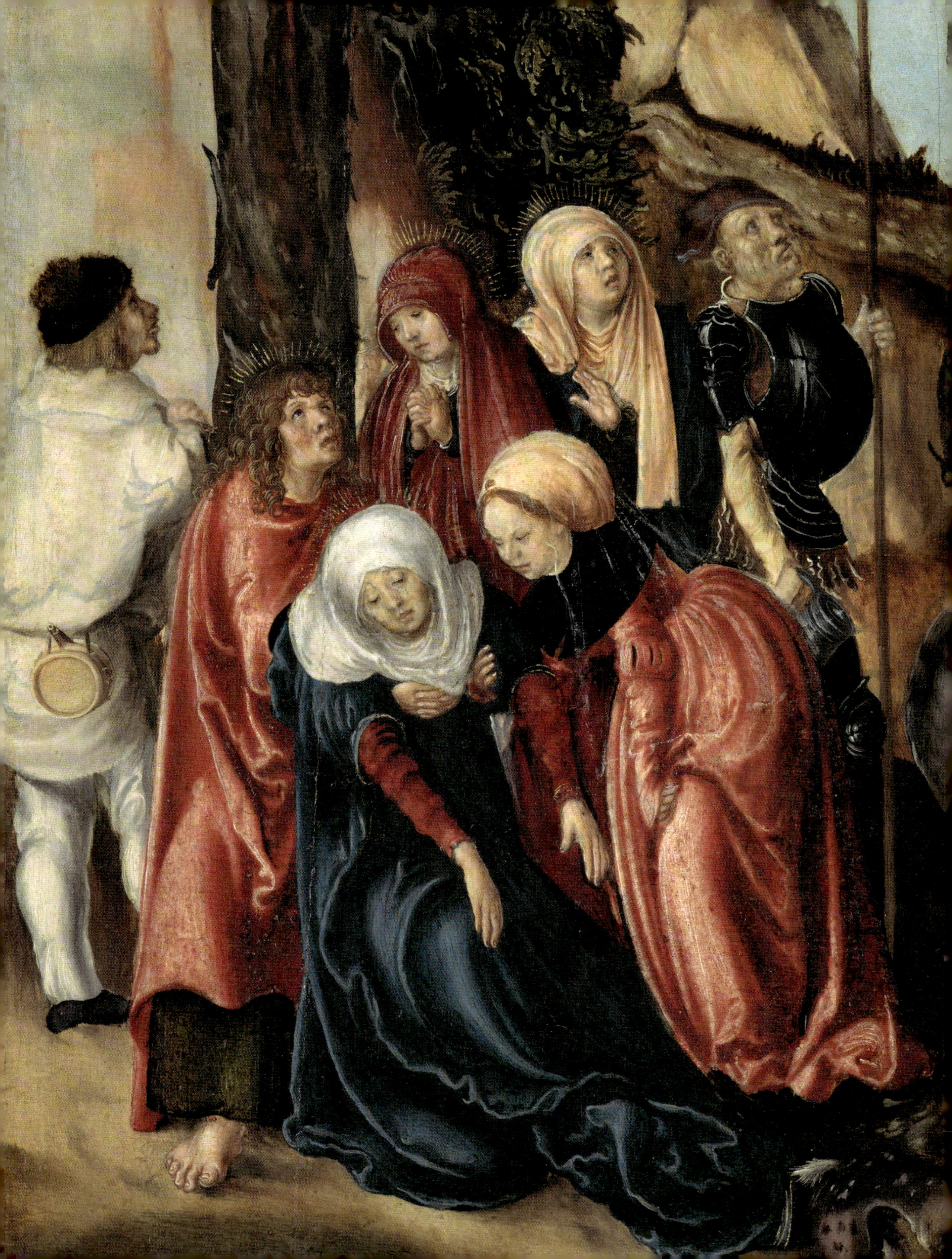

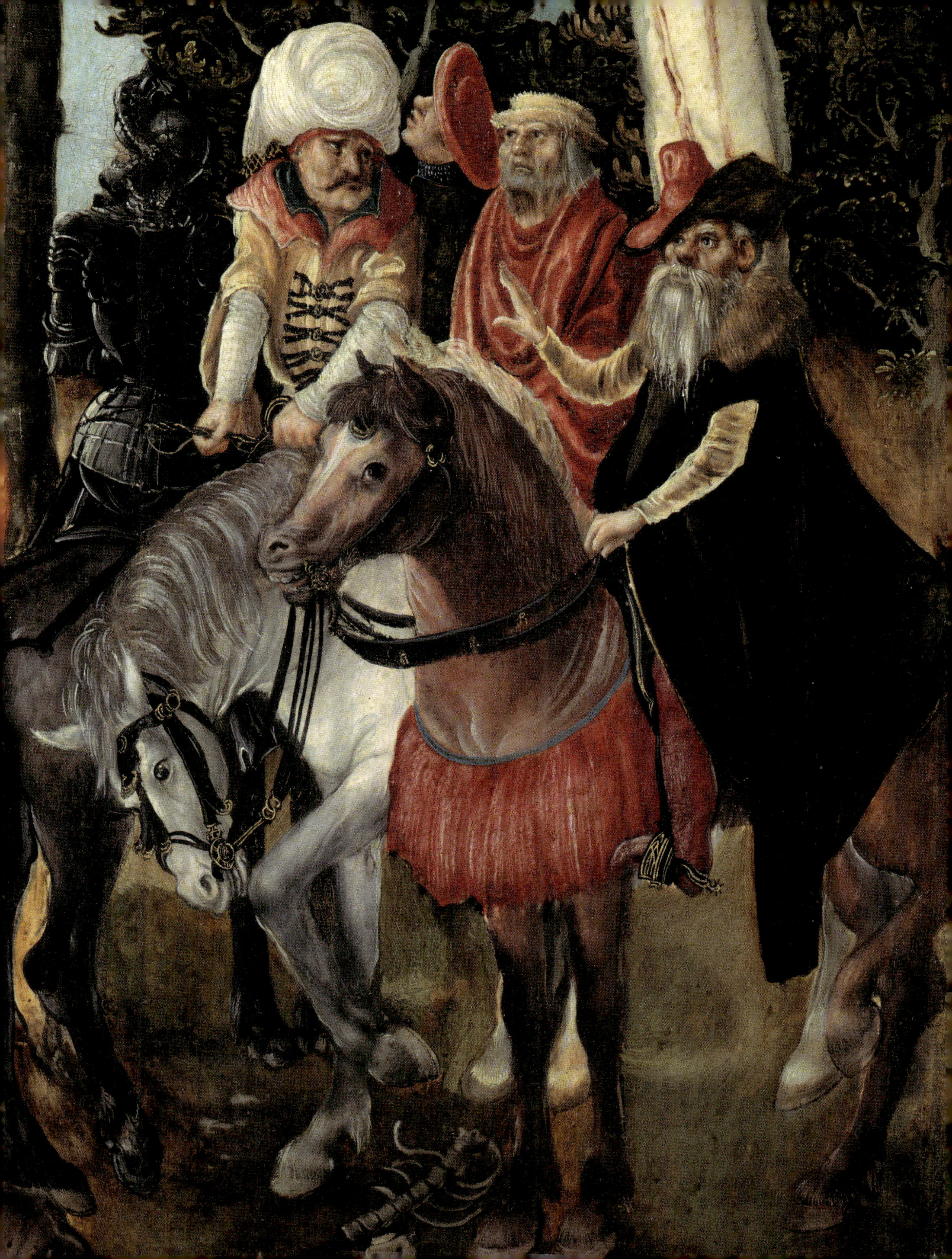